The Global Economy in the 199

The 1990s were an extraordinary, contradict   .....g period of economic development, one evoking numerous historical parallels. But the 1990s are far from being well understood, and their meaning for the future remains open to debate. In this volume, world-class economic historians analyze a series of key issues: the growth of the world economy; globalization and its implications for domestic and international policy; the sources and sustainability of productivity growth in the United States; the causes of sluggish growth in Europe and Japan; comparisons of the information technologies (IT) revolution with previous innovation waves; the bubble and burst in asset prices and their impacts on the real economy; the effects of trade and factor mobility on the global distribution of income; and the changes in the welfare state, regulation, and macro-policymaking. Leading scholars place the 1990s in a fuller long-run global context, offering insights into what lies ahead for the world economy in the twenty-first century.

PAUL W. RHODE is the Zachary Taylor Smith Professor at the Economics Department of the University of North Carolina, Chapel Hill.

GIANNI TONIOLO is Professor of Economic History at the University of Rome "Tor Vergata" and Research Professor of Economics at Duke University, Durham, North Carolina.

The Global Economy in the 1990s

A Long-Run Perspective

edited by

PAUL W. RHODE AND
GIANNI TONIOLO

CAMBRIDGE
UNIVERSITY PRESS

CAMBRIDGE UNIVERSITY PRESS
Cambridge, New York, Melbourne, Madrid, Cape Town, Singapore, São Paulo

Cambridge University Press
The Edinburgh Building, Cambridge CB2 2RU, UK

Published in the United States of America by Cambridge University Press, New York

www.cambridge.org
Information on this title: www.cambridge.org/9780521852630

© Cambridge University Press 2006

First published 2006

Printed in the United Kingdom at the University Press, Cambridge

A catalogue record for this publication is available from the British Library

ISBN-13 978-0-521-85263-0 hardback
ISBN-10 0-521-85263-3 hardback

Contents

Figures

List of figures

Tables

Contributors

Michael A. Bernstein, Professor of History and Associated Faculty Member, Department of Economics, University of California at San Diego

Nicholas F. R. Crafts, Professor of Economic History, London School of Economics

Barry J. Eichengreen, George C. Pardee and Helen N. Pardee Professor of Economics and Political Science, University of California at Berkeley

Riccardo Faini, Dipartimento di Studi Economico-Finanziari e Metodi Quantitativi University of Rome "Tor Vergata"

Alexander J. Field, Michael and Mary Orradre Professor of Economics, Santa Clara University, California

Robert J. Gordon, Stanley G. Harris Professor of Economics, Northwestern University, Evanston, Illinois

Peter H. Lindert, Distinguished Professor of Economics, University of California at Davis

Paul W. Rhode, Zachary Taylor Smith Professor, Economics Department, University of North Carolina, Chapel Hill

Peter L. Rousseau, Associate Professor of Economics, Vanderbilt University, Nashville, Tennessee

Peter Temin, Elisha Gray II Professor of Economics, Massachusetts Institute of Technology, Cambridge, Massachusetts

Gianni Toniolo, Professor of Economic History, University of Rome "Tor Vergata," and Research Professor of Economics, Duke University, Durham, North Carolina.

Eugene Nelson White, Professor of Economics, Rutgers University, New Jersey

Gavin Wright, William Robertson Coe Professor of American Economic History, Stanford University, California

Preface

In the process of producing this volume the editors incurred numerous debts, which we can only partially repay with an expression of our gratitude here. The original versions of these papers were presented at the joint Duke–University of North Carolina conference on "Understanding the 1990s: the long-run perspective" held at the Terry Sanford Center on the Duke University campus in Durham, North Carolina, from 26–27 March 2004. This conference would not have been possible without the untiring efforts of Peggy East at Duke University. We would also like to thank Nancy Kocher at the University of North Carolina, and members of the program committee Peter Coclanis, Robert Keohane, Thomas Mroz, and Thomas Nechyba. Generous funding was provided by the Dickson Fund for the Study of Economics in History at the University of North Carolina Economics and History Departments, the Kenan Fund of the University of North Carolina Department of History, the Duke University Economics Department, the Duke Center for International Studies, and the European Studies Center. These contributions are greatly appreciated. We would also like to thank the discussants and participants for their valuable remarks, which led to lively discussion and debate at the conference and – ultimately – to better chapters in this volume. Among those deserving special thanks are Andrea Boltho, Michael Bordo, Paul David, Thomas Geragthy, Christopher Hanes, Richard Sylla, Ignazio Visco, John Wallis, and Barrie Wigmore. Finally, we would like to thank Andriy Gubachiov at Duke University and Lynn Dunlop and Chris Harrison at Cambridge University Press for their work in making this volume possible.

1 Understanding the 1990s: a long-run perspective

Paul W. Rhode and Gianni Toniolo

1.1 Introduction

The twentieth century both opened and closed with a bang: the *belle époque* before 1914 and the "roaring nineties" (Stiglitz, 2003) just past. It was only after the First World War that people looked back at the 1895–1914 period with nostalgia as a "beautiful era" of spreading prosperity, peaceful technical progress, low inflation, and modest financial instability. The 1990s, on the contrary, were seen as the "best of times" (Johnson, 2001) by many of those who lived through the decade – at least, those in the United States.[1] Will future historians confirm this view? If the twentieth century is any guide, much will depend on how the twenty-first century unfolds. If peace again prevails, if productivity growth continues apace at the economic center and spreads to the periphery, if means are found to govern the international economy in ways that make the costs of globalization socially acceptable, then the 1990s may well be remembered as a moment in human history when the foundations were laid for a long period of sustainable growth. If, on the other hand, social, political, and economic instability prevails, as it did after the First World War, then people may indeed look back at the 1990s as "the best of times," creating the myth of another *belle époque*. Posterity will magnify the virtues of the last decade in the twentieth century and ignore its shortcomings.

While we cannot anticipate the future verdicts of either public opinion or historians on the 1990s, there can be little doubt that, from a number of political, social, and economic viewpoints, the decade was an exceptional, significant, and defining period in human history. But how exceptional, and how significant? And what was the nature of the new epoch being defined? These are questions that can be answered only from a long-term perspective. As we do not possess the hindsight of future generations, we can only look at the 1990s through the prism of the past. By taking a long-term perspective, often covering the entire twentieth century, the chapters in this book offer a better understanding of the "novelties" of the 1990s that so impressed contemporary observers.

1

Some may quibble with treating the 1990s as a unit of analysis because decades are not natural economic or historical concepts. Developing periodizations using great wars or revolutions as breakpoints is much more common when taking the long view. Accidents of the calendar make it sensible to treat certain decades, such as the 1920s and 1930s, as meaningful historical periods. Watershed events – the end of the First World War, the onset of the Great Depression in 1929, and the beginning of the Second World War – broke the flow of history. But, in general, the use of decades is an artifice. Nonetheless, the 1990s do possess a greater claim that most decades to possessing an economic unity. The period was indeed full of events for which the words "new" and "path-breaking" can hardly be avoided. The most important events, all taking place in the late 1980s and early 1990s, were the end of the Cold War, Europe's move to closer integration, and the start of the meteoric rise of China and India

The end of the so-called Cold War was undoubtedly the most important event in global history since 1945. The fall of the Berlin Wall in 1989 and the events that followed in rapid sequence throughout Eastern European marked such a sharp break with the past that we now speak of a "short twentieth century," encompassing only 1914–1991 (Hobsbawm, 1994), much as we refer to a "long nineteenth century" (1789–1914). It was soon clear that history did not end with the Cold War, and that – if anything – its path would become more complex, uncertain, and challenging as people and leaders ventured into uncharted territory. Historians and political scientists are just beginning to take stock of the implications of the end of the Cold War, while – as mentioned by Peter Temin in chapter 10 – its impacts on the world economy remain to be assessed by economic historians.

A second trend-setting event took place almost unnoticed. In February 1986 the representatives of the (then) twelve European Union member states signed the Single European Act in Luxembourg. This led to the creation of a truly Single European Market, beginning on 1 January 1993. While the relevance of Europe's quiet revolution – which also entailed the creation of the single currency – is little understood outside the "old continent," it is nevertheless likely to be one of the most innovative events for which the 1990s will be remembered.

Two other changes in the early 1990s also have the potential to be epoch-making. In the mid-1980s China's economic reforms, initiated in 1978, threatened to stall. On the one hand, these reform policies were challenged by power-brokers associated with the previous system and, on the other hand, they were deemed inadequate by intellectuals, students, and members of the slowly emerging middle class. The course that would ultimately be followed remained unclear, leading to instability that potentially threatened China's economic growth. In 1989 the situation came to a head with the tragic events of

Tiananmen Square. Following the resurgence of conservative members of the Communist Party, it seemed that economic reforms had suffered a permanent blow. In 1992, however, the fourteenth Party Congress gave its official approval to Deng Xiaoping's policies promoting a market-oriented economy. Since then, Chinese GDP growth has averaged about 8 percent annually.

In India, at roughly the same time (July 1991), Manmohan Singh, finance minister in the Narasimha Rao government, responded to a twin fiscal and foreign deficit crisis by pushing through a thoroughgoing liberalization package. Long-standing trade barriers and regulatory/licensing restraints were removed, foreign investment encouraged, and public assets privatized. Since 1992 India has experienced sustained GDP growth in the range of 5–6 percent annually, and the English-speaking and highly educated segments of its population have begun to participate in and enjoy some of the prosperity of the high-technology boom.[2] Whereas China has emerged onto the world stage as a manufacturing powerhouse, India has adopted the role of specialization in services and advanced technology.

If, from a global perspective, many of the most defining events of the 1990s took place in Europe and Asia, it was in the United States that the decade took on the feeling of an exciting, even inebriating, second *belle époque*. As in the 1920s and 1960s, the popular imagination in the 1990s was enthralled by the dream of a "new economy," promising a cornucopia of high income and productivity growth, low inflation and unemployment, and soaring returns on financial assets.

Early in the 1990s the mood in the United States was tinged with pessimism, out of concern about industrial decline, Asian competition, rising unemployment, and economic inequality. Rising populist sentiments in response to deindustrialization mixed with social disharmony resulting from the so-called "cultural wars" and racial/ethnic strife, and with widespread frustration about political gridlock and an apparent future of unending fiscal deficits. If the United States had triumphed in the Cold War and stunned the world with its military might in the First Gulf War, the Americans seemed to be losing out to foreigners, especially to the Japanese, in terms of economic welfare and competitiveness. The "American Century" appeared destined to an early end.

A few years later, those who returned to the United States after spending some time away were surprised by the U-turn in the country's prevailing mood. Open optimism about the future of the economy had replaced the creeping pessimism. Japan and the "Asian Tigers" were no longer perceived as threats. Innovations in IT were progressing at a breathtaking pace. Spending six months out of the country meant that, on return, one needed to exert a non-trivial effort in updating one's hardware technology and learning to use the new software. By the mid-1990s foreign observers were impressed by the renewed optimism and vitality that characterized large segments of American society. Statistical

Table 1.1 *Average annual growth rates in per capita GDP: the world economy and the United States*

	1820–1870	1870–1913	1913–1950	1950–1960	1960–1970	1970–1980	1980–1990	1990–2000
World	0.53	1.30	0.91	2.78	3.03	1.89	1.29	1.55
United States	1.34	1.82	1.61	1.71	2.87	2.12	2.25	1.94

Source: Maddison (2001, 2003).

evidence for healthy economic performance by the United States and, particularly, a remarkable productivity surge soon confirmed that these impressions were not unfounded. The media announced the birth of a "new economy," based on the internet and the World Wide Web. The "fabulous decade" of growth in the United States highlights how one historical period in a particular economy can have a unique feel, one different from that prevailing in the same economy just a half-dozen years before or after or in other economies at the same instant.

For reasons both geopolitical and economic, therefore, the 1990s were an extraordinary, contradictory, fascinating period of economic development. It is a period, however, that is far from being well understood. Prominent voices, such as that of Joseph Stiglitz, have called for the "economic history of the 1990s to be rewritten." The jury is still out on a number of key issues, including: the causes and sustainability of productivity growth in the United States; the sluggish growth in Europe and stagnation in Japan; how the IT revolution compares with past waves of innovation; the bubble in financial prices and its impact on the real sector; the financial instability in the "periphery"; the effects of trade and factory mobility on the global distribution of income; and the impact of changes in the welfare state, regulation, and macro-policymaking. By taking a long-run perspective on these issues, this book hopes to make the task of the jury easier. We hope that, by providing a better understanding of the features of the world economy in the 1990s that are particularly meaningful or distinctive from a historical perspective, we shall be able to frame the questions most relevant for our economic future more meaningfully.

1.2 The international economy

Thanks to the heroic quantification efforts of scholars such as Angus Maddison (2001), we can now roughly compare the growth rates in GDP *per capita* for the whole of the world economy in the 1990s with past periods. Table 1.1 shows that neither the world nor the United States witnessed exceptional economic performances in the 1990s. It was far from being the best economic decade on record. In fact, growth rates in the 1990s were below the 1950–2000 average both for the world and the United States. As we noted above, any periodization is quite arbitrary and decades should not be taken too seriously as units of observation. The 1990s opened with a fairly long (1989–1992) period of virtual stagnation (zero growth) both worldwide and in the United States. If we take a shorter definition of the 1990s (1992–2000) then the GDP per capita rate of growth was 2.45 and 1.95 percent per annum respectively for the United States and the world. Of course, the ad hoc choice of other starting and ending dates for previous periods would also show different performances. We shall return to this briefly at the end of the chapter.

It is not surprising given this record for per capita GDP growth that Nicholas Crafts (chapter 2) finds that "for the industrial countries as a whole there was no resurgence in total factor productivity (TFP) growth." He concludes that, "despite the excitement of the 'new economy' in the United States and the international take-up of new electronic age technologies, there was no return to the TFP growth of the (1950–70) Golden Age."

Crafts does find that, from other vantage points, the 1990s appear rich in novelties. The most notable potential breakthrough, both from a historical perspective and for its implications for the future of the international economy, is the rise of China to the rank of a world economic power. Between 1990 and 2000 the Chinese economy more than doubled its size in real terms (Maddison, 2003), its share in the world economy growing from 7.8 to 12.5 percent (from 2.7 to 7.0 percent in manufacturing production). Growth acceleration in India was also outstanding by historical standards. As these two countries together accounted in the year 2000 for about 38 percent of the world's population, it may be argued that their recent growth performance brought about probably the biggest single improvement in human welfare anywhere, at any time.

The rapid growth of China and India brought about the second important change in the 1990s, already under way in the previous decade: the end, perhaps the reversal, of the increase in worldwide income inequality that characterized "modern economic growth" (as defined by Kuznets, 1966) since it began in the early nineteenth century. If, as noted by Crafts, "divergence big time" was a key feature of the last century, then the 1990s highlight a true structural break in the economic history of the world. Figure 1.1 shows a measure of inequality (Gini coefficient) for the world economy: the unit of observation is the per capita GDP of individual countries weighted with the share of each country's population in the total world population. The graph measures both the big twentieth-century divergence and the convergence process that began in the 1980s and continued in the following decade. This finding by Boltho and Gianni Toniolo (1999) has subsequently been refined by Bourguignon and Morrison (2002) and Sala-i-Martin (2002). In chapter 2, however, Crafts argues that welfare indicators

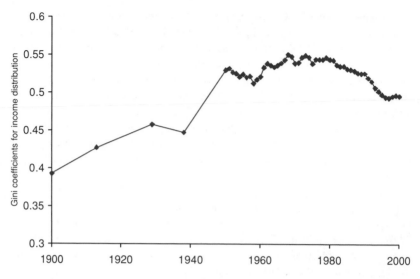

Figure 1.1 Global Gini coefficients, 1900–2000

such as the Human Development Index (HDI), which, in addition to income, takes into account education and mortality, have converged worldwide since the 1950s.

Crafts points out that the whole African continent, and in particular its sub-Saharan part, did not share in the world's output surge of the 1990s. The continent's per capita GDP remained stagnant throughout the decade in real terms, declining from 28 to 24 percent of the world average between 1990 and 2000. At the end of the twentieth century Africa's poverty remained the world's most intractable development issue, underlying the failure of policies thus far undertaken and consigning to the twenty-first century what will probably turn out to be its most relevant economic challenge.

If Africa's economic problems dated back decades, two economic failures were specific to the 1990s: Japan and Russia. The two experiences differ greatly. Japan's performance was disappointing mostly in the light of its previous outstanding growth, which led many to predict in the 1980s that it would pass the United States in the "race for global economic leadership." Between 1990 and 2000 Japanese per capita GDP grew on average only by 0.8 percent per year, as against almost 6 percent over the previous four decades (see tables 4.1 and 4.2 in chapter 4). Although scholars and policymakers disagree sharply over reasons for the "lost decade" in Japan, its beginning is inevitably linked in the popular mind to the bursting of the stock market bubble in December 1989 and the real estate bubble a year later. The asset market deflation hit the core financial sector hard, with the major banks proving unwilling or unable to write down their non-performing loans. The long recession even led the country's consumer price index (CPI) to fall persistently after 1998, a rare event indeed in the postwar world. Studying the shift in Japan's economic performance from "miracle" to "malaise" has spawned a veritable cottage industry. Useful points of entry are Saxonhouse and Stern (2003), which explores wide-ranging debates about the macro-policy responses, and Gao (2001), which traces the institutional/structural roots of stagnation to the strong coordination weak monitoring regime that evolved between banks and large corporations during the high-growth epoch. Among the other important forces depressing growth were: (i) the nation's demographic structure, with low birth rates and a rapidly aging population (see Peter Lindert's discussion in chapter 11); and (ii) the rise of rival manufacturing powers in East Asia during an era of global de-industrialization.[3] (See also Sato, 2002; Hayashi and Prescott, 2002.)

The case of the Russian Federation was one of the most serious economic failures in the 1990s, particularly in the light of the performance of the formerly centrally planned Eastern European economies and of Russia's claim to being a political and military superpower. In 2000 the per capita GDP of Russia was only two-thirds of that of Soviet Russia in 1990. Moreover, welfare indicators such as life expectancy had also dramatically declined and income distribution became vastly unequal. Such a dismal performance came as a surprise to some economists and policymakers, who in the early 1990s had bet on growth acceleration in Russia once market institutions replaced central planning. Economic historians, whose main professional assumptions are that "time matters" and "institutions matter," were much less surprised. "Transition" was not easy for any country. It was, however, easier for those Eastern European countries that had enjoyed before 1939 a relatively modern market economy, with the attendant institutions and entrepreneurial middle class. There was, on the other hand, no heritage of social, economic, and political institutions that the Russians could draw upon in building a free-market economy. These changes will take much longer to take root in Russia than they did in the Eastern European countries that have recently gained access to the European Union.

The economic development of the European Union was also quite disappointing, to those who had pinned hopes on the Single Market and Currency. "Or was it?" asks Riccardo Faini in chapter 4. It was a common perception, on both sides of the Atlantic, during the 1990s that the European economy performed poorly when compared to that of the United States. While the latter's GDP grew at an average annual rate of 3.2 percent, the European Union's managed only an annual average increase of 2.1 percent. Moreover, the world's export share of the large Continental economies sharply declined, while the United States was able to achieve a slight increase in its share of total world trade. More importantly still, labor productivity growth in Europe remained higher than in the United States until the mid-1990s, after which time, however, productivity growth in the United States was more than twice as fast as that of the European Union. It is likely, therefore, that the 1990s witnessed a break in the long-established postwar trends that saw Western Europe and Japan catching up with the United States after losing ground for over a century prior to 1950.

In the long-term perspective, the end – and perhaps the reversal – of Europe's convergence with the United States represents one of the relevant economic changes of the 1990s, with potentially far-reaching implications for the twenty-first century. While acknowledging that Europe's long productivity catch-up came to an end in the second half of the 1990s, Faini warns against viewing these trends with undue pessimism (from Europe's point of view). First of all, demographic trends on the two sides of the Atlantic are very different, and if per capita rather than total GDP is taken into consideration then Europe's relative performance looks distinctly better. During the 1990s population growth was 1.15 percent per annum in the United States and only 0.3 percent per annum in the European Union. If this is taken into account, it remains true that over the 1990s the United States grew more rapidly than Europe on per capita terms, but only by the narrow margin of 0.1 to 0.2 percentage points per annum. In the second half of the decade, the rate of growth in GDP per capita was about the same in the two areas. Moreover, Faini notes, differences in accounting practices and definitions result in a reduction of some 0.2 to 0.3 percentage points in growth differential between Europe and the United States, so that the latter's per capita growth in the second half of the 1990s would again be slower than Europe's. While convergence has by and large come to an end, we are not – or not yet – witnessing the beginning of a great new divergence.

1.3 The productivity surge and the "new economy" in the United States

Even before the purported advent of a "new economy" in the United States, the 1990s saw a revival of intellectual interest in "long waves" of technological progress, particularly in the role of general-purpose technologies (GPTs) as the engines of growth. The GPT concept, formulated by Bresnahan and Trajtenberg (1995) in a highly influential article (written in 1991), captured many of the features of semiconductors. An innovation qualified as a GPT if it was pervasive, spreading to many sectors of the economy; if it was a break-through that had the inherent potential for continuous improvement; and if it fostered complementary innovations in downstream sectors. The concept was in some sense an updating of Joseph Schumpeter's idea of the "great innovation."

This updating proved timely. During the "golden age" of productivity growth, in the 1950s and 1960s, scholars had come to downplay the role of individual great inventions. Edward Denison's pioneering work (1962) on growth accounting had established that in a large, robustly expanding economy no single invention, and indeed no single factor, explains more than a small fraction of total growth. This conclusion was reinforced by the path-breaking work of "new economic" historians Robert Fogel (1964) and Albert Fishlow (1965) on the social savings of the railroad in nineteenth-century America. This transportation innovation, which for many historians had virtually defined the century's progress, could, in Fogel's estimation, account for only two years of economic growth. The idea of a long boom driven by a single epoch-making innovation was on its deathbed.

Even the onset of the "great productivity slowdown" of the 1970s and 1980s, which revived scholarly interest in the long waves, seemed to confirm the lesser role for single great technologies in the growth progress. The stagnation of measured productivity was occurring in the period when new information technologies were rapidly entering offices, factories, and homes. This puzzling phenomenon was well captured in Robert Solow's famous paradox: "We see computers everywhere but in the productivity numbers (Solow, 1987)." The IT sector might well satisfy Moore's (1965) law, which promised a doubling of computing capacity for a given cost every 18–24 months, but it wasn't generating measured increases in output per unit of input.

A number of arguments addressed the puzzling statistical unimportance of this technology, which appeared revolutionary to most who used computers and certainly to all who produced them. One common argument was that the shift of the economy from commodity production to services muted the impact of productivity advances, leading to what is known as Baumol's Disease (Baumol, 1967). Some argued this was due to measurement problems. In many services such as the government sector, output is very hard to measure and is, essentially, proxied by inputs. A second, related argument was that much of the modern productivity advances, even in the commodity-producing sector, took the forms of quality improvements that were poorly measured by existing prices series. A now classic article by William Nordhaus (1997b) on the price of light and the careful empirical work of Zvi Giliches and his associates highlighted such measurement issues.[4] Others argued, more negatively, that the computer did not actually contribute to greater creativity or to more judicious decisions. Instead, the computer just reduced the cost of making revised drafts, leading to more work being produced, not a better final product. Others contended that portable computers and mobile phones increased the number of hours worked rather than output per hour.

In contrast to these pessimistic assessments, a highly influential article by Paul David argued that productivity gains from computers were just over the horizon; it was only a matter of time. David (1990) drew a historical parallel between the impact of the computer and that of the electrical dynamo in the early twentieth century. Although visionaries could see the revolutionary implications of electrical power from the mid-1890s on, the effects would not be realized in meaningful ways until the 1920s. Building on the prior work of Richard Du Boff (1964) and Warren Devine (1983), David noted that the first uses of electricity

Table 1.2 *Productivity in the US nonfarm business sector, 1974–2001*

	1974–1900	1991–1995	1996–2001	Post-1995 change
Growth of labor productivity	1.36	1.54	2.43	0.89
Contribution from capital deepening	0.77	0.52	1.19	0.67
IT capital	0.41	0.46	1.02	0.56
Computer hardware	0.23	0.19	0.54	0.35
Software	0.09	0.21	0.35	0.14
Communication equipment	0.09	0.05	0.13	0.08
Other capital	0.37	0.06	0.17	0.11
Labor quality	0.22	0.45	0.25	−0.20
Multifactor productivity	0.37	0.58	0.99	0.41
Semiconductors	0.08	0.13	0.42	0.29
Computer hardware	0.11	0.13	0.19	0.06
Software	0.04	0.09	0.11	0.02
Communication equipment	0.04	0.06	0.05	−0.01
Other sectors	0.11	0.17	0.23	0.06
Total IT contribution	0.68	0.87	1.79	0.92

NB: Growth in percent per annum.
Source: Oliner and Sichel (2002).

in manufacturing involved plugging the new power source into the shaft-and-belt factory designed around steam engines. Only over time did the new system of production with straight-line product flows, small-horsepower motors, and material handling devices evolve, allowing the full realization of the potential of electrical power. David argued that, in a similar way, the first decades of the diffusion of the computer would be spent in redesigning production to make use of the new technologies. Outweighing the initial benefits of using new hardware or software were the investment costs in updating to version 2 of better hardware or software. Eventually, though, the net gains would be realized.

In the United States, the recent past has borne out David's prediction of an acceleration of productivity growth based on the application of the new computer technologies. Table 1.2 illustrates this acceleration and indicates its proximate causes, using data gathered by Stephen Oliner and Daniel Sichel

(2002). Comparable analyses by Jorgenson and Stiroh (2000) and Jorgenson, Ho and Stiroh (2003) led to roughly similar results. All these studies date the US productivity surge to 1995/96.

The analysis highlights IT's contribution to changes in labor productivity through two channels: (i) capital deepening by investments in computer hardware, software, and communication equipment; and (ii) increases in multifactor productivity within the sectors producing semiconductors, computer hardware, software, and communication equipment. Using Oliner and Sichel's (2002) calculations and the 1995/96 breakpoint, labor productivity increased by about 0.9 percentage points per year between the 1991–1995 and 1996–2001 periods.[5] IT accounted for all of this change (and, indeed, a little more). Multifactor productivity increased from about 0.6 percent per year to 1.0 percent, and again virtually all the acceleration was due to IT. The resolution of the Solow puzzle was accompanied by the widespread celebration of a new technological age.

In chapter 5, Alexander Field places the acceleration of US productivity growth in the second half of the 1990s into a century-long perspective. He finds that the labor productivity advance in the recent period was well below that achieved in the "golden age" of 1947–1973 and was roughly the same as that occurring during the interwar period. Notably, he finds that the 1995–2000 "multifactor productivity growth was less than half what it was during the Depression years" of the 1930s, a period that Field has dubbed the "most technologically progressive decade" in a major recent article (Field, 2003). In this sense, the 1990s experience was far better than that of the 1970s and 1980s, but not truly exceptional in the long-run perspective. His careful sectoral decomposition of growth further indicates that the advance in the 1990s was on a narrower front, concentrated primarily in the computer-producing and intensive computer-using sectors, than productivity growth in earlier periods. Further, Field takes issue with the practice of attributing the labor productivity advance associated with capital-deepening investments in computers to the IT sector, arguing that such productivity-enhancing investments would have occurred in other sectors in any case. He concludes: "We should give the IT revolution its due, but not more than its due."

Adopting the analytical framework of Bresnahan and Trajtenberg, Peter Rousseau's contribution in chapter 6 offers a sweeping comparison of electrification and IT as general-purpose technologies. He finds that electricity and IT both meet the standard criteria as GPTs: they are pervasive, improving, and innovation-spawning. Rousseau dates the introduction of electricity to 1894 and IT to 1971, and notes that productivity growth was lower at the onset of the new GPT eras than in the decades preceding them. After the introduction of each technology, economic innovation – as measured by initial public offerings (IPOs), patents, and investment by new firms relative to incumbents – began to rise. In a head-to-head comparison of the GPTs, Rousseau concludes, on the one hand, that electricity was more pervasive and diffused more rapidly and more evenly through the economy than information technologies. IT, on the other hand, saw more dramatic improvements, with its price falling over a hundred times more quickly than that of electricity. (The power of Moore's law exceeded that of the economies of scale and improvements in fuel economy that contributed to falling electricity prices before the 1970s.) In terms of patents, IPOs, and investments in start-ups, IT also seems to have generated more innovation. The slowdown during the birth phase of the IT GPT was also deeper. Thus, Rousseau regards IT as more "revolutionary." Whereas Field preaches caution about the much-hyped IT revolution, Rousseau appears more optimistic, saying that "continuing price declines and the widespread increases in computer literacy . . . suggest . . . the most productive period of the IT revolution still lies ahead."

Gavin Wright, in chapter 7, widens our focus to link the invention and diffusion of new technologies with labor market conditions. He argues that, throughout the twentieth century, periods of rapid productivity growth have also been periods of strong upward pressure on real hourly wages. The 1920s represent one of the clearest examples. Most accounts, Wright argues, stress the causal link from exogenous productivity advance to higher wages. They neglect the causal link operating in the opposite direction, as the processes of induced innovation and diffusion respond to the high-pressure labor market conditions such as those prevailing from the mid-1990s onwards. Many of the computer-based technologies, for example the inventory-control technologies employed by cutting-edge retailers, had been available in the 1970s and 1980s, but were not fully exploited until the 1990s. Wright argues that "*both* blades of the scissors are required to account for the productivity surge" of the period. This chapter also raises an important caution against equating "technological progress" with changes in total factor productivity. The commonly used measures of TFP suffered not only because they are calculated as residuals – and thus, in Moses Abramovitz's formulation, are really "measures of our ignorance" – but also because they assume that technological change is neutral. Technological change that fundamentally changes the production function or redefines inputs or output is poorly captured by such measures.

1.4 Financial bubbles, policy, and the real economy

American observers living through the "roaring nineties" naturally made comparisons with the "roaring twenties." As in the 1920s (and 1960s), "new economy thinking" led even intelligent observers to conclude that the business cycle was dead and a new age of endless growth was possible. Prosperous times such as the 1990s seemed to give the lie to the textbook macro-economics prescriptions that potential output is best captured by the average of what is actually achieved and that NAIRU (the non-accelerating inflation rate of unemployment) is permanently fixed at roughly 6 percent. The 1990s experience induced even Federal Reserve Bank chairman Alan Greenspan, after a period of initial caution, to believe that more aggressive policies could achieve faster growth without reigniting inflation. In the United States, economic prosperity became the core topic of everyday conversation, just as the "war on terrorism" became in the early 2000s. Venture capitalists touting their most recent IPO as the "next new thing" became the centers of media attention, near-celebrities. In contrast to the 1970s and 1980s, when talk about financial matters focused on how to preserve wealth from erosion by inflation and taxes, in the 1990s (or at least the second half) attention was paid to earning wealth through clever investing and risk-taking.

In his chapter exploring the real side of the economy, Robert Gordon details the striking similarities between the 1920s and the 1990s. Placing the series for the two decades on the same graphs, Gordon observes that the growth paths of income, productivity, and employment were almost identical. Inflation remained low in both periods, calling into question the existence of a Phillips Curve trade-off. Over each decade, new GPTs drove the boom. Gordon's analysis seeks to link the appearance and utilization of the new technology with investment behavior. The core question (inspired by the desire to understand better the economic disaster of the 1929–1933 period and avoid its repetition) is to compare investment in the 1920s and the 1990s. Did a technology-inspired "wave of optimism" lead to "overinvestment" in the 1920s and to the subsequent collapse? Are there signs of similar problems in the 1990s? Gordon concludes that, due to better public policies (including, but not limited to, monetary behavior) and to an economic structure emphasizing the service sector, the modern US economy is much "more stable and less fragile than in the 1920s." In this case, the experience of the 1990s provides valuable lessons for how we can understand the past, how we should interpret the causes of the Great Depression.

To the public mind, the most notable analogy between the 1990s and 1920s was soaring stock prices. And one of the greatest sources of concern was whether the "bubble" and the subsequent "bust" would lead to widespread financial disturbances and, ultimately, to severe economic difficulties. In his chapter examining the financial markets in the 1990s in the mirror of the 1920s, Eugene White asks whether it is possible to distinguish between stock prices changes due to improved fundamentals and those due to what Alan Greenspan famously called "irrational exuberance." He further inquires how, given these difficulties, the Federal Reserves should respond to asset market booms and crashes. White argues convincingly that there are enormous difficulties in identifying the role of fundamentals in forward-looking assets, and yet one can't attribute the rise in equity prices solely, or even primarily, to unfounded optimism. The positive signs of a "new economy" promising a prosperous future were real, both in the 1920s and the 1990s. Thus, a Federal Reserve policy of "benign neglect" towards stock market booms was an adequate response. White does suggest that the contrast between the disastrous aftermath of the boom of the 1920s and the much softer landing after the boom of the 1990s highlights the wiser application of monetary policy today. One of the most striking and telling features of the "bubble" of the 1990s is that no major bank or financial institution failed when it finally burst.

Peter Temin (chapter 10) helps to broaden our perspective by placing the 1990s in a comparison with the 1950s as well as the 1920s. He argues that the common feature that each of these periods shared was a "postwar decade." After the ends of the three great wars of the twentieth century – the First World War, the Second World War, and the Cold War – the world economy was shocked by declines in military expenditures and by dramatic changes in government in the losing countries. Even for the winners, postwar decades were special. In Temin's comparison, the experience in the United States following the end of the Cold War appears closer to that after the First World War than after the Second World War. Both the rise and fall of military spending as a share of GDP was greater in the 1940s than in either of the other episodes. Temin observes that "the 1990s recapitulate the 1920s in the United States: the unsustainable boom in stock prices, international capital flows, and income distribution inequality." In contrast with the Second World War and its aftermath, when income and wage distribution in the United States experienced what Claudia Goldin and Robert Margo (1992) call the "great compression," wage and income inequality was high and rising after the ends of the First World War and the Cold War. In addition, the renegotiation of the social contract that commonly occurs after a war was not so apparent in the 1990s. The peace dividend did not lead to an expansion of the welfare state. One key difference Temin notes with the 1920s and 1950s is that, in the 1990s, the United States was the great borrower, not the great lender. Temin's emphasis on the end of the Cold War is welcome, because, the economics of this conflict has heretofore received little attention (with the exception of Edelstein, 1990). The victorious end of the Cold War and the reduction in the threat of nuclear destruction undoubtedly contributed to the optimism for which the 1990s became known in America.

1.5 Globalization and international policymaking

The word "globalization" was found in the pre-1990 editions of good dictionaries but it became a fashionable quasi-neologism only in the 1990s. Whether describing the world economy or the birth of a universal culture, globalization became the catchword of the last decade of the twentieth century. It is now commonplace to say that human life has become global and that only by "thinking global" we can understand reality at the onset of the twenty-first century. But – asks Barry Eichengreen in chapter 3 – how different was globalization in the 1990s from that of previous periods?

International economic integration is driven by two major forces: transportation and communication costs on the one hand, and institutions on the other. Long-distance transportation and communication costs have shown a secular tendency to fall since the early decades of the nineteenth century. Together with the decline of mercantilism and the introduction of market-friendly policies, the steam-engine-driven transport revolution progressively built up the "first globalization" of the last decades of the nineteenth century. After 1914, even as technical progress continued in the transport industry, wars, depression and strained international relations produced a "globalization backlash" (O'Rourke and Williamson, 1999) that began to be slowly reversed only in the 1950s.

Both the first and the second globalization were the result of the long-term decline in transportation and information costs and of an institutional environment that favored the development of domestic and international markets. Thus, Eichengreen notes: "The expansion of international transactions in the 1990s was the continuation of trends that had been under way for as long as half a century, and their growth pace did not significantly exceed that of the preceding twenty-five to fifty years." Nevertheless globalization in the 1990s was more extensive than it was before 1913. In particular: (i) the ratio of world exports to world GDP was considerably higher in 1990 than it had been in 1913 and rose considerably in the following decade (table 3.1); (ii) whereas in 1913 gross world asset and liability positions were very close to net, in the 1990s the former were much higher than the latter, indicating a large multidirectional flow of capital funds not seen in the first globalization (Obstfeld and Taylor, 2003, p. 145). One area where pre-1913 globalization remains unrivalled is labor mobility. Today's somewhat smaller ratios of migrants to the total population, in spite of much higher wage differentials between countries of emigration and immigration, indicate that today's restrictions on labor mobility are much more binding than they were before the First World War.

If the 1990s were not marked by discontinuities (trend breaks) in the pace of international market unification – a process that, according to Eichengreen, is far from full realization – then why has recent public opinion been so impressed by "globalization"? The reason may be found in the level, rather than the rate of change, of integration in the international economy. By the 1990s the level of integration had crossed the threshold where it affected the daily lives of a large number of people in many countries and altered the distributions of income and wealth. This led, among other things, to political clashes about global markets of an intensity not seen since the first globalization of the nineteenth century. One ironic difference was that, this time round, information technology and cheap travel have globalized even anti-globalization protests.

The new political awareness that international developments matter for the "man in the street" in every corner of the world prompted increasing demands, both in developed and developing nations, for active international policymaking. Three developments, Eichengreen argues, had significant implications for the management of the world economy in the 1990s: growth in emerging markets, capital mobility, and the rise of regionalism.

Eichengreen believes that, in some cases, the challenges to international policymaking were addressed quite successfully, as in the case of the completion of the Uruguay Round (1994) and the creation of the World Trade Organization (WTO). A number of countries pursued policies friendly to foreign direct investment (FDI), which held up well in the face of the financial turbulence of the 1990s. Regionalism developed in ways that proved to be complements to rather than substitutes for the growth of global markets and institutions.

Other problems persist however, notably those deriving from short-term capital mobility and from the need to create an international financial architecture better able to prevent financial crises and to mitigate the impact on the real economy of those that inevitably take place (e.g. the crises in Mexico (1994/95), the Far East (1997/98), Russia (1998) and Brazil (1998/99)). Most problematic of all, international policymaking has so far failed to tackle poverty in the lowest-income countries and significantly reduce the long-term impact of economic activity on the natural environment on a global scale.

As with globalization, deregulation also became a key economic policy catchword of the 1990s. In chapter 12, Michael Bernstein argues that the deregulation movement yielded mixed or negative results, at least in the United States. Changes in the telecommunications sector, which – together with banking and aviation – experienced the greatest deregulation in the 1980s and 1990s, lie close to the heart of the IT revolution. Many observers relate the more rapid adoption of information technology in the United States than in Europe to the break-up of AT&T (1982) in the United States and the continued sway of state-run monopolies in Europe. (The faster diffusion of mobile phones in Europe supports rather than refutes this claim.) But the deregulated telecommunications industry was also closely tied to the American bubble and the bust. In the late 1990s rival firms in this sector built vast fiber optic networks in a competition to win first-mover status in this market of the future. Between 1998 and 2001 global investments in fiber optics totaled over $1 trillion. Yet only 5 percent of this capacity was "lit" by the end of the period, as the demand needed to justify the infrastructure build-up never appeared (see Matheison, 2002a, 2000b; Brenner, 2002, 2003). Faced with this over-investment and accounting/underwriting scandals associated with its financing, many industry leaders, including Worldcom/MCI, Global Crossing, and AT&T, were brought low in the early 2000s. But this was not the only reckoning with telecom deregulation. Bernstein observes that in the United States, even as long-distance rates fell,

(v) As Mark Twain might say, the news of the death of the welfare state has been highly exaggerated. For all the talk about a race to the bottom, the welfare state remains alive and well in the advanced countries and is likely to be adopted by middle-income developing countries as they become wealthier and more democratic. The challenges here will be to make sure that the welfare state does not end up on the rocks of deficit spending and to adjust taxation to minimize its allocative distortions.

(vi) The bursting of the financial bubble in 2000/2001 proved more benign than in previous instances. Even in the complex environment created by the attacks on the twin towers of the World Trade Center the 2000/2001 bust in asset prices had a remarkably mild effect on the real economy of the developed countries. This is a marked contrast to previous episodes, such as 1929/30. It is possible to take this historical "novelty" as an indication that monetary macro-management of the domestic economy and international coordination have improved, perhaps as a result of moving along a learning curve from experiencing past difficulties. This promising development also highlights the value of learning the lessons that history offers.

(vii) International policymaking has not been as successful as its domestic counterpart in preventing financial crises and/or mitigating their impact on the real sector of the economy. It is difficult to judge whether international monetary cooperation has been more effective in the 1990s than in its heyday of the 1960s. The creation of the WTO and the Second Basel Accord are important cooperative successes. At the same time, the succession of financial crises in Mexico (1994/95), the Far East (1997/98), Russia (1998) and Brazil (1998/99) indicates that international economic organizations are not yet entirely adjusted to the current financial environment, characterized as it is by free and large-scale capital mobility. Financial crises are monsters that will never be entirely tamed, but, as has been shown by the experience of the US and European bubbles, much can be done to prevent them from seriously damaging the real economy. What is expected of international policymakers at the beginning of the twenty-first century is a renewal of the multilateral cooperative effort in designing and managing international institutions adapted to operating in a context of floating exchange rates, free capital mobility, and the emergence of substantial new players.

Notes

1. While giving the adjectives "roaring" and "best" an ironical twist, Stiglitz and Johnson imply that they were taken seriously by a large number of people.
2. A debate is raging about whether India's boom dates to the adoption of neo-liberal policies in 1991 or to earlier pro-business reforms in 1980. See Panagariya (2004), De Long (2003), and Rodrik and Subramanian (2003). Both sides recognize that growth rates accelerated in the 1980s (above those in the 1970s) and exceeded 5 percent

per annum. The question is whether, given the prevailing policies, the 1980s growth surge was sustainable.

3. The 1990s witnessed a *global* decline in industrial employment, as recorded by the International Labour Org. (see ILO, 2003). As a sign that de-industrialization was not simply a shift from high-wage advanced countries to low-wage developing countries, note that even in China manufacturing employment fell. That is, reductions in employment in China's state-supported heavy industrial sector exceeded the growth in its newer export-oriented consumer goods sector.

4. See Griliches and Berndt (1993). These concerns, together with the recommendations of the Boskin Commission (Boskin et al., 1996), have led to an explosion in the use of hedonic adjustment, which will probably improve our understanding of the performance of the current economy. But it comes at the cost of making comparisons with growth in earlier periods that are equally deserving of hedonic adjustment. A defense of this differential treatment is that quality changes are greater in the current period than in the past. This is not obvious, prima facie, and cannot be justified unless some attempt is made to apply such adjustments earlier.

5. The World Wide Web was invented in 1989 by a European, Tim Berners-Lee, and first deployed at CERN (the European organization for nuclear research). But the United States felt its effects earlier than Europe. For an industry-by-industry assessment of the prospects for catching up, see the contributions in O'Mahoney and van Ark (2003).

2 The world economy in the 1990s: a long-run perspective

Nicholas Crafts

2.1 Introduction

This chapter considers the 1990s in the context of long-run economic growth performance. Growth in the context of this chapter should be understood to comprise the growth of real living standards as well as real GDP per capita. There were a number of new experiences during the decade that were sufficiently surprising to warrant posing the question: "Do we now need to rethink the conventional wisdom about economic growth?"

The essential background to growth in the 1990s was the unprecedented extension and intensification of globalization in terms of the international integration of capital and product markets, sustained both by reductions in transport and communication costs and also by policy choices. Table 2.1 reports an increase in world merchandise exports relative to world GDP from 12.7 percent in 1990 to 18.8 percent in 2000, more than double the ratio reached before the disintegration of the world economy in the interwar years. Even more impressive has been the surge in international capital mobility, reflected in table 2.1 through the ratio of assets owned by foreign residents to world GDP, which rose from 25.2 percent in 1980 to 48.6 percent in 1990, and further to 92.0 percent in 2000 – about five times the peak reached in the early twentieth century.

Obviously, this was facilitated by the more general adoption of policies of trade openness and financial liberalization. But technological progress also played an important role. The public imagination was captured by the notion of the "*death of distance*" (Cairncross, 2001) as new information and communications technologies (ICT) proliferated. Table 2.2 reports data on the spread of the internet and mobile phones, highlighting both the rapid diffusion in OECD countries and the fact that middle- and low-income economies were rapidly following suit by the end of the decade. At this point ICT had become established as a general-purpose technology deserving to be mentioned in the same breath as steam and electricity (Lipsey, Bekar, and Carlaw, 1998).

Table 2.1 *International trade and foreign investment compared with world GDP*

World merchandise exports/world GDP (%)	
1820	1.0
1870	4.6
1913	7.9
1929	9.0
1950	5.5
1973	10.5
1990	12.7
2000	18.8
Foreign assets/world GDP (%)	
1870	6.9
1913	17.5
1930	8.4
1945	4.9
1960	6.4
1980	25.2
1985	36.2
1990	48.6
1995	62.0
2000	92.0

Sources: Exports – Maddison (2001), updated using WTO (2001); assets – Obstfeld and Taylor (2004).

Table 2.2 *The diffusion of information and communications technology*

	Internet hosts/1000		Mobile phones/1000	
	1995	2000	1990	1999
Finland	42.2	200.2	52	651
United States	21.1	179.1	21	312
Singapore	7.4	72.3	17	419
Germany	6.3	41.2	4	286
Spain	1.8	21.0	1	312
Hungary	1.6	21.6	0	162
South Africa	1.2	8.4	0	132
Brazil	0.2	7.2	0	89
Swaziland	0	1.4	0	14

Source: UNDP (2001).

Table 2.3 *Shares of world manufactured production and exports*

Production (%)

	1880	1913	1953	1973	1990	2000
United Kingdom	22.9	13.6	8.4	4.9	3.8	3.5
Rest of Western Europe	30.8	34.8	17.7	19.6	29.1	26.9
North America	15.1	32.9	46.9	35.1	23.4	26.4
Japan	2.4	2.7	2.9	8.8	16.8	13.8
Other East Asia	n.a.	n.a.	0.8	3.1	4.7	6.4
"British India"	2.8	1.4	1.7	2.1	1.7	1.7
China	12.5	3.6	2.3	3.9	2.7	7.0
Rest of world	13.5	11.0	19.3	22.5	17.8	14.3

Exports (%)

	1876–1880	1913	1955	1973	1990	2000
United Kingdom	37.8	26.9	17.9	7.1	6.1	5.0
Rest of Western Europe	51.3	50.3	36.3	49.5	48.1	37.3
North America	4.4	11.1	26.1	16.1	15.2	17.8
Japan	n.a.	2.4	3.9	10.0	11.5	9.7
Rest of Asia	<1.5	3.8				
South and South-East Asia			2.8	4.6	12.0	15.6
China			0.6	0.7	1.9	4.7
Rest of world	<6.5	5.5	12.4	12.0	5.2	9.9

Sources: Production – Bairoch (1982), UN (1965) and UNIDO (2002); exports – Yates (1959), UNCTAD (1983) and WTO (2001).

In this globalizing world economy the other feature that attracted everyone's attention was the rise of China. Table 2.3 captures this with regard to manufacturing. China's share of world manufactured production rose from 2.7 percent in 1990 to 7.0 percent in 2000 and of world manufactured exports from 1.9 percent in 1990 to 4.7 percent in 2000. This represents the most dramatic arrival on the world scene since that of Japan in the 1960s. At the same time, China's share of the world's stock of foreign direct investment rose from 1.4 percent in 1990 to 5.8 percent in 1999 (UNCTAD, 2003). The opposite side of the coin was a pronounced decline in Europe's share of manufactured exports by about 12 percentage points.

Table 2.4 *Growth rates of real GDP per capita (percent per year)*

	1870–1913	1913–1950	1950–1973	1973–1990	1990–2000
Africa	0.57	0.92	2.00	0.14	0.14
Asian Tigers	0.79	0.29	5.98	6.13	4.83
China	0.10	−0.62	2.86	4.77	6.31
India	0.54	−0.22	1.40	2.60	3.87
Latin America	1.82	1.43	2.58	0.69	1.46
Western Europe	1.33	0.76	4.05	2.00	1.76
United States	1.82	1.61	2.45	1.96	1.95

NB: The "Asian Tigers" comprise Hong Kong, Singapore, South Korea, and Taiwan.
Source: Maddison (2003).

Turning to growth rates, the most notable development was the continuation of rapid growth in China and the acceleration of growth in India, the two most populous countries in the world. Their growth rates far outstripped those of the mature OECD economies during the 1990s, as table 2.4 reports, and were very encouraging by historical standards. Sadly, there was no sign of an onset of rapid catch-up growth in Africa, and the bounce-back of Latin America from the trauma of the debt crisis of the 1980s was disappointingly weak.

Other aspects of the 1990s were also quite remarkable. First, the unexpected collapse of the Soviet empire led to the arrival of some twenty-five "transition economies" with an opportunity to join the catch-up growth club. Over the course of the decade their experience of recession, recovery, and – in some, but not all, cases – take-off into sustained economic growth offered unique insights into the political economy of growth. Second, in some parts of the world there was a savage reversal of one of the main achievements of the twentieth century in the growth of living standards, namely the massive and widespread increase in life expectancy. AIDS hit African countries very hard, and by the end of the decade epidemics of the disease were incipient in both China and India. This has implications for the analysis of convergence and divergence that have not yet been fully digested. Third, the general presumption of the postwar years that Western European growth would outpace that of the United States no longer seemed to be valid from the mid-1990s onwards; this owed something to European deceleration as well as to American acceleration. Why this should happen is a puzzle that conventional growth theories may struggle to explain, given that the new technology was widely available and Europe has continued to invest in all the things that "new economy" theorists expect will raise the growth rate.

With these aspects of the economic history of the 1990s to the fore, I shall examine their implications for ideas about and policies for growth. This assessment will, of course, be preliminary in many ways. It is as yet "too soon to tell" what the implications of the 1990s are for the analysis of economic growth. Nevertheless, the effort will be worthwhile if it highlights key issues that can form a menu for further research.

2.2 Accounting for growth

Growth accounting is a standard technique for identifying the proximate sources of growth in benchmarking exercises. The estimates reported in table 2.5 were designed to facilitate comparisons across countries.[1] In the context of a number of debates in the economic growth literature, the estimates for total factor productivity growth deserve the most attention. It should be accepted that these are subject to measurement error (both from incorrect price indices in obtaining real output growth and from inappropriate assumptions about the specification of the production function), which can make comparisons over time rather than between countries in the same period somewhat unreliable (Crafts, 2003). Nevertheless, the following observations are probably robust to problems of this kind.[2]

First, notwithstanding the advent of ICT, for the industrial countries as a whole there was no resurgence in TFP growth during the 1990s. On the contrary, this decade continued the pattern of modest TFP growth that has characterized the OECD countries since the "golden age" of economic growth that ended in the early 1970s. The lack of responsiveness of OECD TFP growth in the late twentieth century to enhanced investments in human capital and in research and development has been highlighted by Jones (1995) as a challenge to the claims of endogenous growth theory. However, it may also represent a gestation period before the full impact of ICT is realized. In any event, despite the excitement of the "new economy" in the United States and the international take-up of new electronic age technologies, there was no return to the TFP growth experienced in the "golden age."[3]

Second, with the possible exception of China, continued rapid Asian catch-up growth owed proportionately less to TFP growth and more to capital deepening in the 1990s than had been the case for Europe in the "golden age."[4] In both East and South Asia this tendency was accentuated in the 1990s compared with the 1980s. By the 1990s the large capital deepening contribution increasingly relied on very high savings rates as incremental capital to output ratios became less favourable (Crafts, 1999).

Third, during the 1990s TFP growth continued to be negative in sub-Saharan Africa, as it had been in both the 1970s and the 1980s. Moreover, in both

Table 2.5 *Sources of labor productivity growth (percent per year)*

	Total factor productivity	Education	Capital deepening	Labor productivity
1950–1973				
France	3.2	0.4	1.4	5.0
Japan	4.1	0.5	2.8	7.4
United Kingdom	1.4	0.2	1.5	3.1
United States	1.6	0.5	1.0	3.1
West Germany	3.6	0.3	1.8	5.7
1970–1980				
Industrial countries	0.3	0.5	0.9	1.7
China	0.8	0.4	1.6	2.8
East Asia	1.0	0.6	2.7	4.3
Latin America	1.2	0.3	1.2	2.7
South Asia	−0.2	0.3	0.6	0.7
Africa	−0.4	0.1	1.3	1.0
1980–1990				
Industrial countries	0.9	0.2	0.7	1.8
China	4.3	0.4	2.1	6.8
East Asia	1.4	0.6	2.4	4.4
Latin America	−2.3	0.5	0.0	−1.8
South Asia	2.3	0.4	1.0	3.7
Africa	−1.4	0.4	−0.1	−1.1
1990–2000				
Industrial countries	0.5	0.2	0.8	1.5
China	5.3	0.3	3.2	8.8
East Asia	0.6	0.5	2.3	3.4
Latin America	0.4	0.3	0.2	0.9
South Asia	1.2	0.4	1.2	2.8
Africa	−0.5	0.4	−0.1	−0.2

NB: "East Asia" comprises Indonesia, Malaysia, the Philippines, Singapore, South Korea, Taiwan, and Thailand. "Africa" is sub-Saharan Africa.
Sources: 1950–1973 – Maddison (1996); 1970–1980, 1980–1990 and 1990–2000 – Bosworth and Collins (2003).

Latin America and Africa the contribution of capital deepening was very weak, and, compared with Asia, these continents are inferior in both components of labor productivity growth. This suggests that reforms inspired by the Washington Consensus did little to transform growth prospects in the late twentieth century.

Table 2.6 *Levels of GDP per capita in 1990 dollars Geary–Khamis*

	1870	1913	1950	1973	1990	2000
Africa	500	637	894	1410	1444	1464
	(20.4%)	(12.0%)	(9.4%)	(8.4%)	(6.2%)	(5.2%)
Asian Tigers	595	828	955	3631	9975	16010
	(24.3%)	(15.6%)	(10.0%)	(21.8%)	(43.0%)	(56.9%)
China	530	552	439	839	1858	3425
	(21.7%)	(10.4%)	(4.6%)	(5.0%)	(8.0%)	(12.2%)
India	533	673	619	853	1309	1910
	(21.8%)	(12.7%)	(6.5%)	(5.1%)	(5.6%)	(6.8%)
Latin America	681	1481	2506	4504	5053	5838
	(27.9%)	(27.9%)	(26.2%)	(27.0%)	(21.8%)	(20.8%)
Western Europe	1960	3458	4579	11416	15966	19002
	(80.2%)	(65.2%)	(47.9%)	(68.4%)	(68.8%)	(67.6%)
United States	2445	5301	9561	16689	23201	28129

NB: The figures in parentheses give the per capita GDP level as a percentage of that of the United States. Geary-Khamis dollars embody a purchasing power parity (PPP) correction to exchange rate conversions.
Source: Maddison (2003).

Recent research has persuaded many economists that differences in income levels across the world owe a great deal to TFP gaps rather than just reflecting shortfalls in physical and human capital per person (Hall and Jones, 1999; Parente and Prescott, 2000). In other words, the pure neoclassical (Solow) model based on universal technology is inapplicable, and, as such, its forecast of ultimate convergence in income levels is unreliable. Prima facie, the productivity experience of the 1990s appears consistent with this position.

2.3 Divergence big time?

During the twentieth century the gap between the poorest and richest countries in terms of real GDP per capita widened dramatically – the experience has been memorably described as "divergence big time" (Pritchett, 1997). This is reflected in table 2.6, which shows that, whereas Africa was at 20.4 percent of the US level in 1870, this had fallen to 9.4 percent by 1950 and to 5.2 percent by 2000. Over the same periods the absolute gap had risen from 1945 to 8667 to 26,665 in 1990 dollars Geary-Khamis, while the level of real GDP per capita in this metric in Africa in 2000 was about $1000 less than in the United States in 1870. The gap continued to widen through the 1990s.

It is also true that income gaps for China and India have widened greatly since 1870. Whereas the gap with the United States then was about 1900 in

Table 2.7 *Population living on $1 and $2 per day (millions)*

	1981	1990	2001
$1 per day			
China	633.7 (63.8)	374.8 (33.0)	211.6 (16.6)
Rest of East Asia	162.1 (42.0)	97.4 (21.2)	60.3 (11.0)
Eastern Europe and Central Asia	3.1 (0.7)	2.3 (0.5)	17.6 (3.7)
Latin America and Caribbean	35.6 (9.7)	49.3 (11.3)	49.8 (9.5)
Middle East and North Africa	9.1 (5.1)	5.5 (2.3)	7.1 (2.4)
India	382.4 (54.4)	357.4 (42.1)	358.6 (34.7)
Rest of South Asia	92.4 (42.2)	104.9 (38.9)	72.5 (21.1)
Sub-Saharan Africa	163.6 (41.6)	218.6 (44.6)	315.8 (46.9)
Total	1481.8 (40.4)	1218.5 (27.9)	1092.7 (21.1)
$2 per day			
China	875.8 (88.1)	824.6 (72.6)	593.6 (46.7)
Rest of East Asia	294.0 (76.2)	291.7 (63.6)	270.7 (49.2)
Eastern Europe and Central Asia	20.2 (4.7)	22.9 (4.9)	93.5 (19.7)
Latin America and Caribbean	98.9 (26.9)	124.6 (28.4)	128.2 (24.5)
Middle East and North Africa	51.9 (28.9)	50.9 (21.4)	69.8 (23.2)
India	630.0 (89.6)	731.4 (86.1)	826.0 (79.9)
Rest of South Asia	191.1 (87.3)	226.1 (83.7)	237.7 (69.1)
Sub-Saharan Africa	287.9 (73.3)	381.6 (75.0)	516.0 (76.6)
Total	2450.0 (66.7)	2653.8 (60.8)	2735.6 (52.9)

NB: $1 ($2) per day is $1.08 ($2.15) at 1993 PPP prices; figures in parentheses give the percentage of the population.
Source: Chen and Ravallion (2004).

1990 dollars Geary-Khamis, by 2000 it was nearly 25,000 for China and over 26,000 for India. Here, however, the 1990s showed some respite from the divergence experience, in that both China and India (together comprising about 37 percent of the world's population) reduced the percentage gap in income levels with the United States. Even so, this still left them far short of their relative position in 1870.

Nevertheless, the 1990s saw continued progress in terms of a reduction in the incidence of extreme poverty, as table 2.7 reports. The number of people living on less than $1 per day fell to 1.09 billion or 21 percent of the population of the developing world in 2001, a reduction of 126 million since 1990 and of 389 million since 1981. This decrease came entirely from growth in East and South Asia, however, while poverty in sub-Saharan Africa intensified. If a $2 per day criterion is adopted then a striking feature of the data in table 2.7 is the marked

Table 2.8 *Human Development Index averages*

	1870	1913	1950	1990	2001
North America	0.504	0.643	0.774	0.912	0.937
Oceania	0.516	0.708	0.784	0.883	0.935
Western Europe	0.421	0.580	0.707	0.888	0.927
Africa	n.a.	n.a.	0.271	0.456	0.478
China	n.a.	n.a.	0.225	0.624	0.721
India	n.a.	0.143	0.247	0.519	0.590

Sources: Crafts (2002) and UNDP (2003).

increase in poverty in Eastern Europe and Central Asia after the collapse of the Soviet Union.

A major qualification to the "divergence big-time" story is that trends in inequality in other important components of living standards have been quite different. Consider the Human Development Index, which is based on income, longevity and educational standards. Table 2.8 reports estimates of HDI over the long run and shows that gaps between Africa, China and India and the OECD countries have narrowed since 1950. Neumayer (2003) has shown that the non-income components of HDI have exhibited both β- and σ-convergence from the 1960s to the end of the 1990s.

Becker, Philipson, and Soares (2003) use estimates of willingness to pay for reduced risks of mortality to convert gains in life expectancy between 1965 and 1995 into an equivalent in terms of real GDP per capita. They find that proportionate gains for poor countries have tended to exceed those of rich countries; thus, the value of the fall in mortality for Egypt between 1965 and 1995 was worth over 70 percent of 1995 GDP whereas for the United States the figure was about 15 percent. The tendency for convergence in life expectancy then implies unconditional β-convergence for "full income" – i.e. – GDP plus the value of improved mortality per head.

Thus trends in HDI have not exhibited divergence big-time. However, the advent of AIDS in the recent past threatens this outcome. If life expectancy had not been affected by this disease, HDI in Africa would have been 0.531 in 2001, and a calculation similar to that used by Becker, Philipson, and Soases (2003) shows that welfare losses in the worst-affected countries (such as Botswana, South Africa, and Zimbabwe) could be equivalent to around 80 percent of GDP per capita (Crafts and Haacker, 2003). The incidence of HIV infection in China and India at the end of the 1990s was similar to that in the worst-affected African countries about twelve years earlier; if the problem is allowed to develop into

Table 2.9 *The growth of real GDP per capita (percent per year)*

	Globalizers	Non-globalizers
1960s	1.4	2.4
1970s	2.9	3.3
1980s	3.5	0.8
1990s	5.0	1.4

Source: Dollar and Kraay (2004).

a similar epidemic, the welfare losses in these two huge countries really will entail a phase of "divergence big time."

A major reason for divergence in income levels is that during the twentieth century there were big rewards for countries with good institutions and policy; the penalties for getting it wrong have been much higher since the Second World War, when the prize of rapid catch-up growth has been on offer more widely than ever before. The evidence of the growth regressions literature points firmly in this direction and identifies reasons for differences in growth performance between East Asia and Africa or Latin America (Bleaney and Nishiyama, 2002).

Dollar and Kraay (2004) find that in the 1980s, and even more so the 1990s, countries that they classify as "globalizers" enjoyed a far superior growth performance to that of "non-globalizers," as table 2.9 reports. Their classification is based on the expansion of trade relative to GDP, and includes in the former category China and India along with twenty-two other countries. This might be taken to show that globalization was good for growth in the late twentieth century and that a full embrace of globalization throughout the Third World might be an antidote to divergence.

On balance, the evidence does suggest that openness to trade is good for growth, partly directly and partly through its association with improved institutional quality (Winters, 2004). The effects of increased international capital mobility are much more debatable. Broadly speaking, in the absence of a subsequent financial crisis and in the presence of good institutions a positive effect from financial liberalization of up to one percentage point is predicted (Edison et al., 2002), but in the 1980s and 1990s globalization seems to have led to a much greater incidence of financial crises (notably in the Far East in 1997/98) (Bordo et al., 2001), and this has undermined the advantages that might otherwise have ensued (Eichengreen and Leblang, 2002).

In this context, it is noteworthy that China, although pursuing outwardly oriented policies, is still much more a "developmental state" than a fully paid-up member of the globalization club. Indeed, it surely avoided the 1997 crisis only because it had not liberalized the capital account of the balance of payments. Similarly, the Asian Tigers – with the exception of Hong Kong – also fall into this category. The growth of these countries seems to be that of a modern-day Gerschenkronian latecomer, as the well-known accounts by Amsden (1989) and Wade (1990) of growth in South Korea and Taiwan underline. The success of the "globalizers" does not detract from the point that institutional diversity is potentially valuable in the early stages of development in the context of high transaction costs and market failures. The evidence of the 1990s is that globalization continues to have dangers, especially in the form of financial crises, as well as rewards for developing countries.

2.4 Some implications of the ICT revolution

The "death of distance" and its close cousin the "weightless economy" were popular ideas in the 1990s, and were sometimes thought to be coming to pass as a result of the revolution in ICT. The implications would be dramatic, as is stressed by the "new economic geography." When transport and communication costs are either very high or very low economic activity is widely dispersed and there is no penalty to being far away from the center. When transport costs are "intermediate" industrial location decisions feel the pull of centrality through linkage effects and firms find it desirable to be near their suppliers or their industrial customers, as market access is a key advantage (Venables, 1996). Thus, if breakthroughs in ICT meant the death of distance, we would expect a huge migration of economic activity to hitherto low-wage parts of the world. The rise of China might seem to support this hypothesis to some extent, as would the growing practice of offshoring business services.

In fact, the evidence suggests that distance was very much still alive in the 1990s and mattered a great deal for economic interactions, as table 2.10 reports. Add to this econometric evidence that the pull of centrality through linkage effects was steadily increasing in Europe during the 1990s (Midelfart-Knarvik et al., 2000), that distance from markets and suppliers "explained" about 70 percent of the variance in world income levels (Redding and Venables, 2004) and that world market access was highly unequal across the world, as is set out in table 2.10. The implication is that during the 1990s the traditional pattern of the concentration of industrial activity was basically sustained, although with some shifts in the balance between regions, as is suggested by table 2.3.

Of course, ICT clearly had some novel effects. Both offshoring and outsourcing were encouraged. McKinsey Global Institute (2003) has estimated that by 2001 offshored business services amounted to about $26 billion (skewed heavily to India and Ireland), initially focusing on call centers, data processing, accounting, etc., and were growing at the rate of 30 to 40 percent per year. A notable development during the 1990s was the divestment by General Motors

Table 2.10 *Distance, economic interactions, and world market access*

Economic interactions and distance (flows relative to their magnitude at 1000 km)

	Trade	Equity finance	FDI	Technology
1000 km	100	100	100	100
2000 km	42	55	75	65
4000 km	18	31	56	28
8000 km	7	17	42	5

World market access (North America = 100)

North America	100
Western Europe	92
Eastern Europe	87
South-East Asia	52
Other Asia	40
Latin America	35
Sub-Saharan Africa	34
Oceania	21

Sources: Distance – Venables (2001), based on estimated gravity models; access – Redding and Venables (2002).

of its parts division (the reverse of what happened in the 1920s) as outsourcing advanced (Lucking-Reiley and Spulber, 2001). In general, insofar as the internet has increased the range of potential suppliers of inputs, it has reduced the scope for opportunistic behavior and thus the advantages of vertical integration, and has encouraged American companies to import more. But, at the same time as the complexity of the production and design process has also been enhanced, the advantages of proximity for just-in-time production and for transactions that require "handshakes" as opposed to mere "conversations" has also been increased (Leamer and Storper, 2001). Thus, during the 1990s, ICT was changing the role that geography plays in location decisions but not abolishing it. The weightless proportion of GDP was still fairly small.

Although it did not imply the death of distance, technological progress in ICT was a very important aspect of economic growth the 1990s, with the benefits spread quite widely across the world – contrary to the inferences sometimes drawn from growth accounting exercises. This is best appreciated by recognising that because, driven by Moore's Law, the price of ICT equipment fell so rapidly, the gains from technological progress in the ICT-producing countries were transferred to a wide array of users across the world, as is shown by the estimates of "social savings" from ICT by Bayoumi and Haacker (2002).[5]

2.5 After the "golden age": European sclerosis?

Throughout the years from the early 1950s to the mid-1990s labour productivity grew more rapidly in Western Europe than in the United States. In the early postwar period the United States had a large productivity lead, but this was quickly reduced by rapid European catch-up growth during the "golden age," which ended in the early 1970s. In the next twenty years both the United States and Western Europe experienced a productivity growth slowdown, but here too Europe had the faster growth and by the mid-1990s the leading European countries had overtaken the United States in terms of (PPP-adjusted) real GDP per hour worked. At the same time, however, the gap in terms of real GDP per capita between Europe and the United States stayed much the same over the last thirty years, as reductions in hours worked and labor force participation offset the differential productivity performance, as table 2.11 reports.

Since 1995, however, the United States has experienced a productivity growth revival whilst in much of Western Europe productivity growth has weakened markedly such that in recent years the United States has outperformed; see table 2.11. This reversal of relative growth outcomes has coincided with the disappearance of the Solow productivity paradox in the United States, and is clearly related to greater American success in exploiting the productivity potential of ICT. This raises the question of whether the old pattern of faster productivity growth in Europe will reassert itself or whether we have entered a new era in which American productivity growth will permanently be the faster of the two.

There are several possibilities:
 i) European incentive structures have become less favorable for catch-up growth;
 ii) a European productivity surge is just around the corner following an ICT diffusion lag; and
iii) ICT fits less well than earlier technologies with European social capability.

The period between 1950 and 1973 is conventionally known as the "golden age" of European economic growth. Growth rates of real GDP per hour worked were in excess of 4 percent per year for most Western European countries, with the fastest growth experienced by countries with the lowest initial income levels – i.e. – the most scope for catch-up growth. The productivity slowdown after 1973 resulted largely from the exhaustion of the transitory aspects of rapid catch-up growth (Temin, 2002).

Catch-up in early postwar Europe was by no means automatic. It was based on having "social capability" (Abramovitz, 1986) – that is, incentive structures that encouraged innovation and investment. A key feature of the period was that in many countries postwar settlements had developed "social contracts"

Table 2.11 *The relationship between real GDP and labor productivity in the European Union and the United States.*

Sources of the real GDP per capita gap (% United States)

	Labor productivity	Hours worked	Employment	Real GDP per capita
1973				
Germany	−25	0	+4	−21
Ireland	−58	+5	−6	−59
Sweden	−22	−5	+8	−19
United Kingdom	−35	+3	+4	−28
EU15	−31	0	+2	−29
1990				
Germany	−1	−16	−3	−20
Ireland	−30	−4	−15	−49
Sweden	−19	−10	+5	−24
United Kingdom	−22	−6	−1	−29
EU15	−12	−12	−6	−30
2003				
Germany	+4	−24	−7	−27
Ireland	+8	−11	−6	−9
Sweden	−12	−13	+1	−24
United Kingdom	−15	−10	−2	−27
EU15	−8	−14	−7	−29

Growth (% per year)

	Labor productivity	Hours worked	Real GDP
1973–1990			
EU15	2.6	−0.2	2.4
United States	1.2	1.8	3.0
1990–1995			
EU15	2.5	−1.0	1.5
United States	1.0	1.4	2.4
1995–2000			
EU15	1.6	1.1	2.7
United States	1.9	2.2	4.1
2000–2003			
EU15	0.9	0.3	1.2
United States	1.9	0.1	2.0

NB: The "EU15" comprise Austria, Belgium, Denmark, Finland, France, Germany, Greece, Ireland, Italy, Luxembourg, the Netherlands, Portugal, Spain, Sweden, and the United Kingdom.

Source: Derived from Groningen Growth and Development Centre (2005); estimates up to and including 1990 are for West Germany.

that facilitated wage moderation in return for high investment in a corporatist setting accompanied by trade liberalization (Eichengreen, 1996). The quid pro quo for greater exposure to the risks of international economy was enhanced social insurance (Rodrik, 1997).

The legacy of the European postwar settlements as they encountered the turbulent 1970s was a substantial increase in public spending relative to GDP and strengthened regulation of labor and product markets. This had adverse effects on incentive structures, notably through raising taxes and employment protection while undermining competition. Prescott (2004) notes that the divergence in hours worked between Europe and the United States seems to reflect growing disparities in the taxation of labor incomes. By the 1990s restrictions in the supply of goods and of labor resulting from weaker competition may have accounted for about 40 percent of the real GDP per capita gap between the European Union and the United States (Bayoumi, Laxton, and Pesenti, 2004).

However, these adverse effects applied to levels of GDP per capita rather than labor productivity growth and did not constitute an obstacle to continued productivity catch-up of the United States by the European Union through the mid-1990s, even though the unfortunate policy stance was already in place, as table 2.12 reports. Whereas the TFP gap between the European Union and the United States was 20 percent in 1979, by 1995 this had halved to 10 percent (O'Mahoney, 2002). Indeed, since the 1980s European countries have moved towards the deregulation of labor and product markets. Given the existence of agency problems in firms, this could have been expected to speed up the adoption of new technologies (Aghion, Dewatripont, and Rey, 1997) – a prediction that is borne out by the econometric evidence (Nicoletti and Scarpetta, 2003).

The acceleration in American productivity growth has been much discussed and it is generally accepted that it owed a good deal to ICT, notwithstanding the misdirected investments and excessive optimism of the bubble years. The episode has been analyzed by several authors using variants of growth accounting techniques. They show a distinct change of pace in the mid-1990s and attribute this mainly to the impact of ICT (see, for example, Oliner and Sichel, 2002). A growth accounting comparison has found that the contribution of ICT to labor productivity growth in 1995–2000 in the United States was twice that in the European Union, 1.2 percent compared with 0.6 percent per year (van Ark et al., 2003).

Both macro- and micro-level analysis suggest that there were substantial lags in obtaining the productivity pay-offs from investments in ICT. This has been the experience in the United States, where strong TFP growth after 1995 is positively related to ICT investment in the same sector in the 1980s but negatively related to ICT investment in the 1990s (Basu et al., 2003). The much higher long-term returns reported by Brynjolfsson and Hitt (2000) reflect the time that it takes to follow up investment in ICT with changes in organizational structures and to learn about the capabilities of ICT in specific business settings. Moving to new work practices, such as operating with fewer layers of management, introducing flexible job responsibilities, the decentralization of work structures and greater use of teamwork, has been fundamental to high productivity outcomes (OECD, 2001).

This has proved more difficult for Europe in the 1990s, both because of a slow start in ICT investment in the 1980s – seemingly related to market imperfections that raised the price of ICT equipment substantially above the American level (de Serres, 2003) – and because labor market regulation acted as an inhibiting factor. European Union investment expenditures on ICT rose from 2.2 percent of GDP in 1990 to 2.9 percent of GDP in 2000, about what the United States was already spending in 1980 (van Ark et al., 2003).

The relative weakness of investment in ICT in Europe seems also to be related to regulation. Gust and Marquez (2002) have show that ICT investment – but not investment in general – is negatively related to employment protection legislation. The rationale is that employment protection legislation, which raises firing costs, is an obstacle to the upgrading of the labor force and the reorganizing of work practices that are central to obtaining the pay-off from ICT. This may also help to explain why the United Kingdom, with very weak employment protection by European standards, has a relatively strong ICT capital deepening growth contribution (van Ark et al., 2003). Although Europe moved in the direction of reducing employment protection during the 1990s, as table 2.12 reports, at the end of the decade firing costs were still much higher than in the United States.

There is therefore some reason to think that ICT is less compatible with European incentive structures than investment in other types of capital. Nonetheless, it is important not to exaggerate this. The coefficient on employment protection estimated by Gust and Marquez (2002) suggests that if the European Union were as laissez-faire as the United States rather less than half of the gap in the ICT investment/GDP ratio would be eliminated.

Prior to the mid-1990s Europe had a strong record of faster productivity growth than the United States. Of itself, this implies that simplistic arguments about European sclerosis are inadequate. The taxation and regulation that were imposed in the 1960s and 1970s were not so out of line with the United States as to preclude productivity catch-up, although there probably was a cost in lower growth of labor inputs and of real GDP. More nuanced hypotheses concerning regulation do, however, have some validity. In particular, it appears that employment protection regulation and the high price of ICT capital goods held back investment in ICT capital deepening in the 1980s. Given the long lags that appear to characterize the realization of productivity gains from this

Table 2.12 *Supply-side policy stances*

Distortionary Tax Revenues (% GDP)

	1955	1980	1990	2000
Germany	20.2	27.6	27.0	27.3
Ireland	11.8	21.3	19.3	19.5
Sweden	18.2	38.5	40.2	43.0
United Kingdom	19.6	26.2	25.6	25.3
EU median	17.1	27.0	27.8	29.8
United States	19.1	26.3	22.1	24.9

Employment Protection Index (0–2)

	1960–1964	1973–1979	1980–1987	1998
Germany	0.45	1.65	1.65	1.30
Ireland	0.02	0.45	0.50	0.50
Sweden	0.00	1.46	1.80	1.10
United Kingdom	0.16	0.33	0.35	0.35
EU median	0.65	1.35	1.35	1.10
United States	0.10	0.10	0.10	0.10

Product market regulatory reform (0–6)

	1978	1988	1993	1998
Germany	5.2	4.7	3.8	2.4
Ireland	5.7	5.1	4.8	4.0
Sweden	4.5	4.2	3.5	2.2
United Kingdom	4.3	3.5	1.9	1.0
EU median	5.6	5.0	4.2	3.2
United States	4.0	2.5	2.0	1.4

Sources: Tax revenues – OECD (1981, 2002); distortionary taxes are defined as in Kneller, Bleaney, and Gemmell (1999); employment protection – Nickell (2003); regulatory reform – Nicoletti et al. (2001).

new general-purpose technology the adverse implications relative to the United States were probably felt more in the 1990s than the 1980s.

ICT investment seems to have been unusually sensitive to these factors, and thus European policies exacted a price in the context of a new technological era that would not have been paid previously. The message is that social capability depends not only on institutional arrangements and policy choices but on the nature of the technological opportunities that are available.

2.6 Convergence, not divergence, in the twenty-first century?

In a pure neoclassical model, in which all countries have access to the same technology and institutions and adopt market-friendly policies while capital is fully mobile internationally, international economic inequalities should be rapidly reduced as capital flows from rich to poor countries and a process of economic catch-up and convergence ensues.

Lucas (2000) argues that in the globalized world economy of the twenty-first century this vision will start to become more and more relevant, as countries increasingly learn the lessons of history and reject failed (non-market-friendly) policies, adopt institutions that underpin efficient markets and avail themselves of elastic supplies of foreign capital and technology that eliminate the domestic savings and knowledge constraints on growth. The "Lucas paradox" (Lucas, 1990) that capital has generally not flowed from rich to poor countries will evaporate. Countries that join the catch-up club will be able to grow at rates way above those enjoyed by the Asian Tigers. A calibrated version of the model has the interesting property that it produces a long-run trend in world income inequality much like that reported by Boltho and Toniolo (1999), with a peak in the third quarter of the twentieth century, and then goes on in the future to exhibit massive declines in inequality throughout the next hundred years. So, does the experience of the 1990s suggest that Lucas's prediction will come true?

The first obvious difficulty with the argument is that it takes no account of geography. In section 2.4 it was shown that distance still mattered a lot in the 1990s, and that its death has been greatly exaggerated. The prospect that this offers is one of various convergence clubs with different steady-state levels of income rather than a full equalization of per capita income across the world. The income levels that different locations will support seem at present to exhibit a high variance (Redding and Venables, 2004). Nevertheless, the evidence of growth regressions suggests that the direct influence of geography on growth is weak relative to that of institutions and policy (Gallup, Sachs, and Mellinger, 1999).

The second big problem is identified by new institutional economic history (North, 1990). This school of thought would certainly stress the key role that institutions play in informing decisions to invest and/or to innovate. In the absence of well-defined property rights, enforceable contracts and government that is credibly committed to non-predatory behaviour, the neoclassical catch-up process will be aborted. At the same time, this tradition stresses both that bad institutions are frequently persistent and, once in place, can be virtually impossible to depose and also that "informal" institutions (rules of the game based on social norms) are important and generally not amenable to top-down reform.

Table 2.13 *The rule of law governance indicator*

	1996	2002
OECD Europe	1.63	1.65
Asian Tigers	1.34	1.22
EU accession candidates	0.33	0.68
Latin America	−0.12	−0.35
Africa	−0.60	−0.71
Russia	−0.80	−0.78

NB: The indicator is scaled from −2.5 to +2.5.
Source: Kaufmann, Kraay and Mastruzzi (2003).

There is substantial empirical evidence in favor of the claim that property
rights institutions matter and that strong but limited government is the corner-
stone of sustaining long-run growth (Acemoglu and Johnson, 2003). Moreover,
these authors support the proposition that institutions are persistent by stress-
ing the long-run implications of different strategies of colonization contingent
on the disease environment. If this perspective is correct, it is important to note
that there is still a huge variation in the extent to which the rule of law applies
around the world and that, in general, there has been little sign of improvement
in recent years in the least well-governed countries of the world, as table 2.13
reports.

The experience of the transition economies in the 1990s offers some further
support to this pessimistic view but also provides quite an important corrective.
Table 2.13 reports that Russia has a depressingly low score for rule of law, as in
fact do all the CIS (Confederation of Independent States) countries. This seems
to illustrate a case where a bad equilibrium has been established from which
escape will be difficult. By contrast, the Central European and Baltic countries
that acceded to the European Union in 2004 experienced a rapid improvement
in institutions during the 1990s, which is reflected in table 2.13. This represents
a successful use of conditionality in that institutional reform was a sine qua non
for membership of the European Union, a prize that was perceived as valuable
enough to sustain pro-reform coalitions.

Table 2.14 reports long-term growth projections for the transition economies,
based on a modification of the IMF growth regressions methodology (Fischer,
Sahay, and Vegh, 1998) that takes account of institutional quality. Three important points stand out. First, that the CIS countries, which have not for the most
part reformed their institutions successfully, have very poor growth prospects,
bearing in mind that their initial income levels are very low and growth could
be very rapid if circumstances were propitious. Second, the Eastern European

Table 2.14 *Projections for the long-run growth of real GDP per capita in the transition economies (percent per year)*

Eastern Europe		CIS countries	
Bulgaria	2.16	Armenia	2.34
Czech Republic	4.64	Azerbaijan	3.66
Estonia	4.48	Belarus	2.54
Hungary	4.38	Georgia	1.11
Latvia	3.58	Kazakhstan	1.44
Lithuania	3.93	Kyrgyz Republic	2.52
Poland	4.09	Russia	1.78
Romania	3.19	Tajikistan	2.75
Slovakia	5.32	Ukraine	2.49
Slovenia	3.37	Uzbekistan	3.16
Average	3.91	Average	2.38

Source: Crafts and Kaiser (2004).

countries, all now either EU member states or accession candidates, have rather better prospects thanks to the institutional reforms that they have accomplished. Third, even so, it is hard to envisage the double-digit growth that Lucas (2000) supposes is on the cards for countries joining the catch-up growth club. Crafts and Kaiser (2004), using a growth accounting framework, note that unless the accession candidates achieve unprecedented TFP growth they are most unlikely to emulate the growth performance of the Asian Tigers, simply because their demographics are much less favorable.

In sum, the vision that Lucas offers of a world in which convergence takes over and international income inequality is ultimately vanquished still seemed a long way off at the end of the 1990s. In particular, it is very hard to be optimistic about growth prospects either in Africa or much of the former Soviet Union.

2.7 Conclusions

The 1990s saw unprecedented developments in the extent of globalization, partly connected with the blossoming of a new general-purpose technology, ICT, that bears comparison with electricity and steam. The continuation of very rapid growth in China and, to a lesser extent, India has opened up quite new prospects for the balance of world economic activity and for the world distribution of income over the coming decades.

Nevertheless, some aspects of economic growth in the 1990s were seriously oversold in the popular media. It is apparent that the "death of distance" was greatly exaggerated and that the impact of reductions in communication and transport costs on the location of industry was modified somewhat rather than abolished entirely. Similarly, although the impact of ICT on productivity growth was significant, especially in the United States, where even sceptics believe that trend growth has risen by over half a percentage point (Gordon, 2003a), the "new economy" was not the miraculous transformation of growth prospects that its proponents on Wall Street claimed.

Seen in terms of human development rather than the national accounts concept of economic growth, the most disturbing aspect of the 1990s was the catastrophic fall in life expectancy in countries that succumbed to the HIV/AIDS epidemic, with the threat that it might spread to other parts of the world. This threatens to reverse at a stroke one of the most remarkable achievements of the twentieth century, namely the massive reduction of mortality risks in poor countries.

So, what are the lessons of the 1990s for growth economics and for policy-making in the twenty-first century?

First, it is clear that globalization potentially challenges conventional generalizations about catch-up and convergence. If transport and communication costs tend to zero and capital is much more internationally mobile than hitherto, it might be reasonable to suppose that the neoclassical predictions will, after all, become valid. This is the vision offered by Lucas (2000). If this seems implausible then it is important to pin down the reasons why globalization will not deliver this outcome.

Second, it is surely desirable to think about convergence and divergence in terms of living standards rather than GDP per capita. Taking increases in life expectancy into account challenges standard claims about "divergence big time" in the past. However, the effects of AIDS in Africa together with the threat of epidemics in China and India could result in a new type of divergence in the future. This suggests that Nordhaus (2000) is right to urge us to think more about concepts of national income that are utility-based and that international policy initiatives to promote economic development should stress disease control and eradication more than hitherto.

Third, the puzzle of European productivity growth performance in the 1990s suggests that social capability is both more important and more complex than is often recognized. The requirements of a new technological epoch may involve reform. Aspects of the postwar settlements that were helpful in promoting rapid catch-up growth during the "golden age" may subsequently have become liabilities. This indicates that we need to find out more about how yesterday's solutions become tomorrow's problems.

Finally, the encouraging progress in institutional reform made by the transition economies that have recently joined the European Union offers a positive experience of conditionality in substantially improving growth prospects. It would be nice to work out ways in which aspects of this could be replicated.

Notes

I thank my discussant, Ignazio Visco, for comments that have improved this work substantially. The usual disclaimer applies.

1. The estimates for 1950–1973 derived from Maddison (1996) are not strictly comparable with the remainder, which are taken from Bosworth and Collins (2003) and use standardized factor share weights. However, differences in methods between the two studies are not important enough to invalidate their use for the present purpose.

2. Estimates for China present big problems. Those reported in table 2.5 almost certainly exaggerate both output growth and TFP growth, possibly very substantially so; see Young (2003) for a detailed discussion, and an estimate that between 1978 and 1998 labor productivity growth is overstated by 1.7 percentage points per year and TFP growth in the non-agricultural sector is overstated by 1.6 percentage points per year.

3. "Golden age" TFP growth clearly benefited substantially from a number of transitory components stemming from the reorganization and reconstruction of OECD economies and from the widespread catch-up of the United States; see Maddison (1996).

4. The contribution of TFP is understated and that of capital deepening is overstated if, as is probable, the elasticity of substitution between capital and labour was less than one. This bias is relatively large when capital/labour ratios grow rapidly. A correction of up to 0.8 percent per year to TFP growth might be called for which would still leave the thrust of the argument intact; see Crafts (1999).

5. "Social savings" can be thought of as consumer surplus gains. In a closed economy this would approximate to the growth accounting contribution of TFP growth in ICT production, but where ICT products are exported some of this accrues to foreign consumers.

3 Managing the world economy in the 1990s

Barry Eichengreen

3.1 Introduction

Three developments with significant implications for the management of the world economy in the 1990s were growth in emerging markets, capital mobility, and the rise of regionalism. After the "lost decade" of the 1980s growth accelerated in the developing world. Exports from developing countries grew twice as rapidly as production, by nearly 10 percent per annum.[1] Disturbances in emerging markets, including financial crises, became a prominent concern. And emerging market economies, for their part, increasingly insisted on a voice in the management of the international system.

The preceding reference to financial crises points to the second important development, namely rising capital mobility. A growing number of countries relaxed controls on capital movements in the 1980s and 1990s. Advances in information and communications technologies reduced the costs and increased the attractions of investing across borders. In response, net private capital flows to developing countries rose sixfold between 1983–1989 and 1993–1996. Capital mobility promised to extend the benefits of portfolio diversification, consumption smoothing, and higher rates of capital formation to developing countries. But capital flows proved not just large but also volatile. Their management thus proved a major challenge.

The third important development was the rise of regionalism. The 1990s saw the deepening and widening of the European Union. It also saw the establishment of NAFTA (the North American Free Trade Agreement) and the development of Asian regionalism. Increasingly, events such as the EU currency crisis of 1992, which once might have been thought to be in the province of global institutions such as the IMF, were handled regionally.

Of course, these developments were neither without precedent nor without parallel. In the second half of the nineteenth century an earlier cohort of emerging markets, the overseas regions of recent European settlement, had transformed the pattern of international settlements and the global competitive balance. The emergence in the late nineteenth and early twentieth centuries of the largest and most dynamic member of that cohort, the United States, had disturbed the operation of the international monetary system and international capital markets.

Nor was the final decade of the twentieth century the first period of high international capital mobility: as a share of global GNP, net capital flows were, in fact, larger in the century's opening decade. Financial crises, similarly, were far from unprecedented. And the end of the twentieth century was not the first episode of economic regionalism, there having been colonial systems and economic blocs in the nineteenth century and the 1930s as well.

But that these phenomena had precedents does not limit their utility as windows onto the challenges of managing the world economy. Indeed, subtle differences in the nature of these changes and in the policy responses they elicited can help us understand what was distinctive about the global economy and its management in the 1990s.

3.2 How different were the 1990s?

How different, from this point of view, were the 1990s? At one level the 1990s were similar to previous decades in that the rise in international transactions was a continuation of trends that had been under way for a half-century and more. Those trends reflected secularly declining communication and transportation costs, which encouraged the internationalization of markets and policies. They reflected the removal of restrictions on economic freedom, which has been part and parcel of the removal of restrictions on political freedom.

At the same time, there were signs of an acceleration in the growth of international transactions in the 1990s. This is evident in the rates of growth of international trade, international capital flows, and international production. The question is to what extent this reflected an acceleration in the pace of political and technological change as opposed to other changes, such as autonomous shifts in policy.

Although it became fashionable to draw comparisons with earlier episodes, globalization in the 1990s was, in an important sense, more extensive. Exposure to trade was higher – not surprisingly, since transport costs were lower. The internationalization of manufacturing production was more extensive, given lower costs of communication and therefore corporate control. While net capital flows had been large a century beforehand, gross capital flows were smaller, and a narrower range of assets was traded across borders. In the 1990s many of the constraints leading to this earlier pattern were relaxed by the IT revolution, with far-reaching implications for economic management at the national and international levels.

Table 3.1 *Merchandise exports as percentage of GDP in 1990 prices, 1870–1998*

	1870	1913	1929	1950	1973	1990	1998
France	4.9	7.8	8.6	7.6	15.2	20.5	28.7
Germany	9.5	16.1	12.8	6.2	23.8	32.4	38.9
Netherlands	17.4	17.3	17.2	12.2	40.7	51.1	61.2
United Kingdom	12.2	17.5	13.3	11.3	14.0	19.6	25.0
Spain	3.8	8.1	5.0	3.0	5.0	11.7	23.5
United States	2.5	3.7	3.6	3.0	4.9	6.8	10.1
Mexico	3.9	9.1	12.5	3.0	1.9	5.3	10.7
Brazil	12.2	9.8	6.9	3.9	2.5	4.2	5.4
China	0.7	1.7	1.8	2.6	1.5	2.9	4.9
India	2.6	4.6	3.7	2.9	2.0	1.6	2.4
Japan	0.2	2.4	3.5	2.2	7.7	12.4	13.4
World	4.6	7.9	9.0	5.5	10.5	12.8	17.2

Source: Maddison (2001, table F-3) and author's calculations based on table C-3.

Table 3.1 shows merchandise exports as a share of GDP for the world and for eleven systemically significant countries. While the rising export/GDP ratio in the 1990s is clearly evident, it is also apparent that this rise was a continuation of a trend extending back to the early 1950s. But by 1973 recovery to the export/GDP ratios of the years prior to the Depression and the Second World War was complete. Thus, the further rise in export/GDP ratios since then must have reflected other forces, such as declining transport costs, the development of global supply chains, and the reduction of tariff and non-tariff barriers (NTBs) to trade.[2] From this point of view, the rise in export/GDP ratios in the 1990s was not unique. It reflected the fact that the world was still far from fully globalized.[3]

At the same time, the rate of increase in the export/GDP ratio was faster. After having risen by less than a quarter in nearly two decades since 1973, the ratio worldwide rose by more than 50 percent in the 1990s. Other changes included export-oriented structural adjustment in Latin America in response to the debt crisis of the 1980s, which ratcheted up the openness of the region's relatively closed countries, and the emergence of China as a major trading power. As a result of these and other factors, it is often asserted that levels of trade dependence were back to 1913 levels at the end of the 1990s. Table 3.1 shows that, in fact, they were actually quite a bit higher.[4]

Flows of labor were stimulated by declining costs of commercial air transportation and telecommunications but constrained by restrictive policies. One way of summarizing the restrictiveness of immigration policy is in terms of the real wage differential between sending and receiving countries – a measure of the incentive to move. In 1880 the US–Italian wage differential was roughly two to one; now the differential between developed and developing countries is on the order of ten to one.

United Nations estimates suggest that the stock of migrants grew by 1.9 percent per annum over the quarter-century from 1965 to 1990, slightly above the rate of growth of the world population, and that the rate of growth of the migrant stock accelerated as the period progressed (table 3.2). In the 1990s, in contrast, the immigrant stock rose by a slower 1.3 percent per annum, reflecting more restrictive policies. What was different about the 1990s, therefore, was not a faster rate of growth of immigration but changes in composition and direction. The advanced countries were the only region to see increases in the immigrant stock over the decade; the migrant population of the less developed regions actually fell by 2 million in the 1990s. Although migration patterns are too diverse to admit of simple generalizations, it might be said the movement of people increasingly took the form of migration from the developing to the developed world. Total gross immigration to the United States, Canada, Australia, and New Zealand rose sharply from an annual average of fewer than 800,000 individuals per year in the 1980s to well over 1,000,000 in the 1990s. Annual immigrant inflows to these countries had been under 600,000 in the 1950s and under 700,000 in the 1960s; this too, then, was a continuation of the broad postwar trend, although the acceleration in the 1990s was noticeable. Nor was this trend limited to North America and Oceania. Net immigration to the European Union rose from 200,000 per annum in the 1980s to roughly 750,000 per annum in the 1990s (Chiswick and Hatton 2003). Western and Southern Europe became destinations for immigrants from Asia, the Middle East, Africa, and the former Soviet Union.

The growth of foreign direct investment and multinational production had been rapid over the entire postwar period; few aspects of this process grew more quickly in the 1990s than in preceding years (table 3.3). An exception is cross-border mergers and acquisitions (M&As), reflecting the growing role of financial markets in international transactions. While there was some sign of an acceleration in the rate at which restrictions on capital inflows and outflows were removed (table 3.4), that trend had already been under way since the mid-1970s or early 1980s in the industrial countries and since the early or late 1980s in the developing world. Reflecting this rise in capital mobility, the 1990s saw the growth of current account balances and the shrinkage of the Feldstein–Horioka puzzle (the high correlation of national savings and investment rates).[5] Similarly, the period saw a rise in foreign assets as a share of world GDP from 25 percent in 1980 to 49 percent in 1990 and 92 percent in 2000 (Obstfeld and Taylor, 2003, table 2.1).

Capital mobility was another feature of the 1990s with important consequences for international economic management. Some have argued that

Table 3.2 *Analysis of the migrant stock by region, 1965, 1975, 1985 and 1990*

| Region | Thousands | | | | Estimated foreign-born population | | | | | | | | | | |
| | | | | | As a percentage of total population of region | | | | Annual rate of change (percent) | | | As a percentage of migrant stock world total | | | |
	1965	1975	1985	1990	1965	1975	1985	1990	1965/75	1975/85	1985/90	1965	1975	1985	1990
World total	75214	84494	105194	119761	2.3	2.1	2.2	2.3	1.2	2.2	2.6	100.0	100.0	100.0	100.0
Developed countries	30401	38317	47991	54231	3.1	3.5	4.1	4.5	2.3	2.3	2.4	40.4	45.3	45.6	45.3
Developing countries	44813	46117	57203	65530	1.9	1.6	1.6	1.6	0.3	2.1	2.7	59.6	54.7	54.4	54.7

Source: Zlotnik (1998).

Table 3.3 *Selected indicators of FDI and international production, 1982–1999*

Item	Value at current prices (billions)			Annual growth rate (percent)				
	1982	1990	1999	1986–1990	1991–1995	1996–1999	1998	1999
FDI inflows	58	209	865	24.0	20.0	31.9	43.8	27.3
FDI outflows	37	245	800	27.6	15.7	27.0	45.6	16.4
FDI inward stock	594	1761	4772	18.2	9.4	16.2	20.1	18.8
FDI outward stock	567	1716	4759	20.5	10.7	14.5	17.6	17.1
Cross-border M&As[a]	n.a.	151	720	26.4[b]	23.3	46.9	74.4	35.4
Sales of foreign affiliates	2462	5503	13564[c]	15.8	10.4	11.5	21.6[c]	17.8[c]
Gross product of foreign affiliates	565	1419	3045[d]	16.4	7.1	15.3	25.4[d]	17.1[d]
Total assets of foreign affiliates	1886	5706	17680[e]	18.0	13.7	16.5	21.2[e]	19.8[e]
Exports of foreign affiliates	637	1165	3167[f]	13.2	13.9	12.7	13.8[f]	17.9[f]
Employment of foreign affiliates (thousands)	17433	23605	40536[g]	5.6	5.0	8.3	11.4[g]	11.9[g]

3.3 The emergence of emerging markets

Table 3.5 shows that the share of developing countries in world trade rose by a third over the decade, from 24 percent at its beginning to 32 percent at its end. A small number of recipient countries similarly came to account for a growing share of North–South capital flows. Between 1990 and 1996 sixteen emerging markets accounted for nearly three-quarters of all net private capital flows to the developing world (IMF, 1997, 76). One implication was that policy towards developing countries bifurcated into policy towards middle-income countries with ready access to international markets for exports and finance versus policy towards low-income countries in need of debt relief and export-oriented structural reform (discussed in section 3.4 below). Another implication was that Third World countries, regardless of the category into which they fell, insisted on more voice in the institutions of global governance.

An illustration is the Uruguay Round of trade negotiations, signed in April 1994. In contrast to its predecessors, this was the first trade round in which the developing countries formed a significant negotiating group. Exports had come to figure more importantly in their growth strategies, highlighting the issue of market access. Developing countries thus worked together with some of the smaller industrial economies to craft a compromise agenda. In contrast to previous multilateral trade rounds, they did not insist on strict reciprocity as a condition for concessions. In turn this facilitated cross-issue bargaining.

Developing countries also provided impetus for the creation of the World Trade Organization, which they saw as a way of limiting the scope for unilateral action by the larger powers, including the United States. Their immediate objectives included steps to outlaw voluntary export restraints, such as those on clothing and textiles, which had grown into the Multi-Fiber Arrangement (MFA), and to facilitate agricultural trade liberalization. Lobbying as a block, they succeeded in including in the Uruguay Round an agreement to phase out a variety of voluntary restraints and orderly marketing agreements. They secured small steps in the direction of reducing agricultural protection, such as the tariffication of border measures. In return, developing countries "gave" market access for service industries and the extension of the multilateral trade regime to intellectual property. This is not to suggest that there were no divisions among the developing countries. But their collective voice figured more prominently than in earlier General Agreement on Tariffs and Trade (GATT) rounds, reflecting their growing importance as exporters and importers.

Just as emerging markets worried that the GATT was too weak to prevent arbitrary action by the large industrial countries, they complained about institutional weaknesses in the International Monetary Fund (IMF), the World Bank, the Bank for International Settlements. The BIS was an extreme case: though its Committee of Banking Supervisors was charged with formulating

Table 3.3 (*cont.*)

Memorandum:								
GDP at factor cost	10611	21473	30061^h	11.7	6.3	0.6	−0.9	3.0^h
Gross fixed capital formation	2231	4686	6058^h	13.5	5.9	−1.4	−2.1	−0.3^h
Royalties and fees receipts	9	27	65^h	22.0	14.2	3.9	6.3	0.5^h
Exports of goods and non-factor services	2041	4173	6892^h	15.0	9.5	1.5	−1.8	3.0^h

[a] Data are available only from 1987 onwards.
[b] 1987–1990 only.
[c] Based on a regression of sales against FDI inward stock for the period 1982–1997.
[d] Based on a regression of gross product against FDI inward stock for the period 1982–1997.
[e] Based on a regression of assets against FDI inward stock for the period 1982–1997.
[f] Based on a regression of exports against FDI inward stock for the period 1982–1997.
[g] Based on a regression of employment against FDI inward stock for the period 1982–1997.
[h] Estimates.

Source: UNCTAD (2000, p. 4).

Table 3.4 *National regulatory changes affecting FDI, 1991–1999*

Item	1991	1992	1993	1994	1995	1996	1997	1998	1999
Number of countries that introduced changes in their investment regimes	35	43	57	49	64	65	76	60	63
Number of regulatory changes	82	79	102	110	112	114	151	145	140
of which:									
More favorable to FDI	80	79	101	108	106	98	135	136	131
Less favorable to FDI	2	–	1	2	6	16	16	9	9

Source: UNCTAD (2000, p. 6).

financial markets had been equally globalized before. While they have a point, there is a question mark over how far to push it. Foreign investment loomed large before 1913 in the development of certain countries – the United Kingdom on the creditor side and Canada and Australia on the debtor side – but it loomed much smaller in the accounts of others, such as the United States. Other data, including Obstfeld and Taylor's (2003) estimates of foreign assets as a share of world GDP, suggest that foreign asset stocks were considerably smaller in 1913 than in the 1990s. In part, this is telling us about the difference between gross and net flows: estimates of foreign assets are constructed by cumulating gross flows, whereas current account balances reflect net flows. And gross flows were almost certainly an order of magnitude larger in the 1990s, reflecting diversification on the part of rich-country investors. In addition, it was in connection with gross flows that the impact of information technology was most apparent; the cost of moving financial capital across borders with a click on a computer keyboard was a small fraction of the cost of a cable-based transaction a century earlier. Thus, the 1990s were different from, say, the 1890s by virtue of the growth of short-term gross capital flows in particular.

The impact of advances in IT can also be seen in the volume of transactions on foreign exchange markets, a more specialized indicator of what was happening to gross international capital flows and to short-term gross flows in particular. Official Bank for International Settlements (BIS) estimates suggest that transactions in spots, forwards, and swaps rose by 46 percent between 1992 and 1995 and by a somewhat slower 26 percent between 1995 and 1998.[6] Other measures that adjust volumes for changes in the value of non-dollar transactions suggest that the growth of turnover in fact accelerated between these periods. These were rapid rates of growth from levels that were already historically unprecedented.

The greater ease of transmitting information across long distances encouraged the internationalization of production. The growth of FDI in manufacturing was thus one of the profound differences from the pre-1914, when direct investment had been heavily concentrated in extractive. The development of global supply chains was evident in the growth of FDI in China, while the incentive to produce close to the customer was apparent in the growing volume of M&As between the high-income countries. It is important to emphasize the far greater importance of FDI at the end of the twentieth century. Whereas in 1914 nearly all of the global stock of FDI was located in developing countries and (Dunning, 1983), in the mid-1990s well over two-thirds was located in the industrial countries (UNCTAD, 2000), reflecting the large volume of direct-investment-related transactions among the industrial countries themselves.[9]

Table 3.5 *Percentage shares of world exports*

Region/economic grouping		Exports (f.o.b.)									
	1990	1993	1994	1995	1996	1997	1998	1999	2000	2001
Developed market economy countries	71.51	70.05	68.96	68.64	67.60	66.81	68.44	67.27	64.03	64.12
Developing countries and territories	23.85	27.03	27.63	27.71	28.59	29.38	27.81	29.13	31.98	31.46
Countries in Eastern Europe	4.64	2.92	3.41	3.65	3.81	3.81	3.75	3.60	3.99	4.42

Source: UNCTAD (2002, p. 14).

rules for global financial markets and institutions, emerging market countries were unrepresented. The Asian crisis highlighted the problem by making Asian financial markets the center of regulatory attention. Talk of creating an "Asian BIS" quickly led BIS management to offer admission to Hong Kong, Singapore, and a number of other emerging markets.

Reforms to the IMF and World Bank proved harder nuts to crack. These institutions disbursed real money, which left the advanced countries reluctant to share control. The developing countries and emerging markets that accounted for 85 percent of IMF members and were the subject of 100 percent of its programs had only 40 percent of the votes. Relative to their share of global GDP at purchasing power parities, this left them significantly under-represented in the Fund. Similarly, the 85 percent of IMF members that were not advanced industrial countries had only 50 percent of the seats on the executive board. As the financial problems of developing countries gained prominence in the Fund, questions arose about the representativeness and therefore the legitimacy of its actions. The same was even more true of the G-7, the select grouping of seven advanced industrial countries that had traditionally set the broad agenda for IMF policy. Following the Asian crisis, the United States created the Group of Twenty Two "systematically significant countries," including key emerging markets, to consider reforms of the international financial architecture. But the ad hoc nature of this group, to the composition of which the small members of the G-10, excluded from the G-22, predictably objected, robbed it of legitimacy and prevented it from evolving into an effective mechanism for the governance of the international financial system.

3.4 The rise of capital mobility

A key feature of the 1990s, as noted, was the explosive growth of capital flows. The single largest net flow was, ironically, towards the United States, itself a relatively capital-abundant economy. Foreign capital was attracted by the promise of the "new economy." The combination of strong growth in the United States and capital inflows from abroad supported the dollar, the rise of which reversed itself only when the bloom came off the stock market rose.

But the aspect of capital mobility that most attracted the attention of policymakers was the flow to emerging markets. Debt flows to developing countries recovered following the Brady Plan and the development of a market in emerging market debt securities. Equity flows were stimulated by the liberalization of stock markets and the relaxation of capital controls. Still, while portfolio capital flows got most of the press, foreign direct investment dominated numerically and economically, and increasingly so as the decade progressed. Notwithstanding the growth of portfolio equity flows, investors saw holding minority stakes in foreign enterprises as a risky business. Limiting principal–agent slack across long distances in most cases still implied holding the substantial shares that are the defining characteristic of direct investment. FDI was facilitated by containerization, which reduced transport costs for merchandise, and by the information and communications revolution, which facilitated the control of branch plants abroad and the development of global supply chains. It responded to privatization in developing countries, which allowed the acquisition of former state enterprises, often in resource-intensive activities, and to macroeconomic stabilization and structural reform, which heightened the attractions of investment in other sectors. In contrast to financial capital flows, in the case of FDI the evidence of learning spillovers was more compelling.[10] The implications for financial stability were relatively favorable.[11]

As table 3.6 shows, FDI and medium- to long-term debt flows from private creditors fluctuated in tandem for much of the 1990s, but the latter collapsed in the wake of the Asian crisis. The same pattern is evident in the behavior of bank loans and bonds, although bank lending fell precipitously following the crisis, turning negative in 1999.[12] Banks concluded that syndicated lending to developing countries was dicey and that bonds had better risk-sharing characteristics.[13] Another important if underappreciated feature of the data is the importance of M&A-related flows, which dwarfed lending through banks and the bond market and displayed the same procyclical pattern.

Short-term flows were the most volatile component of the capital account. Whereas the swing in net bank lending following the Asian crisis was from +$50 billion to −$5 billion, the swing in short-term debt flows went from +$60 billion to −$60 billion, more than twice that absolute amount. The share of short-term debt in a country's external obligations was clearly associated with its vulnerability to crisis.[14] This led a number of countries to use capital controls and regulatory policies to lengthen the maturity structure of their external obligations.[15] By the end of the 1990s even the IMF and the US government had acknowledged the prudence of such measures.

This reference alludes to an important respect in which management of the world economy went off-track in the 1990s. In retrospect, the Fund and the United States had pushed with excessive enthusiasm for capital account liberalization. The Clinton Treasury had pressed Asian and Latin American countries to abolish capital controls, and prior to the Asian crisis (and as late as the World Bank/IMF meetings in Hong Kong in September 1997) the IMF was lobbying for an amendment to its charter that would have made capital account liberalization an obligation of member countries. Elsewhere I have reflected on what might explain this naive enthusiasm for capital account liberalization.[16] For present purposes, the important point is that by the end of the decade it had been acknowledged as excessive, and both the US government and IMF had moderated their positions.

Table 3.6 *Net capital flows to developing countries, 1989–2003*

Developing countries	1989	1990	1991	1992	1993	1994	1995	1996	1997	1998	1999	2000	2001	2002
Current account balance	−44.7	−17.8	−72.3	−80.2	−128.6	−85.5	−106.5	−90.0	−91.4	−113.6	−10.7	61.9	27.6	48.3
as a percentage of GDP	−1.2	−0.4	−1.8	−1.9	−3.0	−1.9	−2.1	−1.6	−1.5	−2.0	−0.2	1.0	0.5	0.8
Financed by														
Net equity flows	24.5	28.6	41.4	59.7	116.5	133.2	125.8	161.5	196.0	181.9	194.3	186.7	177.7	152.4
of which:														
Net FDI inflows	21.2	24.1	33.4	45.6	68.2	90.0	105.6	127.9	169.3	174.5	179.3	160.6	171.7	143.0
Net portfolio equity inflows	3.3	4.5	8.0	14.1	48.3	43.2	20.2	33.6	26.7	7.4	15.0	26.0	6.0	9.4
Net debt flows	50.0	58.0	63.5	95.1	108.6	72.0	151.8	114.1	102.1	57.4	13.9	−1.0	3.2	7.2
of which:														
Official creditors	20.5	27.3	30.5	24.7	26.8	15.6	38.8	3.8	13.0	34.1	13.5	−6.2	28.0	16.2
Private creditors	29.5	30.7	33.0	70.4	81.8	56.4	113.0	110.3	89.1	23.3	0.5	5.1	−24.8	−9.0
Net medium- to long-term debt flows	12.8	15.6	13.9	34.5	48.3	41.3	54.1	81.9	84.0	87.4	21.9	14.5	−8.6	−2.9
Bonds	3.2	1.0	8.2	8.6	33.0	28.9	23.4	49.3	38.4	39.7	29.6	17.4	10.1	18.6
Banks	1.8	4.0	4.0	14.8	4.7	8.2	28.6	30.6	43.1	51.4	−5.9	2.6	−11.8	−16.0
Other	7.9	10.5	1.7	11.1	10.7	4.2	2.1	1.9	2.5	−3.6	−1.8	−5.5	−7.0	−5.5
Net short-term debt flows	16.7	15.1	19.0	35.9	33.4	15.0	58.9	28.4	5.0	−64.2	−21.4	−9.4	−16.2	−6.1

Table 3.6 (*cont.*)

Change in reserves (− = increase)	n.a.	−37.4	−53.2	−14.9	−63.8	−60.5	−101.2	−88.9	−54.0	−18.5	−37.7	−51.7	−81.6	−161.3
Memorandum														
Bilateral aid grants (excluding technical cooperation)	19.2	28.2	35.1	30.5	28.4	32.7	32.8	27.8	26.7	28.2	29.4	29.6	29.5	32.9
Net private flows (debt + equity)	54.0	59.3	74.4	130.1	198.3	189.6	238.8	271.9	285.1	205.2	194.7	191.8	152.8	143.4
Net official flows (aid + debt)	39.7	55.5	65.6	55.2	55.2	48.3	71.6	31.6	39.7	62.3	42.9	23.4	57.5	49.0
Workers' remittances	24.5	30.6	31.2	36.3	38.5	43.6	48.1	52.6	62.7	59.5	64.6	64.5	72.3	80.0

NB: Figures are in billions of dollars unless otherwise specified.
Source: World Bank (2002).

To be sure, capital account liberalization was not simply foisted on developing countries from the outside. There were powerful economic and political forces in the affected countries themselves encouraging the liberalization of capital accounts. Policymakers in developing countries saw capital account decontrol as a concomitant of the general strategy of liberalization, stabilization, and privatization. Investors saw it as a signal of policy reform and as a promise of ease of repatriation for their earnings (Bertolini and Drazen, 1997).

With the benefit of hindsight we know that, for capital account liberalization to contribute to growth rather than simply precipitating costly crises, macroeconomic imbalances first had to be removed. The banking system had to be strengthened. The exchange rate regime had to be adapted to the reality of capital mobility, which generally meant adjusting it in the direction of greater flexibility. Unfortunately, these principles were not always appreciated at the time. While many countries did in fact reduce tariffs, strengthen fiscal policies, and deregulate domestic financial transactions prior to liberalizing short-term capital inflows, few reduced government ownership and involvement in the banking system and strengthened prudential supervision and regulation (Williamson and Mahar, 1998). This failure is one way of understanding why the 1990s was a decade of crises. Efforts to count the number of currency and banking crises and to quantify their severity using intertemporally consistent criteria suggest that crises were becoming more frequent, although – some prominent exceptions to the contrary notwithstanding – they were not obviously also becoming more severe (Bordo et al., 2001). There is also some indication, mainly anecdotal, that the problem began dying down towards the end of the decade. It is tempting to credit the progress of emerging markets in adapting their policies to the new environment of high capital mobility – by strengthening their banking systems, accumulating reserves, limiting their dependence on short-term capital, and moving to greater financial transparency and exchange rate flexibility.

It is tempting to assign some credit for reform to the international financial institutions (IFIs) as well. Following the Mexican crisis in 1994 the IMF and World Bank devoted more resources to encouraging transparency and more effective prudential supervision in member countries. The IMF established a Special Data Dissemination Standard for countries active on international capital markets, and the Bank and Fund undertook joint Financial Sector Assessment Programs (FSAPs) and Reviews on the Observance of Standard and Codes (ROSCs).[17] The IMF established an International Capital Markets Department. It reviewed its response to capital account crises. As noted above, it acknowledged the prudence of going slow on capital account liberalization.

But, if there was progress on crisis prevention, there was less movement on crisis resolution. Some advocated expanding IMF lending operations – turning the Fund into an international lender of last resort on the grounds that most capital account crises resulted from panic, pure and simple – while others recommended curtailing them on the grounds that IMF programs only encouraged reckless lending and facilitated future crises. While the evidence for the moral hazard view was hardly overwhelming, it carried the intellectual day. Realizing that it would never be practically possible to limit IMF lending until there were other ways of managing crises at acceptable costs, officials contemplated alternatives for crisis resolution such as adding restructuring-friendly provisions ("collective action clauses") to loan agreements, creating an international bankruptcy court, and establishing a sovereign debt restructuring mechanism through an amendment to the IMF's Articles of Agreement. None of these proposals was implemented in the 1990s, but the intellectual way was paved. 2003 saw the first significant issues of sovereign bonds with collective action clauses in New York by emerging markets such as Mexico, Brazil, South Korea, and South Africa. By the middle of this decade the practice has become commonplace.

The temperamentally less optimistic will observe that little progress was made in creating locks and levies to regulate the tidal waves of capital that periodically flood into emerging markets. In the absence of progress in regulating the volume of global liquidity, the entire burden of adjustment was placed on emerging markets. Nor was progress evident in addressing the inability of emerging markets to borrow abroad in their own currencies. The main options this left developing countries for protecting themselves against currency mismatches was accumulating reserves (an expensive policy, since the yield on US Treasury bonds was significantly less than the cost of funds) or not borrowing abroad in the first place (and thus stymying the transfer of resources from capital-rich to capital-poor countries). The massive accumulation of reserves by Asian and Latin American countries and the decline in portfolio capital flows towards them at the end of the 1990s were indicative of inadequate progress on these aspects of international financial management.

Poor countries, unlike their emerging market counterparts, lacked access to international financial markets. Moreover, both total foreign aid and the share directed towards the poor countries declined in the 1990s. On the other hand, FDI flows to the poor countries rose from the equivalent of 0.4 percent of their GDP in 1986–1988 to 1.1 percent in 1991–1993 and 2.7 percent in 1997–1999, as these countries benefited from the global surge in FDI, took steps to enhance their investment climates, and adopted new laws permitting profit repatriation and limiting double taxation. While foreign investment continued to flow towards mineral- and oil-exporting countries, their share of the poor country total in fact fell over the course of the decade, from nearly 50 to roughly 20 percent. As a result, the Feldstein–Horioka correlation (between savings and investment) fell from 0.7 to 0.4–0.5 between the first and second halves of the 1990s. In addition, poor countries were connected to the international financial system by the growing participation of foreign banks in their economies. Foreign bank assets as a share of total bank assets in poor countries rose from less than 20 percent to more than 40 percent between 1995 and 2000. By the end of the 1990s only fifteen of the fifty-eight countries classified as low-income by the World Bank reported no foreign bank activity (World Bank, 2002, p. 65).

Thus, the view that the poorest countries were wholly disconnected from the international financial system and therefore dependent on aid flows is exaggerated. That said, their lack of securities market access, in conjunction with low savings capacity and pressing capital needs, continued to support the case for official aid. Against this backdrop the decline in official flows and, in particular, the decline in the share of total aid going to the poorest countries were particularly disturbing. Aid fell by 10 percent in real terms between 1990 and 2000 (see table 3.7). It fell by a third as a share of donor country GNP over a decade when the number of persons in developing countries living on less than $1 a day showed little downward trend. On top of this, the share of total aid going to low-income countries fell by a tenth from the early 1980s to the late 1990s.

The stagnation of aid flows reflected donor skepticism about the effectiveness of concessionary transfers. Where governance was poor and corruption was rampant, aid might be dissipated, or worse. In an influential paper for the World Bank (using pre-1994 data and widely circulated prior to publication), Burnside and Dollar (2000) found that aid had a positive impact on growth in developing countries with good fiscal, monetary and trade policies but little effect in the presence of poor policies. This finding influenced World Bank and donor country policy in the late 1990s, suggesting how foreign aid programs might be restructured and under what circumstances it made sense to augment the aid going to particular countries. Unfortunately for this new consensus, subsequent research (e.g. Easterly, Levine, and Roodman, 2003) suggested that the aid–growth nexus was more complex and that simple formulas such as "aid only countries that already have strong policies and institutions" had limited utility.

3.5 The rise of regionalism

The modern wave of European integration had been under way since the second half of the 1940s. By the 1980s integration had become a touchstone of European policy – it was the household remedy that Europe's leaders administered for every ache and pain. At this point their most important source of discomfort was chronic slow growth and high unemployment ("eurosclerosis"). European officials responded by reinvigorating the integration process and committing to the creation of a unified internal market by 1992. To be sure, they did not all share a common vision of what that internal market should entail or how it would solve the problem of eurosclerosis. While some saw it as a way of eliminating regulatory barriers to growth and introducing the chill winds of competition,

Table 3.7 Net official aid to developing countries, by type and source, 1990–2001

Aid	1990	1991	1992	1993	1994	1995	1996	1997	1998	1999	2000	2001
Overseas Development Assistance (ODA) and official aid	45.1	49.5	46.4	41.7	48.1	46.3	39.7	36.1	39.0	42.3	40.7	39.3
Grants (excluding technical cooperation)	30.1	35.1	30.5	28.3	32.7	32.8	28.1	26.6	27.9	30.2	29.9	29.6
Bilateral	26.5	29.5	23.9	22.5	24.6	26.2	21.8	19.8	20.5	22.0	22.6	22.5
Multilateral	3.6	5.6	6.6	5.8	8.1	6.6	6.3	6.8	7.4	8.2	7.3	7.1
Concessional loans	15.0	14.4	15.9	13.4	15.4	13.5	11.6	9.5	11.1	12.1	10.8	9.7
Bilateral	8.3	6.3	8.5	6.7	6.5	4.9	3.0	1.5	2.9	4.6	3.6	3.0
Multilateral	6.7	8.1	7.4	6.7	8.9	8.6	8.6	8.0	8.2	7.5	7.2	6.7

NB: All figures in billions of dollars.
Source: World Bank (2002).

others saw it as a way of avoiding a race to the bottom and reinventing the European social model on a continental scale. But, if rationales varied, results were uniform in that policies led to a more integrated and unified market.

Monetary union, the goal set out in the Delors Report in 1989, was similarly an aspiration of long standing. What was different in the 1990s was that the single market heightened the urgency of the task. By requiring European countries to dismantle capital controls in order to create a unified European capital market, it ruled out alternatives such as narrow fluctuation bands and pegged but adjustable exchange rates. Flexible rates being a source of political tension and transactions costs, preserving the single market required a forced march to monetary union.

The result of reinvigorated economic and monetary integration was a strengthening of regional institutions for managing economic affairs. This was evident in the case of the European Central Bank, which became the vehicle used by the majority of European countries for managing their interest rates, exchange rates, and financial flows. But the point is more general. As a result of the single market, the European Commission acquired a larger role as the guardian of competition. As a result of economic and monetary union (EMU), the Commission and the Council of Ministers acquired more responsibility for the surveillance of European fiscal policies. When currency and financial crises erupted, European governments handled them regionally rather than turning to the IMF, as had been the practice in earlier decades.[18]

Fears of a "Fortress Europe" notwithstanding, there was little evidence that regional integration was inconsistent with global integration. Cross-section data suggest that EU member states traded more with the rest of the world as a result of their regional arrangement (see, for example, Eichengreen and Taylor, 2003, table 1, columns 3 and 6). European regionalism was embedded in the GATT system. Europe was still broadly sympathetic to the notion of global trade liberalization, agriculture aside; the only difference made by the single market was that the European Union now negotiated with one voice.

Nor did deepening and widening prove incompatible. Warnings that a European Union struggling with the structural challenges of deeper integration would be unable to digest new members proved unfounded. There were good reasons for thinking that the accession of Austria, Finland, and Sweden in 1995 would go down easily, but it is more striking that neither the commitment to the single market nor the fact of monetary union slowed the European Union's negotiations with the transition economies of central and Eastern Europe, eight of which were offered treaties of accession at the beginning of the following decade.

The other important regional initiative was the North American Free Trade Agreement. Free trade between the United States and Canada was hardly earth-shattering: industries such as motor vehicles and parts had long-standing cross-border links, and economic structures and living standards were not dissimilar.

Free trade with Mexico was another matter. In part the impetus came from declining information and transportation costs, which reduced the difficulty of controlling branch plants in foreign countries; for US producers, Mexico was an obvious place to outsource assembly operations. In part it derived from the European example and the desire to insure against the danger of a Fortress Europe. In part it reflected the wish in Washington to lock in policy reform south of the border. It reflected the coming to power of a new generation of Mexican policymakers (not a few with Ph.Ds. in economics from leading US universities) who realized that their country's future depended on inward foreign investment and merchandise exports – that is, on internationalization.

For the United States, NAFTA remains small potatoes; the Mexican (and, for that matter, the Canadian) economy is simply too small to have a major impact. For Mexico, NAFTA has been associated with a sharp increase in exports to the United States and an even sharper increase in inward FDI. On the other hand, NAFTA's advent on 1 January 1994 was followed in short order by a disastrous currency and financial crisis. One way of understanding this crisis is in terms of the management of capital flows and the sequencing of liberalization (that is, in terms of the discussion of the preceding section). Opening the economy to capital inflows before exchange rate policy is made more flexible and both macroeconomic and regulatory policies are strengthened is a recipe for disaster. Thus, when in March 1994 the assassination of presidential candidate Luis Donaldo Colosio caused foreign investment flows to turn around, the exchange rate collapsed, the banking system was devastated, and living standards tumbled. Even now, Mexican real wages have not recovered to pre-NAFTA levels.

Ultimately, the debate over NAFTA turns on dynamic effects. While economists and policymakers remain optimistic, hopes that Mexico would quickly move out of assembly-for-export operations into higher value-added exports with tighter links to the domestic market were initially disappointed; despite some evidence of positive vertical spillovers (Lopez-Cordova and Moreira, 2003), the main response was a boom in assembly operations. The optimistic view is that one decade was too short a time to observe the desired dynamic effects. On the other hand, the fact that growing numbers of production and assembly operations outsourced from the United States now seem to be shifting to China lends a more negative cast to the debate.

NAFTA is more weakly institutionalized than the European Union. It has side agreements for environment and labor standards but no body with regulatory powers like those of the European Commission or policymaking prerogatives comparable to the Council's. This reflects its more limited economic scope: there is little appetite for moving from a free trade area to a single market with a common set of policies and regulations. It also reflects the more limited political aspirations of the partners; as yet, there is no evident desire for political integration.

The progress of regionalism was slower in Asia. Income levels, development stages, and economic and political systems were more diverse than in Europe or even the Western Hemisphere. Trade links were less concentrated regionally. Intra-regional capital flows figured less importantly as a share of foreign investment. The putative leader of the integration process, Japan, was in the doldrums. More generally, the balance of power in the region was in flux, with the Asian crisis dealing a setback to the Tigers and other countries having to adjust to the rapid rise of China. Asia also lacked a tradition of integrationist thought comparable to Europe's. The legacy of the Second World War was very different; countries did not draw the European lesson that integration was the way to prevent another war. The United States did not promote integration within Asia; in contrast to its strategy in Europe, it preferred bilateral security ties.

In 1993 the six founding members of the Association of South-East Asian Nations (ASEAN) agreed to form an ASEAN Free Trade Area (AFTA) and to establish a common effective preferential tariff (CEPT). But their agreement permitted members to exclude so-called sensitive goods, as they continue to do. While the initial AFTA program also required members to remove non-tariff barriers progressively, it did not indicate how NTBs affecting trade in products covered by the CEPT were to be identified or eliminated. It allowed countries to maintain extensive exclusion lists of products deemed sensitive to tariff reduction. That there was not more progress reflected the fact that AFTA did not include the three most important trading countries in the region: China, South Korea, and Japan. As a result, little headway was made by attempts to extend regional cooperation to the promotion of foreign direct investment and financial market development.

Another reason for slow progress was that Asian integration remained weakly institutionalized. Cooperation is characterized by consensus decisionmaking, a presumption of non-intervention in national affairs, and an understanding that countries will not criticize their neighbors (the so-called "Asian way"). This emphasis on consensus and good manners constrains efforts to apply peer pressure for faster action. In the absence of stronger regional institutions, Asia was in no position to speak with one voice at global venues or to challenge multilateral approaches to global governance.

The obvious test for Asia's regional aspirations was the financial crisis of 1997/8. When the crisis struck, governments responded not by circling the wagons but by turning to the IMF. Although Japan did provide some assistance, it was the Fund that crafted the rescue programs and designed the conditionality. While controversy continues to swirl over the efficacy of these programs, there is a widespread feeling that they could have been better tailored to Asia's distinctive circumstances. In particular, IMF programs could have been better attuned to the strength of the region's budgets, the weakness of its banks, the highly geared nature of its corporations, and the fragility of its political systems.

As early as the autumn of 1997, dissatisfaction with the design and effects of IMF programs led to proposals for an Asian Monetary Fund (AMF). Asian countries understood better their own distinctive characteristics, the argument ran, and in addition an Asian Fund would relieve them of the embarrassment of having to go crawling to Washington, DC. But the United States and the IMF opposed the AMF initiative on the grounds that the Asian way would lead to weak conditionality, inadequate adjustment, and moral hazard. Cynics suggested further that the US government and the Fund were reluctant to agree to an initiative that might compromise their control. In response to their objections, the AMF idea was abandoned. The inability to rebuff US objections reflected both the weak institutionalization of Asian regionalism (there was no existing institutional foundation on which to build an AMF quickly) and Asia's extensive interdependence with other regions.

The realization that Asian regionalism would never be consequential without the involvement of the continent's large economies led to an increasing level of activity in ASEAN+3 (where the "plus-three partners" were China, South Korea, and Japan). There was also growing activity in the region's pre-existing intergovernmental networks. The results included the Chiang Mai Initiative (CMI), a regional arrangement of swaps and credit lines, negotiated in 2000, and the Asian Bond Fund, a regional initiative to promote the development of regional financial markets, sealed in 2003.[19]

It remains to be seen how consequential those developments will be for the management of the world economy. Will the Chiang Mai Initiative evolve into an Asian Monetary Fund? Will the Asian Bond Fund lead to a single currency for Asia? Perhaps. But negative answers are also plausible; the diversity of Asia's political and economic systems and its extensive links with other parts of the world militate against purely regional solutions.

3.6 Conclusions

The 1990s is frequently portrayed as a decade of globalization. One purpose of this chapter has been to suggest that the distinctiveness of the period has been exaggerated by observers not fully acquainted with longer-term developments. In important respects the expansion of international transactions in the 1990s was the continuation of trends that had been under way for as long as half a century, and the pace of their growth did not significantly exceed that of the preceding twenty-five to fifty years. The principal exceptions were international transactions sensitive to advances in information and communications technologies, which themselves accelerated markedly in the 1990s. These technological advances sharply reduced the costs of international financial transactions. They also sharply reduced the costs of foreign sourcing and multinational production, encouraging the articulation of global supply chains. Again, the novelty of these developments should not be exaggerated. Similar practices have been seen before. But both qualitative and quantitative evidence suggest that their growth accelerated in the 1990s.

Even where there was no break in the trend and no obvious acceleration, cumulative effects alone sufficed to render these developments of growing prominence and concern. In turn, this created challenges for economic management. Could the further liberalization of trade be successfully fostered? Could capital flows be managed in ways that magnified their benefits instead of their costs? Could enthusiasm for regional integration be reconciled with existing inter-regional interdependencies? Could the high-income countries and multilateral institutions devise policies to ameliorate poverty and stagnation in low-income countries?

In some cases these challenges were addressed reasonably successfully. The Uruguay Round was completed in 1994. The World Trade Organization was established as a mechanism for overseeing a more rules-based trading system and addressing issues such as services trade and intellectual property. Countries pursuing policy reforms attracted foreign direct investment, which held up well in the face of global financial turbulence. Regionalism developed quickly but in ways that complemented global markets and institutions rather than undermining their operation.

In comparison, there was less progress in managing financial capital flows. Few of the changes in private contracts and IMF policies tabled as responses to this problem had been implemented by the end of the decade. Little progress was made in reducing poverty in the poorest countries, official aid to which, in fact, declined as the decade progressed. No progress was made in addressing governance problems at the IFIs.

Optimists will argue that, even where progress in the 1990s was halting, the stage was set. The IMF continued to rethink its response to capital account crises and adopted a more cautious approach to capital account liberalization. It initiated a debate on sovereign debt restructuring that ultimately led the markets to add restructuring-friendly provisions to their loan contracts. The advanced industrial countries, and notably a United States galvanized by the events of 11 September 2001, committed themselves to increases in aid. Each of these developments, it can be argued, reflected the continuation of a process of adaptation begun in the 1990s. Whether that decade proves a source of durable lessons and sustained momentum for addressing these issues, of course, remains to be seen.

The new century will bring new challenges. Initially, at least, these are likely to emanate from the same technological and political developments that differentiated the 1990s from preceding decades. Thus, the continuation of the advances in ICT that fostered the expansion of international financial transactions and global supply chains in the 1990s is now encouraging the internationalization of services (the outsourcing of white-collar jobs). The emergence of additional emerging markets, led by the expansion of the modern goods- and services-exporting sectors in China and India, is adding the equivalent of another middle-sized advanced industrial country to the global economy each year. However tempting it is to assert that history provides valuable lessons, it is likely that the 1990s provide, at most, broad guidance for dealing with these challenges.

Notes

1. World Bank (2001, p. 15). Sachs and Warner (1995) list more than thirty developing countries as switching from closed to open trade regimes between 1985 and 1995.
2. Thus, the World Bank (1995) reports that the costs of oceanic freight transport fell by fully 70 percent between the 1920s and the 1990s. The fall in the cost of air freight was even faster.
3. For instance, had global integration been complete, a United States that accounted for 20 percent of global production would have imported 80 percent of the goods and services consumed by its residents. The actual number was more on the order of 10 percent; again, see table 3.1.
4. Other metrics point to the same conclusion: see Bordo, Eichengreen and Irwin (1999).
5. Consensus results pointed to a decline in this correlation from the point estimate of 0.9 originally obtained by Feldstein and Horioka (1980) to estimates on the order of 0.6. See Sinn (1992).
6. See BIS (1998). In contrast, the BIS's next survey, of foreign exchange market turnover in April 2001, showed a decline from the previous survey of some 14 percent when volumes are measured at constant exchange rates. This presumably reflected the growing role of electronic brokers, the declining tolerance for open foreign exchange positions after the turbulence of August–September 1998, and the advent of the euro.
7. Thus, a rise in the dollar reduces the value of non-dollar transactions unless a correction is made for changes in the exchange rate.
8. Dunning (1983) estimates that 55 percent of the foreign capital stake in this period was accounted for by the primary sector and only 15 percent by manufacturing. A commonplace explanation is that monitoring and control are least problematic in such sectors, where both inputs and outputs are, in the main, tangible. This, of course, is just another perspective on the phenomenon noted above, namely the growing importance of intra-industry as opposed to inter-industry trade.
9. Dunning suggests adopting the contemporary definition of developing countries when considering the data prior to the First World War, in which case their share rises to more than four-fifths. This further accentuates the contrast with today.

10. Studies suggest that spillovers are mainly vertical (inter-industry, affecting buyers and suppliers) rather than horizontal (intra-industry, affecting competitors) and that they are contingent on the absorptive capacity of the recipient economy. See, *inter alia*, Aitken and Harrison (1999) and Kugler (2000).

11. See Frankel and Rose (1996). Hausmann and Fernandez-Arias (2000) caution against using the share of FDI in a country's total capital inflows as a measure of its financial health. "Unhealthy" (financially riskier) countries attract less total capital but actually import more of it in the form of FDI.

12. The "other" entry under net debt flows from private creditors reflects mainly the change in trade credits.

13. The banks also adjusted by purchasing subsidiaries in developing countries and establishing local branches, which they could use to fund their local lending with local (and local currency) deposits.

14. While there is some dispute over whether that association was causal (since if investors fear a crisis they have an incentive to shorten the tenor of their claims), there is little question that heavy reliance on short-term debt could heighten the severity of a crisis.

15. Chile's non-interest-bearing deposit requirement is a favorite example of this policy. A few countries mistakenly pursued policies with the perverse effect of encouraging short-term inflows and paid the price. Thus, South Korea opened its banking system to short-term inflows in the mid-1990s while continuing to limit inward FDI, the idea being that the country did not want to compromise control of its corporate sector. The December 1997 crisis was a direct result.

16. See DeLong and Eichengreen (2002). As noted there, the Clinton Treasury's sympathy for capital account liberalization flowed from its belief in free and open markets. It reflected the experience and predisposition of a Treasury Secretary drawn from Wall Street. It was consistent with the belief that controls created opportunities for corruption. It reflected the belief that domestic financial liberalization had important benefits. It followed from the administration's commitment to trade liberalization, including trade in services.

17. It is too early to tell how much difference these programs make for country credit worthiness and financial stability. Empirical analyses of the early evidence include Gelos and Wei (2002), Glennerster and Shin (2003), and Christofides, Mulder and Tiffin (2003).

18. Thus, the United Kingdom and Italy had drawn resources from the IMF in the 1970s, and Denmark had engaged in a reserve tranche purchase as recently as 1987.

19. Up to 10 percent of the drawings available to a country under the CMI can be provided for a limited period without it having entered into an IMF agreement, but subsequent disbursements will be linked to an IMF program and therefore to the government's success in meeting IMF conditions, thus meeting U.S. and IMF insistence that a regional support arrangement should not undercut the effectiveness of IMF conditionality. That these developments occurred after the decade that is the subject of this chapter is perhaps not surprising, given that the Asian crisis to which they were a response broke out in that decade's final years.

4   Europe: a continent in decline?

Riccardo Faini

4.1 Introduction

Euro-pessimism is back. The last bout of optimism about the economic prospects of the European Union came at the beginning of 2001, following the launch of the Lisbon reform agenda (which was supposed to modernize the EU economy and make it the most dynamic and competitive in the world) and the first indications of a significant slowdown of the US economy. At that time many European ministers expressed their belief that Europe, and the European Union in particular, was poised to become the engine of growth for the world economy.

Economic performance has not been kind to such forecasts. Between 2001 and 2003 average economic growth in the Union was slightly above 1 percent, versus 2 percent in the United States. Prospects for 2005/2006 are not much better, with US growth according to the OECD projected at 3.5 percent against 2.3 percent in the European Union. Looking backward does not offer much consolation either: between 1990 and 2000 GDP increased at an average annual rate of 3.2 percent and 2.1 percent in the United States and in the European Union respectively. Focusing on the performance of the Euro area rather than on the Union would only make the gap with the United States larger.

Adding to the concerns of the Euro-pessimists is the steady erosion of the EU export share in world markets. Between 1990 and 2001 Germany's export share fell from 12.1 percent to 8.1 percent. Italy and France did not fare better, with their share declining respectively from 5.1 percent and 6.1 percent in 1990 to 3.9 percent and 4.8 percent in 2000. Again, the contrast with the United States is striking: over the same period, the US share in world export markets rose from 13.1 percent to 14 percent.

Labor productivity is also mentioned as a further, and perhaps more fundamental, indicator of Europe's long-term decline. During the 1980s labor productivity rose at a faster rate in the European Union compared to the United States, thereby contributing to bridging the income gap between the two areas.

Even in the first half of the 1990s the European Union maintained its lead in productivity growth: 1.7 percent on an average annual basis versus 1.4 percent in the United States. However, between 1997 and 2002 the United States definitely outperformed the European Union, with labor productivity growth rising to 2.2 percent in the former and falling to 1 percent in the latter.

In this chapter, we take a closer look at the European performance. We take issue with most of the indicators – GDP growth, world export share, productivity growth – that have been used to demonstrate the facts of Europe's decline. We focus mainly on the Euro area, since this is where performance has been most disappointing and macroeconomic conditions less heterogeneous.

We concentrate on long-term issues and do not consider macroeconomic policies as a significant culprit in Europe's allegedly poor economic performance. This is not because we believe that aggregate demand policies are ineffective in boosting economic activity but, less fundamentally, because we see no evidence that such policies have been unduly restrictive during the second half of the 1990s. Indeed, both short- and long-term real interest rates were lower in Europe than in the United States from 1995 until at least 2001. Similarly, fiscal policy cannot be blamed for stifling Europe's growth. Contrary to widespread allegations, fiscal policy was not procyclical during the run-up to EMU (Gali and Perotti, 2002). Afterwards, between 1999 and 2001, the cyclically adjusted budget deficit worsened by one full percentage point of GDP. By and large, therefore, the macroeconomic policy stance was broadly supportive of economic activity.[1]

The chapter is organized as follows. In the next section we briefly review demographic trends in Europe and the United States and show that the growth gap is significantly smaller when expressed in per capita terms. We then perform two simple exercises. First, in section 3, we correct GDP growth for accounting differences and find that, while a marginal factor in explaining the gap in aggregate growth figures, such correction can significantly alter the relative trends in per capita growth. Second, in section 4, we decompose GDP per capita into its main components, namely hourly productivity, hours worked per employed person, employment rate, and a demographic factor. We find that the composition of the income gap between the United States and the euro area has undergone a radical modification over the last thirty years. Most of the gap is now accounted for by differences in the numbers of hours worked per employed person. Whether this is due to a greater preference for leisure in Europe or to more stringent institutional constraints in the labor market there is a key topic for future research. In section 5, we look at the behavior of export shares in world markets. The key finding there is that fluctuations in oil prices and the nominal euro/dollar exchange rate can explain most of the fall in Europe's world market shares. Interestingly enough, the appreciation of the euro since 2001 seems to be associated with a marked recovery of world export shares. Finally, in the

Table 4.1 *GDP growth in the United States, Japan, and the euro area*

	1981–1990	1991–2002	1991–1996	1997–2002
United States	2.9	2.88	2.53	3.22
Euro area	2.4	1.92	1.52	2.32
Japan	4.0	1.2	1.8	0.6
Differentials				
US–euro area	0.5	0.96	1.01	0.90
Japan–euro area	1.6	−0.7	0.3	−1.7

Source: IMF (various issues).

concluding section, we return to the issue of Europe's productivity slowdown and its inability, in contrast to the United States to combine sustained employment growth with continuing productivity gains. We argue that this may represent, at least to some extent, a transitory phenomenon, due to the large inflow of a young, educated, but largely inexperienced labor force. Of course, even this optimistic interpretation would not free Europe's policymakers from the task of persevering on the road to labor and, in particular, product market liberalization.

4.2 Demographic trends and economic performance

In 1970 Germany, France, and Italy, the three largest countries in the euro area (EU3),[2] accounted respectively for 2.12 percent, 1.37 percent, and 1.46 percent of world population. Thirty years later their share of world population had declined to 1.36 percent, 0.99 percent, and 0.95 percent respectively. This is a massive decline. In percentage terms, the shares in world population dropped by almost 40 percent for France, 54 percent for Italy, and 56 percent for Germany. In aggregate terms, the EU3 share fell by 50 percent, against 20 percent for the United States.

By and large, therefore, old Europe suffers first and foremost from a demographic decline. During the 1980s the population increased at an average annual rate of 1 percent in the United States and only 0.3 percent in the euro area. During the 1990s population growth in the United States even accelerated, to 1.15 percent, and the gap with the euro area rose to more than 0.8 percentage points. Clearly, under these circumstances, comparing aggregate GDP growth is simply misleading. To control for the differences in demographic trends we must do the obvious thing, namely focus on the evolution of per capita rather than aggregate income. Doing this changes the picture, at least to some extent.

Consider table 4.1. Already in the 1980s the United States surpassed the euro area in terms of aggregate GDP growth, 2.9 percent against 2.4 percent. The

Table 4.2 *Per capita GDP growth in the United States, Japan, and the euro area*

	1981–1990	1991–2002	1991–1996	1997–2002
United States	1.9	1.73	1.38	2.07
Euro area	2.1	1.60	1.20	2.00
Japan	3.4	1.0	1.5	0.4
Differentials				
US–euro area	−0.2	0.13	0.18	0.07
Japan–euro area	1.3	−0.7	0.3	−1.6

Source: IMF (various issues).

gap gets significantly bigger during the 1990s, rising from 0.5 percentage points to almost one percentage point. If we focus on per capita growth however, the picture changes considerably (table 4.2). First, during the 1980s, growth in GDP per capita was faster in the euro area than in the United States, 2.1 percent versus 1.9 percent. This was a period, therefore, when the euro area was converging towards the (higher) US norm. The process came to a halt, however, and actually went into reverse during the 1990s. Per capita growth in the eurozone fell by half a percentage point, from 2.1 percent to 1.6 percent. In the United States, the decline in per capita growth is much less pronounced, from 1.9 percent to 1.7 percent. As a result, per capita growth is now higher in the United States than in the euro area.

This is both good and bad news from a European point of view. The good news is that the gap in GDP growth clearly understates the relative performance of the euro area economy. The bad news is that, even on a per capita basis, the euro area is now growing more slowly than the United States. We have seen that the US–euro area differential in aggregate GDP growth increased by half a percentage point during the 1990s compared to the previous decade. Basically, one-third of the increase in the gap is due to faster population growth in the United States. The rest appears to reflect the worsening performance of the European economy.

Further insights come from decomposing the 1990s into two sub-periods (columns 3 and 4 of table 4.1). As expected, we find that US growth accelerates strongly, from some 2.5 percent in the first part of the decade to 3.2 percent between 1997 and 2002, despite a substantial slowdown in 2001. Per capita GDP also exhibits a similar acceleration from 1997 onwards (table 4.2). Somewhat surprisingly, however, we see that both aggregate and per capita growth in the euro area accelerates even more, by 0.8 percentage point. As a result, in the second half of the 1990s the difference in per capita growth between the euro area and the United States becomes virtually negligible.

Summing up so far, when corrected for population growth, Europe's performance was better than that of the United States in the 1980s, worsened markedly during the first half of the 1990s and, in more recent years, has been at par with that of the United States. Before delving more into the determinants of such performance, we must take a small detour and check whether accounting conventions explain part of these differences.

4.3 Do accounting conventions matter?

The harmonization of national accounts definitions has been a decisive factor in allowing meaningful cross-country analyses. Nonetheless, substantial differences persist, even among industrial countries.

The OECD Department of Statistics has recently summarized the most significant accounting differences between the United States and other, mainly European, industrial countries (Ahmad et al., 2003).

The first differences have to do with the treatment of military equipment. Prior to 1996, all government spending in the United States was recorded as current expenditure. GDP was therefore underestimated as it excluded the depreciation component of public investment. In 1996, however, when US national accounts were duly amended, the extension of the coverage of investment was more extensive than recommended by international conventions, as it also included those assets that are used exclusively for military purposes. The effect on the level of GDP may not have been sizable – 0.6 percent according to the OECD. Its impact on growth may be even smaller – 0.03 percent over the past decade. Both effects, however, are likely to grow larger given the recent military build-up undertaken by the current US administration.

Financial intermediation services to households are a further item that is treated differently in the United States, where it has been included since the late 1980s, from how it is in Europe and Japan, where – contrary to international conventions – it is excluded, mainly because of measurement difficulties. The impact on the GDP level is considerable: 2.3 percent; that on GDP growth is not negligible: 0.1 percent.

The third contentious area is the treatment of software. International conventions recommend that purchases of software, including any own-account production, should be capitalized. The key issue is how to measure software investment. Most European countries use a demand approach, relying on the way businesses record investment. An alternative approach, used in the United States, is to measure the total supply of software services and then estimate the portion of such services with characteristics of assets. The impact on the level of GDP is substantial. Given the disproportionate growth of software expenditure, differences in the measurement of software also have a sizable impact on growth. According to the OECD, had the United States used the European demand-based approach, growth in 1997–98 would have fallen by a substantial amount – up to 0.2 percent.

Last but not least, Europe and the United States differ in their use of hedonic prices. This is perhaps the most notorious correction. Perhaps surprisingly, its GDP effects are not particularly significant. Moreover, even the sign of such correction is not unambiguous. For instance, if hedonic prices are used for intermediate imported goods, the hedonically corrected volume of imports will increase with a corresponding reduction, *ceteris paribus*, in the volume of net output. Overall, according to the OECD, the impact on US growth is relatively small: 0.1 percent. More crucially, it is offset by a parallel correction in US national accounts. Following international recommended practices, the United States combines the use of hedonic prices with Laspeyres instead of Fischer indices, the latter being used instead by European statistical offices. Laspeyres indices lead to a fall in the measured growth rates of approximately the same order of magnitude as the increase associated with the reliance on hedonic prices.

Overall, allowing for the different accounting definitions leads to a reduction in the US growth rate of around 0.2–0.3 percentage points. As emphasized by Ahmad et al. (2003), this correction results only in a fractional reduction of the aggregate growth differential – almost one percentage point during the 1990s – between the United States and the euro area. However, the impact on the difference in per capita GDP growth is quite significant. Moreover, there is a further and quite crucial effect on the dynamics of the convergence process between Europe and the United States. Recall that most of these accounting corrections have little or no impact on measured growth during the 1980s, their main effect being to lower US growth during the 1990s, particularly in the second half of that decade. This has a number of substantive implications. First, the decline during the 1990s in the relative performance of the euro area with respect to the United States was less pronounced than previously thought, as it reflects to some significant extent different accounting procedures. Second, it is no longer evident that the US economy grew at a faster rate than that of the euro area during the first half of the 1990s. Even a small reduction in US per capita growth during that period would put it at par with the euro area performance. Hence, it can no longer be taken for granted that the early 1990s witnessed a cessation, and even less a reversal, of the convergence process between the euro area and the United States. Finally, and perhaps more crucially, in the second half of the decade US per capita growth would, again, be at par with – or even below – that in the euro area.

Table 4.3 *Productivity growth in the United States and the euro area*

	1981–1990	1991–2002	1991–1996	1997–2002
United States	1.10	1.81	1.43	2.18
Euro area	1.90	1.34	1.70	0.98
Differential	−0.80	0.47	−0.27	1.20

Source: IMF (various issues).

Table 4.4 *Employment growth in the United States and the euro area*

	1981–1990	1991–2002	1991–1996	1997–2002
United States	1.80	1.07	1.10	1.03
Euro area	0.50	0.58	−0.18	1.33
Differential	1.30	0.49	1.28	−0.33

Source: IMF (various issues).

4.4 A simple growth decomposition

We have seen that, once different accounting conventions are allowed for, per capita growth in the euro area has not fallen behind that of the United States, and may even have surpassed it in the most recent years. Should Euro-optimism be back center stage, therefore? The answer is "no," in spite of the fact that, as far as we can see, the convergence process with respect to the United States is still making (slow) progress.

The problem arises from the composition of growth. Consider tables 4.3 and 4.4, which report productivity and employment growth in the United States and in the euro area for both the 1980s and the 1990s. As before, we distinguish two sub-periods during the latter decade. Three facts stand out. First, productivity growth has steadily accelerated in the United States, from 1.1 percent in the 1980s to 1.43 percent in the first half of the 1990s and to 2.18 percent in 1997–2002. It has, however, decelerated in the euro area, from 1.9 percent in the 1980s to 1.7 percent and 1 percent in the first and the second half of the 1990s respectively. Second, employment continued to grow in the United States, with both unemployment falling and the employment rate rising at the same time as the surge in productivity growth. The euro area shows quite a distinct pattern. Productivity growth held up quite well between 1991 and 1996 when employment was contracting at an average annual rate of 0.18 percent.

However, when, thanks to wage moderation and greater labor market flexibility, employment started increasing rapidly in the euro area as well, productivity growth virtually collapsed. Looking at TFP growth, a more appropriate measure of productivity, would only strengthen this conclusion. OECD research (OECD, 2003a) shows that TFP growth rose in the United States, from 0.9 percent in the 1980s to 1.3 percent in the second half of the 1990s, but fell quite dramatically in many European countries: from 1.9 percent to 1.1 percent in France, from 1.5 percent to 0.8 percent in Germany, and from 1.5 percent to 0.7 percent in Italy.

In a nutshell, while the US economy was able to combine fast employment growth with an extraordinary productivity performance, the euro area economy appears to be facing a difficult trade-off between fast productivity growth, and hence sustained wage growth, and rapid employment growth but stagnant real wages.

The role of productivity growth, as well as of other factors, is also apparent in a more complete decomposition of income growth. At any point of time, income per capita can be expressed as the product of hourly productivity, hours worked per employed person, the employment rate (defined as the ratio of employment to the working age population) and demographic factors (i.e. the ratio of the working age population to total population). Formally:

$$y = Y/P = Y/H * H/L * L/WAP * WAP/P = \pi * h * l * \mathrm{wap} \qquad (1)$$

where Y is GDP, P is population, H is total hours, L is employment, and WAP is the working age population (defined as the population of age fifteen to sixty-five years). Accordingly, $y = Y/P$ is income per capita, $\pi = Y/H$ is hourly productivity, $h = H/L$ is hours worked per employed person, $l = L/WAP$ is the employment rate, and $\mathrm{wap} = WAP/P$ is the complement to 1 of the dependency ratio ("demography" henceforth). In growth terms, we have:

$$y' = \pi' + h' + l' + \mathrm{wap}' \qquad (2)$$

where a prime indicates a proportional rate of change.

We can use equations (1) and (2) to track the evolution of the income gap between the United States and the euro area. We rely on PPP-corrected data. No attempt is made, however, to control for different accounting conventions. Table 4.5 confirms that our earlier findings of section 4.2 carry over to a PPP-corrected basis. Indeed, between 1979 and 1990 per capita GDP rose at a slightly faster rate in the euro area than in the United States, 2.1 percent versus 1.9 percent. Between 1991 and the 1996 per capita GDP growth was faster in the United States, while the reverse holds true for the most recent period.

Further insights come from decomposing per capita income growth according to equation (2) (as in rows 3–10 of table 4.5). We find that between 1979 and 2001 differences in productivity growth gave a key contribution to the reduction of the income gap between the euro area and the United States. The

Table 4.5 *The sources of growth*

		1979–2001	1979–1990	1991–1996	1997–2001
			(average percentage change)		
Per capita growth	United States	1.81	1.88	1.86	1.99
	Euro area	1.89	2.07	1.52	2.42
Hourly productivity	United States	1.54	1.17	1.56	2.92
	Euro area	2.09	2.36	2.65	1.09
Hours per person	United States	−0.04	0.0	0.10	−0.38
	Euro area	−0.62	−0.65	−0.69	−0.61
Employment rate	United States	0.30	0.72	0.27	−0.71
	Euro area	0.24	−0.08	−0.31	2.02
Demography	United States	0.01	−0.01	−0.08	0.19
	Euro area	0.19	0.45	−0.10	−0.07

Sources: OECD (2003b, 2003c).

1997–2001 period stands, however, as an exception, as the United States greatly outperformed the euro area in this respect. The behavior of the employment rate is the mirror image of productivity. Over the full sample, the growth in the employment rate was substantially larger in the United States than in the euro area, with the latter making up for some of the gap during the late 1990s. The most striking fact, however, is the contribution to income growth of hours worked. In the United States, the number of hours worked per employed person remained virtually unchanged between 1979 and 1996. Only in the last few years does it show a (modest) decline, from 1849 to 1821 hours. In the euro area, instead, the number of hours is on a steady downward trend, from 1745 in 1979 to 1521 in 2001.

We can use equation (1) to measure the proportional contribution of the different factors to the US–euro area income gap (figure 4.1). Productivity differentials were quite important at the beginning of the period, as they accounted for 57 percent of the gap. Faster productivity growth in Europe meant, however, that this factor played a lesser role over time. Indeed, in 1997 productivity per hour was actually higher in the euro area than in the United States. More recent trends have favored the United States, however, and in 2001 the productivity differential once again gave a positive contribution to the income gap between the euro area and the United States. At the same time, though, its role was much reduced. Indeed, in 2001 the key factor in explaining the income gap between the two areas was the number of hours worked per employed person. Its contribution to the overall income gap has grown steadily. It was quite modest in 1979, 13 percent, but accounted for more than half, 57 percent, of the gap by 2001. The contribution of the employment rate also increased over time, until 1997, but following the employment surge in the euro area after 1997 it is now much less significant. Finally, and perhaps surprisingly, the contribution of demography has, so far, been to reduce the income gap between the eurozone and the United States. This may look surprising in light of the aging of the euro area population, but most likely it reflects the more than proportionate reduction of the youngest cohorts, less than fifteen years old. This trend is not likely to persist, however, as it will soon be outweighed by the increasing share of the cohort of those over sixty-five.

Figure 4.1 raises more questions than it provides answers. Let us focus on two issues. First, we have seen how hours worked per person provide a crucial and growing contribution to the income gap between the two areas. Does this mean that Europeans have a somewhat higher preference for leisure? This is an area where future research would yield a large dividend. On the one hand, it is true that a larger fraction of employed people would like to work longer hours in Europe than in the United States (Sapir et al., 2003). Taken at face value, this could be taken as an indication that Europe's short working time reflects labor market rationing rather than a greater preference for leisure. On the other

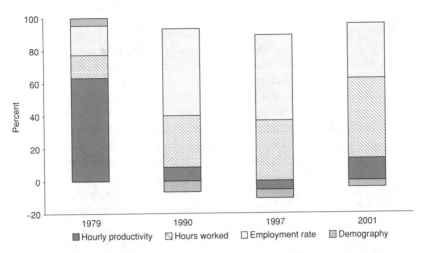

Figure 4.1 Decomposing the income gap between the euro area and the United States
Source: Own calculations, based on OECD data.

hand, these effects are relatively minor, with only 2 percent of total employment in Europe expressing a desire for working more hours, versus 1 percent in the United States (OECD, 2003b). Given that in the euro area part-time employment represents 17.1 percent of total employment, and assuming that part-timers work only half of the standard hours, we can estimate that average hours per employed person would increase by 1 percent if hours were no longer rationed and part-time work was no longer involuntary. Even then, worked hours per employed person would still contribute 50 percent to the income gap between the euro area and the United States. By and large, therefore, labor market rationing does not appear to be a significant factor behind Europe's short working time and, hence, its remaining income gap with respect to the United States.

Alternatively, a large and increasing tax burden may have discouraged European households from supplying labor. While the marginal tax rate on labor was basically constant in the United States between 1970–1974 and 1993–1996 at around 40 percent, it increased during the same period from 41 percent to 64 percent in Italy, from 49 percent to 59 percent in France, and from 52 percent to 59 percent in Germany. According to Prescott (2004), the rise in Europe's marginal tax rates can explain most of the fall in its labor supply. However, as highlighted by Blanchard (2004), Prescott's results depend crucially on an unrealistically high wage elasticity of labor supply. Moreover, in a number of countries not considered by Prescott[3] – in Ireland, for instance – both the marginal tax rate on labor and the supply of labor show a rising trend over the period.

The second issue is the behavior of productivity. We have seen how the euro area was unable to combine employment and productivity growth. The key question is whether this trade-off is temporary. Standard growth accounting shows that the quality of the labor force increased significantly in Europe after 1997, as the new entrants into the labor force were quite well educated. The other side of the coin is that, for a given rate of output growth, the rate of increase in total factor productivity growth fell even more given the increase in the (quality-adjusted) labor input. On this count, therefore, there are good reasons to be concerned that the slowdown in productivity growth reflects a fall in the rate of technological advance and bodes ill for the future growth prospects of the European economy. At the same time, though, it cannot be neglected that the new entrants into employment were mostly young and quite inexperienced. The recorded fall in TFP growth may therefore be a statistical artifact, to the extent that no (or inadequate) allowance is made for experience. Over time, as the new entrants acquire more experience, Europe's productivity growth may rebound, softening the trade-off between productivity and employment growth. This is an additional area that clearly deserves further research.

Summing up, the evidence for Europe's decline is somewhat less than fully compelling. First, much of the remaining gap is accounted for by differences in hours worked. It remains to be seen whether the latter reflects a greater preference for leisure in Europe or, alternatively, tighter constraints in the smooth functioning of the labor market. Second, while it is undeniable that productivity growth fell in Europe and surged in the United States, it is perhaps too early to tell whether the European slowdown is a temporary or a permanent phenomenon. Moreover, whatever the answer, it remains true that the opening up of the productivity gap with respect to the United States offers new prospects for Europe to catch up. Whether Europe will be able to take this opportunity will also depend on its ability to reform its economy. Finally, our analysis casts light on the role of demography. This factor is all but neglected in most empirical analyses. So far it has provided a positive contribution to the reduction of the income gap between the euro area and the United States. This fact, however, should not be taken as a reassuring indication of future trends. Over the next few decades, demography is likely to make a negative contribution to the convergence process between the two areas.

4.5 Is Europe losing competitiveness?

Competitiveness, as is well known, is an ill-defined concept (Krugman, 1994). Nonetheless, it is a continuing source of concern for most policymakers. In particular, the loss of market share in world exports is often lamented as an unambiguous indication of the decline in Europe's competitiveness in the international arena.

That Europe's role in world trade has been declining is difficult to deny. OECD data show that, between 1990 and 2001, all the eurozone countries suffered a major drop in their share of world exports. Germany suffered the largest fall, with its share shrinking from 12.1 percent in 1990 to 8.1 percent in 2000. France and Italy, the next largest countries in the euro area, did not fare much better. Italy's share fell from 5.1 percent to 3.9 percent between 1990 and 2000, France's from 6.1 percent to 4.8 percent. The contrast with the United States is striking: during the same period the United States succeeded in expanding its contribution to the world export market, from 13.1 percent to 14 percent.

Are policymakers' concerns about the erosion of Europe's weight in world trade warranted? The answer is, as usual, nuanced. Obviously, for given relative prices, the loss of world export share indicates that the elasticity of Europe's exports with respect to world demand is less than unitary. Indeed, even when measured in volume terms, Europe's export share has contracted markedly. This, in turn, can be taken either as an indication that Europe's price competitiveness is being eroded – as Europe's prices and costs tend to increase somewhat more rapidly than in other countries, world consumers shift out of its exports – or, more fundamentally, that Europe's specialization is biased towards slow-growing sectors. In both cases, Europe would be losing competitiveness. The fact, furthermore, that the erosion of market share coincided with a substantial real depreciation for the euro area, a fact that by itself should have increased Europe's share in volume terms, is typically taken as further compelling evidence for Europe's decline.

By and large, these conclusions should be taken with a grain of salt. First, it is not altogether clear that a region, such as the eurozone, where population and hence aggregate output tend to grow at a slower pace than in the rest of the world will be able hold indefinitely its share of the world export market. While it is true that small countries tend to be more open, there are no reasons to believe that the share of exports in GDP would grow sufficiently large as to offset the impact of the fall in the share of world output. Indeed, it is noteworthy that exports per capita in Italy and Germany rose at a faster rate than in the United States and in the world economy in general.

Secondly, and more fundamentally, how the value share in world exports changes over time depends on a set of factors, many of which have little relationship to competitiveness. Consider, for instance, the impact of a nominal appreciation of the dollar exchange rate with respect to the euro. The higher value of the dollar will tend to boost the value of trade outside the euro area. Conversely, the fall in the value of the euro will depress the value of intra-European trade. This is a simple valuation effect with no implications for competitiveness, however defined. Its relevance can be seen from figures 4.2 and 4.3, where the link between the dollar/euro exchange rate and the share of Italy and Germany, respectively, in world export markets is highlighted. We see immediately how

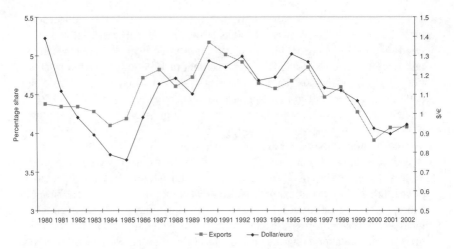

Figure 4.2 Italy's share of non-oil world exports and the dollar/euro exchange rate
Source: Own calculations, based on WTO data.

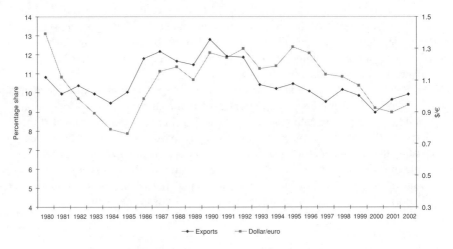

Figure 4.3 Germany's share of non-oil world exports and the dollar/euro exchange rate
Source: Own calculations, based on WTO data.

both countries suffered a substantial loss in their market shares during the early 1980s, when the dollar was appreciating quite rapidly. Most of these losses were reversed during the period of dollar depreciation, only to resurface again in the second half of the 1990s following the recovery of the US currency. Interestingly enough, over the last three years Germany's share of world exports has

Table 4.6 *Determinants of countries' shares of world exports*

Dependent variable	$\ln(X_i/X_w)$	$\ln(X_i/X_w)$
$\ln(RER)$	0.08 (1.65)	0.05 (0.69)
$\ln(\$/€)$	0.25 (7.72)	0.27 (7.40)
$\ln(p_{oil})$	−0.13 (7.61)	−0.14 (7.29)
D_{90}	−	0.06 (0.66)
Adj. R^2	0.98	0.98
Sample	1980–2002 France, Germany, Italy	1980–2002 France, Germany, Italy

X_i: Current price of exports of country i (i = France, Germany, Italy).
X_w: World exports.
RER: Real exchange rate.
$\$/€$: dollar/euro nominal exchange rate.
P_{oil}: Oil price.
D_{90}: Dummy variable (1 during the 1990s, 0 otherwise).
NB: t-statistics in parentheses.

risen again, from 8.1 percent to 9.4 percent, in line with the new strength of the euro. France, but not Italy, has also succeeded in reversing the downward trend in its world export share.

Oil prices represent a further complicating factor in the analysis. Indeed, an increase in the price of oil tends to boost the value of oil trade and, *ceteris paribus*, reduces the share in world exports of oil-importing countries. In an attempt to control for this factor, both figures 4.2 and 4.3 focus on non-oil exports.

Further evidence can be gained from a simple econometric exercise. We run a standard regression where the share of world *nominal* exports is a function of the real exchange rate, the dollar/euro nominal exchange rate, the oil price, and a set of country dummies. The sample includes three countries (France, Germany, and Italy) and runs from 1980 to 2002. The data are simply pooled in a fixed-effect framework. The results are presented in table 4.6. The notion that the nominal exchange rate strongly affects the behavior of the export share even after controlling for the real exchange rate is strongly supported by the estimation results. Similarly, oil prices have a negative and significant impact on the countries' shares of world exports, as expected. We also test whether export behavior changed significantly after 1990 with a view to detecting a more fundamental loss of competitiveness for the major euro area countries. The results do not support such a hypothesis. On the contrary, we find that the dummy variable for the 1990s has a positive sign for Italy (not shown in the table), suggesting that during that decade Italy's export behaved somewhat

Table 4.7 *The United States' and Europe's growth in historical perspective*

	(annual average growth rate)	
	Europe	United States
1870–1913	1.25	1.79
1913–1929	0.97	1.65
1929–1950	0.79	1.55
1950–1973	3.61	2.40

Source: Gordon (2004a).

better than the estimated norm. However, the same dummy variable is not significant for France and Germany, or for the EU3 as a whole.

To sum up, there are no obvious indications of a structural loss in competitiveness for euro area countries. The evolution of their export share in world markets is well explained by the behavior of the nominal dollar/euro exchange rate. The recent recovery in world export share for Germany and France also points to the paramount role of valuation effects. Finally, there is no indication that export shares suffered from a negative structural break during the 1990s.

4.6 A long-run view

The vicissitudes of Europe's convergence with respect to the United States can be interpreted better in a longer-run perspective. As shown by Gordon (2004b), from 1870 until 1950 Europe has been steadily losing ground with respect to the United States (table 4.7). The availability of land and of natural resources, a large internal market, the bounds of a common language, a well-designed patent system, and an effective regulatory framework all combined to foster productivity growth at a rate that old Europe was unable to achieve. Interestingly enough, the productivity gap rose during the Great Depression, when the halt to immigration flows and the collapse of world trade hit Europe more than the United States.

Matters changed after the Second World War, when Europe was finally able to exploit (with a twenty-year lag compared to the United States!) the technological advances that had been made at the beginning of the twentieth century. The catch-up of Europe with respect to the United States continued well after the postwar reconstruction was over, fueled by the creation of a large and increasingly integrated internal market. Figure 4.4 documents how, between the early 1950s and the mid-1970s, the income gap between the United States and the

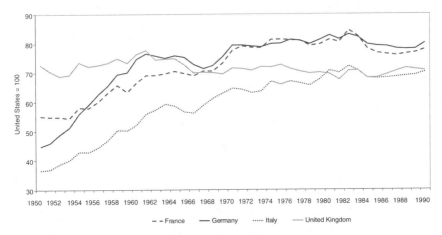

Figure 4.4 Converging with the United States? Relative income per capita
Source: Groningen Growth and Development Centre (2005).

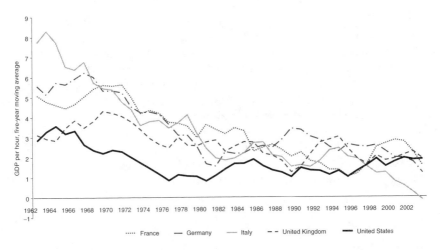

Figure 4.5 Productivity growth
Source: Groningen Growth and Development Centre (2005).

largest European countries fell markedly. For instance, the ratio between Germany's and the United States' income per capita rose from 44.8 percent in 1950 to 70 percent in 1960 and 80 percent in 1975.

Figure 4.4 also shows that Europe's catch-up with the United States came to a virtual stop around the mid-1970s. Interestingly enough, productivity growth,

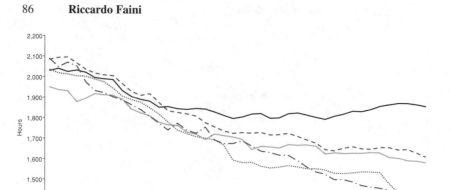

Figure 4.6 Annual hours worked
Source: Groningen Growth and Development Centre (2005).

which had been substantially higher in Europe than in the United States after 1950, stayed that way even after the mid-1970s, when the income convergence process stopped. The lack of income convergence in spite of more rapid productivity growth is fully explained by Europe's abysmal labor market performance (the employment rate fell from 62.9 percent in 1970 to 58.8 percent in 1995, against a rise from 63.6 percent to 74.4 percent in the United States during the same period) and by its record with regard to working hours, the relative decline of which with respect to the United States began precisely during the mid-1970s (see figure 4.6). After 1995, however, following the spread of information technologies, US productivity growth has been faster than in Europe. By and large, these findings are fully in line with those of section 1.

4.7 Conclusions

The evidence for Europe's relative economic decline is less compelling than commonly thought. First, demographic factors must be fully controlled for. Population growth has been systematically higher in the United States than in the euro area, with the gap widening further in the 1990s compared to the 1980s. Accordingly, the differential in aggregate growth rates tends to provide a seriously distorted picture of the relative economic performance of the two areas. Second, while it is true that since 1990 per capita income growth in the United States has been somewhat higher, and certainly not lower, than in the euro area, matters look different when allowance is made for differences in accounting conventions. Indeed, when this is done it is no longer true to say that the convergence process in per capita income between the euro area and the United States has virtually stalled during the last thirteen years. Interestingly, we find that, after controlling for accounting definitions, the convergence process slowed down but continued during the early 1990s. Third, while the differential in the level of per capita income between the euro area and the United States is still large, around 30 percent in purchasing power terms, its causes have radically changed over time. In the early 1970s, productivity differentials were the main factor behind the income gap. In 2001, however, it is the hours worked per employed person that play a predominant role. As noted earlier, whether the fewer working hours in Europe reflect a greater preference for leisure or institutional constraints in the labor market is a promising avenue for future research.

Finally, the fact remains that Europe has been unable to combine fast productivity growth with sustained employment creation. Since 1997 European total employment has been growing quite rapidly, at the expense, however, of productivity performance. This disappointing performance has much to do with inadequate spending on research and development (R&D), poor educational achievements, and inadequate regulation of the labor and product markets. We have not pursued in this chapter this line of inquiry, as it has been fully explored elsewhere (OECD, 2003a; Visco, 1994). We suggest, however, that the poor productivity performance in Europe may perhaps reflect the absorption of a young, educated, but largely inexperienced workforce, following a number of significant changes in labor market regulations. It may also reflect Europe's inability to absorb quickly new technological breakthroughs. We have already seen how Europe lagged at least twenty years behind the United States in benefiting from the wave of technological innovations at the beginning of the twentieth century. If some of these factors hold true, there are perhaps reasons to be optimistic about future productivity prospects, since both wages and productivity are likely to rise in line with experience and the delayed impact of new technologies should be felt in the relatively near future. Equally, however, none of this frees Europe's policymakers from the task of persevering on the reformist road.

Labor and – even more – product market liberalization should loom high on the agenda for these policymakers. There are good reasons to believe that labor market reforms have strong distributional implications and will, therefore, be fiercely resisted. While product market liberalization may also hit sectoral interests, its distributional impact may be less resented if it is undertaken over a broad range of sectors (Blanchard and Giavazzi, 2003). Moreover, there are good reasons to believe that labor market distortions are "derived" distortions. Product market reforms would make labor demand more elastic and limit the amount of rents to be claimed through restrictive labor market regulations.

A further priority should be the strengthening of educational achievements. Lamenting the obsolete nature of the European pattern of specialization and the inadequate level of spending in research and development is of little use. Some of the proposed remedies, such as protectionist measures against foreign competition and the launching of ambitious programs to foster investment in R&D, may even worsen rather than alleviate the problem. In the end, both the pattern of specialization and the level of spending in R&D reflect the limited abundance of skills in Europe and, more broadly, its pattern of comparative advantage. Upgrading the levels of skills and promoting lifelong learning would also help in reducing unemployment and lengthening the average working life.

Finally, financial market reforms are key to Europe's ability to benefit from new technological and market opportunities. US financial markets, in particular the development of venture capital, were instrumental in diffusing the more recent IT advances. This is an area where European institutions have a bigger say and progress is likely to be swifter than in those fields where, instead, national governments jealously guard their privileges.

Notes

I am grateful to Andrea Boltho, Sergio de Nardis, Marco Magnani, Pierferdinando Targetti, Gianni Toniolo, Ignazio Visco, and Vincenzo Visco for their comments and suggestions.
1. For a differing point of view, however, see Boltho (2003).
2. Alone, they represent two-thirds of the euro area population. Germany includes East Germany throughout the period.
3. Prescott (2004) focuses only on the G7 countries. Aiginger (2004) underscores the need to consider a broad set of European experiences.

5   Technical change and US economic growth: the interwar period and the 1990s

Alexander J. Field

5.1 Introduction

Looking back over the twentieth century, the years 1948–1973 stand out as the "golden age" of labor productivity growth and living standard improvement in the United States – the result of a combination of respectable multifactor productivity (MEP) growth and robust rates of capital deepening. The period 1973–1989, in contrast, was the most disappointing, because of the virtual collapse of multifactor productivity growth during these years. The contrast between these periods gave rise to a raft of studies trying to pinpoint the causes of the slowdown in MFP growth and, as a consequence, labor productivity growth. More recently, attention has shifted towards determining the contribution of the IT revolution to the revival of productivity growth in the 1990s.

Most of these studies, however, embrace an historical perspective that reaches back no further than 1948, the year in which most of the standard series maintained by the Bureau of Labor Statistics (BLS) begin. This chapter, in contrast, pushes the time horizon back to the beginning of the twentieth century, with particular attention to the period following the First World War and preceding US entry into the Second World War in 1941. It combines a summary of the magnitude and sources of productivity advance during the interwar years (for more details, see Field, 2003, 2006a) with a comparative examination of progress during the last decade of the century.

Because of the influence of cyclical factors on productivity levels, it is common in historical research to restrict calculations of productivity growth rates to peak-to-peak comparisons. For the most recent episode, this requires measurement from 1989 to 2000. Many students of the productivity revival prefer, nevertheless, to measure from 1995. Although 1995 is not a business cycle peak, the acceleration in output growth after 1995 does make the revival look more striking. Whether it is desirable or appropriate to choose one's start date with the objective of making the contrast between recent and past history more dramatic is, of course, an open question.

Table 5.1 *Compound annual growth rates of MFP, labor, and capital productivity in the US private non-farm economy, 1901–2000*

	MFP	Output/hour	Output/adjusted hour	Output/unit capital input
1901–1919	1.08	1.71	1.44	0.01
1919–1929	2.02	2.27	2.33	1.09
1929–1941	2.31	2.35	2.21	2.47
1941–1948	1.29	1.71	1.42	1.32
1948–1973	1.90	2.88	2.64	0.18
1973–1989	0.34	1.34	1.03	−1.24
1989–2000	0.78	1.92	1.41	−0.61
1973–1995	0.38	1.37	0.98	−0.98
1995–2000	1.14	2.46	2.08	−0.84

NB: "Output per adjusted hour" uses an hours index that has been augmented to reflect changes in labor quality or composition. In creating this index, different categories of labor are weighted by their respective wage rates.

Sources: 1901–1948 – Kendrick (1961, table A-XXIII; the unadjusted data are from the column headed "Output per man hour," the adjusted data from the column headed "Output per unit of labor-input," and capital productivity is "Output per unit of capital input"); 1948–2000 – Bureau of Labor Statistics, www.bls.gov, series MPU750021, MPU750023, MPU750024, and MPU750028; these data are from the multifactor productivity section of the website, accessed 12 April 2004; the labor productivity section contains more recent data and is updated more frequently.

That said, the recent achievement is impressive when measured in relation to the period of slow growth that preceded it. But, even if we show the recent acceleration in its best light, by measuring from 1995 to the peak of the cycle in 2000, the end-of-century labor productivity advance remained well below "golden age" rates. Perhaps more surprisingly, it remained in the same range as that registered during the interwar period (see table 5.1). And multifactor productivity growth was less than half what it was during the Depression years.[1]

The seminal studies by Abramovitz (1956) and Solow (1957) showed that, in comparison with the nineteenth century, a large gap opened up in the first half of the twentieth century between the growth of real output and a weighted average of inputs conventionally measured. This gap, termed the "residual," was subsequently interpreted by Abramovitz as reflecting a shift to a knowledge-based type of economic development, which, from the vantage point of the middle of the century, was expected to persist (Abramovitz, 1993, p. 224).

By and large it did so for another quarter-century. But the sixteen-year period of slow productivity growth generally dated from 1973 forced, or should have forced, a reassessment of the view that the Abramovitz and Solow studies had identified a permanent sea change. The end-of-century revival of productivity growth, in turn, has focused attention on what caused the growth of the residual to accelerate and how much of it could be laid at the feet of IT.

This chapter focuses on the two major cycles of the interwar period (1919–1929 and 1929–1941) and the more recent 1989–2000 period. All three periods experienced comparable labor productivity growth rates. The respective contributions of multifactor productivity growth and capital deepening were, however, quite different, as were the sectoral locations of rapid advance.

5.2 Overview of twentieth-century growth trends

For the moment, let's look forward from 1929. With some simplification the labor productivity growth history of the United States between 1929 and 1995 can be thought of as consisting of three periods in which the respective contributions of MFP growth and capital deepening were quite distinct. The years 1929–1948 witnessed exceptionally high rates of MFP growth, but little capital deepening.

Between 1948 and 1973 lower but still respectable MFP growth combined with a revival of physical capital deepening to produce the highest rates of labor productivity growth in the century, and a golden age of living standard improvement. Between 1973 and 1995 capital deepening continued at somewhat slower rates but multifactor productivity growth in the US economy effectively disappeared. Labor productivity rose, but at greatly reduced rates (1.37 percent per year) compared with the 2.88 percent annual growth clocked during the golden age (see table 5.1; data are for the private non-farm economy (PNE)). At the end of the century labor productivity growth again approached golden age rates, principally as the result of a revival of MFP growth.

5.3 The rise in output per hour during the Depression: causes and consequences

A number of economists have been aware of the rise in output per hour during the Depression, but most of the attention in explaining this has been on the effects of the selective retention of workers, particularly during the 1929–1933 downturn (Margo, 1991). By 1941, however, when recovery had finally pushed unemployment rates into single-digit levels, much of this should have been unwound. There were secular improvements in labor quality during the Depression years as well, but a comparison of columns 2 and 3 of table 5.1 suggests that such improvements can explain only a small fraction of the growth in output per hour between 1929 and 1941.[2] Clearly, other factors had to have been operative – and these could not have included physical capital deepening, as can also be seen from table 5.1.

Since there was virtually no increase in private sector inputs conventionally measured between 1929 and 1941, MFP advance accounted for *all* of the 32 percent increase in the real output of the private non-farm economy over these years. And, since there was no private sector capital deepening, the same was true for the increase in output per hour. Masked by the continuing levels of high unemployment, an impressive expansion of the potential output of the US economy was taking place.

Does the claim that the Depression years witnessed the highest MFP growth rates of the century include consideration of the end-of-century "new economy" boom? The short answer is that it does. My offices at a university in the heart of Silicon Valley offered a ringside view of the investment boom, the rising share prices, and some of the hyperbolic claims that drove both. For better or for worse, this enthusiasm led to a reorganization of the federal government's statistical apparatus in an effort to make it more sensitive to the possible contributions of the IT revolution to growth.

But the data from the end of the twentieth century, even after incorporating the use of hedonic methods to adjust for quality changes, tell a more nuanced story. Revolutionary technological or organizational change – the sort that shows up in MFP growth – was concentrated in distribution, securities trading, and a narrow range of industries within a shrinking manufacturing sector. MFP advance within industry was largely localized within the old SIC 35 and 36,[3] sectors that include the production of semiconductors, computers, networking, and telecommunications equipment. Aggregate MFP growth remained modest by the historical standards of the twentieth century.

Evidence from the beginning of the twenty-first century suggests the possibility of more substantial MFP payback in the IT-using sectors, albeit delayed (*Wall Street Journal*, 2003). Labor productivity grew at 3.04 percent per year continuously compounded from 1995 through 2004 (BLS series PRS85006093, accessed 19 June 2005). This represents very strong performance, particularly after 2000. At the time this chapter was written, however, we did not have MFP estimates beyond 2002, so it remains unclear how much of early twenty-first-century growth must be due to an increase in the labor composition contribution due to selective retention (which would not persist at this rate through a full recovery), or how much the capital deepening contribution may have changed since the heady days of 1995–2000. Capital services grew at 5.38 percent per year between 1995 and 2000, and their rate of increase has certainly slowed. But hours, which grew at over 2 percent per year between 1995 and 2000, declined at 1.85 percent per year between 2000:2 and 2003:2. Even with subsequent recovery, hours in 2005:1 were still 3 percent below their peak in 2000. Until we have the most recent capital services numbers we can't know what has happened to the capital/hours ratio. Between 2000 and 2002 (the latest year for which we have capital services data) capital services per hour rose very rapidly – a total of 12.4 percent – as the numerator continued to rise and the denominator declined. We will need to have the economy approach closer to potential output, and have the data for it, before we can have a clearer picture of the sustainability of these recent trends. The bottom line is that, measuring from 1989 through the end of the boom in 2000, aggregate MFP growth, including that in the IT-using sectors, although more than double the rate in 1973–1989, was only a third that registered between 1929 and 1941 (see table 5.1).

Why 1989? And why 2000? Multifactor productivity data is available only on an annual basis. According to the National Bureau of Economic Research (NBER) business cycle chronology, the peak of activity in July 1990 was followed by a recession that bottomed out in March 1991, followed by the long expansion of the 1990s, culminating in the peak 120 months later (March 2001). But 2001 was also a year of economic downturn, with the trough reached only eight months afterwards, in November that year. Similarly, 1990 included five post-peak months. Since we are using annual data, I measure from the last full year of expansion (1989) before a downturn to the subsequent final full year of expansion before a downturn (2000).[4]

It is well known that MFP and labor productivity grew at an accelerated pace during the second half of the 1990s, and it has become conventional to measure to and from 1995, even though the year was not a business cycle peak. The argument against 1995 is that it is not a peak, a point reflected in the controversy surrounding Gordon's claims that much of the end-of-century improvement reflected a cyclical acceleration in both labor and multifactor productivity common in later stages of a business expansion (Gordon, 2003c). Nevertheless, there does seem to be a break in the series *circa* 1995, and, in deference to current practice, table 5.1 also reports MFP advance over the last five years of the century. Here the compound average annual growth rate comes in at 1.14 percent per year. This is three times the anemic MFP growth registered between 1973 and 1995. But it is still substantially below golden age rates and, even more remarkably, less than half the rate registered between 1929 and 1941.

5.4 The role of manufacturing

If we are discussing contributions to achieved productivity levels in the interwar period, it is appropriate to place a good deal of emphasis on a growing

Table 5.2 *The growth of MFP, labor, and capital productivity in manufacturing in the United States, 1919–2000*

	MFP	Output/hour	Output/adjusted hour	Output/unit capital input
1919–1929	5.12	5.45	5.45	4.20
1929–1941	2.60	2.61	2.46	2.96
1941–1948	−0.52	0.20	0.03	−1.82
1949–1973	1.49	2.51	n.a.	−0.03
1973–1989	0.57	2.42	n.a.	−1.22
1989–2000	1.58	3.56	n.a.	0.16
1973–1995	0.66	2.61	n.a.	−0.82
1995–2000	2.09	4.07	n.a.	0.08

Sources: 1919–29 – Kendrick (1961, table D-1, p. 464); 1929–1941 and 1941–1948 – output and labor input are from Kendrick (1961, tables D-1 and D-2), capital input is based on the index for manufacturing fixed capital in the BEA's Fixed Asset Table (4.2, www.bea.doc.gov/bea/dN/FAweb/Index2002.htm), MFP is calculated based on an assumed share of 0.7 for labor, 0.3 for capital; 1949–2000 – Bureau of Labor Statistics, series MPU300001, MPU300002, MPU300003, accessed 22 November 2004.

manufacturing sector that by 1941 comprised almost a third of the economy. I estimate that 84 percent of MFP growth in the private non-farm economy between 1919 and 1929 and about 48 percent of the growth between 1929 and 1941 originated in manufacturing (see below). For 1995–2000 manufacturing's contribution was about 39 percent of private non-farm MFP growth, but that total and manufacturing's percentage point contribution to it were much smaller than was true in the interwar period.

Although Kendrick does not provide enough information to allow the calculation of MFP growth rates within manufacturing for the 1929–1941 and 1941–1948 sub-periods, one can do so for the sector as a whole using Kendrick's estimates for output and labor input combined with capital input data from the Bureau of Economic Analysis's (BEA's) Fixed Asset Tables (see table 5.2).[5] These calculations show MFP growth within the sector over the 1929–41 period to have proceeded at the rate of 2.60 percent per year. This is higher than in any subsequent period of the twentieth century. It does, however, represent a halving of the 5.12 percent rate registered over the 1919–1929 period, years in which the flexibility offered by the unit drive electric motor facilitated the shift to a single-story layout and the assembly line production of automobiles and a host of new electrically powered consumer durables (Devine, 1983;

Table 5.3 *The employment of scientists and engineers in US manufacturing,*
1927–1940

	1927	1933	1940
Chemicals	1812	3255	7675
Electrical machinery	732	1322	3269
Petroleum	465	994	2849
Non-electrical machinery	421	629	2122
Primary metals	538	850	2113
Transport equipment	256	394	1765
Food/beverages	354	651	1712
Stone/clay/glass	410	569	1334
Fabricated metal products	334	500	1332
Instruments	234	581	1318
Rubber products	361	564	1000
Totals, eleven industries	5917	10309	26489
Totals, manufacturing	6274	10918	27777

Sources: National Research Council data, cited in Mowery (1981); Mowery and Rosenberg (2000, p. 814).

David and Wright, 2003; Field, 2004). My calculations also suggest, consistent
with arguments advanced in Field (2003, 2005), a decline in the level of MFP
in manufacturing over the 1941–1948 period.

Technical advance in manufacturing during the 1929–1941 period was not
as rapid and not as uniformly distributed across two-digit industries as was
true during the 1920s. The performance in the Depression years looks more
impressive, however, when contrasted with what took place in the second half
of the century, including the "new economy" period at the end of the 1990s.
Although technical progress was broadest and most uniformly high during the
1920s, advance within manufacturing was taking place across a broader frontier
during the Depression than was the case in the 1990s.

MFP advance in manufacturing during the Depression years was increasingly dependent on organized research and development. Table 5.3 summarizes National Research Council (NRC) data on the employment of scientists
and engineers in US manufacturing. Total R&D employment increased from
6,274 in 1927 to 10,918 in 1933, and then almost tripled in the next seven years,
reaching 27,777 in 1940.

Margo has documented the lower incidence of unemployment among professional, technical, and managerial occupational classifications as compared,

for example, with unskilled or blue-collar labor, or those with fewer years of schooling (Margo, 1991). This is indirect evidence that the sharp increase in R&D employment during the Depression was driven more by an outward shift in the demand for this type of labor than by a shift in its supply.

According to the Bureau of Economic Analysis, the real net manufacturing capital stock was less than 10 percent higher in 1941 than it had been in 1929, while, according to Kendrick, hours had risen 15.5 percent over the same period (Kendrick, 1961, appendix, table D-II). So, at the same time that the aggregate capital labor ratio in the sector fell, the relative demand for scientists and engineers increased. During this period complementarity was between high-end labor and the disembodied technical change that was such an important feature of the Depression years – a contrast with the capital–skill complementarity emphasized by Goldin and Katz (1998).

Table 5.3 lists the eleven two-digit industries that employed at least 1,000 scientists and engineers in 1940. The chemical industry tops the list by a wide margin, followed by electrical machinery and petroleum. These three industries alone account for almost half the total R&D employment on the eve of the Second World War. Absent from the list are tobacco, textiles, apparel, lumber, furniture, paper, publishing, and leather – industries that, with the possible exception of tobacco manufacture, one can identify with the first industrial revolution, before the Civil War. Although the emphasis here is on R&D-intensive industries such as chemicals, which turned in stellar productivity results during the Depression, it should be noted that a number of these latter industries, including tobacco and textiles, also turned in very respectable MFP performance over the period.

The overall trends revealed in the employment data are echoed in other R&D indicators. Between 1929 and 1936 the annual rate of founding of new R&D labs (seventy-three) exceeded the comparable statistic between 1919 and 1928 (sixty-six), and real spending on R&D in manufacturing more than doubled during the 1930s, with an acceleration at the end of the decade (Mowery and Rosenberg, 2000, pp. 814, 819).

Between 1929 and 1941, as noted, MFP growth in manufacturing fell by half compared with 1919–1929 (see table 5.2). There are two closely related questions here. On the one hand, why did MFP growth fall from 5.12 percent per year to 2.60 percent per year? The main explanation is that the across-the-board gains from exploiting small electric motors, and reconfiguring factories from the multi-story pattern that mechanical distribution of steam power required to the one-story layout made possible by electrification, were nearing exhaustion by the end of the 1920s. By 1929 79 percent of manufacturing horsepower in the United States was already provided by electricity (Devine, 1983). It's not that productivity levels in manufacturing were going to fall as a result of this exhaustion, it's just that one could not hope to continue to generate 5 percent per year growth in the residual from this source.

The related question, then, is, why didn't MFP growth in manufacturing fall more? Here the answer has to do with the contributions of a maturing and expanding privately funded research and development system that had begun with Thomas Edison at Menlo Park. The lion's share of private R&D spending was then – and is now – done in manufacturing, and a variety of new technological paradigms, most notably in chemical engineering, were ripe for exploitation.

The growing importance of the manufacturing sector – it generated about a quarter of national income in 1929, almost a third in 1941 – helped counterbalance the within-sector decline in MFP growth in terms of the ability of the sector to contribute to high and, indeed, accelerating MFP growth in the aggregate economy during the 1930s. Still, this roughly 2.6 percentage point decline in the MFP growth rate in the sector worked in the opposite direction, reducing the overall importance of manufacturing in aggregate MFP growth. Clearly, one had to have substantial accelerations in MFP growth in other sectors in order to produce the 2.31 percent continuously compounded growth rate reported in table 5.1 for the private non-farm economy.

That acceleration came principally within transportation and public utilities (about a tenth of the economy) and to a lesser degree within wholesale and retail distribution (about a sixth of national income). The remaining sectors, on net, contributed somewhat less. Agriculture is excluded from this analysis since we are examining the performance of the private non-farm economy, but we know that the farm sector's productivity growth in the 1930s also lagged behind that of the rest of the economy (see Field, 2003).

With the exception of water transport, productivity performance in transportation and public utilities between 1929 and 1941 was stellar (Field, 2006a). Of the 4.67 percent per year MFP growth in the sector, trucking and warehousing accounted for almost 40 percent of the total (1.80 percentage points), railroads an additional 26 percent (1.22 percentage points). Thus, almost two-thirds of the sectoral advance took place in surface transportation, and trucking and warehousing alone accounted for approximately 10 percent of MFP growth in the entire PNE.

It is useful to contrast the effects of the boom in street, highway, and other infrastructure construction during the 1930s with those of the rather different government-financed capital formation boom that took place during the 1940s. The latter effort poured more than $10 billion of taxpayer money into GOPO (government owned, privately operated) plants. Almost all this infusion was in manufacturing, and a large part went for equipment, particularly machine tools, in such strategic sectors as aluminum, synthetic rubber, aircraft engines, and aviation fuel refining (Gordon, 1969). Most of this was then sold off to the private sector after the war. This boom in equipment investment was associated with negative MFP growth in manufacturing between 1941 and 1948 and, partly as a result, a slowdown in PNE MFP growth overall (see Field, 2005, 2006a). In contrast, the infrastructure spending during the 1930s had positive spillovers in the private sector, particularly in transportation and distribution.

The achievements of the 1930s built on foundations put in place during the Depression years as well as work done in the 1920s and earlier. By establishing the groundwork for subsequent advance, the period also restocked the larder. For example, almost all the development work carried out by Philo Farnsworth on the quintessential postwar consumer commodity was carried out during the Depression, supported by venture capital funding. The new product (television) was introduced to a wide public in 1939 at the New York World's Fair, but the demands of war forestalled its full exploitation until after 1948.

Overall, of the 2.31 percent CAAGR (compound average annual growth rate) of MFP in the private non-farm economy between 1929 and 1941, 48 percent was contributed by manufacturing, 24 percent by transport and public utilities, and 18 percent by wholesale and retail distribution, with the remainder of the PNE contributing about 11 percent (see Field, 2006a).

We can now summarize the main distinctions between 1919–1929 and 1929–1941 with respect to aggregate MFP growth and its sources. First, MFP growth in the 1920s was almost entirely a story about manufacturing. Comparing the latter with the earlier period, there was a significant drop in the share of MFP growth in the private non-farm economy accounted for by manufacturing, from 84 percent in the 1920s to 48 percent in the 1929–1941 period. This was primarily due to a halving of within-sector MFP growth, only partially compensated for by the expanding size of the manufacturing sector. There was also a change in the sources of advance – away from the one-time gains associated with the final stages of electrification to those associated with exploiting the results of organized and expanding research and development efforts. This interpretation is supported by the aforementioned R&D employment and expenditure data (see table 5.3) and by chronologies of major process and product breakthroughs (Kleinknecht, 1987; Mensch, 1979; Schmookler, 1966; Field, 2003), which all show peaks during the 1930s, particularly its latter half.

5.5 The end-of-century episode

The aim of the second part of this chapter is to examine the end-of-century episode in historical perspective, and, in particular, to consider how much of the recent productivity growth and its acceleration should be credited to the *enabling technologies* of the IT revolution. If we want to take the measure of the IT revolution, we need to try and imagine a world in all respects similar save for the availability of these enabling technologies. In their absence, saving flows would have been congealed in other *not quite as good* capital goods. Output and productivity growth rates would have been somewhat lower, and one would like to know by how much.

Common practice in estimating the IT revolution's impact on labor productivity to date has been to sum three components: a contribution within the IT-*producing* industries to MFP growth, a contribution within the IT-*using* industries to MFP growth, and a portion of the effect on labor productivity of capital deepening associated with the accumulation of IT capital (Oliner and Sichel, 2000; Jorgenson, Ho, and Stiroh, 2003).

There can be few conceptual objections to the first two of these components. We should credit to the enabling technologies most of the MFP growth in the semiconductor and computer/network equipment manufacturing industries (SIC 35 and 36) and, where it can be demonstrated, a portion of non-cyclical MFP growth in IT-using industries such as securities trading and wholesale and retail distribution. The inclusion of the third component is more problematic, although it is endorsed by many, including Barro and Sala-I-Martin (1995, p. 352) and Klenow and Rodriguez-Clare (1997, p. 608).

The objection to including a portion of the capital deepening effect is this. What one is trying to do here is to estimate the social saving of the IT revolution. In its absence, saving flows would have been congealed in a slightly less beneficial array of physical capital goods. One wants to emphasize that breakthroughs such as the integrated circuit, and continuing advances in the manufacture of semiconductors, display screens, and mass storage devices, have saved us real resources in generating quality-adjusted IT services. We will pick that up in MFP growth in the IT-producing sectors. The very rapid MFP growth in these sectors is indeed the reason why the relative prices of semiconductors and goods embodying them have plummeted.[6]

We also want to ask whether the fact that saving flows were congealed in this slightly superior range of physical capital goods, as opposed to others, enabled a set of resource savings in other parts of the economy. This we will pick up in MFP growth in the IT-using sectors (these are typically referred to as spillovers or productive externalities).

But, unless we can make the argument that the enabling technologies of IT raised the rate of return to new investment projects at the margin, *and* that there was a response of aggregate saving rates to this rise, the capital deepening effect should ultimately be credited to saving behavior, and not to the enabling technologies.[7] It is, of course, conceivable that the enabling technologies of the IT revolution led, by raising the incremental return to investment and perforce saving, or by redistributing income to households with higher saving propensities, to an increase in the total flow of accumulation as a percentage of GDP at either the US or the world level, in which case it becomes more difficult cleanly to distinguish between the roles of saving and technical change in fostering labor productivity growth.

The evidence is, however, that investment in these goods did not crowd out consumption goods. Rather, it crowded out other not quite as good capital goods both within the United States and outside the country. Although we can comfortably posit an upward influence of IT innovations on marginal returns to investment and thus saving (this was, after all, the rationalization for rising stock market values during the 1990s), we would also need to argue, in order to justify the inclusion of the third component, that saving responded. And we would be hard-pressed to do so.

There is a large literature on the responsiveness of saving to after-tax interest rates. Theoretically, as in the case of the response of labor supply to increases in after-tax wages, there is the possibility of both an income and a substitution effect. Empirically, the evidence is inconclusive, although consistent with a conclusion of little net effect. As far as the income distribution mechanism, there is no question that there was a trend towards greater inequality in the last quarter of the century, particularly in the United States, and marked by a widening gap in the wages of highly and less highly educated workers. But there is no evidence that this redistribution resulted in an increase in private sector saving rates.

Some argued, particularly in the late 1990s, that saving rates were improperly measured because they did not include unrealized capital gains. But the conventionally measured saving rate was largely invariant both to the expansion of stock market valuations in the 1990s and their collapse in the early twenty-first century.

Between 1995 and 2000 consumption spending in the United States increased by 34 percent, from \$4,969 billion to \$6,683.7 billion nominal.[8] Consumption rose not just absolutely but as a share of a rising GDP, from 67.2 percent to 68 percent. At the same time, the growth of IT capital services accelerated from 0.41 percent per year (1973–1995) to 1.03 percent per year (1995–2000). Part of this acceleration came at the expense of the services of other components of the stock within the United States, the growth of which declined from 0.30 percent per year in the earlier period to 0.06 percent per year (US Council of Economic Advisors, 2001, p. 29). How was the boom in capital formation, much of it IT capital, financed?

Table 5.4 shows that between 1995 and 2000 there was a \$611.6 billion increase in gross private domestic investment as well as an increase in government investment of \$81.6 billion. How was this financed? Not by an increase in personal saving, which fell by a third, or by retained business saving (net business saving), which fell by a quarter. Gross business saving rose, however, as a consequence of a \$274.3 billion increase in corporate and unincorporated

Table 5.4 *Changes in the uses and sources of saving in the United States,*
1995–2000

	1995	2000	Change in uses	Change in sources
Gross private domestic investment	1143.8	1755.4	611.6	
Gross government investment	238.2	319.8	81.6	
Personal saving	302.4	201.5		−100.9
Retained business earnings	203.6	152.6		
Depreciation allowances	743.6	1017.9		
Gross business saving[a]	963.6	1170.5		206.9
Gross government saving	−8.5	435.8		444.3
Net foreign investment	−98.0	−395.8		297.8
Statistical discrepancy	26.5	−128.5		−155.0
Totals			693.2	693.1

[a] Includes wage accruals and disbursements not shown separately.
NB: All numbers are billions of dollars, nominal. This table is based on a rearrangement
of the open economy investment savings identity. Private domestic investment must
be financed by the sum of private domestic saving, government saving, and inflows
of foreign saving (capital account surplus or current account deficit). Note that negative net foreign investment is entered as a positive number in the sources of saving
column.
Source: US Council of Economic Advisors (2003, table B-32).

capital consumption allowances. This reflected the large portion of the gross
investment surge comprised of relatively short-lived IT capital goods, which
increased the importance of short-lived capital goods in the capital stock. We
thus experienced a net change in gross private saving of $106.1 billion.

The increase in gross domestic investment was $693.2 billion. After taking
into account the effect of changes in gross private saving, a saving gap of
almost $600 billion remains. It was filled through two main mechanisms. First,
a movement in the consolidated government surplus from −$8.5 to $435.8
billion – a swing of $444.3 billion in the surplus direction, and, second, a
deterioration of net exports from a deficit of $38 billion to one of $395.8 billion,
a swing of $297.8 billion. The remaining gap between the changes in the sources
and uses of saving is accounted for by an increase of $155 billion in the statistical
discrepancy.

The end-of-century investment boom was enabled on the one hand by the
willingness of foreign wealth holders to divert their saving flows from investment in their own countries or elsewhere and make it available to the United
States, and on the other hand by the tax policies of the Clinton administration

and the second half of the George W. Bush administration. Their fiscal policies, in particular modest tax increases in conjunction with an economy operating at close to capacity, provided the foundation for the big increase in government saving.

It is conceivable that, although the IT accumulation spurt was not associated with a rise in the private saving rate within the United States, it was associated with a rise in the world saving rate. This seems unlikely, and no one has made this case. We are left with the conclusion that, by and large, the IT capital accumulation spurt in the United States represented a substitution not away from consumption but away from other not quite as good capital goods, both within the United States and abroad.

Whether the flows necessary to finance capital accumulation came from national saving or from outside the country is irrelevant from the standpoint of productivity trends within the United States. But it does have welfare implications, particularly for the future. Reliance on foreign borrowing meant that the United States was able to forgo the sacrifice of current consumption that would otherwise have been the price of capital deepening. The borrowing will turn out to have been a good deal for the country if the increases in output per hour associated with the additional capital deepening exceed the increases in debt service per hour of labor input. But there is no guarantee that this will be the case; it depends on how much of the additional investment turns out to have been well directed. In any event, the gains in output per hour obtained through foreign borrowing will not be manna from heaven, given the obligation of debt repayment.

Within the United States there was indubitably an acceleration in overall capital deepening, comparing 1995–2000 with 1973–1995. Capital services per quality-adjusted hour grew at 2.93 percent per year in the latter period, as compared with 1.96 percent per year in the former. Thus, the slowdown in non-IT capital accumulation was more than compensated for by the rising rate of IT capital accumulation. One could argue that the drop in US private saving simply compensated collectively for the rise in government saving. But this seems doubtful, since the saving rate has been trending downwards for decades through periods of government deficit and surplus. It is more likely that, in the absence of the tax increases of the early 1990s, the deterioration of the current account would have been even worse.

If the enabling technologies of the IT revolution diverted towards the United States some portion of world saving flows that would not otherwise have come this way *even though US and world saving rates remained largely unaffected and may actually have declined*, it would technically be correct to say that we should grant to the IT revolution that part of the growth in labor productivity associated with IT's share of capital deepening. But, if we care about labor productivity because we care ultimately about consumption per person in the

United States, this is a misleading calculation. Much of the capital deepening has associated with it a liability tied to increased foreign indebtedness. This is in sharp contrast with the contributions to labor productivity growth of the first two components of the traditional triad used to measure IT "contributions."

5.6 The IT contribution and social saving controversies

The framework for reckoning the impact of the IT revolution advocated in this chapter, particularly its emphasis on MFP to the exclusion of the portion of the increase in labor productivity attributable to IT's share of capital deepening, runs counter to current practice. It can be better appreciated by comparing the challenge of coming to terms with IT in the 1990s with one of the critical disputes that gave rise to the new economic history. This involved the attempt to estimate the social saving of the US railroads. W. W. Rostow (1960) argued that railroads were "indispensable" to American economic growth. Both Albert Fishlow (1965) and Robert Fogel (1964) wanted more precision. They tried to imagine worlds otherwise similar save for access to the blueprints needed to build railroads. They calculated alternative channels for saving flows (into canal building and river dredging, for example) and ultimately how much lower US GDP would have been in this alternative world.

The social savings calculations that came out of those debates four decades ago were designed to impress upon us first of all the fact that, because saving flows were congealed in railroad permanent way and rolling stock, as opposed to other forms of physical capital such as canals, GDP was indeed higher than it otherwise would have been. *But not by a whole lot.* Fogel argued, for example, that 1890 US GDP was about 4 percent higher than it would have been in the absence of the availability of the railroad. What kind of an increment to MFP over a quarter of a century would one have needed to produce a GDP (or output per hour) in 1890 4 percent higher than it otherwise would have been? About 0.15 percent per year, continuously compounded.

In fact, Abramovitz's and Kendrick's analyses of nineteenth-century growth after the Civil War suggest, as was true for the 1973–1995 period, that, at least up until 1889, almost all the growth in real output can be accounted for by growth in inputs conventionally measured. It would make little sense to suggest that we have underestimated the contribution of the availability of railroad blueprints to growth in living standards in the nineteenth century because we have not accounted for the share of the increment to output per hour attributable to that portion of capital deepening associated with investments in locomotives, rolling stock, and permanent way.[9]

The key message of the classic works by Fishlow and Fogel was that, in the absence of the railroad, saving flows would have been congealed elsewhere, with results for the economy that would have been almost, but not quite, as good. We should take the same approach to reckoning the importance of the IT revolution.

In defense of what has become the conventional approach, some labor productivity is certainly, in an accounting sense, attributable to capital deepening. And a large fraction of the capital deepening, particularly at the end of the 1990s, was indeed associated with the accumulation of physical IT goods: computers, servers, fiber optic cable, routers, etc.[10] But, since the counterfactual suggested here imagines saving behavior largely unaffected by the presence or absence of the IT blueprints, our estimate of the portion of labor productivity growth attributable to saving (as opposed to technical innovation) should be largely independent of the particular forms in which saving flows were congealed.

It should, to be fair, also be independent of the sources of that saving. With respect to the labor productivity growth caused by capital deepening, it is irrelevant whether the saving came from outside the country. But, from the standpoint of their contribution to US standards of living, labor productivity gains from capital deepening financed by foreign borrowing come encumbered in a way that similar gains financed by domestic saving do not.

It is true that, if we are operating below capacity, and a new attractive invention offers profitable opportunities for new investment, it is reasonable to talk about the extent to which the innovation increases real output through its effect on the amount of real capital formation. From an aggregate perspective, such investment will be largely self-financing (just as, in the presence of accommodative monetary policy, will be government deficits). Under these circumstances, we can argue that it is investment that drives saving.

But, once the economy reaches potential output, the old rules of microeconomics again apply. Choices have opportunity costs, and saving constrains investment rather than the other way around. This has always been the rationale for policy changes designed to increase the after-tax return to saving, and, if the elasticities are right, saving flows – policies that make sense from a long-range growth perspective but are contra-indicated if one is below capacity. By and large, in growth accounting one tries to abstract from cyclical effects, and study the effect of saving and innovation on the increase of potential output. We want to know, in the long run, what the effect of the IT-enabling technologies is on the growth of potential output. If we are concerned with contributions to long-run growth, an appeal to the role of IT capital formation role in "contributing" to increases in real output based on these Keynesian arguments is misplaced.

It is analogous to emphasizing, as did Rostow, the stimulus to the iron and steel and lumber industries caused by late nineteenth-century railroad construction. That emphasis obscured the fact that, once the economy was at potential output, these resources had alternate uses, and the enormous costs of constructing the railroads raised the hurdle they had to overcome to make a positive contribution to GDP. They managed to do so, as Fogel and Fishlow demonstrated, by speeding up the turnover of inventories in the economy and by enabling a superior exploitation of regional comparative advantage. But it was close.

5.7 MFP growth versus the capital deepening effect

How important, in terms of their impact on labor productivity, were the respective roles of MFP and capital deepening over the 1995–2000 period? There are a couple of ways of looking at this. The first is to ask how much of the *acceleration* in labor productivity growth each is responsible for. For the private non-farm economy, that acceleration, comparing 1995–2000 with 1973–1995, was 1.09 percentage points, and about three-quarters of this is attributable to MFP acceleration.

The contribution to the output per hour growth of the labor composition change was about the same during the two periods (slightly lower between 1995 and 2000). Comparing 1995–2000 with 1973–1995, capital services growth accelerated from 3.94 percent per year to 5.38 percent per year. Growth in hours rose from 1.58 to 2.09 percent per year. As a result, the rate of capital deepening increased from 2.36 to 3.28 percent per year between 1995 and 2000.

But, assuming a capital share of 0.32,[11] this 0.92 percentage point increase should have accounted for an increase in the growth of output per hour of a modest 0.29 percentage points. In fact, the growth of output per hour rose 1.09 percentage points, from 1.37 to 2.46 percent per year. Almost all the balance – about three-quarters of the total – was due to MFP acceleration.[12]

A second approach is to ask what portion of labor productivity growth (2.46 percent per year) each is responsible for. Between 1995 and 2000 MFP growth was 1.14 percent per year. The rate of capital deepening was 3.28 percent per year. Multiplied by 0.32, this yields a capital deepening contribution of 1.05 percent per year. The remainder, about 0.27 percent per year, is the contribution of labor quality improvement. Looked at from this perspective, we can say that MFP growth accounted for less than half – about 46 percent (1.14/2.46) – of labor productivity growth between 1995 and 2000. Table 5.5 summarizes these calculations.

There is no hard and fast guide to what metric we should prefer here, although for an individual country it seems to me that the more meaningful measure is IT's contribution to the rate of improvement, not the rate of improvement of the rate of improvement, of labor productivity. For comparisons between countries, we should also be interested in levels.

5.8 MFP growth in the IT-producing and -using sectors

In spite of the various frameworks that researchers have used to measure the overall impact of IT on productivity growth, there is now enough consensus to

Table 5.5 *The MFP contribution to labor productivity growth and acceleration in the United States, 1995–2000*

Labor productivity growth, 1995–2000[a]	2.46
MFP[a]	1.14
Capital deepening[a]	1.05
Labor composition[a]	0.26
Labor productivity growth acceleration, 1995–2000 vs. 1973–1995[b]	1.09
MFP[b]	0.76
Capital deepening[b]	0.32
Labor composition[b]	−0.01

[a]Percent per year.
[b]Percentage points.
NB: Components do not sum exactly to aggregates due to rounding errors.

Table 5.6 *Contributions to labor productivity acceleration in the United States*

	1995–1999 over 1987–1995	1995–2000 over 1975–1989
Total acceleration	1.33	1.61
Wholesale trade	0.37	0.27
Retail trade	0.34	0.46
SIC 35 (includes semiconductors)	0.12	0.23
SIC 36 (includes computers)	0.17	0.08
Securities trading	0.25	0.32

NB: All figures are percentage points.
Sources: McKinsey Global Institute (2002); Nordhaus (2002, table 6, p. 233).

make some non-controversial statements about trends in MFP growth and their sources at the end of the century. First, in spite of some initial skepticism (see Jorgenson and Stiroh, 2000), it is clear that MFP growth – and, largely because of it, labor productivity growth – did accelerate between 1995 and 2000. Second, it is generally agreed that an important contributor to labor productivity growth and its acceleration was MFP advance associated with technical change in the semiconductor industry and in the manufacture of such products as computers, networking devices, and telecommunications equipment that embodied them. This shows up in very rapid (and accelerating) rates of MFP growth in SIC 35 and 36.

Third, it is likely, although the inferences are more indirect and the statistical support weaker, that some of the IT-using sectors, in particular wholesale and retail trade and securities trading, began to throw off significant MFP growth. Two analyses of the contributions to the acceleration of labor productivity growth (McKinsey Global Institute, 2002, and Nordhaus, 2002; see also US Council of Economic Advisors, 2001) are suggestive. The McKinsey study focuses on four years' growth (1995–1999) whereas Nordhaus covers five (1995–2000), and the base periods on which the acceleration is calculated differ. Both rely on BEA value-added data in the numerator, although the McKinsey study uses persons employed rather than hours in the denominator.

Both nevertheless find that distribution contributed substantially to the acceleration of labor productivity growth, and substantially more than did manufacturing, although the two studies reverse the relative contribution of wholesale and retail trade on the one hand, and SIC 35 and 36 on the other. Of course, one can't reason directly from decompositions of labor productivity acceleration to conclusions about MFP acceleration. Rates of capital deepening may have been exceptionally rapid in these sectors, explaining much of the acceleration of labor productivity growth. Indeed, at least through 2000, the data support this view.

Distribution was an extremely heavy user of IT capital. Largely as a consequence, its overall use of capital services soared. An index of capital services input in wholesale distribution rose 18.8 percent a year between 1973 and 1995 and 20.5 percent a year between 1995 and 2000. Hours in wholesale rose only 1.32 percent per year from 1995 to 2000. Therefore, capital deepened in the sector at a rate of 19.2 percent per year over the last five years of the century, far higher than the average for the economy. Similar calculations for retail distribution show capital deepening at 15.3 percent per year over these years.[13]

The BLS "industry productivity indexes and values table" shows labor productivity growth in wholesale trade rising from 2.82 percent per year (1987–1995) to 4.17 percent per year (1995–2000). In retail trade the comparable numbers are 1.95 percent per year (1987–1995) to 3.72 percent per year (1995–2000). So labor productivity growth in distribution did accelerate.

The problem for the residual is that, assuming a capital share of 0.32, the very high rates of capital deepening more than account for the labor productivity growth, implying negative MFP growth in both sectors overall. Moreover, this negative growth accelerated in the 1995–2000 period, along with the acceleration in capital deepening. The bottom line is that, while heavy capital deepening in distribution did cause an acceleration in labor productivity growth in the sector, it is uncertain whether the results through 2000 fully justify the massive IT expenditure.

Some of this uncertainty and pessimism may be due to an overestimate of how much "true" computer prices dropped, and thus an overestimate of how much real IT output (and investment) grew. This is a controversial suggestion, since a number of economists have actively pressured the BLS to make more use of hedonic methods to estimate the rate of quality improvement (and implied price decline) and praised it for what efforts it has made (see, for example, Nordhaus, 1997a).

The most compelling argument as to why these methods might lead to some overestimate of real product growth is that, in products where the quality has improved, users are typically forced to purchase bundles of attributes, not all of which they may actually desire or value. No one disputes that the issues of quality improvement and the introduction of new products are important challenges in constructing realistic estimates of real product growth. But some of the resulting estimates do not seem to satisfy a reasonableness test.

Hedonic price techniques have yielded end-of-century estimates in the range of −27 percent per year for the rate of decrease of quality-adjusted computer prices (Berndt, Dulberger, and Rapaport, 2000). This rate of price decrease would reduce a 1999 computer priced at $2000 to $500 over five years. Thus, if one used a laptop in 1999 and another in 2004 selling at the same nominal price, the BEA would conclude, based on the price data received from the BLS, that there had been a fourfold increase in the ratio of capital services to hours in one's work. Readers can judge, based on their own experience, whether or not this is reasonable.

For the sake of argument, grant that the BLS estimates of the rates of decline of IT capital prices may have resulted in an overestimate by the BEA of real product growth in the sector. Although this would, of course, boost MFP growth in the IT-producing sectors, it has the effect of worsening it in IT-*using* industries. One of the advantages of adopting the framework for reckoning the importance of IT proposed in this chapter is the elimination of the possible "incentive" to push for more rapid rates of estimated price decline to make IT's contribution appear larger.

Overestimating the real growth of IT services will, of course, also overestimate the capital deepening component of its contributions within what has become the conventional triadic approach. Since the framework advocated in this chapter credits most of the effect of capital deepening on labor productivity to saving, rather than the availability of IT technology, one is left with the effect on MFP growth in the IT-producing sectors, plus the effect in the IT-using sectors, such as distribution, if it can be demonstrated. An overestimate of real IT output growth will increase the former component, while it will reduce the latter. The two effects may largely cancel out.[14]

For the analysis of smaller subsectors of the economy, however, the effects will not cancel out, and the standard value-added approach as applied to subsectors has been criticized precisely because it can be so sensitive to errors in deflation (see Basu and Fernald, 1995). For subsectors the BLS prefers its

KLEMS (capital, labour, energy, materials, services) methodology, which uses growth of gross output rather than value-added measure, and subtracts weighted input growth rates for purchased materials, energy, and business services as well as hours and capital input. Their MFP estimates for the sector are unpublished and incomplete. But the unofficial data show MFP rising at 0.8 percent a year in wholesale although not at all in retail between 1992 and 1997.[15] It is likely that, were data available through 2000, calculated rates of growth of MFP between 1995 and 2000 would be higher.

With respect to retail distribution, the McKinsey study argues that virtually all the gains in labor productivity have been attributable to "big box" retailers such as Costco, Wal-Mart, and Circuit City. And it is the relative ease with which these can be put in place in the United States, as compared with the relative difficulty with which this can be done in Europe and other parts of the world, that Gordon has cited as a principal explanation of cross-country differences in MFP growth in distribution, and, perforce, the economy as a whole (Gordon, 2003a).[16]

Although the McKinsey group was willing to lay at IT's doorstep only about half the gains in wholesale and retail distribution (assuming one could demonstrate them), it is important to keep in mind that these were gains in *labor* productivity. The evidence for uncompensated productivity spillovers – increases in value added attributable to IT that aren't captured by the equipment or software manufacturers – is still weak. There are enough straws in the wind, however, to speculate that we are in fact in the midst of a second IT revolution in distribution, a revolution the trace of which on sector MFP data has been temporarily clouded, or even obliterated, by the over-deflation of IT prices.[17]

5.9 Summary: the 1990s and the 1930s

Let's now try and bring together what we can say about the 1995–2000 episode and how it relates to the 1929–1941 period. In this instance, because of the paucity of disaggregated sectoral data outside of manufacturing, I divide the private non-farm economy into three subsectors: manufacturing, wholesale and retail trade, and other. Excluding agriculture, government, non-farm housing, and the non-profit sector, the private non-farm economy accounts for 72.4 percent of value added. Using year 2000 sectoral shares, one can calculate a manufacturing weight (share of PNE) of 0.214 and a wholesale and retail trade weight of 0.223.

Again, the calculations begin with BLS numbers for MFP growth for the PNE between 1995 and 2000 (1.14 percent per year), and the BLS estimate for manufacturing as a whole of 2.08 percent per year (see tables 5.1 and 5.2). For wholesale and retail trade, one lacks data on MFP growth. As noted, unpublished estimates using the KLEMS methodology show 0.8 percent per year between 1992 and 1997 in wholesale, and no growth in retail. Allowing for

Table 5.7 *Sectoral contributions to MFP growth in the United States, 1995–2000*

	Share of PNE	Sectoral MFP growth	Contribution to PNE MFP growth	Share of PNE MFP growth
Manufacturing	0.214	2.08	0.45	0.39
Trade	0.223	0.70	0.16	0.14
Other	0.563	0.94	0.53	0.47
Total	1.000		1.14	

NB: "Private non-farm economy" excludes non-farm housing, health, agriculture, and government, which leaves 72.4 percent of value added. This is approximately the BLS's current definition of the PNE.

Sources: Sectoral shares – www.bea.doc.gov; MFP growth in manufacturing – see table 5.2; MF in trade – see text.

some acceleration towards the end of the decade in both wholesale and retail, and considering the relative weights of wholesale and retail, one can hazard an estimate of 0.7 percent per year for the sector between 1995 and 2000.

Multiplying sectoral shares by sectoral MFP growth rates, one can estimate that of the 1.14 percent per year growth of MFP within the PNE between 1995 and 2000, 0.45 percentage points originated in manufacturing, most of it due to the IT-producing industries, and 0.14 percentage points in distribution. Given the rest of the PNE's weight of 0.563, we can back out an implied MFP growth within it of 0.94 percent per year contributing the remaining 0.53 percentage points. This "other" category includes stand-out sectors such as securities trading, as well as laggards such as construction and trucking. Table 5.7 summarizes these calculations.

Suppose that one now credits all of the MFP growth in manufacturing between 1995 and 2000 to the enabling technologies of the IT revolution, and a third of that in distribution and the rest of the economy.[18] We would then conclude that 0.68 percentage points of the 1.14 percent MFP growth between 1995 and 2000 could be credited to IT innovations. Thus, we would attribute about 28 percent of labor productivity growth between 1995 and 2000 (0.68/2.46 percent per year) to the enabling technologies of the IT revolution.

How does this analysis compare with the recent decomposition by Jorgenson, Ho, and Stiroh (2003)? First, the BLS data for the private non-farm economy cover less than three-quarters of their aggregate. Jorgenson, Ho, and Stiroh include what the BLS excludes: the farm sector, government, housing, and (presumably) the non-profit sector.[19] These excluded sectors were slower-growing, and as a consequence their output aggregate grows at 4.07 percent between 1995 and 2000, versus 4.54 percent for the BLS PNE. Their hours series grows at 1.99 percent versus 2.09 percent for the PNE. Their labor quality adjustment is also lower: 0.22 percent versus 0.37 percent per year. Finally, their MFP growth estimate is much lower (0.62 versus 1.14) and their output per hour rises more slowly (2.07 percent versus 2.46 percent) (Jorgenson, Ho, and Stiroh, 2003, table 2). The difference in labor productivity growth rates is less than the difference in MFP growth rates because their implied rate of capital deepening (3.88 percent per year) is higher than for the BLS PNE (3.28).

All these comparisons speak to the extent to which the sectors excluded by the BLS and added back in by Jorgenson and Stiroh (1999) tend to be slower-growing and, in the aggregate, relatively unprogressive technologically.

Of their 2.02 percent per year growth in labor productivity between 1995 and 2000, they attribute 0.85 percentage points to IT capital deepening and 0.45 percentage points to IT-related MFP growth. In other words, they "attribute" about two-thirds of labor productivity growth ($1.30/2.02 = 0.64$) to IT. Conceptually, their analysis is more favorable to IT because, like Oliner and Sichel (2000), they credit the sector with a (large) portion of the effect on labor productivity of capital deepening. But in another respect their approach is less favorable than that advocated in this chapter, because they credit IT innovations with *none* of the MFP growth outside the IT-producing sectors, even though, in contrast to some of their earlier analyses, they do now acknowledge some MFP growth in the rest of the economy. If one applied my framework to their data, one would add the 0.45 percentage points of IT-related MFP growth and a third of the "other" MFP growth ($0.17/3 = 0.056$) to obtain 0.51 out of a total of 2.02 percent per year attributable to the enabling technologies of IT. This is approximately one-quarter of the total.

Comparing "new economy" economic growth with the MFP boom period of the interwar years, the following conclusions stand out. The 1920s, the 1930s, and the 1990s all saw contributions to MFP growth from manufacturing but the percentage point contribution to PNE growth in the recent episode was much lower (0.45 percentage points per year, versus 1.24 percentage points per year between 1929 and 1941 and 1.69 percentage points in the 1919–1929 period. Although rapid MFP advance within manufacturing was somewhat more localized in the 1930s than it had been in the 1920s, it was very narrowly concentrated at the end of the century.

Distribution played an important role in both the 1930s and the 1990s, although its percentage point contribution was three times larger in the Depression. Perhaps most striking, however, in comparison with the 1930s, the 1990s lacked the broad-based and very rapid advance in transportation and public utilities that characterized the 1930s. Although sectoral MFP estimates are not available across the board, labor productivity data, such as that contained in US Council of Economic Advisors, 2001, show growth rates declining, comparing 1995–1999 with 1989–1995, in trucking and warehousing, communications, and electric, gas, and sanitary services. For trucking and warehousing, labor productivity actually fell (US Council of Economic Advisors, 2001, table 1.2).

Finally, we need to re-emphasize that, for the private non-farm economy as a whole, aggregate MFP advance in the 1929–1941 period was more than twice as fast as in 1995–2000, more than three times as fast as in 1989–2000. For the 1930s, the question of whether or not to include a technology-driven capital deepening effect on labor productivity is moot, since there was effectively no capital deepening, at least in the private sector.

5.10 Taking the measure of the IT revolution

What has been incontrovertibly revolutionary about the IT revolution has been the operation of Moore's law: the ability to manufacture computers, peripherals, and telecommunications equipment in such a fashion that output has risen much more rapidly than inputs conventionally measured. The plummeting costs of producing quality-adjusted central processing units and memory, mass storage, and display devices have been for the late twentieth century an even more dramatic version of what spinning jennies and water frames were for the late eighteenth century in Britain. There is some evidence that the rate of technical progress in semiconductors accelerated even further after 1995, as the interval required to double performance dropped from eighteen months to twelve months. The revolutionary character of advances in the IT industries shows up as higher and accelerating MFP and, perforce, labor productivity growth in SIC 35 and 36. Even allowing for the possibility of some overshooting in the estimate of output growth resulting from the use of hedonic techniques, we can happily and uncontroversially credit the revolution with these gains, which flow directly through to improvements in the material standard of living.

It is also likely that some – although by no means all – of the MFP advance in wholesale and retail distribution, securities trading, and some other sectors of the economy was made possible by IT investments, and we should credit the enabling technologies of the IT revolution with an appropriate share of these gains as well, where we can demonstrate them. But, because the IT-producing sectors are small in relation to the aggregate economy, and because the gains in the IT-using sectors have been somewhat more modest, the boost to the growth of overall output per hour remains modest in comparison, for example, with the impact of MFP growth in the 1930s

This accounting does not attribute a portion of the effect of capital deepening to IT innovation – arguing that this is attributable to saving. An objection is that technical improvement, whatever its sources, might have affected saving behavior by raising the rate of return to incremental investments and thus, assuming there were a positive elasticity of the saving rate with respect to the real after-tax interest rate, an increase in saving flows. Or, because of a bias in technical change, capital's share might have risen, leading to a redistribution of income, to households with higher saving propensities. Versions of these arguments have been made for the period after the Civil War in the United States, when, it has been suggested, such innovations as the railroad and Bessemer and Siemens Martin steel elicited an upward surge in aggregate saving behavior that propelled the economy to higher labor productivity levels as predicted by the Solow model (David, 1977; Williamson, 1973, p. 591).[20]

There was indeed an acceleration of gross capital formation in the last half of the 1990s, associated with a more than doubling of real investment in computers, telecom equipment, and software between 1995 and 2000.[21] And the national saving rate did rise, barely, because government saving compensated for a continued decline in private sector saving. It is doubtful that private saving rates fell because tax rates were raised (the Ricardian equivalence argument), since saving rates fell in the last quarter of the century through periods of government deficit and surplus alike. And no one has claimed that the changes in fiscal policies in the early 1990s that led to a rise in government saving were a response to IT innovations, as a rise in the private saving rate might have been. Finally, the gap between private saving and national investment not filled by the increase in government saving was filled by a diversion of saving flows from outside the country towards the United States, not necessarily an augmentation of the world saving rate.

These are the grounds for attributing the effect of capital deepening on labor productivity largely to the forces of thrift rather than innovation. In the absence of IT, saving flows would have been congealed in a set of not quite as good capital goods – an argument that can be, and has been, made for the railroad in the nineteenth century.

Many of the frameworks used to guide thinking about the impact of the IT revolution were developed during a period of sustained stock market exuberance when there was enormous pressure among academics and within government statistical offices to resolve the Solow paradox (computers were showing up everywhere but in the productivity statistics.) We need to make sure that our vision is not clouded by the legacies of the IT public relations offensives of the 1990s.

One manifestation of the effectiveness of that campaign has been a change in the way that government statistics on fixed assets are collected, classified, and presented. In the BEA's "Fixed Asset Tables," for example, the assets produced by information technology industries are now listed first, in separate and detailed categories. But why are saving flows congealed in IT goods and software more or less important than those congealed in structures, machine tools, vehicles, nuclear fuel rods, or any of the other fixed asset categories? One might reply, "Because IT is a special type of capital good, one with a greater propensity to carry or embody or stimulate technical innovation within using sectors."

A problem with this argument is that the rise in the equipment share in capital formation in the United States, which began after the Second World War (Field, 2006b), has been associated with a generally declining rate of MFP growth. To the degree that it is true, we will pick up these effects in MFP growth within the IT-using sectors.

Another intellectual legacy of the IT boom has been the widespread and largely uncritical acceptance of the usefulness of the concept of a general purpose technology and the recognition of IT or computers as its principal instantiation (Bresnahan and Trajtenberg, 1995). While it is undoubtedly true that some advances are more important than others, to call something a GPT has, in many instances, been to suggest about a class of innovations or industries that there was more to them than apparently met the eye, or showed up in aggregate statistics. The enthusiasm for the concept runs the danger of placing too much emphasis on specific innovations awarded this designation.

One of the difficulties with GPTs is the potential multiplicity of candidates. Steam, electricity, and IT are most frequently identified, but chemical engineering, the internal combustion engine, radio transmission and the assembly line have all also been mentioned. The identification of one or several GPTs often offers an appealing narrative hook, but the criteria for designating them are not universally agreed upon, in spite of continuing efforts to nail them down. For example, why isn't the railroad also a GPT? Gordon (see chapter 8) suggests that use by both households and industry is a criterion. This works for electricity and the internal combustion engine. But steam?

Here is another concern. Bessemer and Siemens Martin processes were industry-specific, and would clearly not pass muster as GPTs. They offered, to use David's words, "complete, self-contained and immediately applicable solutions" (2004, p. 22). This was not the case for the product the production of which they enabled. Does that make steel a GPT? It took Carnegie and others time to persuade users that they should make skyscrapers, plate ships, and replace iron rails with it. Cheap steel in turn encouraged complementary innovations such as, in the case of taller buildings, elevators.

If one follows the impact of product and process innovations far enough through the input–output table, one will eventually find products or technological complexes used as inputs in many other sectors, with the potential to generate spillover effects in using sectors. These processes, products, or complexes are the consequence of many separate breakthroughs as well as learning by doing, much of which has been sector-specific. IT, for example, has required advances in software, sector-specific semiconductor manufacturing, and the thin film technology and mechanical engineering that underlies most mass storage.

Because of the potential for multiplying GPT candidacies and the lack of an authoritative tribunal applying uniform rules passing judgment about which ones qualify, economic and technological history may well be better off without the concept. Our enthusiasm for GPTs suggests that we may still not have absorbed entirely the lessons of the Rostow–Fogel–Fishlow debate about the "indispensability" of the railroad. Whereas IT has probably been responsible for a larger increase in MFP growth between 1995 and 2000 than was the railroad in the twenty-five years after the Civil War (compare here the estimate of 0.15 percent per year for the railroad with the 0.68 percent per year I attribute to IT between 1995 and 2000), overall MFP advance at the end of the twentieth century was still much slower than it had been during the 1930s.

It is important to distinguish between the proposition that it sometimes takes a long time for the productivity benefits of new technological complexes to be reaped and the concept of a GPT. One can accept the former without necessarily embracing the usefulness of the latter. The full benefits of IT may indeed involve considerable delays before they are realized. My intent in this chapter, however, has been to focus on what the statistical record allows us to conclude has actually been achieved, not on what might happen, or what we would like to believe will happen, in the future. The end-of-century productivity revival needs to be understood on its own terms. We should give the IT revolution its due, but not more than its due.

Notes

For comments on earlier versions of this work, I am grateful to Nick Crafts, Stanley Engerman, Robert Gordon, Robert Solow, and Gavin Wright. I also thank seminar and conference participants at Duke, Virginia, Indiana, Michigan, Yale, UCLA, the All Ohio Economic History Seminar, the World Cliometrics conference in Venice, and the Economic History Association meetings at San Jose, California.

1. Some scholars restrict the term "Depression" to the years 1929–1933. This chapter treats it as extending over the twelve-year period 1929 to 1941, during which output was persistently depressed below its potential. In 1941 unemployment dipped into the single-digit range (9.9 percent) for the first time in more than a decade. Even so, this was 6.7 percentage points above the 3.2 percent recorded for 1929, and 6.1 percentage points above the 3.8 percent recorded for 1948, so 1929–1941 does not make for an ideal peacetime peak-to-peak comparison. The data in table 5.1 are reported without a cyclical adjustment for 1941. A recent paper (Field, 2005) includes one, based on a regression of the change in MFP on the change in the unemployment rate in percentage points between 1929 and 1941. This regression is then used to predict MFP had unemployment in 1941 been at the 1948 level. Because of the strong procyclicality of productivity during the Depression years, the adjustment raises MFP growth for the 1929–1941 period to 2.78 percent per year, and lowers it for the 1941–1948 period to 0.49 percent. This adjustment serves to accentuate further the distinctiveness of the 1929–1941 period.
2. For a more extended discussion of this issue, see Field (2004a).
3. The Standard Industrial Classification (SIC) codes are being replaced in post-1997 reporting with North American Industrial Classification System (NAICS) codes, but I use the older vocabulary throughout this chapter.

4. The story told here is only weakly sensitive to using 1990 rather than 1989 (the level of MFP in the private non-farm economy was identical, so the annual rates calculated would rise slightly if we measured from 1990), although choosing 2001 rather than 2000 reduces the calculated growth rates, since MFP fell between 2000 and 2001.

5. "Chain-type quantity indexes for net stock of nonresidential fixed assets by industry group and legal form of organization," US Bureau of Economic Analysis (2003), or www.bea.doc.gov/bea/dN/FAweb/Index2002.htm.

6. The "dual" approach to estimating MFP growth looks at relative price changes across sectors as an alternate means of inferring its incidence.

7. Assertions or assumptions of such a link are numerous. "Ongoing technological advances in these (IT-producing) industries have been a direct source of improvement in TFP growth, as well as an indirect source of more-rapid capital deepening" (Jorgenson and Stiroh, 2000, p. 128). "The spread of information technology throughout the economy has been a major factor in the acceleration of productivity through capital deepening" (US Council of Economic Advisors, 2001, p. 33).

8. All the subsequent discussion of the financing of the 1995–2000 investment boom uses nominal data, which ensures that the saving–investment identities hold for each year. Inflation was relatively modest over this period.

9. In this respect as well the railroad/infrastructure investment boom of the late nineteenth century was analogous to the IT boom of the late twentieth century: both triggered, and were associated with, inflows of capital from outside the country.

10. Estimates of the amount of the surge in physical capital formation have been augmented by the BLS's 1999 reclassification of business software acquisition as capital formation (as opposed to its previous treatment as an intermediate good).

11. The BLS capital share for 1995 is 0.3268; for 2000, 0.3109.

12. Alternatively, converting everything to an adjusted-hours basis, we can calculate a 1.06 percentage point increase in the rate of capital deepening (capital growth less adjusted-hours growth), implying that the increase in the rate of capital deepening should have been responsible for a 0.36 percentage point increase in the growth in output per adjusted hour (0.34×1.06). Adding in the increase in MFP growth (0.76 percentage points), one concludes that output per adjusted labor hour should have increased a total of 1.10 percentage points ($0.36 + 0.76$).

13. The source is the Bureau of Labor Statistics: for capital, "Capital and related measures from the two-digit database, 1948–2001"; for hours, "Industry productivity indexes and values table," 5 November 2003.

14. Overestimating the real flow of IT goods increases the estimated growth of real output and of real output per hour, as well as the capital stock and thus the rate of capital deepening. IT goods are, however, a much larger fraction of investment than they are of output; the effect on estimated MFP growth is therefore ambiguous, although it is likely to reduce it.

15. I am grateful to Larry Rosenblum of the BLS for making these data available to me.

16. In a paper broadly consistent with this view, Foster, Haltiwanger, and Krizan (2002) have argued that most of the productivity advance in retail trade has been the result of "more productive entering establishments displacing much less productive exiting establishments."

17. For discussion of an earlier revolution associated with the simultaneous deployment of the telegraph and the railroad, see Field (1987, 1992, 1996) and Chandler (1977).
18. The McKinsey study places a great deal of emphasis on the Wal-Mart effect, both in terms of its growing share of retail trade and through its role as an object of imitation by such firms as Target. But, although the report grants that much of the company's success is based on advanced inventory control methods obviously enabled by IT investment, it also stresses that much is based on management innovations such as worker cross-training. The implication is that, although it is defensible within manufacturing to credit virtually all the MFP growth to IT, outside manufacturing this is not so. Many of the productivity-enhancing management improvements could and probably would have been implemented in the absence of new IT technology.
19. Their output measure also includes an estimate of the imputed service flow from consumer durables.
20. According to David, the nineteenth-century traverse was "set in motion by Thrift, that is, by a pronounced rise in the proportion of output saved." In some passages he appears to treat it as exogenous, in others as a response to an upward movement in the real interest rate. In Abramovitz and David (1973), the authors speak of "technologically induced traverses." The implied argument seems to be that new blueprints lead to an increase in real returns to investment, which induces an upsurge in the saving rate, propelling one to a different steady state involving higher output per hour. In Abramovitz and David (2000), the authors suggest that the bias in technical change led to an increase in capital's share, which redistributed income to households with higher propensities to save, and this is the mechanism that led to the upsurge in the saving rate. Williamson's 1973 paper is more consistently based on an analysis of the consequences of an upward shift in saving propensities: "For still unknown reasons the saving rate rose markedly during the Civil War decade" (p. 593).
21. Some of this surge was driven by "Y2K" concerns, presumably a one-time event. Some of it was wasted, or, as in the case of fiber optic cable in the telecom sector, overbuilt.

6 General-purpose technologies: then and now

Peter L. Rousseau

6.1 Introduction

Gaining a better understanding of how technology affects long-run growth and aggregate fluctuations is an enterprise that has never strayed far from the top of the growth economist's research agenda, yet technological change often remains modeled as incremental in nature, adding only a trend to standard growth models. Experience has shown, however, that such change can come in bursts, with flurries of innovative activity following the introduction of a new core technology. This observation has led economists to reserve the term "general-purpose technology" to describe fundamental advances that transform both household life and the ways in which firms conduct business. Looking back over the past two hundred years or so, steam, electricity, internal combustion, and IT seem to qualify as such core technologies. They have affected entire economies. Going back further, the very ability to communicate in writing and, later, to disseminate written information via the printed page also seem to fit well into the notion of a GPT.

The idea that GPTs are somehow different from the more incremental refinements that occur in between their arrivals may be an appealing way to organize thinking about long-run economic fluctuations, but requires establishing some objective criteria for determining just what features a technology must possess to qualify as a GPT as opposed to a more run-of-the-mill invention. This chapter adds some quantitative rigor to the identification of GPTs by looking at two candidates, electrification and IT, using criteria that have been suggested in recent research on the subject. At the same time, I consider similarities and differences between the two candidate GPTs and the conditions surrounding their diffusion in the US economy and use the findings to assess, by comparison and extrapolation, general economic conditions in the 1990s and the potential for IT to transform the world economy in the twenty-first century.

Up until the end of the "dot-com" boom of the late 1990s, the IT "revolution" had been heralded as one of the key forces ushering in the so-called "new

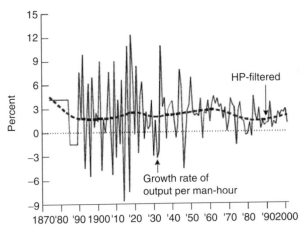

Figure 6.1 Annual growth in output per man-hour in the United States, 1874–2001

economy," which was to be associated with a period of unprecedented productivity growth. Doubts were raised as to whether IT would live up to expectations when these gains did not materialize rapidly in standard measures of productivity. Will such judgments turn out to be premature? Can history help us in thinking about the question? Jovanovic and Rousseau (2002a, 2002b) argue that the early decades of the twenty-first century will see higher productivity than the 1950s and 1960s, while Gordon (2000b) is more pessimistic. A few basic facts set the tone for the debate and reveal some fascinating possibilities.

As David (1991) pointed out some years ago, if electricity and IT are indeed GPTs, neither delivered productivity gains immediately upon arrival. Figure 6.1 shows the growth in output per man-hour in the US economy from 1874 to 2001, with the dashed line representing long-term trends as generated with the Hodrick–Prescott (HP) filter.[1] Productivity growth, at least as viewed through the HP filter, seems to have been relatively high in the 1870s, when steam was the dominant power source for industry, but fell as electrification arrived in the 1880s and 1890s. It was only in the period after 1915, which saw the diffusion of secondary motors and the widespread establishment of centralized power distribution systems, that measured productivity numbers began to rise. Figure 6.1 also shows that Intel's 1971 invention of the 4004 microprocessor (the key component of the personal computer), if taken to be the start of the IT era, did not reverse the decline in productivity growth that had begun more than a decade earlier.

Associating a point in time with a GPT's "arrival" depends on what one exactly means by this term. If defined with an objective measure, such as attaining a 1 percent share of horsepower in the manufacturing sector, then sometime around 1895 seems appropriate for electricity's arrival. This also corresponds roughly with the start-up of the first hydroelectric power generator at Niagara Falls, New York, in 1894, and I will use this formally in the analysis that follows as the year of electricity's "arrival." It would be reasonable to argue, however, that electricity actually arrived earlier – perhaps in 1882, when Thomas Edison brought the first centralized electric generator online at the Pearl Street station in New York City. For IT, it is true that mainframe computers had existed for two decades before the invention of the 4004 chip in 1971, and had even been used to project the winner of the 1952 US presidential election. Yet, if measured by the attainment of a 1 percent share in the industrial sector's stock of equipment, 1971 remains the most likely candidate for dating IT's "arrival."

Since the period of rapid diffusion for electricity seems to end around 1929, which is when net adoptions in households and firms level off, this seems a natural place to date the "end point" of the GPT era. Yet the Great Depression certainly influenced the slowdown, and many homes remained without electricity for some time thereafter, so valid arguments could be made for a later end date. On the other hand, new adoptions of IT continue to rise in 2004, so – on that criterion – the IT era presses onward.

6.2 Defining GPTs

The objective of this chapter is to look for quantitative parallels and differences in economic conditions that existed between the earlier part of the twentieth century, especially the 1920s, and the 1990s. This sets the stage for considering the extent to which the commonalities or differences may be related to the introduction of electricity and IT as GPTs. The periods of rapid adoption of the two technologies both contain a growth slowdown at the outset, but productivity rose later in the diffusion of electricity and appears to have picked up early in the twenty-first century. If the two GPT eras are indeed similar in some "fundamental" respects, this could mean that growth rates will pick up over the next several decades.

Making such an inference, however, even preliminarily, requires documenting as many of these similarities or differences as possible. My strategy will be, first, to consider how electricity and IT measure up as GPTs according to criteria established by Bresnahan and Trajtenberg (1995), and then to examine the time series behavior of other economic indicators that should respond to the introduction of a breakthrough technology.

Bresnahan and Trajtenberg argue that a GPT should have the following three characteristics.
(1) *Pervasiveness*: the GPT should spread to most sectors.
(2) *Improvement*: the GPT should get better over time and, hence, should keep lowering the costs of its users.

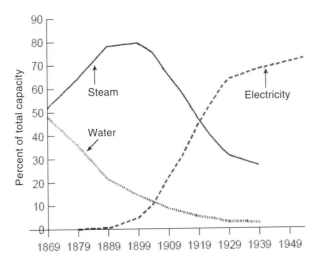

Figure 6.2 Shares of total horsepower generated by the main sources in US manufacturing, 1869–1954

(3) *Innovation-spawning*: the GPT should make it easier to invent and produce new products or processes.

Most technologies possess each of these characteristics to some degree, and therefore a GPT cannot differ qualitatively from these other technologies. But the extent to which technologies have all three should determine which ones are strong candidates for being classified as GPTs.

6.3 Pervasiveness of the GPT

To examine the pervasiveness of electricity and IT, I begin with aggregate measures of each technology's diffusion in industrial firms generally and then turn to an analysis of individual sectors. A summary of diffusion in the household sector follows.

6.3.1 Net adoption in industry

Figure 6.2 shows the shares of total horsepower in manufacturing driven by water, steam, and electricity from 1869 to 1954.[2] The period covers the decline of waterwheels and turbines, as well as most of the life cycle of steam power. It is striking how quickly steam power, which involved low fixed and high variable costs, faded from use after electrification arrived. The decline of water power, on the other hand, which involved high fixed and low variable costs, was much more gradual and its rate of decline was not accelerated by electricity's

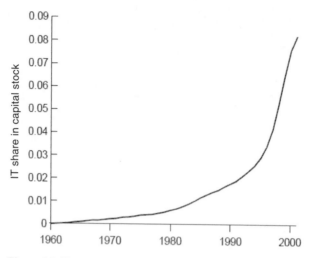

Figure 6.3 Shares of computer equipment and software in the US aggregate capital stock, 1960–2001

arrival. The relative brevity of the entire steam cycle, which rises and falls within fifty to sixty years, suggests that the technology that replaced it, electricity, was important enough to force change rapidly among manufacturers. The fact that a new source (e.g. solar power?) has not yet emerged to replace it identifies electricity as one of the breakthrough technologies of the modern era.

Figure 6.3 shows the diffusion of computers in US industry as measured by the real share of IT equipment and software in the real aggregate capital stock.[3] Computer and software purchases appear to have reached the first inflection point in their "S-curve" more slowly than electrification in the early years of its GPT era, but it is striking how much more rapidly the IT share has risen over the past few years.

Figures 6.2 and 6.3 are not directly comparable. The vertical axis in figure 6.2 measures the shares of total horsepower in manufacturing, whereas the vertical axis in figure 6.3 is the real share of IT equipment and software in the real aggregate capital stock. But, even if these measures are somewhat different, the nature of the two diffusions suggest that the IT era will last longer than the thirty-five years of electrification.

Even though electrification and IT seem to exhibit a common characteristic of pervasiveness when looking at aggregate data, the nature of their absorption across sectors in the US economy differs considerably. Figure 6.4 shows the shares of total horsepower electrified in manufacturing sectors at ten-year

Table 6.1 *Rank correlations of electricity shares in total horsepower by manufacturing sector in the United States, 1889–1954*

	1889	1899	1909	1919	1929	1939	1954
1889	1.000						
1899	0.707	1.000					
1909	0.643	0.918	1.000				
1919	0.686	0.746	0.893	1.000			
1929	0.639	0.718	0.739	0.871	1.000		
1939	0.486	0.507	0.571	0.750	0.807	1.000	
1954	0.804	0.696	0.650	0.789	0.893	0.729	1.000

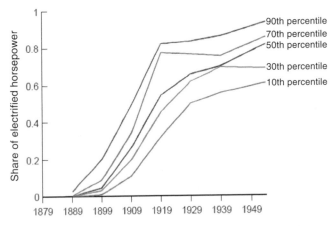

Figure 6.4 Shares of electrified horsepower by US manufacturing sector in percentiles, 1890–1954

intervals from 1889 to 1954 in percentile form.[4] The percentiles are determined by sorting the electricity shares in each year by sector and, given that only fifteen sectors are represented, plotting the second, fifth, eighth, eleventh and fourteenth largest shares in each year. Electrical adoption was very rapid between 1899 and 1919 but slowed thereafter, with the dispersion in the adoption rates largest around 1919.

The main message of figure 6.4, however, is that electrical technology affected individual manufacturing sectors with a striking degree of uniformity. Moreover, table 6.1, which shows the rank correlations of electricity shares across sectors and time, indicates that there was little change in the relative ordering of the manufacturing sectors either. This means that sectors that were the heaviest users of electricity in 1890 remained among the leaders as adoption slowed down in the 1930s. Indeed, the adoption of electricity was sweeping and widespread.

The slow adoption rates for electricity in the first decade of the twentieth century and the rapid increases in adoption rates and their dispersion across sectors over the next ten years probably reflect a shift in the way that industries put their new electrical capacities to use. Prior to the common use of secondary electric motors (i.e. 1915 or so), firms in many industries, including New England textiles, simply replaced their steam-driven generators with electric ones. Since the steam generators had already been designed to drive a series of shafts and belts that powered looms, spinning machines and other equipment (see Devine, 1983), very little refitting was needed to hook up an electric generator as the primary power source. But this did not in itself encourage further expansion of power distribution systems and secondary (i.e. stand-alone) electrical devices. It just did not make economic sense at that time to incur the fixed costs of setting up the infrastructure needed to electrify homes and industrial plants fully until various electrical devices became more readily available. Once the potential was seen, however, sectors that would become the leaders in the use of secondary motors quickly took the steps to electrify, while others were slower to pick up on the advantages.

Figure 6.4 also helps in dating electricity as a GPT. Linear extrapolation between the years 1890 and 1900 suggests that, in 1894, about 1 percent of horsepower in the median industry was provided by electricity. This places the "arrival" of electricity in the year that the Niagara Falls power facility was put into service. Whether or not this is the right percentage for dating the start of the electrification era, I will use the same percentage for the median industry to date the beginning of the IT era.

The spread of information technology was also rapid, but does not appear to have been as widespread as electricity. Figure 6.5 shows the share of real IT equipment and software in the real net capital stocks of sixty-two sectors from 1960 to 2001, once again plotted as annual percentiles.[5] In the case of IT, some sectors adopted very rapidly, and by 1975 six of them (the ninetieth percentile) had already achieved IT equipment and software shares of more than 5 percent. Other sectors lagged, with some not adopting IT in a substantive way until after 1985.

On the other hand, the rank correlations of the IT shares across sectors, shown in table 6.2, are about as high as those for electrification. On the face of it, then, electrification would appear to have been the more sweeping GPT-type event, because it diffused more rapidly and evenly in the US economy, whereas IT diffused rapidly in some sectors and not so rapidly in others. Nonetheless, the recent gains in IT shares show that the diffusion of this technology has yet to slow down in the way that electrification did after 1929.

Table 6.2 *Rank correlations of IT shares in capital stocks by sector in the United States, 1961–2001*

	1961	1971	1981	1991	2001
1961	1.000				
1971	0.650	1.000			
1981	0.531	0.806	1.000		
1991	0.576	0.746	0.847	1.000	
2001	0.559	0.682	0.734	0.909	1.000

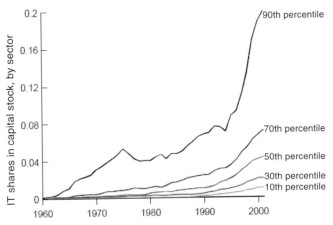

Figure 6.5 Shares of IT equipment and software in the US capital stock by sector in percentiles, 1960–2001

6.3.2 Net adoption by households

Households also underwent electrification and the purchase of personal computers during the respective GPT eras. Figure 6.6 plots the cumulative percentage
of households that obtained electric service and that owned a personal computer
in each year following the "arrival" of the GPT.[6] Dating electricity as arriving
in 1894 and the personal computer in 1971, figure 6.6 indicates that households
adopted electricity about as rapidly as they are adopting the personal computer.
By the time that the electricity era was thirty-five years old (in 1929), nearly
70 percent of households had it. A comparison with figure 6.4 shows that this
is just a little higher than the 1929 penetration of electrified horsepower in
the median manufacturing sector. As in the case of firms, the electrification of
households reaches a plateau in 1929, then resumes its rise a few years later.

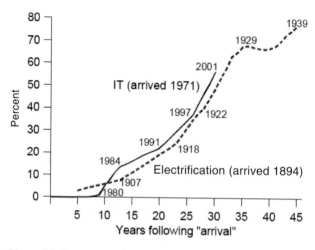

Figure 6.6 Percentage of US households with electric service and personal computers during the two technological epochs

There is no indication yet, however, that the diffusion of the computer among either households or firms is slowing down.

In some ways it is puzzling that IT's diffusion has not been much faster than that of electrification. As the next section of this chapter shows, the price of computing is falling much more quickly than the price of electricity did. Affordable personal computers came out in the 1980s, when the technology was some fifteen years old. On the other hand, households had to wait longer for affordable electrical appliances. As in industry, it was only after 1915, when secondary motors in the form of household appliances began to be invented, that the benefits of electrification began to outweigh the costs for a majority of households.

6.4 Improvement of the GPT

The second characteristic that Bresnahan and Trajtenberg suggested is an improvement in the efficiency of the GPT as it ages. Presumably this would show up in a decline in prices, an increase in quality, or both. How much a GPT improves can therefore be measured by how much cheaper a unit of quality gets over time. If the new technology is embodied in capital and begins to account for an increasing share of the net capital stock, the price of capital as a whole should be falling more rapidly during a GPT era, but especially capital that is tied to the new technology.

Figure 6.7 shows a quality-adjusted series for the general price of equipment relative to the consumption price index since 1885, constructed from a number

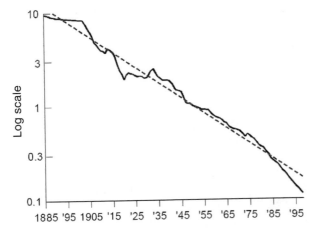

Figure 6.7 The relative price of equipment with respect to consumption goods in the United States

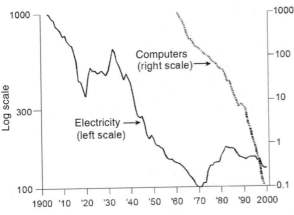

Figure 6.8 US price indices for the products of two technological revolutions

of sources and with a linear time trend included.[7] Equipment prices fell more rapidly than trend between 1905 and 1920, and again after 1975. The 1905–1920 period is also the one that experienced the most rapid growth of electricity in manufacturing (see figure 6.4) and in the home (see figure 6.6). The post-1975 period follows the introduction of the personal computer.

Figure 6.8 plots the price of the components of the aggregate capital stock tied to the two GPTs. Because deflators for electrically powered capital are not available in the first half of the twentieth century, declines in the relative prices associated with electricity itself are compared with the quality-adjusted price of computers, once again relative to the consumption price index.[8] The use of the left-hand scale for electricity and the right-hand scale for computers underscores the extraordinary decline in computer prices since 1960. While the electricity price index falls by a factor of ten, the computer price index falls by a factor of 10,000. It can be said that the electricity index, being the price of a kilowatt-hour, understates the accompanying technological change because it does not account for improvements in electrical equipment, and especially improvements in the efficiency of electric motors. Such improvements may be contained in the price series for capital generally. Yet, based on the price evidence in figure 6.8, both electricity and computers might qualify as GPTs, but computers appear to be more "revolutionary."

6.5 Ability of the GPT to spawn further innovation

The third characteristic that Bresnahan and Trajtenberg associate with GPTs is an ability to generate additional innovations. Any GPT will affect all sorts of production processes, including those for invention and innovation. Some GPTs will be biased towards helping to produce existing products, others towards inventing and implementing new ones.

Electricity and IT have both helped reduce the costs of making existing products, and they both spawn innovation. The 1920s in particular saw a wave of new products powered by electricity, and the computer is now embodied in many new products as well. But, as the patenting evidence will bear out, IT seems to have more of a skew towards contributing to further innovation.

6.5.1 Patenting

Patenting should be more intense after a GPT arrives and while it is spreading due to the introduction of related new products. Figure 6.9, which shows patents per capita issued on inventions annually from 1890 to 2000, shows two surges in activity – between 1900 and 1930, and again after 1977.[9] Moreover, the decline in patenting during the Second World War years and the acceleration immediately thereafter suggest that there is some degree of intertemporal substitution in the release of new ideas away from times when it might be more difficult to popularize them and towards times better suited for the entry of new products.

Is it mere chance that patenting activity was most intense during the periods of rapid net adoption of the candidate GPTs? Moser and Nicholas (2004), using patent data for a sample of 121 publicly traded firms, show that the growth rate of patents related to electricity in the 1920s was nearly triple the growth rate

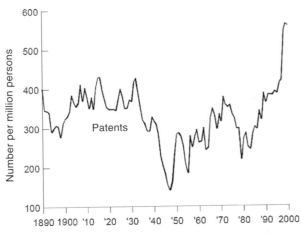

Figure 6.9 Patents issued on inventions in the United States per million persons, 1890–2000

of those associated with chemicals, and 50 percent higher than the growth rate of mechanical patents. Though this is consistent with electricity accounting for a large part of the rise in aggregate patents shown in figure 6.9, they go on to argue that, when measured by the number of forward citations between 1976 and 2002, chemical innovations were at least as long-lived and general as electrical ones. Their assertion that electricity is not truly a GPT seems strong, however, given that the early patents associated with such a sweeping technological advance would likely be unrelated to patents granted more than fifty years later on highly diverse inventions that share only alternating current as a power source.[10]

Another question related to the use of the patent data is whether they reflect fluctuations in the number of actual inventions or simply changes in the law that raise the propensity to patent. The distinction is important, because, over longer periods of time, patents may reflect policy rather than invention. Kortum and Lerner (1998) analyze this question and find that the surge of the 1990s was worldwide but not systematically related to country-specific policy changes. They conclude that technology was the cause of the surge.

6.5.2 Investment in new firms

If new technologies are more easily adopted by new firms that are unencumbered by costs sunk in old technologies and the rigid and firm-specific organization capital required to operate them, there should be waves of new listings on

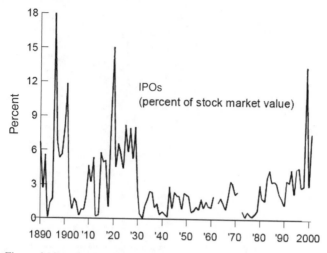

Figure 6.10 Annual IPOs in the United States as a percentage of stock market value,
1890–2001

the stock exchange during GPT eras. Figure 6.10 shows the value of firms
entering the New York Stock Exchange (NYSE), the American Stock Exchange
(AMEX), and NASDAQ in each year from 1890 through 2001 as percentages
of total stock market value.[11] As predicted by Helpman and Trajtenberg (1998),
IPOs surge between 1895 and 1929, and then after 1977, which again closely
matches the dating of the two periods of rapid adoption of the GPTs.

The solid line in figure 6.11 shows the ratio of the IPO rate (from figure 6.10)
to the aggregate investment rate for the US economy.[12] As the ratio of private
investment to the net stock of private capital, the denominator of the ratio
is the aggregate analog of the numerator, which covers only the stock market.
Figure 6.11 shows that, during the electrification era, investment by stock market
entrants accounted for a larger portion of stock market value than overall new
investment in the US economy contributed to the aggregate capital stock. This
is consistent with the adoption of electricity favoring the unencumbered entrant
over the incumbent, who may have incurred substantial adjustment costs in
using the new technology. I say this because aggregate investment, while indeed
including investment by new firms, has an even larger component attributable
to incumbents. Moreover, the solid line in figure 6.11 was highest in the early
years of the electrification period, which is when these adjustment costs would
have been greatest.

Although the solid line in figure 6.11 has so far stayed below unity for most
of the IT era, it has rapidly risen to a higher level in recent years. This could be

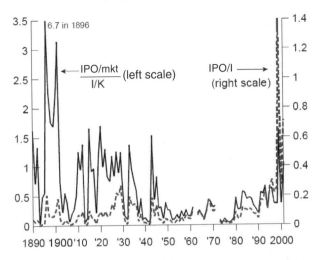

Figure 6.11 Investment in the United States by new firms relative to incumbents, 1890–2001

because IT adoption involved very large adjustment costs for both incumbents and entrants in the early years until the price of equipment and software fell enough to generate a wave of adoptions by new firms.

Stock markets in the United States were still rather small in the early part of the twentieth century, and were certainly less developed than in, say, the 1990s. This means that a given amount of IPO value in the electrification era could account for a larger percentage of total stock market capitalization than it would in today's deeper markets. This suggests that the left-hand side of the solid line in figure 6.11 is not directly comparable with the right-hand side. The dashed line reverses this bias by showing the ratio of IPOs to total investment. Since more new firms choose to list on the stock market now than a century ago, a given level of new investment should generate a higher level for the ratio of the IPO value to aggregate investment now than during the electrification era. After recognizing the biases associated with the two ratios, it becomes clear that new investment did indeed outstrip that of incumbents in both GPT eras.

6.5.3 The speed with which ideas reach the market

According to the "innovation-spawning" characteristic, when a GPT arrives it gives rise to new projects that are unusually profitable. When such projects arrive, firms will be more impatient to implement them. When it is new firms that come upon such projects (rather than incumbents), they will feel the pressure to

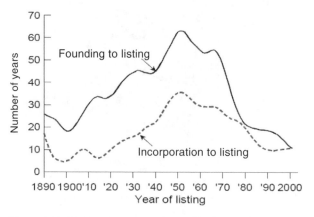

Figure 6.12 Waiting times to exchange listing in the United States, 1890–2001

list sooner. This argument is developed and tested by Jovanovic and Rousseau in a recent paper (2001b). They argue that the electricity and IT era firms entered the stock market sooner because the technologies that they brought in were too productive to be kept out of the market for very long.

Figure 6.12 shows HP-filtered average waiting times from founding or incorporation to exchange listing for the 1890 – 2001 period.[13] The vertical distance between the solid and dashed lines shows that firms often take years, and even decades, after their foundings to list on a stock exchange. Jovanovic and Rousseau (2001b) interpret this delay as a period during which the firm, and possibly its lenders, learn about what the firm's optimal investment should be. But, when the technology is highly innovative, the incentive to wait is reduced and the firm lists earlier, which is what the evidence shows.

6.5.4 Shifts in market share

As a GPT takes hold, we should expect to see firms coming to market more quickly and the market leaders getting younger as well. In other words, every stage in the lifetime of the firm should be shorter. This stands in contrast to the view expressed by Hopenhayn (1992), for whom the age distribution of an industry's leadership is invariant when an industry is in a long-run stochastic equilibrium. That is, the average age of, say, the top 10 percent of firms is fixed. Some leaders hold on to their positions, and this tends to make the leading group older, but others are replaced by younger firms, and this has the opposite effect. In equilibrium the two forces offset one another and the age of the leadership stays the same. Keeping the age of the leaders flat requires, in other words, constant replacement.

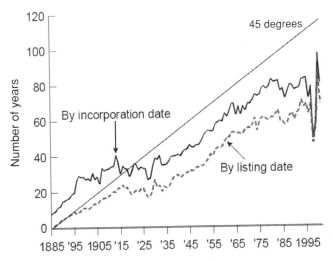

Figure 6.13 Average age (in years) of the largest US firms with market values that sum to 10 percent of GDP, 1885–2001

Figure 6.13 plots the value-weighted average age of the largest firms with market values that sum to 10 percent of GDP. A firm's age is measured as the number of years since incorporation and since being listed on a major stock exchange. Figure 6.13 shows that, overall, the age of the leaders is anything but flat. It sometimes rises more rapidly than the 45-degree line, indicating that the age of the leaders is rising more rapidly than the passage of time. At other times it is flat or falling, indicating replacement.

Based upon years from incorporation, for example, the leading firms were being replaced by older firms over the first thirty years of the sample, because the solid line is then steeper than the 45-degree line. In the two decades after the Great Depression the leaders held their relative positions as the 45-degree slopes of the average age lines show. The leaders got younger in the 1990s, and their average ages now lie well below the 45-degree line. But the lines are flat or falling during the electricity and IT periods, indicating that replacement at these times was high.

6.6 GPTs, interest rates, and consumption

If unanticipated, the arrival of a GPT is good news for the consumer, because it brings about an increase in wealth. How quickly wealth is perceived to rise depends on how quickly the public realizes the GPT's potential for raising output. The rise in wealth would raise desired consumption. But, at the same time,

Figure 6.14 The ratio of consumption to income in the United States, 1870–2001

interest rates should rise to absorb and postpone the rise in aggregate demand. In this section, I examine how these macroeconomic aggregates responded to the introduction of electricity and IT.

Figure 6.14 shows the ratio of consumption to GDP since 1870.[14] The arrival of electricity around 1894 seems to mark the start of an upturn in consumption. If the plot were extended backwards to 1790, this rise would also be seen as ending a long-term decline in the ratio. And, although the level of the series falls during the Great Depression and the Second World War, never to return to its pre-1930 levels, consumption takes another sharp upward turn near the start of the IT revolution and continues to rise.

Economic theory predicts that interest rates should rise to choke off a shift in desired consumption, with no effect on actual consumption. This is not observed in the data. Rather, both actual consumption and interest rates rise. Figure 6.15 shows the *ex post* real interest rate on 60 to 90-day commercial paper from 1870 to 2001, along with an HP trend. Real interest rates were about the same during the two GPT eras, averaging 2.6 percent during the electrification era (1894–1930) and 2.8 percent for the IT era (1971–). They averaged −0.2 percent in the middle decades of the twentieth century.[15] That interest rates did not begin to rise during the electrification period until the 1920s suggests that some of the GPT's potential was unforeseen, possibly allowing actual consumption to rise. Interest rates were also high before electricity's arrival in 1894, but this probably reflects a lack of financial development more than any technological cause, and may have given rise to the overall negative trend in real interest rates observed since 1870.

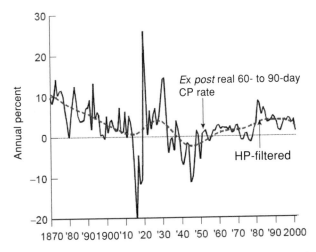

Figure 6.15 The *ex post* real interest rate on commercial paper in the United States, 1870–2001

6.7 Conclusions

This chapter has compared electrification and IT as GPTs with the aim of gaining some insight into what the future may bring in terms of aggregate productivity. Based upon the criteria chosen and the evidence presented here, both electricity and IT were pervasive, improving, and innovation-spawning, and thus seem to qualify as GPTs. Productivity growth was lower in both GPT eras than in the decades preceding them, and measures of invention such as IPOs, patents, and investment by new firms relative to incumbents were on the rise.

At the same time, electricity was more pervasive, affecting sectors more quickly and more evenly than IT, while IT improved more dramatically, with computer prices falling more than a hundred times more rapidly than the price of electricity. IT also seems to have generated more innovation than electricity, and the initial productivity slowdown was deeper in the IT era. All this might lead one to regard IT as the more "revolutionary" GPT.

Why, then, was IT adopted more slowly? Jovanovic and Rousseau (2002a) note the rapid decline in computer prices and hypothesize that this caused firms to delay adoption in anticipation of updating their capital later at lower cost. In other words, the gains forgone by not adopting IT right away were smaller than the gains expected from waiting. But as computer prices continued to fall through the 1990s, the threshold for adoption was crossed by most firms and households, leading to a surge in new computer purchases. And it is only now that this wave of adoption is appearing in measures of aggregate productivity.

In all, the differences between the two technologies seem to be quite important. Yet the evidence clearly supports the view that technological progress is uneven, that it does entail the episodic arrival of GPTs, and that GPTs bring on turbulence and lower growth early on and higher growth and prosperity later. The IT era has already outlasted that of electrification, but, even six decades after what Field (2003) has called the "most technologically progressive decade of the century" (i.e. the 1930s), electricity has yet to become obsolete. Given the multitude of firms and households that have still not quite adopted IT, its continuing price decline and the widespread increases in computer literacy among children and adults worldwide suggest that perhaps the most productive period of the IT revolution continues to lie ahead.

Notes

This chapter is based on work carried out in association with Vanderbilt University and the National Bureau of Economic Research. The author thanks the National Science Foundation for financial support, and seminar participants at Indiana University and the March 2003 meeting of the NBER's program on the Development of the American Economy for comments on earlier versions. This chapter is part of a broader project on electrification and stock markets with Boyan Jovanovic of New York University.

1. Output per man-hour in the business, non-farm sector is from John Kendrick (U.S. Bureau of the Census, 1975, series D684, p. 162) for 1889–1947, and from the US Bureau of Labor Statistics (2002) for 1948–2001. For 1874–1889, Kendrick's decadal averages for 1869–1879 and 1879–1889 are used, assuming a constant growth rate from 1874–1884 and 1885–1889.

2. Shares of total horsepower capacity in manufacturing are ratios of each power source (DuBoff, 1964, table 14, p. 59) to the total (table 13, p. 58). DuBoff estimates these quantities in 1869, 1879, 1889, 1899, 1904, 1909, 1914, 1919, 1923, 1925, 1927, 1929, 1939, and 1954, and I linearly interpolate between them.

3. The ratio in figure 6.3 is formed by summing the capital stocks of sixty-two industrial sectors from the detailed non-residential fixed asset tables in fixed 1996 dollars made available by the US Bureau of Economic Analysis (2002). IT capital includes mainframe and personal computers, storage devices, printers, terminals, integrated systems, and pre-packaged, custom, and own-account software. The total capital stock is the sum of all fixed asset types.

4. The shares of electrified horsepower include primary and secondary electric motors, and are computed using data from DuBoff (1964, tables E-11 and E-12a through E-12e, pp. 228–35).

5. The sectoral capital stocks are from the detailed non-residential fixed asset tables in constant 1996 dollars made available by the US Bureau of Economic Analysis (2002).

6. Data on the spread of electricity use by consumers are approximations derived from U.S. Bureau of the Census (1975) *Historical Statistics* (series S108 and S120). Statistics on computer ownership for 1975 through 1998 are from Gates (1999,

p. 118) and from the U.S. Bureau of the Census (various issues) *Current Population Survey* thereafter.

7. Krusell et al. (2000) build an index of equipment prices from 1963 using the consumer price index to deflate the quality-adjusted estimates of producer equipment prices from Gordon (1990, table 12.4, col. 2, p. 541). Since Gordon's series ends in 1983, they use vector autoregression (VAR) forecasts to extend it through 1992. I start with Krusell et al. and work backwards, deflating Gordon's remaining estimates (1947–1962) with an index for non-durable consumption goods prices derived from the National Income Accounts. Since a quality-adjusted series for equipment prices prior to 1947 is not available, the average price of electricity is used as a proxy for 1902–1946, and an average of Brady's (1966) deflators for the main classes of equipment for 1885–1902. The pre-1947 composite is then deflated using the BLS consumer prices index of all items (U.S. Bureau of the Census, 1975, series E135) for 1913–1946 and the Burgess cost of living index (U.S. Bureau of the Census, 1975, series E184) for 1885–1912.

8. The quality-adjusted price index for IT is formed by joining the "final" price index for computer systems from Gordon (1990, table 6.10, col. 5, p. 226) for 1960–1978 with the pooled index developed for desktop and mobile personal computers by Berndt, Dulberger, and Rappaport (2000, table 2, col. 1, p. 22) for 1979–1999. Since Gordon's index includes mainframe computers, minicomputers, and PCs, while the Berndt, Dulberger, and Rappaport index includes only PCs, the two segments used to build the price measure are themselves not directly comparable, but a joining of them should still reflect quality-adjusted prices trends in the computer industry reasonably well. The index is set to 1,000 in the first year of the sample (i.e. 1960). Electricity prices are averages of all electric energy services in cents per kilowatt hour from the *Historical Statistics* (U.S. Bureau of the Census, 1975, series S119, p. 827) for 1903, 1907, 1917, 1922, and 1926–1970, and from the *Statistical Abstract of the United States* (US Department of Commerce, various dates) for 1971–1989. A constant growth assumption is used to interpolate between missing years in the early part of the sample. For 1990–2000, prices are US city averages (June figures) from the Bureau of Labor Statistics (www.bls.gov). The index is once again set to 1000 in the first year of the sample (i.e. 1903).

9. Patents are those for "utility" (i.e. invention) as recorded by the US Patent and Trademark Office for 1963–2000, and from the US Bureau of the Census (1975, series W-96, pp. 957–59) for 1890–1962. Population figures, which are measured at mid-year for the total resident population, are from US Bureau of the Census (1975, series A-7, p. 8) for 1890–1970, and from the US Bureau of Economic Analysis (2002) thereafter.

10. Moser and Nicholas (2004) admit that "electricity patents were broader in scope than other categories of patents at their grant date, and that they were more 'original' than their counterparts according to the chronology of citations" (pp. 388–9).

11. The data used to construct figure 6.10 and others in this chapter that use stock market valuations are from the University of Chicago's Center for Research on Securities Prices (2002 – CRSP) files for 1925–2001. NYSE firms are available in CRSP continuously, AMEX firms after 1961, and NASDAQ firms after 1971. Jovanovic and Rousseau (2001a) extended the CRSP stock files backwards from

their 1925 starting year by collecting year-end observations from the NYSE listings of *The Annalist, Bradstreet's, The Commercial and Financial Chronicle*, and *The New York Times*, and these data are used to determine aggregate IPO and stock market values for the pre-CRSP years.

12. To build the investment rate series, I start with gross private domestic investment in current dollars from the US Bureau of Economic Analysis (2002) for 1929–2001, and then join it with the gross capital formation series in current dollars, excluding military expenditures, from Kuznets (1961b, tables T-8 and T-8a) for 1870–1929. The net capital stock is constructed using the private fixed assets tables of the US Bureau of Economic Analysis (2002) for 1925–2001. Then, using the estimates of the net stock of non-military capital from Kuznets (1961a, table 3, pp. 64–5) in 1869, 1879, 1889, 1909, 1919, and 1929 as benchmarks, the percentage changes in a synthetic series for the capital stock, formed by starting with the 1869 Kuznets (1961a) estimate of $27 billion and adding net capital formation in each year through 1929 from Kuznets (1961b), are used to create an annual series that runs through the benchmark points. Finally, the resulting series for 1870–1925 is joined to the later BEA series.

13. Listing years after 1925 are those for which firms enter CRSP. For 1890–1924, they are years in which prices first appear in contemporary newspapers. See Jovanovic and Rousseau (2001b, p. 340) for additional information on sources and methods. The 6,112 incorporation dates used to construct figure 6.12 are from *Moody's Industrial Manual* (1920, 1928, 1955, 1980), Standard and Poor's *Stock Market Encyclopedia* (1981, 1988, 2000), and various editions of Standard and Poor's *Stock Reports*. The 4,221 foundings are from Dun and Bradstreet's *Million Dollar Directory* (2002), Moody's, Kelley (1954), and individual company websites.

14. The series for consumption and GDP are from the US Bureau of Economic Analysis (2004) for 1929–2001, Kendrick (1961, table A-IIb, cols. 4 and 11, pp. 296–7) for 1889–1929, and Berry (1988, table 9, pp. 25–6) for 1790–1889. The BEA figures are for personal consumption, but the Kendrick and Berry figures include the government sector as well. Since consumption in the government sector was much smaller prior to the First World War, I suspect that the downward trend in the nineteenth century is a result of changing private consumption patterns rather than a reduction in the government sector's consumption.

15. Commercial paper rates are annual averages from the FRED database of the Federal Reserve Bank of St Louis (2002) for 1934–2001, and from Homer and Sylla (1991) for earlier years. The *ex post* return is obtained by then subtracting inflation in the implicit price deflator for GNP, taken from the US Bureau of Economic Analysis (2002) for 1929–2001 and from Berry (1988) for earlier years.

7 Productivity growth and the American labor market: the 1990s in historical perspective

Gavin Wright

7.1 Introduction

Like most academic disciplines, economics has become highly specialized. The purpose of this chapter is to interpret the productivity record of the 1990s in historical context, by drawing together evidence from several lines of research that tend to proceed separately from each other: the economic history literatures on the diffusion of new technologies and institutional change in the labor market; work in labor economics on real wages and wage inequality; and the evidence from growth economics on alternating surges and pauses in the pace of productivity change. Together, these perspectives point towards a linkage between the productivity surge that began during the mid-1990s and the high-pressure labor market conditions that prevailed during the same period.

The objective is not to develop a comprehensive historical interpretation of American technology and productivity, only to suggest that the labor market has been neglected in earlier accounts. I maintain that it deserves a central role in the story of the 1990s and, for that matter, the preceding century.

7.2 Conceptual issues

In virtually any reasonable model of the labor market, higher wages will lead to an increase in the marginal and average productivity of workers. The effect may operate through the choice of technique in production, through factor substitution within a given technique, or through compositional shifts towards more productive workers and higher-value activities; but the correlation should definitely be positive. Thus, when we observe that American real wages were 30 to 50 percent higher than those in Britain in the early nineteenth century, it is not surprising to learn that productivity levels in American manufacturing were considerably higher as well, even at those early dates.[1]

A more challenging question is whether higher wages can generate a faster *rate of increase* in productivity as well as a one-time shift in the productivity

level. The proposition that America's early development of labor-saving technologies was attributable to labor scarcity was advanced by H. J. Habakkuk
in his 1962 classic, *American and British Technology in the Nineteenth Century*. The Habakkuk thesis seems consistent with the evidence *prima facie*, since
American productivity grew rapidly in the face of higher labor costs, overtaking
the British before the end of the century. But, although subsequent research has
identified many features of the emergent "American system of manufactures,"
it cannot yet be said that a precise analytical linkage between labor scarcity
and productivity growth has been established. Perhaps the best brief summary
of this literature would be that the developers of American technology – the
institutional foundations of which would require a much broader historical
discussion – were induced by high labor costs to orient their search for new
techniques towards the labor-saving segment of the spectrum of possibilities.
Because technological development is intrinsically collective or network-based
in character, it tends to follow particular historical "trajectories" that are adaptive
to prevailing economic conditions, of which the labor market was one important element. Because new technologies had to save labor to be successful, the
pace of technology was correlated with productivity growth, whichever way
the causal connection might run. Through mechanisms such as this, economic
historians have succeeded in connecting high American wages to rapid productivity growth, but, clearly, the linkages are specific to a particular historical
context.[2]

Inspired by these historical narratives (at least in part), some theorists have
explored more formalized conceptualizations. In the context of the endogenous
growth model that he pioneered, in which knowledge spillovers cause the rate
of technological progress to be positively related to the rate of investment, Paul
Romer (1987) shows that, when new technologies are strongly labor-saving, a
fall in wages may reduce productivity growth by reducing incentives to invest
in new knowledge. The implication, as Romer notes, is that a policy that forces
up wages and the cost of employment might have a positive effect on the
rate of productivity or even output growth, perhaps at the cost of increased
unemployment.

The Romer model maintains the assumptions that labor is a homogeneous
factor, and that the labor-saving bias of new technology is given exogenously.
To address modern concerns about rising inequality, Daron Acemoglu (1998,
2002) focuses on the incentives facing firms that generate new technologies,
which may choose to direct their efforts towards augmenting or avoiding the use
of different *types* of labor, or different worker attributes. His central argument
is that, if the market for new technologies is imperfectly competitive, there will
be a "market size effect," channeling innovations in directions that make intensive use of somewhat *more* abundant factors. Thus, an exogenous increase in
the supply (or potential supply) of educated workers can generate technologies

designed to be used by such workers, because the profit opportunities for technology producers are consequently greater at that end of the spectrum. Acemoglu's approach points out the dangers of interpreting the direction of technological change by analogy to simple models of supply and demand: through the market size effect, an increase in the relative supply of educated workers may generate innovations that raise the relative demand for these workers, perhaps even increasing their relative wage in the new equilibrium.

A prime example of the Acemoglu effect would be the marked increase in the relative supply of American high school graduates between 1909 and 1929, a consequence of the "high school movement" and the end of mass European immigration during and shortly after the First World War. These labor market changes coincided remarkably with what Claudia Goldin and Lawrence Katz call the "origins of technology–skill complementarity." Modern studies generally report that new techniques are relatively intensive in skilled labor, and this property is often taken as an intrinsic feature of advanced technologies. But Goldin and Katz (1998) show that such complementarity was associated with specific new technologies such as electric motors and continuous-process methods, which enjoyed rapid diffusion during the 1920s. Although the Goldin–Katz study has the shortcoming that the new pattern "originated" in the very first year of their data (1909), evidence from the mid-nineteenth century reveals a different relationship between new technology and labor demands at that time. Atack, Bateman, and Margo (2004) find that, between 1850 and 1880, new large-scale establishments were associated with lower median wages and greater use of unskilled labor.[3]

These findings point towards a modified depiction of the Habakkuk phenomenon. Although American industrial technologies may have been labor-saving on balance, they were also designed for a new type of labor force, moving away from skilled craftsmen or artisans in favor of more elastically supplied unskilled workers, predominantly European immigrants in the late nineteenth century. Thus, the routinized, effort-intensive manufacturing jobs of the late nineteenth century may be understood as a technological adaptation to the changing characteristics of the labor force. Indeed, we may say that the pace of immigration was at least partially endogenous to the expansion of such jobs, the two sides of the market being jointly determined. Although these effects may be described as "deskilling," the analysis does not imply that the overall quality of the American labor force was deteriorating. For one thing, firms that generated new technologies (such as machine tools) were much more skill-intensive than the technology consumers, drawing increasingly on employees with advanced training. Further, the trends within manufacturing cannot be extrapolated to the economy as a whole, because the rising volume of commerce generated many positions for which educated, literate employees were required, as well as opportunities for self-employment. In light of these divergent sectoral trends, it is not difficult to see why the *fin de siècle* was an era of widening inequality in the United States.

Taken together, this body of thought and evidence implies that the direction, and perhaps the pace, of American technology has been subject to historical change; and that these shifts may be understood as responses to economic incentives, broadly conceived. But, when we come to apply this perspective to the twentieth century, the discussion also carries some methodological implications. The first is not to assume a tight, non-varying association between productivity change and new technological knowledge. Not only do new techniques require time for diffusion (itself a process governed by incentives) but the productivity implications of new technical applications may vary with labor market conditions. If technological change can be induced by changing factor supplies, and yet also fosters concomitant changes in the growth of those very factors, then there is no good alternative to examining both sides of the labor market simultaneously, with all the indeterminacy and context-specific contingency that such an approach entails.

The common practice of equating the "rate of technological progress" with change in total factor productivity is particularly hazardous. The shortcomings of TFP as a measure of technological change are frequently noted but almost as often overlooked. The core problems go well beyond the observation that TFP is measured as a residual, and hence vulnerable to errors originating in the measurement of all the included inputs and outputs. Even if our measurements were ideal, TFP tracks technological change only if new technology is "neutral" with respect to the factors of production. However convenient such an assumption is for growth accounting, it is refuted by American history. Alan Olmstead and Paul Rhode, for example, show that the vast expansion of US wheat acreage between 1839 and 1909 would not have been possible in the absence of progress in biological knowledge, primarily changes in crop varieties and cultural practices (Olmstead and Rhode, 2002). More broadly, Moses Abramovitz and Paul David's interpretation of nineteenth-century American economic growth relies crucially on the concept of biased technological change, which persistently raised the rate of return on capital and thus helped to sustain high national investment rates (Abramovitz and David, 2000). When one ponders the list of world-class American innovations making their appearance during that era, the low measured TFP growth for the century stands as a *reductio ad absurdum* for the notion that TFP measures the rate of technological change.

7.3 Phases of American productivity growth

The patterns to be explained are displayed in table 7.1. Although the time periods may be divided and subdivided in various ways, the periodization shown is relatively standard and adequate for present purposes. Growth rate fluctuations

Table 7.1 *Growth rates of US GDP per capita and GDP per hour worked, 1870–2004*

	GDP per capita	GDP per hour worked
1870–1913	1.82	1.92
1913–1950	1.61	2.48
1950–1973	2.45	2.77
1973–1995	1.76	1.14
1995–2000	2.87	2.10
1995–2004	2.29	2.45

Sources: Maddison (2001, pp. 186, 352); Groningen Growth and Development Centre (2005).

in GDP per capita deviate from those in GDP per hour worked for extended periods, because of changes in standard work hours (1913–1950) and in labor force participation (1973–1995). But, if we focus on GDP per hour worked as the core (albeit drastically simplified) measure of productivity, we see a sixty-year phase of accelerated growth after 1913, followed by a plunge to historic lows after 1973. A breakout from the productivity doldrums occurred in the late 1990s, though the growth rates did not reach those of the 1913–1973 era, labeled by Robert Gordon as the "one big wave" of American economic history (Gordon, 1999).

7.3.1 The "new economy" of the 1920s

The American productivity explosion of the 1920s has been widely discussed. Paul David and I have found that the trend in manufacturing productivity growth jumped from 1.5 percent per year to 5.1 per cent during 1919–1929, a discontinuity that we associate with the diffusion of electric power during that decade (David and Wright, 2003). Although the use of electricity in American factories dates from the 1880s, its impact on power processes was long delayed. This diffusion narrative is multifaceted, including chapters on utilities regulation, capital market innovation, infrastructure investment, and – most fundamentally – the need for new physical structures in order to take advantage of electricity's potential for reorganizing and streamlining the flow of materials through industrial plants. When all these aspects of the technology supply-side are acknowledged, however, we still find that the productivity effect cannot be fully appreciated without also considering the incentives to channel electrification in strongly labor-saving directions.

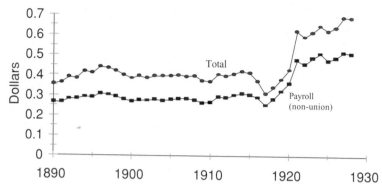

Figure 7.1 Real hourly wages in US manufacturing, 1890–1928
Sources: US Bureau of the Census (1975, series D766, D768) (originally from
Douglas, 1930), deflated by wholesale price index (series E40); 1927–1928 – from
Douglas and Jennison (1930).

Perhaps the single clearest indicator of change in the labor market is the sharp
increase in the real hourly manufacturing wage, shown in figure 7.1. The real
price of labor in the 1920s (relative to the cost of materials and products in the
economy – i.e. from the employer's perspective) was between 50 and 70 percent
higher than it had been a decade earlier. The one-time jump could be viewed as
an accident of timing, because commodity prices collapsed at the end of 1920
while nominal wages were still on a rapid upward trajectory. A lag in nominal
adjustment can hardly be the full explanation, however, because real wages did
not decline gradually but remained at this new high plateau, and in fact drifted
upwards between 1921 and 1928. Evidently, there were important "real" factors
at work as well. The most immediate of these was the end of mass European
immigration, which had averaged more than 1 million per year during the decade
prior to 1914, but was blocked during the war and then decisively closed by
legislation in 1920 and 1924. The rise in real wages ushered in a sweeping
change in the functioning of labor markets, reflected in a fall in turnover and an
upgrading of hiring standards. In comparison to their prewar counterparts, the
manufacturing wage earners of the 1920s were more mature; more likely to be
married with dependents; had more years of schooling in America and a better
command of English; and were more committed to the United States as a place
to live, and to industrial work as a lifetime occupation (Jacoby, 1983; Owen,
1995).

Complementarity between technological change and the high-wage economy is suggested by the fact that both wage increases and productivity change
were heavily concentrated in manufacturing. Clerical and service employees
did not enjoy comparable real wage jumps, presumably because these labor

markets were much less affected by immigration. Nor did these sectors experience a productivity revolution at that time. Within manufacturing, complementarity is shown by the yeast-like character of the acceleration, broadly dispersed across industries, and the marked *positive* correlation between changes in capital productivity and labor productivity. The "general-purpose" character of electrification with respect to the labor market is illustrated by its widespread use in materials handling, an operation common to virtually all manufacturing. According to Harry Jerome's survey of mechanization in American manufacturing, fully half of all reported labor-saving changes were in handling rather than processing operations, even though handlers numbered less than one-fifth of non-supervisory workers (Jerome, 1930, pp. 179–90).

7.3.2 *The 1930s and the New Deal*

The 1920s have often been seen as prosperous but short-lived, a decade of feast to be followed by the desperate famine of the Great Depression. Alexander Field's recent research, however, shows that the productivity revolution continued through the 1930s, if anything broadened and deepened with the passage of time. Although Field's emphasis is on TFP, the distinction is virtually irrelevant for present purposes, because capital formation was so limited in the Depression years. According to Field, comparisons across roughly comparable business cycle peak years reveal that labor productivity growth in the private sector was slightly faster between 1929 and 1941 than it had been between 1919 and 1929. The pace actually slowed in manufacturing (though still robust at 2.60 percent per year), but rapid productivity gains spread during the 1930s to many other sectors, particularly transportation, public utilities, and wholesale and retail trade (Field, 2003, and this volume, Chapter 5).

What sense can we make of the persistence of productivity growth in the midst of depression, obviously a radical contrast to the labor market conditions of the 1920s? As different as the decades clearly were, there were also important underlying continuities, most importantly the steady rise in the real price of labor. Figure 7.2 displays the evidence for manufacturing. Nominal wages were sticky downwards during the contraction of 1929–1933, perhaps as a consequence of the stronger attachments between firms and workers, so that real wages barely budged even as unemployment rose.[4] Hourly wages then increased across the board between 1933 and 1935, as a result of the hours and wages provisions of the National Industrial Recovery Act (NIRA), which covered virtually all of the private non-farm economy.[5] Although these effects receded when the NIRA was declared unconstitutional in 1935, additional labor measures soon took their place, with similar impact. The Wagner Act restored the provisions encouraging the organization of labor unions, with dramatic success. Expanded federal work-relief programs in effect put a floor under wage

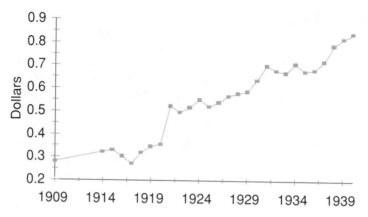

Figure 7.2 Real hourly US manufacturing wages, 1909–1940
Sources: Rees (1960, p. 3), deflated by wholesale price index (US Bureau of the Census, 1975, series E40).

levels, a policy that was formalized as the minimum wage in 1938 with the passage of the Fair Labor Standards Act. In short, real hourly wages rose because a steady stream of policy measures put upward pressure on wage rates, primarily (but by no means exclusively) at the low end of the distribution.

Many economists have noted that rising wage rates probably set back the process of recovery from the collapse of 1929–1933, promoting the widespread impression that mass unemployment would have to be accepted as a chronic, intractable feature of advanced capitalism. This critique undoubtedly has merit. But it has been less well appreciated that these high-wage policies also fostered the continuation of the process of labor force upgrading, begun during the 1920s. For example, the employment of scientists and engineers in manufacturing nearly tripled between 1933 and 1940, dwarfing the expansion of earlier years (Mowery and Rosenberg, 1998). Sanford Jacoby reports that the pace of employment reform quickened with the passage of the NIRA, as large corporations established personnel departments, expanded the training of foreman, and instituted centralized hiring and transfer systems, including systematic job evaluations, merit ratings, and promotion charts (Jacoby, 1985). Few of these managerial innovations were truly new, but they were accelerated during the 1930s because of continuing upward pressure on the cost of labor.

Thus, despite the radical contrast in political auspices, there were underlying continuities between the "welfare capitalism" of the 1920s and the pro-labor reforms of the 1930s, the common element being the "progressive" commitment to a high-wage economy. Herbert Hoover himself was a high-wage man, arguing against wage cuts during the downturn. David Fairris reports a strong

1920s association between productivity growth, reduction in injury rates, and the prevalence of company unions – correlations that carried over (albeit with different institutional forms) into the late 1930s (Fairris, 1997, pp. 22–46, 75–88). Pro-labor measures such as the Davis–Bacon Act of 1931 (requiring that "prevailing wages" be paid on federal and state construction projects) and the Norris–LaGuardia Act of 1932 (outlawing "yellow-dog" anti-union contracts) went into effect well before Franklin Roosevelt took office in 1933. Throughout the interwar period restrictions on the use of "child labor" and increases in the compulsory schooling age combined with the expansion of public schools to exclude teenagers from the labor market and raise the age and educational quality of the workforce (Osterman, 1980, pp. 62–74). Progressive labor policies were promoted by the New Deal using a rhetoric of economic recovery (usually some form of the purchasing power theory), but they are better seen as a continuation of the shift to a high-wage national regime, which drew support from many segments of the political spectrum.

An important difference between the decades was that the wage pressure of the 1920s was largely a labor market phenomenon, with an incidence that was mainly in manufacturing (the destination of most European workers). The wage increases of the 1930s were driven much more by legal and regulatory measures, which were felt more broadly throughout the economy. Thus, the spread of productivity change across sectors is quite consistent with the thesis of this chapter.

To be clear, the argument is not that productivity growth can be "reduced" to compositional change in the labor force, in growth accounting terms. These were genuine productivity-enhancing improvements, "technological progress" in the broad sense, including organizational reforms to retain and allocate labor more effectively, taking advantage of its better education and greater maturity. But technological change was "biased" towards human capital, an effect that is obscured if not missed entirely when labor attributes are collapsed into an index of labor force quality.

7.3.3 The postwar "golden age"

Although New Deal labor market policies may have slowed recovery from the Great Depression, they also set the stage for the high-wage, high productivity growth, human-capital-oriented regime of the postwar years. Decisions by the National War Labor Board confirmed the compression of wage differentials from the 1930s, and the renewal and broadening of minimum wage coverage maintained upward pressure on entry-level wages (Goldin and Margo, 1992). Diffusion of the high school norm continued through the 1950s, finally reaching the southern states at that time. At the other end of the distribution, postwar policies gave major federal support both to science-based technological

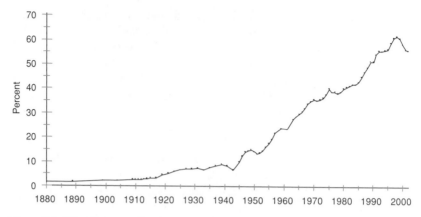

Figure 7.3 US college enrollment as a percentage of the population aged eighteen to twenty-four, 1880–2002
Sources: 1880–1988 – US Department of Education (1993, table 24); 1989–2002 – US Department of Commerce (various dates).

development and to expanded higher education. Figure 7.3 displays evidence on the dramatic rise of college enrollments as a share of the eighteen- to twenty-four-year-old population. The surge began in 1946 when the GI Bill of Rights took effect, but the greatest increases occurred between the mid-1950s and the mid-1970s.

These developments have frequently been discussed as aspects of American economic leadership, on the one hand, or the history of inequality on the other (Nelson and Wright, 1992, pp. 1950–4; Goldin, 2001). But presumably they are also relevant for the extraordinary productivity performance of the postwar era: nearly 3 percent per year for a quarter-century. Small wonder that regular annual increases in productivity and real wages seemed to be routinized and technology-driven. Although both sides of the labor market were buttressed by vigorous public policies – federal research support programs channeled through numerous agencies, and financial subsidies for higher education from both national and state governments – the fundamentally positive economic association between human capital and science-based technology was reflected in the expansion of private corporate R&D funding, and in the response of enrollments to the derived demand for technically trained personnel. Many of the institutional specifics were markedly changed from the interwar years. Yet this broad complementarity imparts an essential unity to the "one big wave," extending from the 1920s until the early 1970s.

Can we say, then, that there were inherent limits to the half-century of high productivity growth, that its demise was historically inevitable? Viewing the wave as a complementary coevolution of technology and labor upgrading adds a degree of specificity to the oft-stated but rarely elucidated proposition that the country was "running out of new ideas" by the 1970s. Most often, this possibility is discussed with respect to the development and diffusion of major innovations. In the case of electrification, for example, it is clear that the transition from steam power to electricity was largely complete by the 1950s. Increased utilization of fixed capital – an effect of electrification that augmented both labor and capital productivity – made a substantial contribution to growth from the 1920s through the 1960s, and subsequently receded as an obvious upper limit was approached (Foss, 1981, p. 6; 1985, p. 59). A second set of advances (at least in measured productivity) that may have faced inherent limits was the cluster of complementary innovations associated with the transition to the automobile, such as highways, supermarkets, and suburbs. In this case the constraints on further progress may not have been purely technological, but rising energy costs undoubtedly impinged on further geographic spread during the turbulent 1970s. The same issues arise with respect to a third technology cluster, the stream of new products based on petroleum, flowing from the merger of modern science with America's long-standing strength in minerals, and ranging from petrochemicals to plastics to pharmaceuticals (Gordon, 2000b, pp. 59–60). In all these examples the complementarities are not difficult to identify, but the nature of the learning process and the bases for diminishing returns are more challenging. Such exercises are inherently speculative, because it is in the nature of dynamic technological societies for new trajectories to replace old ones, generally in directions that were unanticipated by scientific and economic experts alike.

Linking new technology to the labor market allows us to use more objective measures. Innovators may not have been "running out of ideas" in an engineering sense, but opportunities for high-pay-off *economic* applications of new technologies may have been diminishing, because a process of upgrading educational standards has built-in limits. If we measure labor force quality as the fraction of the workforce reaching a given level then, obviously, the adjustment must end at some point. The diffusion of the high school norm was largely complete by 1960, and even the return to higher education may have been entering a region of diminishing returns (though clearly not an upper limit) in the 1970s.[6] These measures may seem artificial, since schooling benchmarks are not true limits to human capacities. But they may track real-world co-adaptations between job specifications and worker attributes. Peter Rangazas (2002) notes that the relative size of schooling investments (e.g. the share of GDP, the fraction of teenagers' time spent in school) rose dramatically to around 1970, making the obvious point that such ratios cannot rise indefinitely. Rangazas argues that a significant portion of US productivity growth was thus "transitional" in character and hence unsustainable.[7]

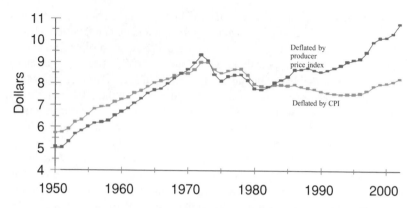

Figure 7.4 Real hourly wages in the United States in 1982 dollars, 1950–2002
Sources: US Council of Economic Advisers (2004, table B-47; 1992, table B-42; 1990, table C-44); Producer Price Index for finished goods from US Department of Commerce (various dates).

7.4 The productivity slowdown

Whether limited internally by diminishing returns or externally by something else, one can hardly overlook the historical correspondence between the 1970s drop-off in productivity growth and the end of the fifty-year wave of labor force upgrading and rising real wages. The reversal of trend in labor quality was sufficiently dramatic by 1984 for Michael Darby to declare the entire slowdown "a case of statistical myopia," writing that "simple demographic adjustments [age, sex, and educational attainment] eliminate any decline in technical progress" (Darby, 1984). Associating productivity with labor market developments is a valuable insight, too often neglected. But to collapse the labor market in this (exogenous) way is to explain the phenomenon away, not to explain it historically.

But history seldom cooperates with economic science by serving up natural experiments that neatly illustrate the forces at work. The technology–productivity trajectories of the 1920s through the 1960s may have been headed towards endogenous slowdown, but this "soft landing" was not played out because the course of history was interrupted by the dramatic external events of the 1970s. The energy crisis of that decade was acutely disruptive to American technological progress, but not along margins of labor quality, or at least not directly so. The subsequent experience of "stagflation" and social turmoil only added to the dislocation. Nominal wage increases continued, but real wage growth came to an end through inflation, as suggested by figure 7.4. Although the inflation may be characterized as a clash between aspirations and

Table 7.2 *Measures of wage inequality for weekly wages in the United States: full-time, full-year workers*

	Percentiles of log wage distribution			
	90–10	90–50	50–10	Gini coefficient
Males				
1963	1.19	0.51	0.68	0.250
1971	1.16	0.55	0.61	0.270
1979	1.27	0.55	0.72	0.277
1987	1.47	0.65	0.82	0.313
1995	1.54	0.74	0.79	0.343
Males and females				
1963	1.27	0.57	0.70	0.272
1971	1.31	0.62	0.68	0.293
1979	1.35	0.66	0.69	0.299
1987	1.44	0.70	0.74	0.320
1995	1.54	0.76	0.78	0.340

Sources: Katz and Autor (1999), p. 1475; 1963–1995 – US Bureau of the Census (various issues).

economic reality, the new constraints were far from clear at the time. Only with more years of observation than were available to Darby did it become evident that the country had entered into a more lasting period of slower productivity growth.

The literature on labor markets during this era, however, is mainly about inequality. The onset of the productivity slowdown and average real wage decline coincided with a general widening of wage differentials in the economy. Table 7.2 displays summary measures of inequality in weekly wages, all showing a steady increase dating from the 1970s. Discussions of this phenomenon have taken the general form of compiling factors contributing to increased inequality, and then debating estimates or opinions on the relative importance of each one. A standard list includes skill-biased technological change; international trade; immigration; and a sub-folder of "institutional" developments, such as the fall in the real minimum wage and the decline of unions. Of the explanations on the list, skill-biased technology has been most popular among economists. Although it is not possible to review this entire literature here, anyone who has read this far will know that the author does not find claims of an exogenous skill bias in technology either plausible or persuasive. Many studies reporting this finding focus on manufacturing; but most manufactured goods are tradable, so the bias of new technologies adopted in that sector was shaped

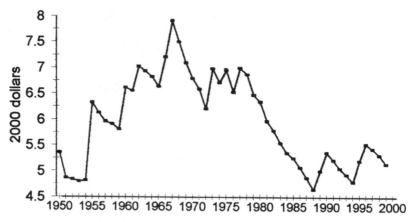

Figure 7.5 Real federal minimum wage in the United States, 1950–2000
Sources: US Department of Commerce (2001, p. 405); wage data from US
Employment Standards Administration, deflated by the CPI-U.

by the country's changing comparative advantage niche in the world economy,
as opposed to imperatives inherent in the technology itself. Because manufacturing had recovered its former productivity pace by the 1980s, it was clearly
not representative of the broader economy. David Card and John DiNardo point
out that the experience of the 1990s, when wage inequality stabilized despite
continuing progress in computer technology, is deeply challenging for the skill-
biased technical change thesis (Card and DiNardo, 2002).

Rather than attempt to track down each one of these purportedly separable and
independent causal factors, I propose a simpler unifying hypothesis: both the
decline in average real wages and the rise of wage differentials are attributable
to the advent (perhaps reinstatement would be the more appropriate term) of
"flexible labor markets," reversing fifty years of labor market policy. Merely as
one illustration of the extent of the policy swing, figure 7.5 displays the change
in the real minimum wage between 1950 and 2000. It is common to consign this
item to a minor bit role in the drama, on the grounds that a relatively small share
of the workforce actually works for the minimum wage and would therefore
be directly affected by these changes. But David Lee shows that, when one
takes into account the full wage distribution, drawing evidence from cross-state
variation in the minimum wage's "bite," this factor alone can account for nearly
all the increased dispersion in the lower tail, and up to 80 percent of the increase
in "within-group" inequality during the 1980s (Lee, 1999).[8]

One need not take a strong position on the impact of the minimum wage
per se in order to recognize that an economic "regime change" began in the

1970s. Many, if not all, of the items on the conventional list of contributing factors may be understood as endogenous or complementary components of the larger transition to a new equilibrium package. Thus, the decline in average levels of US unemployment (relative to those in Europe) was associated with the opening of lower-wage jobs that would previously have been prohibited, as well as with reduced coverage of unemployment insurance. The rise of immigration between the 1950s and the 1990s – from 2.5 million to more than 9 million for the decade – clearly put downward pressure on the unskilled wage. But it was not an exogenous development. Most immigrants came to the United States in response to job opportunities with limited entry qualifications, made possible by effective deregulation of the labor market. Much the same can be said for the rise of labor force participation and working hours per capita, both major factors in maintaining income growth in the face of declining real wages per hour (table 7.1).

Obviously, the transformation of women's role in the economy has had many causes and components, social as well as political and economic. But it has also been complementary to the rise of part-time employment and temporary work, one of the fastest-growing segments of the American labor market (Golden, 1996; Autor, 2004). According to Linda Bell and Richard Freeman, the best explanation for Americans' addiction to long hours and hard work is the "inequality hypothesis," the incentives offered by wage differentials to work one's way up the distribution (Bell and Freeman, 2001). John DiNardo, Nicole Fortin and Thomas Lemieux (1996) find that "labor market institutions [particularly the real minimum wage and de-unionization] are as important as supply and demand considerations in explaining changes in the US distribution of wages." But, when we allow that many important changes in supply and demand were themselves attributable to labor market institutions, it is clear that their conclusion is an understatement.

There is nothing particularly novel about depicting American "flexible labor markets" as a package of complementary elements. In labor economics this formulation is known as the "unified theory." As compared to Europe, American labor markets feature less collective bargaining, less generous unemployment insurance benefits, easier lay-offs, and fewer government regulations; with the results that wages are more flexible, wage differentials greater, and average unemployment levels lower (Blau and Kahn, 2002, pp. 3–6, 219–27). What is often missed in these analyses, however, is the fact that these features of the US labor market – or, at least, the extent of their international distinctiveness – are relatively recent, a marked change from the more unionized and regulated labor markets of the 1950s. Blau and Kahn, for example, write that differences in labor market institutions between the United States and Western Europe were "largely the same" in the 1960s and early 1970s, concluding that the difference must not lie in institutional performance *per se* but in the responsiveness of institutions to "shocks." Chief among these shocks, they list the slowdown in productivity growth dating from the early 1970s (p. 5).

It is evident from figure 7.4 that a regime change occurred after 1973. In addition to an historical perspective on labor market institutions, what is offered here is the further suggestion that this regime change was itself an important contributor to the post-1973 productivity slowdown. The much-discussed issue of possible upward bias in the consumer price index is not particularly relevant for the present point. We are not evaluating the well-being of workers but the stimulus to implement labor-saving technology. Even relative to producer price indices (i.e. from the employer's perspective), real hourly wages had not recovered to their early 1970s peak by 1990. American employers had far less incentive to economize on labor after 1973 than in prior decades. The first blows to real wages in the 1970s may have originated in energy markets and inflation. But one does not require advanced expertise in American history to know that a major change in the political landscape set in after 1980, especially where labor was concerned.

7.5 The 1990s

Although not as eye-catching for the general public as the dot.com boom, the surge of productivity in the late 1990s has received almost as much attention from economists. Already two important points of consensus have emerged: that the acceleration was broadly dispersed within the economy, including service sector industries long thought to be impervious to productivity growth; and that it was closely linked to the diffusion of computer-based information technology. Thus, William Nordhaus finds that "there has been a substantial upturn in on-new economy productivity growth... It is clear that the productivity rebound is not narrowly focused in a few new economy sectors." Similarly, Kevin Stiroh concludes: "Eight of ten sectors show productivity growth increases, and relatively large sectors like wholesale trade, retail trade, and services all show sizable gains." Jack Triplett and Barry Bosworth announce with enthusiasm that "Baumol's Disease" – the hypothesis that productivity improvements in services are inherently less likely than in goods-producing sectors – has been cured, citing rapid productivity growth in these areas after 1995. Andrew Sharpe and Leila Gharani report that "the productivity renaissance in the service sector is broadly based, with four of the six basic service sector industries showing at least a one percentage point increase in labour productivity growth between the 1989–1995 and 1995–1999 periods."[9]

Why should such a sudden break from the past have cropped up in so many disparate industries at the same historical juncture? Productivity analysts are simply not in the habit of connecting their measurements to the state of the labor market. Stiroh, for example, considers two possible explanations. The first is that some lag was needed in order to implement IT successfully and reap the productivity pay-off, citing firm-level studies emphasizing adjustment costs, learning lags, and delays in complementary innovations. The second is that firms do not focus on the present but invest in IT in anticipation of future productivity gains (Stiroh, 2001, pp. 32–3). No role for labor market conditions either way. For another example, consider Martin Neil Baily's comment on Robert Gordon's econometric work:

I see nothing in the actual data for the 1990s to suggest that productivity began to accelerate before 1996, but in Gordon's results using filtering methods . . . the productivity acceleration started in the early 1990s. Maybe that is correct. I have to admit there seems to be no smoking-gun explanation of the shift in trend that can account for a sudden trend break in 1996.[10]

If you look to the labor market, you can find a smoking gun in the mid-1990s. Figure 7.4 shows that real hourly wages finally began to rise at precisely that time, after more than two decades of decline. The fall was less marked when wages are deflated by producer prices, but by that measure (representing the cost of an hour's labor relative to goods in the economy) the jump in the late 1990s was particularly sharp. The wage evidence may be buttressed by several supplementary indicators confirming that, despite the deregulated institutional structure of the US labor market, demand pressures began to press against available supplies at that time. Unemployment rates fell below 4 percent – levels reached only briefly in the 1960s and well below the norm for the 1950s. Labor force participation reached a peak, and the ratio of employment to population reached an all-time high in 2000 (figure 7.6). Should it be surprising that employers turned to labor-saving technologies at this time?

Clearly, the productivity surge drew upon new IT technologies, as shown by numerous studies. Stephen Oliner and Daniel Sichel attribute nearly 70 percent of the acceleration in labor productivity (from 1991–1995 to 1996–1999) to the direct and indirect effects of information technology.[11] Stiroh reports that IT-intensive industries experienced productivity growth about one percentage point per year faster than other industries, while non-IT-intensive industries showed essentially no acceleration (Stiroh, 2001, p. 34). Triplett and Bosworth (2003) find, contrary to stereotype, that "the most intensive IT industries in the US economy are overwhelmingly services industries." Although most economic studies take a "black box" approach, proxying IT diffusion with measures of capital investment, there are some indications that organizational restructuring using IT technology was particularly important. Triplett and Bosworth note that intermediate inputs made a substantial contribution to labor productivity growth in the 1990s, reflecting increased reliance on "contracting out." Studies of labor intermediation suggest that the rise of temporary help agencies was significant in improving the efficiency of the labor market, including both employee screening

Figure 7.6 Employment ratios in the United States, 1948–2004
Sources: US Bureau of Labor Statistics (2005); Labor Force Statistics from the Current Population Survey (http://data.bls.gov/servlet/SurveyOutputServlet).

and flexibility in response to demand fluctuations (Katz and Krueger, 1999, pp. 48–53; Segal and Sullivan, 1997, pp. 127–31).

Such sophisticated managerial systems depended crucially on new information technologies. But was the acceleration *driven* by the progress of that technology? Because of their mutual interdependence, it may be impossible to answer this question definitively, but the timing of the break suggests that the proximate impetus came from labor market pressures. Particularly suggestive is the evidence presented by Jessica Cohen, William Dickens, and Adam Posen (2001, pp. 234–40) in their survey on the diffusion of a new set of practices known as high-performance work organization (HPWO). Examples include job rotation, pay for knowledge, autonomous teams, total-quality management, and quality circles. The central objectives are to increase the firm's ability to move workers between jobs within the firm and to facilitate the matching of new hires to jobs. The adoption of HPWO dates from the 1980s but it accelerated in the late 1990s. Of nine interviews with human resource managers, "two interviewees explicitly denied that advances in IT were an independent motivating force, and all but one of the others either did not mention IT or downplayed its effect, characterizing it as limited to administrative matters . . . The one remaining subject did draw the connection that 'E-commerce has been important in speeding up the business cycle.'" The authors associate the latter comment with competitive product-market pressures, which raised the value of flexibility to the firm.

Similarly, McKinsey's analysis of US productivity growth during 1995–2000 found that the bulk of the acceleration in wholesale and retail trade was directly or indirectly attributable to managerial innovation at one firm, Wal-Mart. IT was important at Wal-Mart, but the McKinsey report (2001) stresses that IT was only one of many management tools; IT was often "a necessary but not sufficient enabler of productivity gains."

7.6 The identification problem

Economists reading this account may wonder about the direction of causal effect. We teach our students that wages are determined by productivity in the long run. So, if wage growth and productivity growth are historically associated, how can we say that productivity was driven by wage pressures rather than the other way around?

The earlier historical episodes are particularly helpful in this regard. In the interwar period wages increased for reasons exogenous to productivity. In the 1920s real wages jumped upwards because of a dramatic fall in prices, super-imposed on a labor market that was adjusting to a major change in immigration policy. Under the New Deal in the 1930s wages were directly increased by policy, clearly not prompted by surging labor demand. In both decades accelerated productivity growth is best viewed as a lagged response to increased labor costs by employers, who used technology and organizational change to raise productivity to match the new higher wage levels.

In the postwar era real wages were driven less by policy and more by market processes. Even then, market forces were complemented by policies such as the rise in the minimum wage and the extension of its coverage, and wage increases were to some extent "institutionalized" in union contracts. But, when real wages and productivity rise together over an extended period such as this one, we should certainly characterize them as jointly determined. The "end of the era" in the 1970s suggests, however, that a painful adjustment process was required before wage behavior adapted to the new economic reality. The high-growth era really had come to a close, but neither workers nor policymakers realized this, as they continued their efforts to restore real wage gains in the late 1970s, beyond what the economy could deliver (figure 7.4). When recovery materialized in the 1980s the discontinuity in the trajectory of real wages was considerably more marked than in productivity, suggesting that the primary impetus came from the labor market. Acemoglu (2002) portrays the extended absolute decline in the real wages of low-skilled workers as a "puzzle" for economists, and his research survey concludes that the role of technology in this trend is indirect – i.e. in its interaction with changes in labor market institutions and the organization of firms.

The real-wage turning point in the mid-1990s is most plausibly attributed to macroeconomic conditions, when an accommodating Federal Reserve allowed employment to press against labor supply for the first time in a generation. Although the macroeconomy was propelled in part by speculation in technology stocks, we have no evidence that this surge was triggered by a trend break in advance of the underlying technologies themselves. On the contrary, historical studies of applications of computer technologies to the American workplace stress the long-term, incremental, evolutionary character of the process. In retail trade – a prime illustration of mid-1990s discontinuity in productivity – James Cortada lists eleven key IT applications in the retail industry *circa* 1995–2001, including electronic shelf levels, scanning, electronic fund transfer, sales-based ordering, and internet sales. Cortada (2004, p. 307) then notes that, "with the exception of e-business, the list could have come from the 1970s and 1980s, and that is the key point."

To be clear, the emphasis on labor markets here is not intended as an alternative to scenarios highlighting the need for learning and adaptation before the potential from new technologies can be fully realized. Many micro-level studies confirm that productivity gains from IT require a package of complementary adjustments, often quite radical reorganizations of internal communications and new types of interaction with suppliers and customers (Brynjolfsson and Hitt, 2000, pp. 25–30). The example of electrification in the 1920s is often invoked in such studies, and the same analogy applies here. Computer-based technologies may have arrived at new levels of reliability and capability by the 1990s, so that the same effects could not have been expected a decade or so before. But the key point is that the incentive to channel the applications of this potential towards labor productivity is separable from adoption decisions *per se*. Retail operators such as Wal-Mart, J. C. Penney, and Gap were innovative IT adopters for decades, calculating inventory, accounting and delivery costs with increasing precision. They turned their innovative energies towards productivity when the price of labor time began to rise in the mid-1990s. Thus, *both* blades of the scissors are required to account for the productivity surge.[12]

7.7 Conclusions

Throughout the twentieth century periods of rapid productivity growth have also been periods of strong upward pressure on real hourly wages. The productivity surge of the late 1990s provides the latest illustration of this empirical regularity. Of course real wages and productivity are mutually interactive, but in each of the major phases one can point to distinct historical circumstances operating in the labor market, suggesting that the primary causal influence ran from the labor market to productivity rather than the other way around. At a minimum, this channel deserves a more prominent place in productivity history than it has received thus far. It has been largely overlooked, perhaps because of prevailing patterns of specialization within the economics profession.

Pursuing this proposition poses a challenge for conventional econometric research, because it is not advanced as a general economic law, valid for all historical times and places. A claim that higher wages always generate productivity-enhancing innovations would be seriously faulty. Within the historical scope of this chapter, such a claim is refuted by the experience of the 1970s, when upward pressures on wages led mainly to higher inflation and unemployment. Perhaps the older technological paths were largely exhausted in the 1970s, and they may not have been well suited for the changed economic situation anyway. Newer technological responses were not then readily at hand. Unfortunately, such diagnoses are far easier to construct after the fact than before, because we lack reliable measures of "technological potential" at a particular point in time and so can only infer potential after observing the technology in practice.

Sometimes we do know, however, that best-practice technology is in flux, and that new methods are emerging that have not yet widely diffused. That is one way to read the extensive discussion of the "productivity paradox" from the 1970s to the mid-1990s. In these situations, history shows that the detailed factor-using properties of new technologies are highly malleable, subject to influence by labor market conditions at the time of adoption. Theorists since John R. Hicks have attempted to understand the linkages among technological progress, factor-saving bias, and labor market conditions. As yet they have not arrived at a satisfactory or consensus model. But that shortfall is no reason to neglect the empirical regularities that gave rise to the theoretical project.

Notes

For helpful suggestions on an earlier draft, I thank Peter H. Lindert, Howard Pack, Paul W. Rhode, and William Sundstrom. But I am solely responsible for all views expressed.

1. On wage levels, see Adams (1970) and the summary in James and Skinner (1985, pp. 537–9). For a comparison of labor productivity as of 1840, see Broadberry and Irwin (2004).
2. This is a drastically condensed summary of a large literature. For an explicitly search-based interpretation of the Habakkuk thesis, see David (1975, chap. 1). On the network character of American technology, see Wright (1999).
3. An earlier study showing that larger establishments were associated with the greater use of women and children during the "early industrialization" period (1820–1850) is Goldin and Sokoloff (1982).
4. O'Brien (1989). For evidence that downward stickiness was not limited to large manufacturing firms, see Simon (2001).
5. Weinstein (1980, pp. 29, 52, 60) finds that the NIRA increased nominal hourly wages by as much as 26 percent during this period, relative to levels that would otherwise have prevailed.
6. Goldin (2001, p. 285) reports that the return to a year of college education declined between 1970 and 1980, before rising in the 1980s.
7. Rangazas (2002) does not include higher education in his analysis, nor does he consider complementarity between human capital and technology.

8. See also DiNardo, Fortin and Lemieux (1996) on the impact of the real minimum wage.
9. Nordhaus (2002, p. 242); Stiroh (2001, pp. 32–3); Triplett and Bosworth (2003, pp. 23, 30); Sharpe and Gharani (2000, p. 6).
10. Baily (2003, p. 282). According to the published account, none of the discussion of Gordon's paper considered the labor market as a potential cause of "exploding productivity growth" in the 1990s.
11. Oliner and Sichel (2000, p. 19). They also report that the broad picture is similar in three other studies (p. 14).
12. Note that accelerated productivity growth continued beyond the end of the boom, as shown in table 7.1. Although this persistence is at first surprising, one should also note that the rise of real hourly wages costs also continued through 2002 (figure 7.4). Thus, the correlation is quite consistent with the theme of this chapter.

8 The 1920s and the 1990s in mutual reflection

Robert J. Gordon

"The Great Depression of 1929 to 1940 in the United States was the greatest event in the history of business cycles. It devastated rich and poor alike. It destroyed wealth in the billions, tossed one-quarter of the 1929 labor force onto the shoals of unemployment, evaporated the hopes and aspirations of millions, left a majority of American families near destitution for a full decade in an event that was totally unnecessary, because properly applied monetary and fiscal policy could have cured the recession in 1930/31, not a decade later in 1941."[1]

8.1 Introduction

The similarities in American economic performance between the decades of the 1920s and 1990s are tantalizing. Particularly when 1919 is aligned with 1990 and 1929 is aligned with 2000, the evolution of many key macro-variables over the intervening decade match remarkably closely. Growth in real GDP, real GDP per capita, employment, and productivity were almost identical, the conventionally measured unemployment rate was identical in 1928 and 1999, inflation was negligible (1920s) or low (1990s), and the late 1920s stock market boom is the only such episode in the century that comes close to the stock market's ebullience in the late 1990s. Like the 1990s, the 1920s witnessed prosperity, a productivity revival, low unemployment, and low inflation. Both decades featured an explosion of applications of a fundamental general-purpose technology, electricity and the internal combustion engine in the 1920s and computer hardware, software, and networking communications technology in the 1990s. Both decades appear to mock the existence of a Phillips curve trade-off between inflation and unemployment.

The evolution of the economy after 1929 was entirely different from its evolution after 2000, however, except for a short-run mirror image in the stock market collapse. Viewed in their antiseptic blandness, the raw data portray an economy in 1929 poised for continuous expansion and a leap forward in the

American standard of living. Yet the four years after 1929 produced an economic disaster without parallel before or since in economic history. This chapter goes beyond the superficial similarity of the 1920s and 1990s to search for worms in the apple of the 1920s. While accepting the role of domestic monetary policy and international monetary relations in explaining the magnitude of the 1929–1933 collapse, we identify lesser-known aspects of the 1920s that made the economy more vulnerable to bad policy than was the case with the economy of the late 1990s.[2]

The aim of this chapter is to find interesting features and puzzles about the 1920s that might be illuminated in contrast with the 1990s. The emphasis is on understanding what happened between 1919 and the summer of 1929, and there is no attempt here to revisit the well-trodden turf of the disastrous conduct of the Federal Reserve after the stock market crash, or the well-known set of factors that caused the Great Depression to be so deep – e.g. the relative roles of the Fed and the "gold standard," bank failures and the absence of bank deposit insurance, the Smoot–Hawley Tariff, or the British abandonment of the gold standard in September 1931. Instead, we focus on the similarities and differences between the 1920s and 1990s pertaining to the economy prior to 1930. The 1920s and 1990s shared a common success, a distinct acceleration of productivity growth in comparison with the previous two decades. The 1920s and 1990s shared common failures, especially overinvestment and the stock market bubbles. The 1990s illuminate the 1920s especially in the demonstration that aggressive monetary and fiscal expansion limited the 2001 recession to the shallowest drop in real GDP in the postwar era, leading to the presumption that similar policies could have had similar effects in 1930/31.

The pivotal role of ICT investment in the boom of the late 1990s leads us to place our major emphasis on a re-examination of investment in the 1920s. Was there "overinvestment" in equipment or structures in the 1920s by comparison with other decades in the twentieth century? We integrate the previously diffuse literature on a business cycle interpretation of investment in the 1920s with the productivity-based literature on GPT in the 1920s, always placing the 1920s in the perspective of the same variables for the 1990s.

8.2 The aligned data on the 1920s versus the 1990s

8.2.1 Growth rates

Our comparison of data on the 1920s and 1990s begins with table 8.1, which displays annualized growth rates of numerous macro-variables for the two decades, 1990–2000 versus 1919–1929, and also breaks down the 1920s into its quite different sub-intervals of 1919–1923 and 1923–1929. Subsequently we will look at the *levels* (as contrasted to growth rates) of selected indicators.

Table 8.1 *Growth rates of selected macroeconomic variables in the United States, 1919–1929 and 1990–2000*

	1990–2000	1919–1929	1919–1923	1923–1929
National Income Accounts				
1. Nominal GDP	5.3	3.0	2.6	3.2
2. Real GDP	3.2	3.4	3.6	3.2
3. GDP deflator	2.0	−0.4	−1.0	0.0
4. Consumer price index	2.8	−0.1	−0.3	0.0
Productivity-related, non-farm private business sector				
5. Output	3.7	3.6	4.1	3.3
6. Hours	1.7	1.3	1.4	1.1
7. Output per hour	2.0	2.4	2.6	2.2
8. Hours per employee	0.0	−0.2	−0.2	−0.2
Income side				
9. National income	5.5	3.1	2.7	3.3
10. Employee compensation	5.7	3.4	3.9	3.1
11. Rent	10.9	2.1	6.6	−0.8
12. Dividends	8.8	7.8	7.1	8.3
13. Interest	3.5	5.5	6.6	4.8
Employment and unemployment				
14. Employment	1.3	1.7	2.0	1.4
15. Labor force	1.1	1.8	2.2	1.6
16. Working-age population	1.0	2.1	2.5	1.8
Money and credit				
17. Money supply (M2)	4.0	5.1	−1.1	9.2
18. Velocity of M2	1.3	−2.1	3.7	−6.0
19. Standard and Poor's 500 stock index	14.5	9.9	−0.8	17.0

Sources: See appendix.

Our primary focus in table 8.1 is on the first two columns, comparing 1990–2000 with 1919–1929. Here we find that *real* variables share growth rates that are amazingly similar while *nominal* variables grow at slower rates in the 1920s, reflecting the complete absence of inflation in that decade. Among the variables that grow at essentially the same rate in the 1990s as in the 1920s are real GDP (line 2), non-farm private business output, hours, and output per hour (lines 5–7), and the nominal money supply (line 17). Hours per employee (line 8) were stable in the 1990s, in contrast to a steady rate of decline in the 1920s that continued the long-term reduction in non-farm private hours per employee from sixty per week in 1889 to forty per week in 1957 (Kendrick, 1961, table A-IX, p. 310).

However similar are the growth rates in the second section for the non-farm private business sector, the 1920s exhibit a clear superiority in productivity growth within the manufacturing sector. While productivity growth in manufacturing was impressive in the 1990s the performance of the 1920s was even better, particularly the great leap forward in manufacturing productivity achieved between 1919 and 1923. The overall growth rate of manufacturing productivity of 5.4 percent per year during the 1920s was more than *quadruple* the pathetic rate of 1.3 percent per year registered in the previous three decades (1889–1919), supporting Paul David's oft-discussed "delay" hypothesis (1990, 1991), further developed in David and Wright (2003), that there was a long delay in achieving the productivity pay-off in manufacturing of the invention of electric power in the 1870s. Clearly, there was more going on in the 1920s than bringing electric motors to the individual work station, and Henry Ford's invention of the assembly line in the preceding decade deserves credit as well.[3]

Since inflation was zero in the 1920s, as contrasted with a modest 2 to 3 percent in the 1990s (lines 3 and 4), all nominal growth rates in the 1920s were substantially lower, including nominal GDP (line 1), components of national income (lines 9 through 13), and the velocity of M2 (line 18). One conspicuous exception is interest income, which grew more rapidly in the 1920s despite the absence of any significant changes in interest rates during that decade. Employment and the labor force grew more rapidly in the 1920s than in the 1990s, reflecting a growth rate of the working-age population that was more than twice as fast (line 16).

Perhaps the most intriguing similarity between the two decades is the run-up in stock market prices towards the end of each period (see line 19). For the two decades as a whole, stock price appreciation in the 1920s was much slower (9.9 percent) than in the 1990s (14.5 percent). This reflects in part the absence of any increase at all in stock prices between 1919 and 1923. If we chop off the first four years of each decade then the increase in stock prices between 1923 and 1929 (17.0 percent per annum) is remarkably similar to that between 1994 and 2000 (18.9 percent per annum). In fact, in real terms (deflating by the GDP deflator) the late decade run-ups are almost identical: 17.0 percent for 1923–1929 and 16.9 percent for 1994–2000.

8.2.2 A long-run comparison of levels and ratios

Some macroeconomic issues are addressed by growth rates, as in table 8.1. Others are better illuminated by raw numbers and ratios. The top section of table 8.2 provides the values of nominal and real GDP, the GDP deflator, and the CPI

Table 8.2 *Levels of selected macroeconomic variables in the United States, 1919–1929 and 1990–2000*

	1919	1929	1990	2000
National Income Accounts				
1. Nominal GDP ($ billions)	76.9	103.6	5803.1	9817.0
2. Real GDP (2000 $ billions)	614.9	865.2	7112.5	9817.0
3. GDP deflator (2000 = 100)	12.5	12.0	81.6	100.0
4. Consumer price index (1967 = 100)	51.8	51.3	391.4	511.8
Employment and labor force				
5. Employment (millions)	39.2	46.2	118.8	135.2
6. Labor force (millions)	39.7	47.7	125.8	140.9
7. Working-age population (millions)	70.4	86.6	189.2	209.7
8. Unemployment rate (percent)	1.4	3.2	5.6	4.0
9. Labor-force participation rate (percent)	56.4	55.1	66.5	67.2
10. Real GDP per employee (2000 $ thousands)	15.7	18.7	59.9	72.6
Interest rates and stock market				
11. Treasury bill rate (percent)	4.9	4.4	7.5	5.9
12. Real treasury bill rate (percent)	4.9	4.4	4.3	4.2
13. S&P 500 stock price index (1941–1943 = 10)	8.8	26.0	335.3	1427.2
New industries				
14. Automobile registrations (millions)	7.6	26.7	188.7	221.5
15. Electricity generation (billion kWh)	52.3	116.7	2816.7	3606.5
16. Computer use at home or work (millions)	–	–	73.7	174.0

for the beginning and end years of the 1920s and 1990s. Here we are impressed at how much everything grew between 1929 and 1990, with compound annual growth rates of 6.6 percent for nominal GDP, 3.5 percent for real GDP, and 3.1 and 3.3 percent, respectively, for the two inflation measures. Compared to the six decades between 1929 and 1990, the decade of the 1990s exhibited slightly slower real GDP growth and inflation, while the 1920s exhibited the same real GDP growth with zero inflation.

The next section of table 8.2 displays data on labor market outcomes. Of most interest is the unemployment rate, which was lower in both 1919 and 1929 than in any year of the 1990s. The labor force participation rate was substantially higher in the 1990s than the 1920s, reflecting the flow of women into the labor force that occurred during the postwar era. A crude measure of productivity, real GDP per employee, grew by almost a factor of five between 1919 and 2000. But its growth rates in the 1920s (1.8 percent per annum) and 1990s (1.9 percent) were not faster at all than in the intervening decades 1929–1990

(1.9 percent) – perhaps a surprising result in view of the common impression that productivity growth was particularly strong in the 1920s and 1990s.

The next section of table 8.2 displays interest rates and a stock market index. It is perhaps surprising to find that the nominal treasury bill rate was lower in 1929 than in 2000. This difference is more than explained by different inflation rates, and the real interest rate in 2000 was almost identical to that in 1929 and 1990.[4] Clearly, the respect in which the 1920s and 1990s differed most from the intervening decades (1929–1990) was in the behavior of the stock market. The increase in the S&P 500 stock market index, expressed in real terms, adjusting for the actual change in the GDP deflator, was a soaring 11.3 percent per year in the 1920s and 12.4 percent in the 1990s, dwarfing the puny 1.0 percent annual realized real return during 1929–1990.

In addition to their distinction in the decadal league tables of stock market returns, the decades of the 1920s and 1990s are perhaps best known for the diffusion of new technologies. While the internal combustion engine and electric power generation had been invented in the 1870s and 1880s, the 1920s represented the true breakthrough. Motor vehicle registrations more than tripled between 1919 and 1929, and electricity generation more than doubled. In the 1990s the number of Americans who reported using personal computers at home and/or at work more than doubled, growing at roughly the same rate as electricity generation in the 1920s.

8.2.3 Charts

In this section we display the aligned data over a longer period, comparing 1913–1932 with 1984–2003. The longer data period allows us to remain aware not only of how much the evolution of the economy differed in 2000–2003 from 1929–32, but also how much more volatile was the economy in the last years of the First World War (1917–1918) and in the period of speculative boom and depression (1919–1921), than in the aligned years 1988–2002.

With the 1913:1984 to 1932:2003 alignment, figure 8.1 displays the astonishing similarity of real GDP growth in the 1920s and 1990s. With a base year of 1929 = 2000 = 100, we note that the growth rate of real GDP was identical over the intervals 1913–1929 and 1984–2000, or, alternatively, between 1919–1929 and 1990–2000. However, the much greater cyclical volatility of the earlier period stands out in the chart. Taking the ratio of the 1913–1932 index number for real GDP to the 1984–2003 number (as plotted in figure 8.1), there was an additional GDP gap in 1914 compared to 1985 of −8.0 percent, in 1921 compared to 1992 of −9.7 percent, and in 1932 compared to 2003 of a gigantic −29.7 percent. The boom of the mid-1920s also outpaced the mid-1990s, with ratios of the real GDP index in 1923, 1924, and 1926 to the corresponding years of the 1990s of +3.3 to +3.5 percent. While Christina

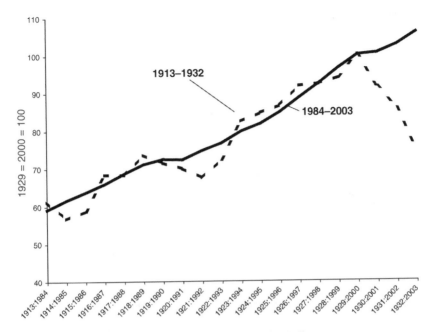

Figure 8.1 Real US GDP growth, 1913:1984 to 1932:2003 alignment

Romer (1990) has suggested that the standard data overstate the volatility of the pre-1929 economy relative to the post-1947 economy, from our narrower perspective there seems little doubt that the macroeconomic environment was far more volatile during 1913–1923 than in 1984–1994, the "aligned" equivalent period.

Figure 8.2 shows that productivity growth in 1919–1929 was identical to 1990–2000. However, the two halves of the decade appear to have the reverse timing, displaying a slowdown in the 1920s versus an acceleration in the 1990s. Productivity growth in the 1920s slowed from annual rates of 2.7 percent in 1919–1924 to 1.5 percent in 1924–1929. In the 1990s the half-decades exhibited the exact reverse behavior, with an acceleration from 1.6 percent in 1990–1995 to 2.4 percent in 1995–2000. The two eras also differed in that productivity growth was much faster during 1913–1919 than in the aligned years 1984–1990, with respective annual growth rates of 2.2 and 1.5 percent.

The Lebergott (1964) unemployment data used by most economists are much more volatile between 1913 and 1929 than in the recent period, as shown in figure 8.3. Excluding the wartime effect of 1918–1919, the peacetime range was between 1.8 percent (1926) and 11.7 percent (1921). The equivalent range over the 1984–2003 interval was between 4.0 percent (2000) and 7.5 percent

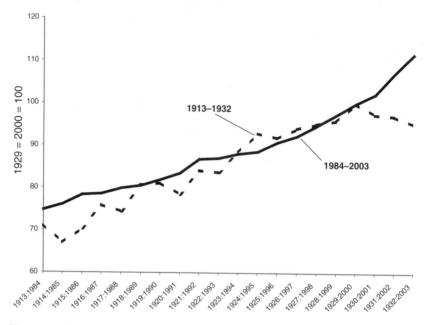

Figure 8.2 US productivity growth, 1913:1984 to 1932:2003 alignment

(1984 and 1992). We should qualify the comparison in figure 8.3 by noting that Lebergott does not allow for cyclical variability in the labor force participation rate. Thus he includes what we now call "discouraged workers" as part of unemployment, whereas in the postwar BLS data they are allowed to drop out of the labor force and are not counted as unemployed. This imparts a modest excess volatility to the pre-1929 Lebergott unemployment data.[5]

Excess volatility is also displayed, in figure 8.4, by the inflation rate, with the CPI rising at an annual rate of 14.7 in 1919–1920 and declining at a rate of 11.3 percent in 1920–1921. Yet, as shown in tables 8.1 and 8.2 above, the price level was almost identical in 1919 and 1929, and the annual rate of inflation between 1922 and 1929 was a mere 0.5 percent.

The final graphical comparison, in figure 8.5, displays the S&P 500 stock market index. The eight-year rise to the peak, starting in 1921 and 1992, is absolutely identical, as is the four-year rise to the peak, starting in 1925 and 1996. The pattern of advance is slightly different, with a late surge of 24 percent per year in the last two years of the 1920s episode (1927–1929), whereas in the 1990s the maximum growth in any year occurred earlier (26 percent in 1996–1997). The comparison in figure 8.5 somewhat overstates the similarity of the 1920s and 1990s, due to the absence of inflation in the earlier decade. The

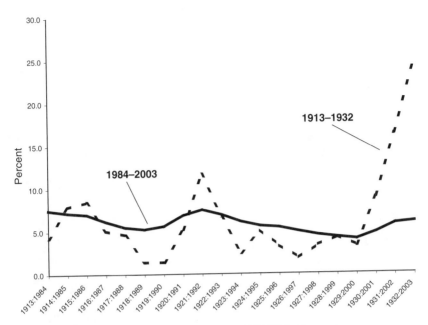

Figure 8.3 US unemployment rate, 1913:1984 to 1932:2003 alignment

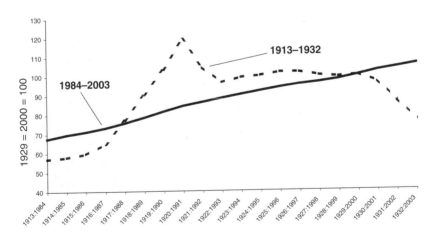

Figure 8.4 US consumer price inflation, 1913:1984 to 1932:2003 alignment

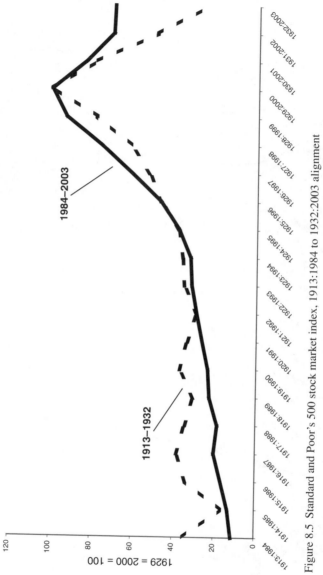

Figure 8.5 Standard and Poor's 500 stock market index, 1913:1984 to 1932:2003 alignment

overall increase in the stock market index when deflated by the GDP deflator is 258 percent in 1921–1929 compared to 197 percent in 1992–2000.

8.3 GPTs and the productivity growth acceleration of the 1920s

The 1920s are a Janus-faced decade that defies simple characterization. At one level, it was a quintessential decade of success, as was the 1990s. The 1920s were a "golden age" of productivity growth (Kendrick, 1961; David and Wright, 2003), as were the 1990s (Jorgenson and Stiroh, 2000; Oliner and Sichel, 2000, 2002). Productivity growth accelerated after decades of dismal quiescence, productivity growth in manufacturing outpaced the average of the private non-farm economy, inflation was low, monetary policy adopted benign neglect, and in the "golden spring" of the terminal year of the decade of success – that is, the springs of 1929 and 2000 – all was rosy and nothing could go wrong.

Yet the two decades ended very differently: the 1990s with a short, mild, recession that brought with it an explosion in productivity growth, albeit a jobless recovery, the 1920s with the catastrophe that has perplexed macroeconomists ever since. Our task in this chapter is to go beyond the well-worn explanation that monetary policy failed in 1929–1932. It did – but why was monetary policy called upon to do anything? Why was there anything to react against? Was there one (or more) "rotten apple" in the 1920s that explains the economy's post-1929 hangover, one with which monetary policy was not prepared to deal?

The Janus-faced 1920s call for a multi-part analysis. Three previously unrelated sets of literature require an attempt at a logical integration. First is the analysis of the productivity growth acceleration of the 1920s, which carried on to the mid-1960s and was the underlying source of the investment boom of the 1920s (David and Wright, 2003; Gordon, 2000a). The second strand is the traditional set of business cycle models based on the multiplier and accelerator; this treats every investment boom as inherently temporary and carrying with it the seeds of its own destruction (Schumpeter, 1939; Samuelson, 1939; Hicks, 1950; Gordon, 1951). Excess investment was the key ingredient that brought the 1920s boom to an end and condemned the economy to a significant downturn, with an effect that was significantly magnified by the stock market bubble. The third strand is best known: the analysis of the domestic banking crisis and monetary policy failure associated with Friedman and Schwartz (1963), and the complementary analysis of the international monetary collapse, developed furthest by Eichengreen (1992a, 1992b). Logic calls for these three strands to be discussed in this order. Along the way, we will identify numerous similarities between the 1920s and 1990s – involving innovation, productivity growth, an unsustainable investment boom, and a stock market bubble – and extreme differences involving banking and monetary policy.

8.3.1 The productivity growth acceleration and its interpretation

The fundamental similarity between the 1920s and 1990s was identified by Paul David (1990, 1991) before the 1990s had even begun! In his perceptive likening of the computer to the "dynamo," he developed what others have labeled the David "delay hypothesis." This was originally proposed as an explanation of the co-existence in the 1970s and 1980s of slow productivity growth together with the spread of computers, a puzzle that by then had become known as the Solow "computer paradox" – that "we can see the computer age everywhere but in the productivity statistics." In David's analogy, the invention of electricity and the electric power generation station in the 1870s and early 1880s required decades of development and cost reduction before the full implications for productivity and efficiency could be brought to fruition, and this occurred in the 1920s, when productivity growth accelerated, especially in manufacturing.

Subsequent to the initial David contribution, Bresnahan and Trajtenberg (1995) popularized the term "general-purpose technologies" for technical advances with wide applications throughout the economy. The steam engine was the original GPT, but doubtless the most important in history were the core inventions of the "Second Industrial Revolution" of 1870–1900, electricity and the internal combustion engine (ICE). Gordon (2000b) has questioned whether the chief GPT innovations of the late 1990s, the web and internet, "measure up" to the pivotal inventions of the Second Industrial Revolution.

David (1990, 1991) identifies several factors that led to delay in the exploitation of the potential of electric power and that finally released this potential after the period 1914–1917, when there was a significant decline in the real price of electricity made possible in part by a shift from isolated sources of electricity generation at individual industrial plants to central station generating capacity. Continuous technological improvements in central station generating equipment, together with a loosening of the political regulation of electric utilities, created the price decline that in turn "propelled the final phase of the shift to electricity as a power source in US manufacturing, from just over 50 percent in 1919 to nearly 80 percent in 1929" (David and Wright, 2003, p. 140). The technique for using electric power also changed in the 1920s as well, from reliance on "group drives" to individually powered machines, which then made possible a redesign of factories into single-story factory layouts. This analysis of the sources of the 1920s productivity miracle in manufacturing can be linked to the business cycle literature on the 1920s investment boom, which recognizes electrification as one source of the boom in both equipment investment and commercial and industrial construction (see Gordon, 1974, p. 22).

For instance, the doubling of electricity output in the 1920s (table 8.1 above) called for significant investment in the utility industry. David and Wright (2003, pp. 141–2) call attention to the effect of these developments in raising the productivity of capital – i.e. reducing the capital–output ratio. Gordon (2000a) notes the contribution of the increasing average productivity of capital to the acceleration of multifactor productivity growth, which he dates to the entire period between 1913 and 1964.[6] Ironically, an increase in the productivity of capital would tend to reduce the share of investment in real GDP, and, after a transition period of high investment in the 1920s, contributed to the weakness in investment in the 1930s. Both the 1920s and 1990s were characterized, at least after the fact, as periods of glut and oversupply in capital equipment.

David and Wright (2003, pp. 156–61) emphasize the need for the fundamental reorganizing and rethinking of business practices in both the 1920s and 1990s. In this they anticipate the recent literature on unmeasured "intangible investment" (business practice reinvention, personnel training) that has been applied to the late 1990s productivity revival by Yang and Brynjolffson (2001) and Basu et al. (2003). David and Wright justify their emphasis on electricity by noting that the productivity acceleration in manufacturing during the 1920s was very widely dispersed across almost every sector of manufacturing, and they contrast this "yeast-like" advance to the "mushroom-like" nature of productivity growth in the 1970s, 1980s, and 1990s, when productivity growth was much faster in some industries, particularly in the manufacture of computers and semiconductors, than in others – e.g. most industries in non-durable manufacturing such as leather, tobacco, textiles, and apparel.

8.3.2 Qualifications

Two aspects of the analysis by David and Wright (2003) require qualification, particularly in looking for the sources of the investment boom of the 1920s and its subsequent collapse. First, in their attention to the electrification of manufacturing, they fail to pay sufficient attention to the effects of the other great GPT of the late nineteenth century, the internal combustion engine, in generating investment in the 1920s. In part, the role of the ICE comes through a revolution in manufacturing technique parallel in importance to the individual-drive electric motor, namely Henry Ford's 1914 invention of the assembly line.[7] Part of the productivity revolution in manufacturing in the 1920s came from the direct effect of all the new factories and equipment needed to boost motor vehicle production from 1.9 million in 1919 to 5.6 million in 1929.[8] Yet much of the influence of the ICE was outside manufacturing, with mobility made possible by the automobile and motor truck creating whole new areas ripe for residential investment, and creating new opportunities to construct facilities for wholesale and retail trade. Clearly, the data of table 8.1 indicate that productivity growth in the 1920s was less impressive outside manufacturing than inside that sector, but here we are interested not just in the role of the GPT innovations as a source of productivity growth but also as a source of investment opportunities that fueled the investment boom of the 1920s.

The David–Wright analysis, while lacking sufficient emphasis on the role of the ICE, joins together with electricity a second major source of the productivity acceleration of the 1920s, namely the "sharp increase in the relative price of labor" (David and Wright, 2003, p. 142). The previous literature had not placed any significant emphasis on labor markets in facilitating the productivity acceleration or investment boom of the 1920s. Credit must be given to the research of Goldin and Katz (1998) emphasizing the uniquely American development of secondary education, which spread high school diplomas to most of the population during the period between 1910 and 1940, and this must have had a pay-off in productivity growth in the decades after the First World War.

Otherwise, however, the David–Wright position does not accord with the facts. If there had been a significant upward shift in the relative price of labor that was not justified by the acceleration in productivity growth then, by definition, labor's share of national income would have increased significantly. But, as shown in table 8.1, over the 1919–1929 period employee compensation rose only 0.3 percent per year more rapidly than national income – almost the same as the 0.2 percent annual surplus registered in the 1990s. Doubt must be registered about the factual accuracy of David and Wright's claim (p. 142) that "the [real] hourly wage of industrial labor was 50 to 70 percent higher after 1920 than it had been a decade earlier." Kendrick (1961, table 26, p. 114) shows that the real price of labor per unit of labor (i.e. the real wage) increased by only 1.4 percent per year during 1919–1929 – significantly slower than the rate of 2.1 percent registered between 1899 and 1919.

8.4 Investment in the 1920s: boom and collapse

The Keynesian tradition of business cycle theory associated with Samuelson (1939), Hicks (1950), and many others identifies fluctuations in fixed investment, and to a lesser extent consumer durables, as the primary impulse that drives the business cycle and makes repeated but non-periodic fluctuations inevitable. In Samuelson's mathematically driven version (1939), the economy is condemned to explosive or damped cycles unless parameters are at precise knife-edge values, leading postwar business cycle theorists to deduce that the absence of damped or explosive cycles must imply a contribution of irregular shocks outside the model. In Hicks's (1950) version the evolution of output is constrained by a capacity ceiling and floor based on the eventual need to replace depreciating capital. Both these models lack a government or foreign sector, nor do they allow for any role of monetary or fiscal policy.

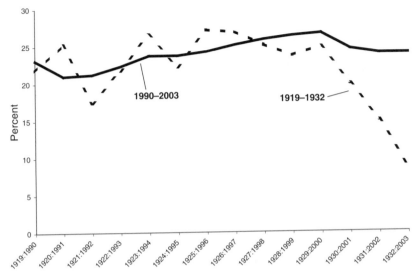

Figure 8.6 The share in real US GDP of consumer durables plus total investment,
1919:1990 to 1932:2003 alignment

8.4.1 Investment in the 1920s and in the 1990s

This traditional Keynesian view traces the magnitude of the Great Depression
back to the investment boom of the 1920s. One way to assess the significance of the investment boom is to compare the 1920s with the 1990s, when
in the last part of each decade there was a notable and unsustainable expansion
of investment in producers' equipment and software. Our first comparison in
figure 8.6 shows the share in real GDP of spending on consumer durables plus
all investment, including the change in inventories. The shares in GDP are
remarkably similar, peaking for the 1920s in 1925 with a GDP share of 27.1
percent and peaking for the 1990s in 2000 with a share of 26.3 percent. The
share in 1926 is almost the same as in 1925, and in 1999 almost the same as in
2000.

The yearly pattern is quite different, however. The investment share rose
slowly and steadily throughout the 1990s, whereas in the 1920s the share was
quite volatile and peaked four years before the end of the expansion. The shrinkage in the share from 27.1 percent in 1925 to 24.8 percent in 1929 suggests in
the context of the multiplier–accelerator model, that weakness in fixed investment was already exerting downward pressure on aggregate demand in 1929,
temporarily masked by strength in consumption and inventory change. The
behavior of the investment/GDP ratio was totally different after the peak of

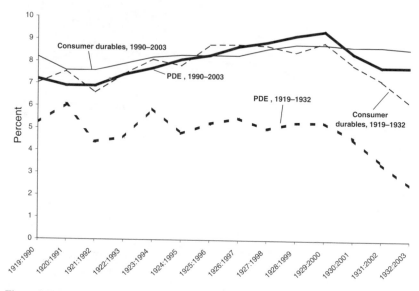

Figure 8.7 The shares in real US GDP of producer durable equipment and consumer durables, 1919:1990 to 1932:2003 alignment

the expansion, declining only from 26.3 percent in 2000 to 23.9 percent in 2003, but from 24.8 in 1929 to a historically unprecedented 8.4 percent in 1932.

The next three figures exhibit the decomposition of consumer durable spending and total investment into five components. Shown in figure 8.7 are the ratios for producer durable equipment (PDE – including software in the 1990s) and consumer durables. Surprisingly, the equipment boom of the 1920s is a pipsqueak, with a PDE share of about 5 percent, compared to the 1990s when the share of PDE (including software) climbed from about 7 percent in 1990 to about 9 percent in 2000. A second surprise is that, despite all the consumer durables for sale in the 1990s that had not yet been invented in the 1920s, the share of consumer durable spending in the two decades is remarkably similar, tracking along in the 8 to 9 percent range during 1923–1929 and 1994–2000. The sharp collapse after 1929 contrasts sharply with 2000–2003, when monetary ease buoyed sales of automobiles and other consumer durables.

A further surprise is contained in figure 8.8, which shows that residential structures investment was not particularly high in the 1920s, with a peak ratio to GDP of 4.8 percent in 1928, very close to the 1999 level of 4.6 percent. Previous discussions implying an unusually high residential investment ratio in

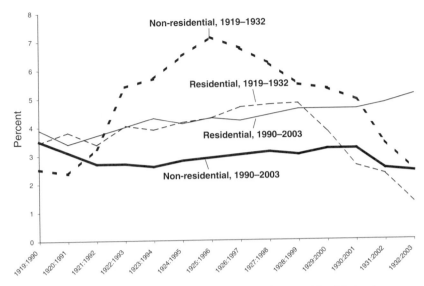

Figure 8.8 The shares in real US GDP of residential and non-residential structures investment, 1919:1990 to 1932:2003 alignment

the mid-1920s are simply incorrect, and are doubtless influenced by base-year-relative price bias implied when residential construction in the 1920s is restated at the high relative prices of the 1970s or 1980s.[9] If anything in the 1920s was excessive, it was not residential investment but non-residential investment, with a peak ratio of 7.1 percent in 1925, drifting down to 5.5 percent in 1929, and then collapsing to 2.4 percent in 1932. In the more recent decade the same ratio was 3.5 percent in 1990 and 3.2 percent in 2000. Taken together, the total share of residential and non-residential structures investment peaked at 11.4 percent in 1926, and by 1929 had already declined to 9.1 percent, before collapsing to 3.7 percent in 1932.

Perhaps the greatest difference between the 1920s and 1990s is to be found in the time path of inventory investment, small and steady as a ratio to GDP in the 1990s, as shown in figure 8.9, but large and volatile in the 1920s, with GDP ratios ranging between +5.5 percent in 1920 and −1.0 percent in 1924. Inventory investment contributed significantly to the Great Contraction, with a collapse in the GDP ratio from +1.5 percent in 1929 to −4.0 percent in 1932. The behavior of inventory investment in the 1990s could not have been more different, with a range during the 1990s only between 0.0 percent in 1991 and a maximum of 0.9 percent in 1994 and 1997, and with a decline in the recession year 2001 only to −0.4 percent.

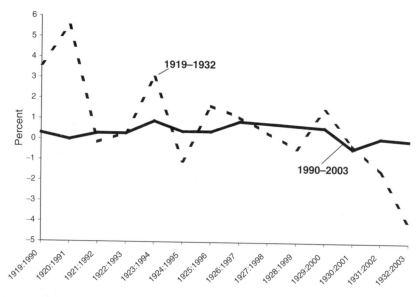

Figure 8.9 The share in real US GDP of inventory change, 1919:1990 to 1932:2003 alignment

8.4.2 The interpretation of investment behavior in the 1920s

One reaction to the display of the investment ratios in figures 6–9 might be "so what?" The share of all components of spending must sum to 100 percent, so why does it matter whether the investment ratio rises or falls? The significance of the ratio requires a Keynesian (or IS-LM) interpretation in which economic fluctuations are driven by shifts in "autonomous spending," whether investment, government spending, exports, or the autonomous component of consumption. The rest of spending, the consumption of non-durables and services, is passive, responding through the consumption function and the multiplier to the autonomous demand shifts. This framework is entirely compatible with a parallel emphasis on the role of monetary and fiscal policy. Monetary policy enters as a driver of consumer durables and investment spending, while fiscal policy enters as a source of autonomous spending shifts, and through the effect of tax changes in shifting the consumption function.

Why was there an investment boom in the 1920s, and which factors apply to the 1990s as well? Gordon (1974, p. 27) lists seven factors that caused the high level of investment in the 1920s: (1) "pent-up demand" created by the diversion of resources to military spending during the First World War; (2) direct and indirect effects of the automobile; (3) demands related to other new industries, including electric power, electrical equipment, radio, telephone, air transport, motion pictures, and rayon; (4) the rapid pace of technological change and resulting rise in productivity; (5) the rise to the peak in a long building cycle; (6) a "wave of optimism"; and (7) elastic credit supply. Factors (3) and (4) are compatible with the David–Wright (2003) emphasis on electricity and the productivity acceleration, while factor (2) is consistent with our emphasis above on the ICE as an additional GPT in addition to electricity.

The traditional literature on investment in the 1920s (Gordon, 1951; Hickman, 1974) emphasizes factor (5), the "overbuilding" in residential construction, which was in part due to the failure of market participants to work out the implications of slower future population growth implied by restrictive immigration legislation of the early 1920s. Hickman (1974) uses a dynamic simulation to conclude that, sheerly on the basis of an autonomous demographic shift, housing starts would have declined from 1925 to 1930, even with no decline in income, by 49 percent.[10] Nevertheless, in the context of figure 8.8, this earlier literature appears to overemphasize residential investment and underemphasize the larger rise in, and subsequent collapse of, non-residential investment in structures.

Most of the factors on the R. A. Gordon list of seven can also be applied to the investment boom of the 1990s, except for the first: pent-up demand caused by a previous war. The invention of the internet, web, and mobile telephone, and the spread of personal computers, were the GPTs that drove the investment boom, especially during 1996–2000. A "wave of optimism" repeated the timing of the 1920s stock market bubble with a nearly perfect repetition of timing and magnitude, and credit was even easier, in the sense that growth in the money supply did not repeat in 1999–2000 the deceleration of 1927–1929.

A more sophisticated analysis of total investment in the 1920s, combining both residential and non-residential structures, is provided by Gordon and Veitch (1986, pp. 316–17). They create a unique database, consisting of quarterly data for the components of GDP covering the interwar period (1919–1941), and analyze these data using a VAR model containing structures investment, equipment investment, non-investment GDP (of which 85 percent is consumption), the real monetary base, the money multiplier, and the corporate bond rate. They carry out exogeneity tests showing that structures investment is largely exogenous, with modest feedback from non-investment GDP. There is significant feedback from the monetary variables to both equipment investment and non-investment GDP. There is strong feedback from the spending variables to the monetary variables, while the interest rate is largely exogenous. They conclude that there were two impulse sources in the interwar business cycle, one "financial," working through the interest rate and money multiplier, and another "real," working mainly through investment in structures. Innovation accounting with the same VAR model supports the view that "structures appear to be virtually autonomous" (Gordon and Veitch, 1986, p. 315). In their words, concerning the behavior of structures investment (pp. 316–17):

There is a high plateau in the own innovations series in 1926–27, a gradual downward movement in 1928–29, and a sharp plunge beginning in 1929:3, before the fourth-quarter stock market debacle. Equally interesting is that the own innovation series remains negative throughout 1931–41, supporting the interpretation of "overbuilding" in the 1920s that required a long period of subsequent adjustment in the 1930s.

The parallel VAR analysis of equipment investment in the interwar period reveals a much smaller autonomous own-innovation for equipment investment than for structures, and much more of a role for feedback from both non-investment GDP and the monetary base. The VAR analysis allows an examination of the residuals from these equations, which are the "own-innovations" in each variable. There were large negative innovations in structures investment in 1929:3 and 1929:4, in equipment investment in 1929:4, and in the monetary base in 1929:1. Large negative innovations also occurred in non-investment GDP in 1931:3 and in the money multiplier in 1931:2, 1931:3, and 1931:4. Using these results, Gordon and Veitch reassessed Temin's (1976) well-known anti-monetarist position based on an autonomous downward shift in the consumption function in 1930. Their results appear to contradict the Temin hypothesis, and they state that "we find no evidence that negative residuals for nondurables consumption played a key role in the initial stages of the Great Contraction" (Gordon and Veitch, 1986, pp. 321–2). Their VAR model shows that the cumulative residuals (i.e. the "own-shock") to non-investment GDP, which is almost entirely consumption, in 1929–1930 amounted to only −1.6 percent of its level in mid-1929. In contrast, the cumulative quarterly residuals for structures investment cumulated in 1929–1930 to −25.2 percent and for equipment investment to −17.2 percent of their 1929 levels.

While the Gordon and Veitch residuals cumulated for 1929–1930 are not large, their own results contain support for Temin in a pattern that they did not apparently notice. Their results for non-durable consumption exhibit a sharp shift from a cumulative residual of +3.4 percent in the first three quarters of 1929 to a cumulative −4.5 percent in the subsequent five quarters (Gordon and Veitch, 1986, table 5.9, p. 321). Thus they are correct that the primary deflationary demand impulse prior to the stock market crash was in investment, not consumption; however, their results are also consistent with Temin's emphasis on an autonomous downward shift in consumption beginning with the market crash and continuing through the end of 1930. Their results also support the monetarist position, in that the cumulative own-residual for the monetary base in 1929–1930 was −20.5 percent of the 1929 value. Thus there appears to be a great deal of support, using modern econometrics, that the key downward demand shocks prior to the crash were to fixed investment and the real monetary base, but that consumption contributed significantly to the propagation of the contraction in 1930 and the money multiplier contributed in 1931–1932.

8.5 Domestic and international monetary policy

The analysis of Friedman and Schwartz (1963) is so well known, and the critique of the FS analysis has also been so often discussed (Temin, 1976), that only a few brief comments are required here. The role of money can be divided into three intervals: 1927–1929, 1929–1931, and 1931–1933. Regarding 1927–1929, a consensus has emerged that "increasingly stringent U.S. monetary policy contributed significantly to the onset of the slump" (Eichengreen, 1992b, p. 221). The annual growth rates of both M1 and M2 slowed sharply from 1925 to 1927, and in the case of M1 were negative in both 1927 and 1928 before turning slightly positive in 1929. Interest rates increased, although only modestly by the standards of postwar monetary tightening. Gordon and Wilcox (1981, p. 66) use quarterly data to compute that the growth rate of M2 slowed from 5.2 percent at an annual rate in the five quarters ending in 1927:4 to only 0.6 percent in the seven quarters beginning in 1928:1. After remaining at 4 percent or below from mid-1924 to January 1928 the Fed's rediscount rate was raised in several steps from 3.5 percent in that month to 5 percent in July 1928, and then, with one final increase, to 6 percent in August 1929.[11]

Tightening by the Fed helped to create the Great Depression, because of the role of US foreign lending in recycling European balance of payments deficits, and because the return of the gold standard forced countries to respond to a loss of gold by domestic monetary tightening. The Fed's tightening in the United States coincided with a stabilization of the French franc. As described by Eichengreen (1992b, p. 221):

As the U.S. and France siphoned off gold and financial capital from the rest of the world, foreign central banks were forced to raise their discount rates and to restrict the provision of domestic credit in order to defend their gold parities. Superimposed upon already weak foreign balances of payments, these shifts in U.S. and French policy provoked a greatly magnified shift in monetary policy in other countries.

Eichengreen quantifies the restrictive impulse, showing that the annual growth rate of monetary aggregates in Europe and Latin America fell in 1927/28 by five percentage points and by an additional five percentage points in 1928/29.

After the 1929 stock market crash there was a two-way transmission of negative demand shocks between the United States and other countries. The restrictive foreign monetary policies that had been partly caused by the Fed's actions reduced US exports.[12] The stock market crash itself depressed consumption, as emphasized by Temin (1976) and supported by the results of Gordon and Veitch. Beginning in 1930 bank failures became a separate source of deflationary pressure, and their effect worsened after the United Kingdom left the gold standard and devalued the pound in September 1931.

The 1970s and early 1980s were characterized by a debate involving Temin, Schwartz, Darby, and others about the causes of the Great Contraction, as to whether "only money mattered" or "money didn't matter at all." The anti-monetarist camp, led by Temin, focused largely on the behavior of consumption and, strangely, neglected the more important autonomous influence coming from fixed investment. But statistical results, including those of Gordon and Veitch discussed above and related work by Gordon and Wilcox (1981), support a role for both autonomous demand shocks and feedback from restrictive monetary policy. Gordon and Wilcox conclude (1989, pp. 67, 74):

Though monetary growth decelerated in 1928 and 1929, such a monetary slowdown had happened before and can only account for 18 percent of the observed decline in nominal income in the first year of the contraction and 26 percent cumulatively in the first two years. . . [B]oth monetary and nonmonetary factors mattered. . . nonmonetary factors were of prime importance in 1929–31. . . different monetary policies in the United States after 1931 would have reduced the severity of the contraction.

Their comment about 1931–1933 is supported by a comparison of the behavior of M2 and nominal GDP in the United States with an aggregate of seven major Western European nations. Both M2 and nominal GDP began to rise after 1931 in Europe, whereas both continued to decline through 1933 in the United States.

8.6 Other similarities and differences between the 1920s and 1990s

8.6.1 Financial speculation and accounting fraud

The 1920s and 1990s were uncannily similar not only in the magnitude and timing of the stock market boom and collapse in both decades but also in the fragility of the financial system. The stock market boom was sustained in 1999 and 2000 by an overstatement of corporate profits, subsequently revealed to involve corruption, cheating, and accounting scandals that brought familiar televised scenes of corporate executives in handcuffs and the collapse of one of the United States' "'big five'" auditing firms. A wave of mergers, acquisitions, initial public offerings, and venture capital investments was part of the speculative froth of financial markets in the late 1990s, followed by the bankruptcy of many of the new "dot-coms" and equity price declines of 90 percent or more for the hi-tech corporations that succeeded in avoiding bankruptcy.

Similarly, a major part of the new equity issues in the late 1920s rested on a fragile base. "The major part, particularly from 1926 on, seems to have gone into erecting a financial superstructure of holding companies, investment trusts, and other forms of inter-corporate security holdings that was to come crashing down in the 1930s" (Gordon, 1974, p. 35).[13] Also similar in the 1920s and 1990s were large profits by investment bankers and a stimulus to consumer demand coming from capital gains on equities. Equity speculation, as in the 1990s, led to overinvestment in some types of equipment and structures in the 1920s, just as the 1990s witnessed a glut of investment in fiber optic cable, other telephone equipment, and dot-com software. The glut of investment goods created during the 1920s were to "hang over the market" for the entire decade of the 1930s.

The evolution of the economy after 2000 was, of course, entirely different from that after 1929, and previously we have attributed this to the aggressive easing of monetary policy, which sustained a major boom in residential construction and in sales of consumer durables sufficient largely to offset the decline of investment in equipment and software. A second difference was the aggressive easing of fiscal policy in 2001–2003 through a succession of reductions in federal income tax rates, including the tax rates on capital gains and dividends. A third major difference was that equities could be margined up to 90 percent in the late 1920s, compared to 50 percent in the 1990s, raising both the level of speculative frenzy in 1927–1929 and the extent of wealth destruction when the crash finally came.

An aspect of the 1920s that has no counterpart in the 1990s is the weakness of the banking system, due in part to regulations that prevented banks in many states (such as Illinois) from establishing branches. In 1924 only eleven states allowed statewide branching (White, 2000, p. 749). Regulations set the stage for the banking collapse of 1930–1931, as the prohibition on branch banking created a system of thousands of individual banks with a fragile dependence on the ups or downs of economic conditions in their local community, often tied to particular forms of agriculture (White, 2000, p. 750).

Two other institutional aspects of the 1920s also differed from the 1990s. One glaring difference is the absence of deposit insurance. When the banks failed, beginning in 1930, the lifetime savings of many American households evaporated, aggravating the decline in aggregate demand. Second, the stock market boom and collapse was exacerbated by loose margin requirements that allowed investors to borrow 90 percent of the value of stocks, in contrast to the 50 percent rule in effect during the 1990s.

8.6.2 Weakness in agriculture

One aspect of the 1920s emphasized by previous authors is the overexpansion of agriculture during the boom days of 1919–1920, when agricultural exports to destitute Europe exploded, only to be followed by a collapse of agricultural incomes and prices after European agricultural capacity recovered (see Gordon, 1974, pp. 36–7). Weakness in agricultural prices helped to keep overall inflation low, in an era in which agriculture was a much larger share of output and employment than in the 1990s. Thus, the boom of the 1920s was largely an urban phenomenon, and the weakness of agricultural prices and incomes lay the seeds for the role of the farm sector in the post-1929 collapse, exacerbated by the worldwide decline in commodity prices.

Both R. A. Gordon and Olmstead and Rhode (2000, fig. 12.1, p. 701) emphasize the fact that agricultural productivity stagnated in the 1920s and took off after the mid-1930s as the full mechanical revolution made possible by the tractor took place. Olmstead and Rhode point to the rapid penetration of motor vehicles on the American farm by 1929 (with a 1919–1929 increase from 48 to 78 percent; fig. 12.3, p. 712) but the much slower diffusion of electricity into rural America. This reinforces our point made above, that David and Wright (2003) overstate the importance of electricity relative to the internal combustion engine in the productivity achievement of the United States in the 1920s.

8.6.3 Wage flexibility and the Phillips curve in the 1920s and 1990s

One of the most intriguing similarities between the 1920s and 1990s is the coincidence of relatively low unemployment in both decades with low inflation in the 1990s and zero inflation in the 1920s. The reasons for low inflation in the 1990s are well understood. A large literature, beginning with Staiger, Stock, and Watson (1997) and Gordon (1997), identify a decline in the natural rate of unemployment, or non-accelerating inflation rate of unemployment. This decline, which allows the inflation rate to be stable at a lower rate of unemployment, has been attributed to a demographic shift away from teenagers (who naturally tend to have higher unemployment rates), an improvement in the micro-efficiency of labor markets made possible by temporary help agencies, and even the rise in the fraction of young adults incarcerated in prisons, some of whom would otherwise have been unemployed.

Beyond the decline in the NAIRU between 1985 and the late 1990s, Gordon (1998) has drawn attention to supply shocks as explaining both the high inflation in the 1970s and the low inflation in the late 1990s. In both decades movements in exchange rates and import prices pushed inflation up (1970s) or down (1990s). In both decades productivity growth was a key explanatory factor, with the productivity growth slowdown of the 1970s pushing inflation up and the productivity growth revival of the 1990s pushing inflation down. Inflation was also held down in the late 1990s by a more rapid rate of decline in the prices of computers and by a temporary hiatus in medical care deflation.

Inflation in the 1920s is more of a puzzle, because the overall price level was so volatile in 1916–1922 and so stable during 1922–1929. Gordon (1982) interprets rapid price adjustment in 1916–1922 as an "aberration, reflecting the ability of economic agents to change their price-setting practices when they are universally aware of a special event (wartime government purchases and deficit spending) that has a common effect on costs and prices." He interprets the post-1922 behavior as a "return to normal" in which firms focused on microeconomic "industry-specific" disturbances to costs and prices that were now large relative to any remaining macroeconomic disturbance.

It is still unclear from recent research how much the experience of the 1920s differed from that prior to 1914. Eichengreen (1992b, p. 217) and David and Wright (2003, pp. 154–5) emphasize the shift in the nature of US labor markets from flexible casual labor markets to those dominated by implicit contracts and a trade-off between wages and skills. With the rise of high school educational attainment (discussed above), firms now valued their most highly skilled workers and were willing to pay them extra. In this era were planted the seeds of the subsequent efficiency–wage model and also the seeds of nominal wage rigidity.

It is unclear how much the 1920s represented a new era in labor management relations, and to what extent the stability of wages and prices represented a return to norms that prevailed before 1914.

Overall, the low rate of inflation in the 1920s combined the weakness of farm prices, the absence of labor unions, and the direct role of the acceleration of productivity growth in holding down inflation. Our explanation of low inflation in the 1990s shares the element of an acceleration of productivity growth, and the declining importance of labor unions in the 1990s echoes the near-absence of unions in the 1920s.

8.6.4 The income distribution

To insert any discussion about the income distribution in a study of the macroeconomics of the 1920s and 1990s may seem arcane. But there is an old literature that, looking for "rotten" aspects of the 1920s, found an inadequacy of real income among the masses to be a source of subsequent "underconsumption."[14] We have already examined evidence in table 8.1 above regarding the evolution of labor's share in national income and have found that the growth in employee compensation during the 1920s was roughly the same as that of national income.

But the functional distribution of income between labor and capital is not the only dimension of the income distribution. The other dimension is vertical inequality, as measured by the Gini coefficient. Here the economic history literature seems to have developed a conflict regarding the 1920s versus the 1990s. As told by the team of Plotnick, Smolensky, Evenhouse, and Reilly

(2000), the Gini coefficient collapsed during the Second World War and never recovered to anything remotely like its value of 1929 (fig. 4.2, p. 253). But a more recent, and perhaps more careful, study by Piketty and Saez (2003) provides convincing evidence that the postwar increase in inequality that began in the early 1970s had, by the mid to late 1990s, caused every measure of inequality to soar far beyond 1929 values. The key table of results by these authors exhibits an income share of the top 5 percent of the population of 23.68 percent in 1998, compared to 19.76 percent in 1929 (Piketty and Saez, table IV, pp. 26–7). At the very top the contrast is even greater, with an income share of the top 0.1 percent of 4.13 percent in 1998 compared to a share of 2.56 percent in 1929.

Why does the income distribution matter? The initial Keynesian idea was that a highly unequal income distribution would put more income in the hands of the very rich, who had a low marginal propensity to consume, and this would lead to underconsumption – i.e. less consumption than otherwise would be the case with the same aggregate income and a more equal distribution of income. But the fact that the distribution of income in the late 1990s was substantially more unequal than in the late 1920s casts aside the income distribution as one more failed hypothesis to explain why the Great Depression was so sharp and so prolonged. The true significance of the twentieth century's changes in the distribution of income lies elsewhere: not in the topic of aggregate demand and business cycles, but in the time sequence of productivity growth in the twentieth century. The U-shaped evolution of the income distribution, with inequality high before 1929 and in the late 1990s, is a symptom of a set of causal factors that also mattered for productivity growth. Three developments starting in the early 1920s served to make unskilled labor more expensive, deliver a "rent" to high school drop-outs and graduates alike, and create a strong incentive to substitute capital for labor. These three were the New Deal legislation that legitimized labor unions in the mid-1930s, the legislation beginning in the early 1920s that limited immigration (together with the Great Depression and the war, which virtually eliminated immigration), and the movement to high tariffs (Fordney–McCumber in 1922 and Smoot–Hawley in 1930) that, together again with Depression and war, reduced imports to a historical low in relation to GDP. Supported by unions, and freed from competition from unskilled immigrants and foreign unskilled labor embodied in imported goods, American unskilled labor did exceptionally well from the mid-1930s to the late 1960s, and this comes out as a sharp reduction in inequality between 1929 and 1945, followed by a plateau of low inequality and then a steady rise in inequality after 1970, climaxing in the late 1990s. Income inequality is a symptom of other labor market developments, not a cause. Income inequality was a symptom of the rents earned by low-skilled workers in what has been called "the great compression" of the income distribution (Goldin and Margo, 1992).

8.7 Conclusions

This chapter has developed an analysis of the US economy in the 1920s, newly illuminated by the perspective of the economy of the 1990s. The centerpiece of our analysis has been to integrate the previously unconnected contributions of David (1991) and David and Wright (2003), on the productivity growth acceleration of the 1920s, with an earlier business cycle literature associated with Schumpeter (1939), Samuelson (1939), and R. A. Gordon (1951, 1974), which emphasizes the role of overinvestment in the 1920s as setting the stage for the post-1929 collapse.

David (1991) creatively linked the disappointing productivity pay-off from the computer to the earlier history of electric motors and electricity generation. He found good reasons why roughly forty years elapsed between the initial electric power station in 1882 and the explosion of productivity growth in US manufacturing in the 1920s, and reasoned that a similar delay, for similar reasons, could be postponing the productivity pay-off from the electronic computer in the 1970s and 1980s. Anyone who forecasts a phenomenon years before its appearance deserves high praise, and David's predicted productivity resurgence in manufacturing and the broader economy occurred in the decade after 1995.

The electricity–computer analogy developed by David (1991), and taken further by David and Wright (2003), sets the stage for the integration carried out in this chapter. In both the 1920s and the 1990s the acceleration of productivity growth linked to the delayed effects of previously invented "general-purpose technologies" stimulated an increase in fixed investment that, in both decades, became excessive and proved to be unsustainable. The 1990s remind us that, even with better institutions, better information, and better policies, it is possible for "overinvestment" to occur. In 2000–2001 everything collapsed, including hi-tech investment and the prices of hi-tech stocks, and many of the "new economy" dot-com start-ups failed. The uncanny parallel of the stock market boom, bubble, and collapse in 1995–2001 to that in 1924–1930, with the side-by-side tale of emotional speculation, overheated activity by investment bankers, and a parallel tale of pyramid building (in the 1920s) and accounting fraud (in the late 1990s), reminds us that business cycles emerge from the complex interplay of multiple factors, not just one. They are not just about monetary and fiscal policy, but about powerful economic forces against which monetary and fiscal policy can react or fail to react. Monetary policy responded in 2001–2002 with a rapid decline in interest rates, and fiscal policy responded with significant reductions in income tax rates. Monetary policy failed to react in 1929–1933 by allowing banks to fail and the money supply to decline, and a perverse fiscal policy actually increased tax rates in 1932.

This chapter integrates a previous literature claiming that one single factor or another was "the primary cause" of the Great Depression. Econometric time-series analysis based on quarterly data for the interwar period demonstrates that in 1928–1929 the economy was exposed to two major demand shocks, not just one. Negative shocks to investment demand occurred prior to the 1929 stock market crash, and these combined with the negative demand impulse of tighter monetary policy. These two negative shocks were joined after the crash by a significant negative shock to consumption relative to income that persisted through the end of 1930.

Going beyond the parallels between the 1920s and 1990s involving a productivity growth acceleration and the accompanying booms of investment and the stock market, the chapter uncovers other similarities – but also differences. The productivity growth accelerations of the 1920s and 1990s both contributed to the explanation as to why inflation was so low in both decades. An additional explanation for the low inflation is provided by the absence of unions in the 1920s and their eroding presence in the 1990s. The accounting scandals and froth of financial speculation of the late 1990s contributed to financial fragility in a new but similar form to the financial superstructure of inter-corporate security holdings that developed in the late 1920s, and came crashing down thereafter.

But the differences between the 1920s and 1990s also stand out, and these go beyond the differing responses of monetary and fiscal policy to the collapse of investment and the stock market. An important difference was the much larger share of agricultural output and employment in the economy of the 1920s and the weakness of farm prices and incomes throughout most of that decade. In this sense, the boom of the 1920s was largely an urban phenomenon that did not extend across the entire economy, and the post-1929 collapse in commodity prices rippled through the farm sector and created an additional component to the pervasive downward shift in aggregate demand. Another, partly related difference was the higher volatility of macroeconomic indicators in the 1920s, particularly the sharp swings of inventory investment evident in figure 8.9 above. This difference in inventory behavior reflected the larger share of agriculture and manufacturing in the economy of the 1920s and the much lower share of services, and in addition the much more primitive methods of inventory management in the 1920s in contrast to the information age of the 1990s.

Another set of important differences concerns public policy. Financial fragility in the 1920s can be traced in part to three policy-related aspects of the 1990s absent in the 1920s, namely the absence of deposit insurance, the unit-banking regulations in numerous states that prevented the diversification of financial risk across regions, and the stock market margin requirements that allowed speculators in 1928–1929 to borrow fully 90 percent of the value of their equity purchases.

While these three aspects of financial fragility were not innovations of the 1920s and had long characterized the US financial system, there were policy initiatives in the 1920s that undermined the health of the world economy. The 1920s witnessed the advent of protectionism, starting with the Fordney–McCumber tariff of 1922, subsequently to be replaced by the infamous Smoot–Hawley tariff of 1930. This regime of high tariffs contributed to the downward spiral in world trade after 1929. Perhaps as important was the sharp curtailment of immigration initiated by the Immigration Acts of 1921 and 1924, which imposed a corset of nationality quotas. The immigration measures contributed to a sharp decline in the rate of population growth from 21 percent in the decade 1900–1910 to only 7 percent in the decade 1930–1940, thus reducing the demand for housing. In contrast, immigration continued its rapid postwar growth in the 1990s, fueled by a liberal set of laws that allowed the almost unlimited legal immigration of family members, together with ineffective border enforcement that allowed millions of illegal immigrants to join the labor force.

The stability of the American economy after the 2000–2001 collapse of investment and the stock market proves that good public policy matters. And these policies go beyond the narrowly defined operations of monetary and fiscal policy. Such highly diverse policies as banking regulation, deposit insurance, margin rules, tariff reduction, and loose restrictions on immigration all combine to make today's US economy more stable and less fragile than in the 1920s. The successes of 2000–2005 help illuminate the failures of 1929–1933, especially in light of the many similarities between the decades of the 1920s and 1990s.

Appendix: Data

All the data for the 1990s were obtained from the US Council of Economic Advisors (2003), the US Department of Commerce (various dates), Gordon (2003b), and the websites of the Bureau of Labor Statistics (www.bls.gov) and the Bureau of Economic Analysis (www.bea.gov). These data were current as of 12 March 2004 and were retrieved for the period 1984 to 2003.

The BLS data are identified by their BLS series identifier.

Consumer price index, CUUR0000SA0.

For the non-farm private business sector:

Output, PRS85006043;

Aggregate hours, PRS85006033;

Productivity, PRS85006093.

All data obtained from the BEA website came from the National Income and Product Accounts (NIPA). National income data came from table 1.7.5, and data on dividends and interest came from table 1.14.

The *Economic Report of the President* was the source for data on employee compensation (table B-14), proprietor's income and rent (both table B-28), employment, labor force, and population (all from the household survey, table B-35), the treasury bill discount rate (table B-73), and the level of the Standard and Poor's (S&P) 500 index of stocks (table B-95). Nominal and real GDP, the GDP deflator, and money supply (M2) were obtained from Gordon (2003b). The *Statistical Abstracts* were the source for electricity output (table T1065), the fraction of people with access to a computer at home or at work (tables T657 and T1197), and the fraction of people with internet access at home or at work (table T1134). Data for electricity output for 1990 and the 1920s came from Datapedia (series Q152) and for 2000 came from the 2002 *Statistical Abstract* (series T1065).

Data for the 1920s were obtained from the *Macrohistory Database* of the National Bureau of Economic Research (www.nber.org), *Productivity Trends in the United States* (Kendrick, 1961), the Long-Term Exchange Group (LTEG), and Datapedia. These data were retrieved for the period 1913 to 1932. Where possible, the data were "ratio-linked" to the modern data. Given an overlapping year, generally 1929, the data for the 1910s and 1920s were multiplied by the ratio of the modern series to the historical series.

Data from the NBER database are identified by their series number. All data that were in quarterly or monthly form were interpolated to annual averages.

National income, a08167;

Employee compensation, a08181;

Rent, a08184;

Dividends, a08185;

Interest, a08186.

Data from Kendrick (1961) include output, hours, and productivity (table A-XXII), and hours per employee (table A-IX). LTEG was the source for household employment (series A78), the unemployment rate (series B1), the labor force participation rate (series B9), the treasury bill discount rate (series B82), and the level of the S&P 500 (series B84) The number of motor vehicle registrations and electricity output was obtained from Datapedia (series Q152 and S32, respectively).

The expenditure shares for the period 1929–2003 in figures 8.6–8.9 were obtained from the BEA website, series 1.10. Series for the 1920s were constructed initially by linking consumption, investment, government spending, and net exports from Kendrick (1961, table AIIa) to the current BEA chain-weighted numbers, which places all the ratios for the 1920s on the basis of 1929 price weights. Then the subcomponents of consumption and investment were obtained from Balke and Gordon (1986), which in turn developed these measures from the sources cited there.

Notes

This research has been supported by the National Science Foundation. I am grateful to Ian Dew-Becker for excellent research assistance, to conference participants

Barry Eichengreen and, especially, Paul David for thoughtful comments on the conference draft of this chapter, and to my late father R. A. Gordon for asking tantalizing questions about the 1920s that, to this date, have not been satisfactorily resolved.

1. This epigraph is my way of describing the Great Depression in language modeled on Keegan's (1989, p. 5) description of the Second World War as the "greatest event in human history."
2. "Standard" discussions of the causes of the Great Depression include, among many, Eichengreen (1992b, 2000), Friedman and Schwartz (1963), and Temin (1976, 2000). Non-standard sources revived here include R. A. Gordon (1951, 1961, 1974), Gordon and Wilcox (1981), and Gordon and Veitch (1986).
3. The David and Wright (2003, pp. 141, 145) version recognizes the Henry Ford assembly line innovation and treats it as complementary to the electrification of manufacturing, and also related to the change in labor market relations. These topics are treated further below.
4. To calculate the real interest rate, I use the realized zero inflation rate of the 1920s for both 1919 and 1929, the realized 1985–1990 3.2 percent average annual rate of increase in the GDP deflator for 1990, and the realized 1995–2000 increase of 1.7 percent for 2000.
5. Also, since a much larger share of the population was involved in the agricultural sector in the 1920s than the 1990s, the unemployment statistics based on the non-agricultural sector bias downwards the volatility of unemployment for the total economy in the 1920s compared to the 1990s.
6. A systematic feature of economic growth in the twentieth century was a steady rise in the ratio of the equipment capital stock to the structures capital stock; see Gordon (2000a, fig. 2), where this is attributed to "space-saving innovation."
7. David and Wright (2003, p. 145) treat the invention of the assembly line as one of three complementary counterparts of electrification, but they make no comment on the role of the ICE in changing the location of economic activity, with the consequent implications for both productivity growth and investment opportunities in the 1920s.
8. Production figures come from Gordon (1974, p. 28). See also US Bureau of the Census (1975, series Q310 and Q312). The ability of the American economy to produce 5.6 million internal combustion engines in 1929, about 80 percent of the world total, provides a central clue to the production miracle of the United States' Second World War "arsenal of democracy."
9. I confess guilt in this regard, as the author of a remark that I have often repeated: "In four successive years (1924–27) the ratio of real residential construction to real GNP reached by far its highest level of the twentieth century" (Gordon and Wilcox, 1981, p. 78).
10. See Hickman (1974, table 3, p. 307) and Gordon and Wilcox (1981, footnote 34, p. 103), who provide a detailed interpretation of Hickman's simulations. Interestingly, the ratios to GDP in Gordon and Wilcox (table 6) are almost double those in figure 8.8 above, suggesting an important base-year-relative price bias in the data used by both Hickman and Gordon and Wilcox.

11. A contrarian claims that the Fed's tightening in 1928–1929 was minor, did not affect borrowing for "legitimate business purposes." "The tightness in credit affected speculation, but this is another matter." See Gordon (1961, p. 427).
12. US exports were equivalent to about 5 percent of GDP in 1929.
13. A more detailed analysis of financial fragility in the 1920s is provided by White (2000, pp. 752–7).
14. R. A. Gordon (1961, pp. 357–8) briefly describes and dismisses "underconsumptionist" theories, and in his final evaluation of the causes of the Great Contraction (p. 445) ascribes much more credence to overinvestment than underconsumption.

9 Bubbles and busts: the 1990s in the mirror of the 1920s

Eugene N. White

> "History is continually repudiated."
>
> Glassman and Hassett (1999), *The Dow 36,000*

Stock market booms and busts command enormous attention, yet there is little consensus about their causes and effects. The soaring market of the 1990s was seen by many, but certainly not all, as the harbinger of a new age of sustained, rapid economic growth. Optimists saw the bull market as driven by fundamentals, although they differed over what these were; while skeptics warned that it was just a bubble, distorting consumption and investment decisions. Regardless of the boom's origin, policymakers feared that a collapse would have real economic consequences and debated how to cope with the market's retreat.

Although the sheer size of the run-up in stock prices in the 1990s has obscured other bull markets in the popular eye, the boom shared many characteristics with previous episodes, notably the 1920s; and the explanations and policy concerns were similar. As in the 1990s, it was widely claimed that a "new economy" had taken root in the United States. Technological and organizational innovations were viewed as raising productivity, increasing firms' earnings and justifying the wave of new issues. In both periods unemployment was low, with stable prices in the 1920s and very low inflation in the 1990s. Participation in the market increased, as investing in the market seemed safer, with reduced macroeconomic risk and the seeming abundance of high-return opportunities.

Just as the new heights of the 1990s market were often challenged as the product of "irrational exuberance," so too there were critics of the fast surge in stock prices in 1928–1929. Policymakers were concerned about the distortions that the quick run-up in stock prices would have on the economy. The potential presence of an asset bubble raised the question of the appropriate policy response – and in the 1920s the bull market helped to produce a grievously mistaken monetary policy.

As booms and crashes are relatively rare events, this chapter offers a comparison of the 1920s and the 1990s in order to provide perspective on the question of

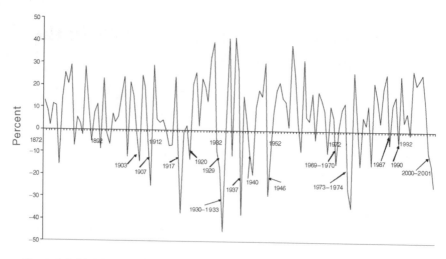

Figure 9.1 Real S&P 500 returns 1871–2003 and twentieth-century crashes

whether the Federal Reserve should respond to booms and crashes. The answer to this question depends critically on the ability of policymakers to identify fundamental components in the stock market. Although considerable energy has been expended to justify stock price movement in terms of fundamentals and measure bubbles, it has proven to be an elusive effort. While this pre-empts a policy response to a boom, the Fed still has a critical role to play in preventing crashes from disrupting the payments system or sparking an intermediation crisis.

9.1   Defining booms and crashes?

Some stock market booms and crashes are well remembered; but, in general, these events are imperfectly defined. While we typically think of the stock market as following a random walk, a boom is viewed as an improbably long period of large positive returns that is cast into sharp profile by a crash. The first questions to address are whether the twenties and nineties stand out in comparison to other booms and crashes, and whether they shared similar characteristics.

To identify booms, we need to look for long periods of positive real stock returns. Figure 9.1 shows the annual real returns on the S&P 500 for 1871 to 2003.[1] Annual data provide the appropriate window to look for bull markets, as they are seen as long upward swings that dominate any brief retreat that might be picked up in data of a higher frequency. The bull market of 1995–1999 stands out, with returns of 27, 21, 22, 25, and 12 percent. If the occurrence of three consecutive years of returns over 10 percent is used as an approximate criterion, booms are relatively rare. The first boom for these data is 1921–1928, which had a long run of positive returns of 20, 26, 2, 23, 19, 13, 32, and 39 percent. Next is 1942–1945, when returns were 11, 18, 15, and 30 percent. The 1950s also had a long bull market with a streak of positive returns: 18, 22, 15, 13, 2, 39, and 25 percent from 1949 to 1956. The years 1963–1965 saw gains of 17, 13, and 9 percent, while 1982–1986 enjoyed returns of 22, 14, 4, 19, and 26 percent. Few contemporaries seemed concerned that the booms of the forties, fifties, or sixties left the market far out of alignment, and it is the fear of a crash underlying a bull market that singles out the 1920s, 1980s, and 1990s.

Mishkin and White (2003) have developed a simple method for identifying crashes, using the three most well-known stock indices to capture the fortunes of different segments of the market: the Dow-Jones Industrial Average (DJIA), Standard and Poor's 500 and its predecessor the Cowles Index, and the NASDAQ. Since October 1929 and October 1987 are universally agreed to be stock market crashes, they were used as benchmarks. In both cases the market fell over 20 percent in one and two days' time. The fall in the market, or the depth, is only one characteristic of a crash. There was no similar sudden decline for the most recent collapse, but no one would hesitate to identify 2000 as the beginning of a major collapse. Thus, speed is another feature. To identify crashes, it is necessary to look at windows of one day, one week, one month, and one year to capture other declines.

This net picked out fifteen major stock market crashes in the twentieth century. These were 1903, 1907, 1917, 1920, 1929, 1930–1933, 1937, 1940, 1946, 1962, 1969–1970, 1973–1974, 1987, 1990, and 2000. These crashes are identified in figure 9.1. Some were clearly driven by political or policy events, but only a few crashes happened after a prolonged boom: 1929, 1946, 1987, and 2000–2001. The crash of 1946 followed rather than anticipated the postwar recession, which hit bottom in October 1945. It generated relatively little concern among contemporaries, unlike the crashes of 1929, 1987, and 2000–2001, which came at the end of heady peacetime booms. The timing and magnitude of the crash of 1987 closely matched 1929. But the rapid recovery of the market, which disguises the crash in figure 9.1, caused policy concerns to abate. The most natural comparison thus appears to be the booms of the twenties and nineties.

Figures 9.2 and 9.3 offer a more detailed comparison of these two episodes, displaying the DJIA, the S&P 500, and its predecessor the Cowles Index. Unfortunately, there is no equivalent for the NASDAQ in the 1920s. To capture some of the movement for smaller, newer firms, an equally weighted index for all common stocks listed on the New York Stock Exchange is included (Fisher, 1966). To make all series comparable, the indices are set equal to 100 in their

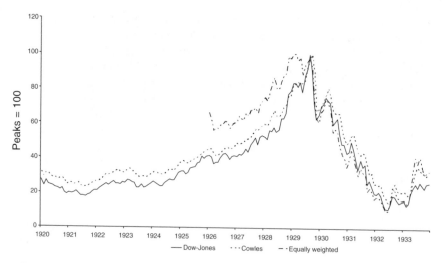

Figure 9.2 Boom and bust, 1920–1933

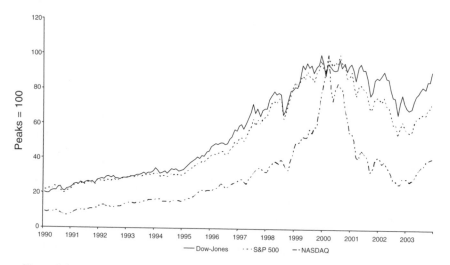

Figure 9.3 Boom and bust, 1990–2003

peak month. These figures highlight the similarities and differences of these two great bull markets. The boom market in 1929 was focused more on the larger companies. Both the Dow-Jones and Cowles indices moved almost in lock step on the way up, although the boom is greater in the bigger Dow-Jones companies. This aspect of the boom is highlighted by the equally weighted index, even though earlier years are missing. The rise is nowhere near as steep and the peak

Table 9.1 *Characteristics of booms and busts in the United States (end-of-month indices)*

	Peak	Trough	Drop	Peak to trough (months)	Recovery to peak date
1920s					
Dow-Jones	Aug 1929	Jun 1932	−0.822	34	Nov 1954
Cowles	Sep 1929	Jun 1932	−0.849	33	Nov 1953
Equally Weighted	Feb 1929	May 1932	−0.896	39	Sep 1945
1980s					
Dow-Jones	Aug 1987	Nov 1987	−0.302	3	Jul 1989
S&P 500	Aug 1987	Nov 1987	−0.311	3	Jul 1989
NASDAQ composite	Aug 1987	Dec 1987	−0.299	4	Jun 1989
1990s					
Dow-Jones	Dec 1999	Sep 2002	−0.339	34	?
S&P 500	Aug 2000	Sep 2002	−0.463	26	?
NASDAQ composite	Mar 2000	Oct 2002	−0.741	32	?

of the market – emphasizing the fate of smaller company stocks – is in February 1929. The crash of October 1929 sent both the Dow-Jones and Cowles indices downwards to join the third index in the bumpy ride to the bottom. Table 9.1 shows the dimensions of the decline for the markets of the twenties, eighties, and nineties. Although starting from different peaks, all indices for the 1920s lost over 80 percent. The recovery to peak was over a decade away, emphasizing the role the Great Depression had in humbling the market.

In contrast to the 1920s, the 1980s boom appears to have been spread across the whole market. All indices crash at the same time, and their recovery is very similar. The 1980s upward rush and initial crash map very closely onto the 1920s; in fact, it is easy to superimpose any two series. In mirror-like movement, the markets recover quickly from the shock. Then, they part company. By July 1989, nineteen months after the peak in the 1980s, the Dow has completely recovered, but at the same distance from the 1920s peak, July 1931, it was 64 percent below that peak.

The rising tide of the 1990s lifted all boats, but the high-tech, small company stocks of the NASDAQ rode the crest. In comparison to the 1920s, when large companies dominated the rising market, or the 1980s, when all rose together, the NASDAQ firms were the center of the boom, rising higher and falling further.

The collapse of the "tech bubble" looks more like the busts of October 1929 and October 1987. From its peak in March 2000 the NASDAQ lost 20 percent within a month. The jagged slump from peak to trough produced a loss of 74 percent; the size and timing matching the collapse from 1929. In table 9.1, it can be seen that the larger, more established companies represented by the DJIA and the S&P 500 experienced the same magnitude of loss as did the indices in 1987 and the initial declines from August to November 1929; but it is slower and more gradual. By the end of 2003 all three indices had recovered partly, but with markedly different success. The absence of a quick recovery *à la* 1987 and the magnitude of the duration of NASDAQ's collapse make the twenties and nineties a natural comparison.

9.2   Bubbles or fundamentals?

Discussion of booms and busts divide observers sharply. There are those who believe that fundamentals are solely responsible for the movements in stock prices, and those who believe that stock prices are largely detached from fundamentals, moved by the fluctuating optimism and pessimism of investors.

Looking back on the boom and bust of the 1920s, Professor John B. Williams of Harvard wrote (Williams, 1938):

Like a ghost in a haunted house, the notion of a soul possessing the market and sending it up or down with a shrewdness uncanny and superhuman, keeps ever reappearing . . . . Let us define the investment value of a stock as the present worth of all the dividends to be paid upon it.

Viewing the same period, John Maynard Keynes (1936) chose to differ:

A conventional valuation which is established as the outcome of the mass psychology of a large number of ignorant individuals is liable to change violently as the result of a sudden fluctuation of opinion which do not really make much difference to the prospective yield . . . [T]he market will be subject to waves of optimistic and pessimistic sentiment, which are unreasoning.

On the threshold of a new bull market, the divide remained. Robert Shiller (1991) observed:

I present here evidence that while some of the implications of the efficient markets hypothesis are substantiated by data, investor attitudes are of great importance in determining the course of prices of speculative assets. Prices change in substantial measure because the investing public en masse capriciously changes its mind.

In contrast, John Cochrane (1991) expounded:

We can still argue over what name to attach to residual discount-rate movement. Is it variation in real investment opportunities not captured by current discount model? Or is it "fads"? I argue that residual discount-rate variation is small (in a precise sense), and tantalizingly suggestive of economic explanation. I argue that "fads are just a catchy name for the residual."

These extreme positions can be maintained because of the observational equivalence in any empirical test between a market driven by a bubble and one that is driven by fundamentals but where there are omitted factors (Flood and Hodrick, 1990). Most models of market behavior are based on the premise of rational expectations, which assumes that (1) individuals have rational information processing and (2) individuals have a correct model of the fundamental structure of the economy. Bubbles or manias may arise if either condition is violated. If the first is violated, there will be an irrational bubble or mania; and, if the second is violated, there will be a rational bubble. With either violation, asset prices will deviate from fundamentals (Blanchard and Watson, 1982). In rational bubbles, market participants may have rational expectations but prices may differ from fundamentals because the sequence of prices in rational expectations models may be indeterminate. Bubbles will be rational as long as the bubble component in the stock price is the expected discounted value of the future bubble. In an irrational bubble, market participants may focus on "noise" instead of fundamentals. Some noise or unsophisticated traders in a market may overwhelm rational or sophisticated investors if the time horizons for arbitrage are finite (De Long et al., 1990). If share prices are moved by a bubble, it will induce distortions into the market, misdirecting investment, and policy intervention may be required.

9.3 Fundamentals and empirical regularities

What were the driving fundamental factors behind the great bull markets of the 1920s and 1990s? Even if one believes either that a bubble or that investor euphoria was the key factor, the natural starting point is deciding how to measure the contribution of fundamentals to prices. Fundamentals require that stock prices equal the present discounted value of expected future dividends. The simplest approximation to this fundamentals-based valuation is the Gordon growth model, which underlies many studies and much popular discussion. While expected future dividends and interest rates may vary considerably, the simple Gordon model assumes constant values for all parameters. Dividends are assumed to grow at a rate g and investors are assumed to require a return of r, composed of a risk-free rate and an equity premium.[2] Usually framed in terms of the aggregate price level of the stock market, P, the Gordon model is

$$P = (1 + g)D/(r - g) \tag{1}$$

While changes in the pay-out rate and the risk-free rate may have made some contribution to upsurges in the market, it is technological change – increasing productivity and leading to higher dividend growth – and changes in the equity premium that are believed to have been the prime movers.

The Gordon model neatly outlines the simple fundamental relationships, yet explaining stock price movements has proved frustratingly difficult. The problem is that, to be rational, prices should be wholly forward-looking, representing the expected future course of dividends appropriately discounted. In a classic article, Shiller (1981) found that stock prices moved far more than was warranted by the movement of dividends, where the *ex post* rational price was equal to the discounted value of the future stream of realized dividends. Even if there were deviations in what was expected from what was realized, the fit should have been good over his long period of observation, 1871–1979; yet the variation of prices exceeded the variation in fundamental prices, violating any reasonable test.[3]

While it has proven difficult to explain the behavior of prices in terms of the movement of future dividends and discount rates, a very different literature has found empirical regularities, explaining the behavior of current prices in terms of past fundamentals. This predictability is surprising, given that prices should be forward-looking; and it provides a further instrument for analyzing the unusual behavior of prices during stock market booms. Fama and French (1988) have found that both the lagged dividend yield and the lagged earnings yield have explanatory power for stock returns (see also Campbell and Shiller, 1988). Lamont (1998) has argued that high dividends predict high future returns because dividends measure the permanent component of stock prices, reflecting the dividend policy of managers. The pay-out ratio (dividend/earnings ratio) forecasts returns because the level of earnings is a measure of current business conditions.[4] It is generally observed that investors require high stock returns in recessions and low returns in booms, and risk premia on stocks covary with the business cycle. As earnings vary with the business cycle, current earnings forecasts future returns, thus both dividends and earnings have information for stock returns. However, the variation explained by these models is very modest.

Table 9.2 gives a closer look at the key ratios for each of the boom periods. Real dividends and earnings climbed to historic highs in 1928–1929, but the market rose so much that the dividend yield and earnings/price ratio fell below traditional levels, and the pay-out ratio moved back to an earlier level. If these two years represented a new era, with higher earnings paying out higher dividends but with a greater share being reinvested, then optimists would seem to have had good cause for paying higher stock prices. Yet, from the empirical regularities, we would anticipate that the fall in the dividend yield would reduce future returns, with the falling earnings/price ratio mitigating it to some degree. For the 1990s the picture was somewhat different. Real earnings per

Table 9.2 *The dividend yield, earnings/price ratio, and pay-out ratio in two booms in the United States*

	Real dividends	Dividend yield	Real earnings	Earnings to price ratio	Pay-out ratio	Real price
1900–1909	7.6	4.6	12.7	7.6	60.4	173.1
1910–1919	8.0	5.9	13.5	10.1	62.4	149.6
1920–1924	5.3	6.3	7.6	8.8	81.9	83.5
1925	6.1	5.7	12.7	11.8	48.0	110.9
1926	7.1	5.5	12.8	9.8	55.6	128.1
1927	8.1	5.7	11.6	8.3	69.4	138.8
1928	9.0	4.8	14.6	7.9	61.6	183.7
1929	10.3	3.9	17.1	6.5	60.2	263.6
1930	11.2	4.5	11.1	4.5	101.0	230.2
1931	10.4	5.1	7.7	3.8	134.4	182.2
1932	7.0	6.0	5.8	4.9	122.0	105.2
1933	6.0	6.2	6.0	6.2	100.0	99.6
1970–1979	13.2	4.1	29.4	9.4	45.5	360.9
1980–1989	13.5	4.6	28.1	9.5	48.6	321.5
1990–1994	15.9	3.2	27.6	5.4	59.8	521.7
1995	16.2	3.0	39.9	7.3	40.6	561.2
1996	17.0	2.4	44.1	6.3	38.5	721.5
1997	17.4	2.0	44.6	5.2	39.0	873.1
1998	17.9	1.7	41.6	3.9	43.0	1080.8
1999	17.9	1.3	51.7	3.9	34.6	1378.0
2000	16.8	1.1	51.8	3.5	32.5	1531.2
2001	16.1	1.2	25.3	1.9	63.8	1378.1
2002	15.8	1.4	30.3	2.7	52.1	1167.3

Source: Robert Shiller's webpage, www.econ.yale.edu/~shiller/data.htm

share jumped, but little was paid out in dividends. Again, the market's surge caused both measures to collapse to unprecedented lows; and the abrupt rise in the market was not anticipated empirically by the changes in the key ratios.

In a telling out-of-sample exercise at the outset of the nineties, Lamont (1998) forecast the cumulative return of buying stocks on 31 December 1994. For his sample period (1947–1994) the unconditional mean excess return over a five-year period was 33 percent. But, using a VAR regression with a starting point of 31 December 1994, the out-of-sample forecast was 1 percentage point below total treasury bills returns to 2000! Even with a potential total forecast error of 21 percent this was well below the performance of the market. His conclusion was that, in the mid-1990s, US stock prices were very high relative to any benchmark. The surprising failure of stock prices to conform to some simple rational model or the empirical regularities requires a closer examination of the fundamentals components of the Gordon model.

9.4   Explanation: technological change

In both the 1920s and the 1990s many bulls heralded the arrival of a "new economy." They saw a higher rate of technological change as the driving force behind a faster-growing economy and a rapidly rising stock market. Surging initial public offerings, many based on technological or managerial innovations, flooded the markets in both periods. Technological innovations were viewed as improving the marginal product of capital, increasing earnings and, hence, dividend growth. A wave of innovations, sometimes characterized as constituting a new general-purpose technology was believed to have placed the economy on a higher growth path.

In his book *New Levels in the Stock Market* (1929), Charles Amos Dice of Ohio State University argued that higher stock prices were the product of higher productivity. Dice identified increased expenditure on research and development and the application of modern management methods as prime factors behind the boom. Irving Fisher (1930) saw the stock market boom as justified by the rise in earnings, driven by the systematic application of science and invention in industry and the acceptance of the new industrial management methods of Frederick Taylor. But not everyone was so sanguine. A. P. Giannini, head of Bancitaly (the future Bank of America), stated in 1928 that the high price of his bank's stock was unwarranted given the planned dividends. Management in some high-flying companies, including Canadian Marconi and Brooklyn Edison, also became alarmed and announced that their shares were overvalued (Patterson, 1965).

As suggested by the somewhat stronger performance of the largest companies in the stock indices in Figure 9.2, the boom of the 1920s was centered on large-scale commercial and industrial enterprises that took advantage of continuous-process technologies. These were coordinated by the emerging system of modern management, which produced more efficient vertically integrated enterprises, capturing economies of scale and scope (Chandler, 1977). Among the "new" industries were automobiles. The Ford Motor Company had pioneered mass production techniques, but General Motors developed a diversified line of production and a more advanced management and organization system, becoming the industry leader. GM's president predicted that its stock price would rise from 180 to 225 and he promised to return 60 percent of earnings to stockholders.

Other new technology industries included radio, movies, aircraft, electric utilities, and banking. Like many fast-growing companies, RCA did not pay dividends but reinvested its earnings. Other prominent new technology companies were Radio-Keith Orpheum, the United Aircraft and Transport Corporation, and the Aluminum Company of America. Central to many of the new technologies was the electricity industry, which was transformed in the 1920s. Utilities had been local industries, but there were now technological opportunities to gain economies of scale in production and transmission, providing incentives to consolidate the industry. In a wave of mergers, banks expanded and acquired other types of financial institutions to provide a wide range of services, yielding advantages of scale and scope. Stock indices available for utilities and banking outstripped the Dow-Jones and S&P 500 indices, much as the tech company stock indices of the 1990s did.

Some students of the 1920s have sought to explain the boom as being primarily driven by technological change raising dividends. Sirkin (1975) has applied a version of the Gordon model to Dow-Jones stocks in the 1920s to see if price/earnings ratios could have been justified by a temporarily higher growth of earnings. Price/earnings ratios had ranged between 12 and 15 before the bull market, while the mean and median at the peak in 1929 were 24.3 and 20.4. Assuming a fixed discount rate of 9 percent, Sirkin has calculated the higher earnings growth and number of years that would be needed to justify peak price/earnings ratios. In his best case, if the higher growth rate of 8.9 percent typical of 1925–1929 had been sustained for ten years, a price/earnings ratio of 20.4 would have been justified, or over-justified; thus he concluded that the market was not overvalued.

Although simple, Sirkin's study is fairly typical of many non-nested exercises, devised to explain the booms of the 1920s and 1990s, that focus on one variable. Sirkin's results are also sensitive to the selection of 1925–1929 as a time-frame for high sustainable earnings. If the years 1927–1929 had been selected to measure reasonable future earnings growth, all the price/earnings ratios he examined would have been justified. This point reflects the fact that earnings are highly variable, compared with the permanent component of dividends.

Donaldson and Kamstra (1996) seek a similar explanation for the 1929 boom and bust, focusing on changes in the expected growth of dividends. In the simple Gordon growth model, dividend growth cannot explain the price peak. Prices move far away from their fundamentals, and simple tests show that one cannot reject the presence of a bubble. However, using pre-1920 dividend data, Donaldson and Kamstra estimate a non-linear ARMA–ARCH (autoregressive moving average – autoregressive conditional heteroskedasticity) model for discounted dividend growth and find that out-of-sample forecasts produce a fundamental price series with a similar time pattern to the actual S&P index. The fit is so close that it is hard to reject expected dividend growth as the driving factor. Yet the discount rate plays no significant role. While Donaldson and

Kamstra use alternatively a constant discount rate and a variable one, they do not allow for any significant variation in the equity premium – a key feature of the boom. Close inspection of their charts reveals that their fundamental peak follows the actual peak, suggesting that the fit may partly reflect the highly persistent behavior of dividends.

In contrast to Sirkin, and Donaldson and Kamstra, Barrie Wigmore (1985) sees no evidence in earnings that could justify the run-up in stock prices. In his detailed survey of the behavior of individual stocks, he points out that, at the market's peak, stock prices average thirty times 1929 earnings, up from ten and at most twenty before the boom. Although thirty was the average, many stocks fell in the thirty to fifty range, with a number over 100. He concludes that "such stock prices were clearly dependent on further price rises rather than on the income generated and distributed by companies ... [A]s the low returns on equity show, these high valuations placed little emphasis on earnings" (Wigmore, 1985, p. 382).

The idea of a new technological age played a key role in the minds of the participants in the 1990s bull market. The rapid changes in computer/information technology and biotechnology were heralded as placing the economy on a higher trajectory. This "new era" vision was supported by some economists. Comparing the computer revolution to the introduction and spread of electricity and internal combustion, Jovanovic and Rousseau (2002a) projected that this general-purpose technology would have an even greater impact on productivity growth. Prices for electricity and automobiles had declined sharply in the 1910s and 1920s, and most quickly after 1924, suggesting a key role for technology in the boom of the 1920s. But price declines for IT products have been much faster, promising higher rates of growth and consumption.

Nonetheless, this rosy future is not strongly supported by more general studies of productivity growth. In a reassessment of long-term multifactor productivity growth, Gordon (2000a) has painted a broad picture of slow growth in the nineteenth century. From an average annual growth rate of 0.39 percent for the period 1870–1890, MFP began to climb, hitting 1.14 percent in 1890–1913. After the First World War it continued its upward movement, rising to 1.42 percent in 1913–1928 before cresting at 1.90 percent in 1928–1950. Gordon argues that this peak of MFP growth was attributable to a cluster of four inventions: electricity, the internal combustion engine, petrochemicals–plastics–pharmaceuticals, and communications–entertainment (telegraph, telephone, radio, movies, television, recorded music, and mass-circulation newspapers and magazines). These were all well established before the Second World War, except for television, and their diffusion and improvements thus contributed to the peak in MFP growth between 1928 and 1950. MFP growth subsided to 1.47 percent in 1950–1964 and then plummeted to 0.89 percent in 1964–1972, hitting bottom at 0.16 percent for the period 1972–1979. The recovery, to 0.59 percent in 1979–1988 and 0.79 percent in 1988–1995 remained far below the peak, leading Gordon to conclude that the contributions from the four earlier GPTs dwarfed today's technology information computer/chip-based IT revolution. Gordon (2000b) has found the most recent increase in MFP, for 1995–1999, to be 1.35 percent, consisting of a 0.54 percent unsustainable cyclical effect and 0.81 percent in trend growth, which he attributed wholly to the computer–IT sector. For the remainder of the economy, MFP did not revive, and other than for durables it actually decelerated.[5] The differences in productivity growth in the late 1990s between IT industries and the rest of the economy look like a potentially good explanation for the greater buoyancy of the NASDAQ compared to the rest of the market. Certainly, it would explain investor response to developments in the IT industry. However, the boom apart from the new economy appears surprising without a major increase in productivity growth, giving skeptics ammunition.

The implications of the modest increase in productivity growth for the value of stocks are to be found in Heaton and Lucas's (1999) study, which parallels Sirkin's exercise for the 1920s. They calculate the growth rates that would be needed to justify the peak price/dividend ratio using Shiller's annual data (1872–1998). For this 126-year period the average price/dividend ratio was twenty-eight and real earnings growth rate was 1.4 percent, implying a discount rate of 5 percent.[6] To match the 1998 ratio of forty-eight with required returns of 5 percent or 7 percent would demand either productivity growth rates of 2.9 percent or 4.9 percent growth in earnings – huge historical leaps, including a doubling of productivity growth, that are not evident in the data. Consequently, Heaton and Lucas are skeptical that any explanation of the 1990s can be based principally on technological change. Like the 1920s, the conclusion for the 1990s is fairly clear: the expected dividend growth was not a major factor driving the boom.

9.5 Explanation: changes in the equity premium

The stock yield or return required for holding stocks has been seized upon by others as the fundamental factor driving stock market booms. Composed of a risk-free rate and an equity premium, the stock yield is believed to be moved primarily by the latter, as the risk-free rate is held to be relatively constant. In the Gordon stock valuation model, where there is a constant expected growth of future dividends, the stock yield is

$$r_t = E(D_{t+1}/P_t) + g \tag{2}$$

The equity premium is then calculated as the difference between the stock yield and a measure of the risk-free rate. This simple formulation points to

Figure 9.4 The stock yield and equity premium in the United States, 1871–2003

the fact that the equity premium is driven largely by share prices, as movements in the growth rate of dividends are relatively small compared to price movements.

Figure 9.4 graphs a measure of the equity premium and the stock yield. The stock yield is based on the S&P 500, while the risk-free rate is composed of three series spliced together: the ten-year constant-maturity US government bond rate for 1941–2003, high-grade industrial bonds for 1900–1940, and high-grade railroad bonds for 1871–1899.[7] The estimated stock yield is equal to the dividend yield and the average growth of dividends. The nominal and real rate of dividend growth were 3.9 percent and 1.7 percent, respectively.[8]

After a long period of relative constancy in the nineteenth century the equity premium rose to over 6 percent after the First World War. During the 1920s it declined back to its previous level, then during the boom it fell to its lowest point yet. If measured on a monthly basis, the equity premium hit an unprecedented 2 percent during the bull market of 1928–1929. The Great Depression elevated the premium to an historic high. By the 1960s it had returned to the nineteenth-century level. The brief period when there appears to be an equity discount is not the result of any decline in the dividend yield but of the unexpected rise in interest rates in the early 1980s. However, since the late 1980s the equity premium appears to have collapsed.[9]

The perception that equities are less risky and hence the equity premium should decline was a common explanation for the nineties boom. Among the most bullish of the bulls were Glassman and Hassett, whose book *The Dow 36,000* (1999) proclaims a "paradigm shift":

Stocks *should* be priced two to four times higher – today. But it is impossible to predict how long it will take for the market to recognize that Dow 36,000 is perfectly reasonable. It could take ten years or ten weeks. Our own guess is somewhere between three and five years, which means that returns will continue to average about 25 percent per year (p. 13).

Their optimism was predicated on equation (2), assuming a real long-term bond rate of 2 percent, and a 2.3 percent real growth rate of dividends, permitting a dividend yield of 1.5 percent to fall to 0.5 percent with a tripling of stock prices (pp. 72–3). Glassman and Hassett argued that a diversified portfolio of stocks was no more risky than an investment in US government bonds. Once investors fully appreciated this fact, the equity premium would vanish as stock prices were bid up. To support their argument, they pointed to the fact that transactions costs had been greatly lowered by mutual funds, 401(k) plans, internet trading, computerization and other innovations that permitted investors to acquire information more easily to diversify their portfolios.

The same factors – increased participation and diversification – that have been used to explain the recent decline in the equity premium were also present in the 1920s. Traditionally, investing in the stock market was restricted to the well-to-do, but the wider public entered the market in the 1920s. Smaller investors were brought into the market as innovations made it easier for them to diversify their portfolios. One important development was the expansion of the investment trusts, precursors to today's mutual funds, which grew in number from forty in 1921 to 750 in 1929. After the stock market collapse of 1929 and the prolonged depression the market was deserted by the small investors, who returned only slowly. By the end of the twentieth century mutual funds facilitated the re-emergence of small investors. Between 1990 and 2002 the number of these funds climbed from 2338 to 7267 and the number of accounts and net assets rose from 61 million with $1065 billion to 251 million with $6392 billion (Investment Company Institute, 2003).

An increase in the stock market participation rate could decrease the required risk premium on stocks, because it would spread market risk over more of the population. The Survey of Consumer Finances showed that the number of shareholders in the United States rose from 52.3 million in 1989 to 69.3 million in 1995, with people entering the market at younger ages (Heaton and Lucas, 1999). In addition, stockholders seem to be more diversified, which would allow holders to demand a lower rate of return. Whereas, very few investors had more than ten stocks in the 1960s (Blume and Friend, 1978), the potential for diversification has increased by mutual fund ownership, yet risk tolerance seems only to have increased slightly from 1989 to 1995. Heaton and Lucas (1999) suggest that individuals who already own stocks are more risk-tolerant than those who do not, implying that the addition of new stockholders might lower the average level of risk tolerance, reducing the effect of wide ownership on the equity premium.

To examine the effects of increased participation and diversification, Heaton and Lucas (1999) calibrate an overlapping generations model where only some households hold equity and there is aggregate and idiosyncratic income risk. They find that substantial changes in participation rates have only a small effect on the equity premium. Diversification is more potent, but this factor has not increased as much as popularly perceived. Mutual funds may have mushroomed, but as late as 1995 only 16.5 percent of equity was owned through mutual funds. Furthermore, households that held stock had almost a half invested in their employing company (Vissing-Jorgensen, 1999). Thus, increased participation and diversification may explain only a limited part of the downward trend in the equity premium.

The sharp decline in the equity premium may also be explained by inflation. Using independent measures of equity risk from cross-sectional data, Campbell and Vuolteenaho (2004) find that inflation explained half of the movement in the dividend yield. The falling dividend yield of the late 1920s was attributable to a drop in risk. The increase in the dividend yield in the 1930s and 1940s was dominated by the increase in risk, overwhelming the effect of deflation, which would have lifted prices. The declining dividend yield of the 1950s and early 1960s was moved primarily by the falling measures of equity risk. But rising inflation from the late 1960s through the 1970s raised the dividend yield. By the late 1980s and 1990s it was falling again, this time because both risk and inflation were declining. Campbell and Vuolteenaho contend that higher inflation was not correlated with any subjective measure of risk that would imply rational pricing. Instead, inflation increased expected long-term real dividend growth because investors formed subjective growth forecasts by extrapolating past nominal growth rates without taking inflation into consideration. The result was that stocks tended to be overpriced when inflation was low and underpriced when inflation was high. Campbell and Vuolteenaho blame this "mispricing" of stocks by the persistent use of the "Fed model" by many contemporary investment professionals, who counseled investors to compare the yield on stocks (the dividend yield) with the yield on treasury bonds plus a risk factor. Use of this model produces some inflation illusion (see also Campbell and Cochrane, 1999). Campbell and Vuolteenaho conclude that, at the end of 1999, when dividend growth and the risk measures justified a dividend price ratio of 3.3, it was observed to be 1.2.

While a huge effort has been expended by financial economists to explain the movement of stock prices in terms of fundamentals, it has had very limited success. Changes in earnings growth and the discount rate cannot fully account for the buoyant markets of the 1920s and 1990s. As Campbell (1999) bleakly explains, "The recent run-up in stock prices is so extreme relative to fundamental determinants such as corporate earnings, stock-market participation, and macroeconomic performance that it will be very hard to explain using a model fit to earlier historical data."

If there had been bubbles in 1929 and 1999, they would have distorted consumption and investment. A boom in stock prices would raise household wealth, helping to drive consumption, and new investment would look more attractive because soaring stock prices would raise the ratio of market value to book value in Tobin's q. In addition, the improvement in the value of collateral would have allowed more firms to borrow. Firms might also switch to equity finance from debt finance because of a lower equity premium. Rising stock prices as a result of increasing investment would have driven up the observed real growth rate, making the apparent productive capacity of the economy greater. If stock prices did not reflect fundamentals, some investments should not have been undertaken, because they did not really have positive internal rates of return. The result would be overinvestment and unusable capacity. Romer (1990) has compared the behavior of consumer spending and stock market wealth in the crashes of 1929 and 1987. She finds that the relationships between stock price variability and consumer spending were similar for both periods, although the continued high level of volatility after 1929 was greater. In the boom and bust, wealth had its strongest effect on consumer durables, raising purchases during the bull market then drastically reducing consumption after the crash. Eichengreen and Mitchener (2003) estimate an investment equation, in which the doubling of Tobin's q that occurred between 1926 and 1929 produces an 18 percent increase in investment, and the collapse afterwards yields a greater effect.

If fundamentals drive the market then there is no unwarranted consumption or investment. Yet studies of fundamentals cast doubt on whether stock market booms are entirely attributable to fundamentals, suggesting that, if one could measure the deviations from fundamentals, there would be a role for incorporating asset prices or some measure of asset mispricing into the Federal Reserve's decision-making.

9.6 What is the optimal policy?

If a consensus had been reached in macroeconomics at the end of the twentieth century, it was that monetary policy should have as its primary goals price stability and growth, with no significant role for asset prices. Thus, Alan Greenspan's 1996 warning that the market was possessed with an "irrational exuberance" astonished many schooled in the history of the Federal Reserve. It had long been held as an article of faith that the Fed had erred, critically, in 1929 when it focused on the buoyant stock market. Tight policy, partly induced by its concern for the market, is generally viewed as having made a mild recession worse, initiating the Great Depression of the 1930s. Greenspan's jawboning was eerily reminiscent of the Federal Reserve Board's policy in early 1929, and opened a debate on whether monetary policy should respond to asset markets.

The question whether the central bank should respond to asset booms and busts is relatively new. The current standard framework for policy is inflation targeting (Bernanke and Mishkin, 1997). Publicly announced medium-term inflation targets are used to set a nominal anchor for monetary policy, allowing the central bank limited flexibility to stabilize the real economy in the short run. In a small, calibrated macroeconomic model, Bernanke and Gertler (2000, 2001) find that an inflation-targeting rule stabilizes inflation and output when asset prices are volatile, driven either by a bubble or technology shock. They conclude that there is no additional gain from responding directly to asset prices, because, although a response to stock prices can lower the variability of the output gap, it may increase the variability of inflation. Additionally, they believe that it is more difficult to identify the fundamental component of stock prices than it is the output gap. In their view, any attempt to address asset volatility runs the risk of imparting instability to prices and output, especially if the measurement of fundamentals is flawed.

Nonetheless, some have argued that asset prices ought to be incorporated directly into inflation targeting. Cecchetti et al. (2000) have proposed that a central bank should adjust monetary policy not only in response to forecasts of future inflation and the output gap but also to asset prices, developing procedures to identify asset price "misalignments." They believe that it is no more difficult to measure stock price misalignments than it is the output gap or the equilibrium value of the real interest rate.[10] Cecchetti et al. estimate the warranted risk premium in 2000 to have been 4.3 percent, which would have justified an S&P 500 level less than half that of the observed level. Their model suggests that, by 1997, the federal funds rate should have been 10.35 percent, as opposed to the actual 5.51 percent. This rate would have kept inflation at under 3 percent, with a small output gap and a risk premium of just under 3 percent.

Bordo and Jeanne (2002) also make a case for pre-emptive monetary policy, with a Taylor rule model where productivity shocks can cause large price reversals. Boom-bust episodes are identified with a simple filter when the three-year growth of real stock prices exceeds a critical value. They are concerned that, during a boom, rising stock prices raise the price of collateral, inducing firms to borrow; while a bust creates financial instability by quickly lowering the value of collateral, yielding a collateral-induced credit crunch. In their view, a central bank should carry out monetary policy in terms of insurance, trading off the loss in output and price stability against the probability of a costly credit crunch and a fall in real output. Bordo and Jeanne find that such a policy, responding to a bull market, sometimes dominates a simpler Taylor rule in its sacrifice of current output against the risk of a credit crunch.

This literature is new and growing, though the consensus remains that the Fed should not incorporate asset prices directly into its policy considerations. While an optimal policy rule may or may not include intervention in response to asset prices, the Fed has been accused of incorrectly responding to the booms of the 1920s and 1990s.

9.7   The role of the Federal Reserve

How did policymakers in the 1920s and 1990s confront the booming markets? Did their policies hinder or aggravate the booms? These issues were part of the debates of both decades.

The bull market of the twenties had its origins in the long economic boom after the First World War. Immediately after the high wartime inflation, the economy experienced a boom and hard recession. It was a wrenching experience for financial intermediaries, with numerous bank failures. Nevertheless, the economy quickly stabilized and began to grow rapidly, with two brief contractions in 1923–1924 and 1926–1927. Overall, between 1922 and 1929, GNP grew at a rate of 4.7 percent and unemployment averaged 3.7 percent. Anchored by the gold standard, prices varied, but there was no trend inflation (US Bureau of the Census, 1975, pp. 135 and 226). The end of the war freed the Federal Reserve from its obligation to assist the Treasury's financing of the war; and the government balanced its budget, cutting expenditures and taxes. Once released from keeping interest rates artificially low the Fed accommodated seasonal demands for credit, and the close coincidence in the timing of the actions of the Fed and the turns in the business cycle imply that it did indeed help to smooth economic fluctuations.

Some argued that the initial stock market boom of 1928–1929 was fueled by expansionary monetary policy driven by international considerations. Having returned to gold at an overvalued prewar parity, the United Kingdom was suffering from high unemployment and a balance of trade deficit. In the spring of 1927 Germany raised interest rates, intensifying the pressure on the British balance of payments. At the same time the Bank of France attempted to halt the appreciation of the franc by selling francs for sterling, which it then attempted to convert into gold at the Bank of England. When, at a secret Long Island conference in July 1927, the Reichsbank and the Bank of France offered only minor concessions to address this threat to the newly restored gold standard, the Fed took the lead and eased monetary policy. Further influenced by the slowdown in the US economy, the Fed cut the discount rate and purchased securities. But the minutes of the Open Market Investment Committee make it clear that the majority worried about how the stock market would react to this policy. One Board member, Edmund Platt, spouted: "Lower [the discount rate] in New York first and to hell with the stock market" (quoted in Clarke, 1967, p. 127).

While this shift in Fed policy was unexpected, it is difficult to see how it could have had a big impact on the stock market. The interest cut was small and brief, as a contractionary policy was initiated in January 1928 with the discount rate ascending from $3\frac{1}{2}$ to 5 percent by August 1928. In addition, there were heavy open market sales. Although the discount rate remained unchanged for another year, monetary policy has been characterized generally as tight for the remainder of the stock market boom. In 1928 and 1929 high-powered money and the CPI fell, and M1 grew only slightly in 1929. In spite of this evidence, many, including Benjamin Strong, president of the Federal Reserve Bank of New York, felt that this tightening was begun too late to halt the advance of the stock market (Clarke, 1967).

Although concerned about protecting international gold reserves, the Federal Reserve was obsessed with the stock market and what it regarded as the excessive expansion of credit for speculation. Following the "real bills doctrine," the founders of the Fed had hoped that the bank's discounting activities would channel credit away from "speculative" and towards "productive" activities. Even in the early 1920s many members of the Board, as well as the banks, were frustrated by the amount of credit that the stock market seemed to absorb and looked for some way to reduce the volume of brokers' loans. Almost all Fed officials agreed about this issue, but they were split over the appropriate policy; and policy inaction, after the August 1928 increase in the discount rate, reflected an intense struggle.

The Federal Reserve Board believed that "direct pressure" or jawboning could be used to channel credit away from speculation. The Board also wanted the Federal Reserve banks to deny access to the discount window to member banks making loans on securities. In February 1929 the chairman, Roy Young, spoke out against speculation and issued a letter to all Federal Reserve banks, instructing them to limit "speculative loans." Brokers' loans by member banks did not increase after this date, but the market was supplied instead by non-member banks, corporations and foreigners. In contrast, the Federal Reserve Bank of New York contended that it could not refuse to discount eligible assets and that it was impossible to control credit selectively. It argued that speculation could be reduced only by raising the discount rate. The Board was not persuaded. Between February and August 1929 it refused New York's eleven requests to raise the discount rate (Friedman and Schwartz, 1963). According to Clarke (1967, p. 155), the New York Fed believed that if the Fed could break the boom early, the adverse effects on the United States would be small compared to the "disastrous consequences for both the domestic and international economies that would result from a prolongation of speculative excesses and from the inevitable and violent collapse of the speculative bubble." Only in August 1929 did the New York Fed finally prevail. Unfortunately, the discount rate was raised from 5 to 6 percent just as the economy was reaching its cyclical peak.

The market, declining since early September, collapsed on Black Thursday, 24 October, and Black Tuesday, 29 October. Margin calls and distress sales of stock prompted a further plunge, while lenders withdrew their loans to brokers, threatening a general disintermediation. The New York Fed promptly encouraged the New York City banks to increase their loans to brokers, made open market purchases, and let its member banks know that they could freely borrow at the discount window. The direct effects of the crash were thus confined to the stock market. The Fed's prompt action ensured that there were no panic increases in money market rates and no threat to the banks from defaults on brokers' loans. While the New York Fed's response has been recognized in hindsight as the correct response, the Board disapproved and censured the New York Fed. In spite of the recession, the Board maintained its tight monetary policy, aggravating the economy's slide and provoking a further decline in the market. The fall in the stock market, by reducing household wealth and the value of collateral, added to the monetary shock that stunned the economy (Friedman and Schwartz, 1963).

The Fed's experience in the 1920s raises three policy questions. The first is whether the Fed's looser policy in 1927 exacerbated the boom at a time when it could have been restrained. Board member Adolph Miller and many critics after the crash blamed the New York Fed for permitting an excessive credit expansion (Meltzer, 2003). Some modern students, including Barry Eichengreen (1992a), have concluded that the Fed erred in loosening its policy, though it is difficult to find a plausible reason for a tighter policy. Although contemporaries worried about speculative excess in the market, mid-1927 precedes the conventional date of the boom's beginning – early 1928. In fact, monetary growth for the year was quite modest, at a little over 1 percent (Meltzer, 2003), and the economy had hit a peak in October 1926. Most contemporary indicators suggested to the Fed that policy should be eased not tightened; the same holds true for a Taylor rule; and Bordo and Jeanne's (2002) measure of excessive asset growth does not identify a boom in mid-1927. Finally, an augmented Taylor rule (Cecchetti, 2003) does not recommend a policy change as the equity premium for 1927 was near its historic average.

The second policy question is how the Fed should have reacted to the crash. New York's prompt intervention in 1929 to prevent the shock spreading to the rest of the financial system is regarded as a canonically correct response (Friedman and Schwartz, 1963). The third policy question is whether the Fed focused too much on the stock market boom after 1928, ignoring the fact that the economy was entering a recession. The scholarly consensus here is that policy was excessively preoccupied with speculation after the crash, inducing the Fed to continue a restrictive policy long after the economy had entered a steep decline.

The lessons learned from the experience of the 1920s have strongly conditioned central bankers' responses to subsequent crashes. As in 1929, the financial system in 1987 came under enormous stress as brokers needed to extend a huge amount of credit to their customers who had been hit by margin calls. Specialists and traders in stock index futures also found it difficult to obtain credit. Fearful that there would be a collapse of securities firms, with ramifications for the clearing and settlements system, the Open Market desk increased bank reserves by 25 percent and the Fed pushed commercial banks to supply broker-dealers and others with credit. While interest rate spreads widened at the beginning of the crisis, they quickly diminished. Finally, the Fed withdrew most of the high-powered money that it had provided as the crisis subsided. In contrast, the slower collapse of the 1990s market produced no calls for intervention as intermediation and the payments system were not threatened. In general, the conclusion that the Fed was mistaken to focus on the stock market after the 1929 crash has convinced most central bankers to take a position of "benign neglect" vis-à-vis asset bubbles.

Thus, it is primarily the first question – whether a central bank should intervene in an asset price boom – that appears to be still open. A comparison of the 1990s with the 1920s is, consequently, useful, as there appear to be strong parallels in economic developments and policy debates. Like the 1920s, the 1990s saw a long period of rapid growth after a period of severe disruptions. The unanticipated inflation of the 1970s and the Fed's decision to wring out inflation in 1979 contributed to a wave of bank and saving and loan failures, cresting in the mid-1980s. By the beginning of the new decade banks had increased their capital accounts and strengthened their balance sheets. After a sharp recession in 1990–1991 the economy experienced its longest expansion on record, from March 1999 to March 2001. Real gross domestic product grew at an annual average rate of 3.3 percent and unemployment averaged 5.5 percent. In many respects, the nineties were the most stable decade after the Second World War (Mankiw, 2002).

In 1993 the chairman of the Federal Reserve Board, Alan Greenspan, announced that the Fed would pay less attention to monetary aggregates than it had in the past, as their behavior did not appear to give a very reliable policy guide. The Fed shifted to interest rate targeting, and in particular the federal funds rate. Most observers believe that the Fed followed some approximation to a Taylor rule, focusing on inflation and growth and leaving other issues that inflamed public debate, including fiscal policy, "irrational exuberance," and international financial crises, to negligible roles (Mankiw, 2002). One of the few exceptions to this consensus is Cecchetti (2003), who claims that, as equity prices boomed, the Federal Open Market Committee (FOMC) adjusted its interest rate targets. Examining the FOMC minutes and transcripts from 1981 to 1997, he measures the relative occurrence of references to the securities markets, and finds that the number rose just as the equity premium was falling. Estimating an augmented Taylor rule with additional variables (the equity premium for the presence of a bubble and a measure of banking system leverage for financial distress), he finds that the FOMC adjusted interest rates in line with changes in the equity premium.[11]

Whether or not the Fed factored the stock market into its policy, independent of inflation and growth objectives, it boldly voiced concerns about the behavior of the market. Well before the IT–NASDAQ boom, the bull market has sounded alarm bells at the Fed, just as it had in 1927–1928. While the price/earnings ratio was increasing, all measures of productivity growth in the early 1990s showed little reason to expect a future surge in earnings and dividends. In 1996 Alan Greenspan castigated the stock market as exhibiting "irrational exuberance." Yet this criticism, seeming to mimic the actions of early 1929, was not followed up by any effort to tame the market. The lesson of the intervention in the 1920s may have restrained the Fed, and it certainly would have been wary about trying to deflate one group of stocks in the technology sector without affecting the whole market. The verbal berating of the market diminished later in the decade when evidence of a productivity upsurge gave the Fed less cause to fear that its low interest rate policy would lead to inflation.

In the higher-growth economy of the late 1990s the Fed's policy has been characterized as one of "forbearance" (Blinder, 2002). However, the Fed did not hesitate when inflationary pressures appeared. Between February 1994 and February 1995 it raised interest rates by three percentage points, after a rapid expansion following the 1990–1991 recession, thereby securing a recession-less "soft landing." Afterwards, policy was largely neutral until the September 1998 collapse of Long-Term Capital Management (LTCM), a $100 billion hedge fund, following the Asian crisis. Fearing that its demise would panic financial markets, the Fed strong-armed the leading New York banks to assist with an orderly liquidation and cut the federal funds rate three times. Some critics have asserted that this action left policy too loose and allowed the boom in the stock market to take off in its final phase. They have argued that it was too late when the Fed finally began to raise interest rates in June 1999. Yet the reduction, of less than 100 basis points in the federal funds rate (and the ten-year bond rate), was not seen at the time as wildly inflaming the boom. Measured by all three indices in figure 9.2, the market had retreated in August 1998 and was largely flat until December 1998–January 1999, when it resumed its ascent; and there was no signal from the dividend yield or price/earnings ratios. Like the loosening of policy in 1927, this action came at a time when the market was quiescent. Given the similar rise in the market when policy was neutral, this action may have been a minor fillip at best.

9.8   Conclusions

This survey of fundamentals-based equity valuation reveals the enormous difficulty of identifying fundamentals in forward-looking assets. At the same time,
little evidence can be mustered to support Shiller's (2000) assertion that the
markets are almost exclusively driven by waves of optimism or pessimism.
Estimates that apportion the degree to which bubbles determine asset prices
relative to fundamentals are, at best, fragile. Perhaps it is not surprising that
"benign neglect" is, typically, the policy accepted both by those who favor
fundamental explanations and those who favor bubble explanations.

The Fed has been blamed for contributing to stock market booms. Two
instances – in 1927, when the Fed helped the United Kingdom stay on the
gold standard, and in 1998, when the Fed responded to the collapse of LTCM –
are sometimes used to argue that the Fed should have pursued a tighter policy
earlier. However, it is hard to regard these relatively modest stimuli as central to
an explanation of the subsequently soaring markets. Furthermore, this criticism
has a 20–20 hindsight quality, as measures of a bubble that should have alerted
policy did not appear until later, in 1928 and 1999.

Fortunately, the Fed in the 1990s was not fixated on speculative credit, as was
the Fed of the 1920s and 1930s, saving it from dangerous deviations from the
appropriate policy targets of price stability and full employment. The Fed has a
limited but vital role in responding to stock market crashes. When the abruptness
of a crash threatens the payments system and intermediation, a classic lender of
last resort role is appropriate, as occurred in 1929 and 1987. In addition, even
if the market's descent is slower and the financial system has weak balance
sheets, intervention may be appropriate in order to prevent a broader financial
crisis. In both cases, however, it is a brief intervention that is required – not a
shift in the Fed's intermediate or longer-term goals.

Notes

1. The most frequently used data for examining booms, crashes and bubbles are the
   series on Robert Shiller's webpage, www.econ.yale.edu/~shiller/data.htm, where
   the return is ln(1 + real return), where the return includes dividends and the capital
   gain.
2. If a constant fraction of the earnings, E, are paid out as dividends, where b is the
   proportion of reinvested earnings, then $D = (1 - b)E$.
3. Critics have attacked the small sample properties of Shiller's tests and his methods of
   detrending (Flavin, 1983; Kleidon, 1986), but in a survey West (1988) has concluded
   that Shiller's results were reasonably robust against these and other criticisms.
4. One concern about using dividends to forecast returns is that, if stock repurchases
   replace dividends, the past history of dividend yields and pay-out ratios will not be
   a good guide to stock returns.

5. Contrasting this skepticism about the IT revolution, Nordhaus (2002) believes that IT provided only a modest contribution to the revival of labor productivity, which was more broad-based. Using income-side GDP measures and four measures of labor productivity, Nordhaus finds that manufacturing productivity growth increased by 1.61 percent from 1977–1989 to 1995–2000, of which the "new economy" contributed 0.29 percentage points. However, Gordon (2002) doubts this finding and recalculates Nordhaus's labor productivity growth, with the result that the computer–IT sector accounted for virtually all the increase.

6. They point out that, at the higher discount rates of 7 to 9 percent that were usually presumed to have prevailed, very high growth rates of between 3.4 and 5 percent would have been required.

7. US government constant-maturity bonds yields are found on www.freelunch.com. The high-grade industrials (series 13026) and McCaulay's railroad bonds (series 13019a) were obtained from the National Bureau of Economic Research website, www.nber.org.

8. The real rate is calculated using the consumer price index. Blanchard (1993) measures the equity premium when the growth of dividends is not fixed; the result, however, is very similar.

9. The disappearance of a substantial equity premium seems to bear out Mehra and Prescott's (1985) claim that, at reasonable levels of risk aversion, it is not possible to justify risk premium any larger than 0.25 percent in the absence of market imperfections.

10. Bernanke and Gertler (2001) are highly critical of Cecchetti et al. and argue that their policy rule requires that the central bank know that the boom is driven by no fundamentals and the exact time when the bubble will burst.

11. If true, this behavior would represent a major change in policy, though the equity premium may be a proxy for aspects of inflation and output growth not captured by the variables in a standard Taylor rule.

10   The 1990s as a postwar decade

Peter Temin

I argue here that the 1990s should be seen as a postwar decade. This description helps to explain some characteristics of the decade and suggests some lessons for today. Charles Feinstein, Gianni Toniolo and I published a paper a decade ago (1994) along similar lines, focusing on three postwar decades. We looked ahead at the 1990s and asserted that it would be a postwar decade like those after the two world wars, coming as it did after the end of the Cold War. The question was whether it would resemble the prosperous aftermath of the Second World War or the parlous aftermath of the First. The 1990s have now passed into history, and I can answer some of the questions we posed a decade ago in anticipation.

I cannot yet answer them all. The 1990s had aspects of both the 1920s and the 1950s; it is hard to say unambiguously that it looked like one or the other. In three important ways, however, the 1990s recapitulate the 1920s in the United States: the unsustainable boom in stock prices, international capital flows, and income distribution. This similarity is worrisome, but not enough to predict the future. Even though the 1930s began with many unresolved problems, the Great Depression was not inevitable; it resulted from the mismanagement of these problems. The question for today is how well policymakers can deal with the problems we can foresee today. The magnitude of the current problems, however, suggests that they are more like those of the 1920s than of the 1950s. I explore two current policies of international relations that were also important in the 1920s: international trade in agricultural goods and exchange rate policies.

The organization of this chapter is as follows. I first review the earlier paper and note the dimensions of economic affairs it discussed. I then update these comparisons with new data from the 1990s, dividing the surveyed areas into those that pose challenges and those that suggest solutions. Finally, I try to peer into my crystal ball.

10.1 Introduction

The earlier paper started with the assertion that the end of the Cold War produced a major shock to the world economy. The world wars of the twentieth century ended decisively, with dramatic changes of government on the losing sides; the end of the Cold War was similarly sudden and dramatic. The result was a massive reordering of government priorities on both sides, a reduction in military spending, and attention to a new set of national and international issues. Our argument was that governments responded far better to the new issues after the Second World War than after the First.

The primary index of the shock to the world economy was the decline in military expenditures, as shown in table 10.1. The data are not complete, as countries tend to change at the end of wars, but the existing data are clear. In the First World War, Germany spent over half its national product on the war at the war's peak; the United Kingdom, 40 percent; the United States, 13 percent. In the Second World War, Germany and Russia both spent a peak level of three-quarters of their national product on the war, while the United Kingdom, Japan, and the United States spent about half. Military expenditures in the Cold War were not nearly as large relative to national products, but they declined sharply after 1989.

Defense spending in the United States fell from over 5 percent of GDP in the 1980s to less than 4 percent in the 1990s. This does not seem like a large shock, but it was not much smaller than the shocks after the First World War. (Spending in the United Kingdom also fell, but it was not possible to compile comparable data for Germany or Russia in the 1980s and 1990s due to changes in the extent of these countries.) The United States did not spend much on the First World War relative to its national product, and it continued to spend on the military after the Second as it became involved in Korea. Moreover, military spending now is more concentrated than in the early twentieth century both regionally and industrially, and reductions have more concentrated effects (Brauer and Marlin, 1992). While the fall in actual spending was not large, it had a large effect on people's attitudes. The end of the Cold War and the US victory were seen as epochal events, giving rise to such vain boasts as Fukuyama's *The End of History* (1992).

The earlier paper looked at the disruptions to various markets in the aftermath of the world wars. International monetary arrangements had to be recreated, over the course of half a decade after the First World War and more quickly after the Second. In each case, exchange rate stability was the goal of postwar planners. World agricultural markets also had been stressed during the wars, and the dramatic change in transport costs after the war flooded the world with cheap grains and other products. Trade arrangements disappeared or were refashioned beyond recognition.

Table 10.1 *Military expenditure as a percentage of NNP or GDP*

	United Kingdom	United States	Soviet Union	Germany	Japan
First World War					
1913	4	1			
1914	9	1		14	
1915	34	1		41	
1916	38	1		35	
1917	38	6		53	
1918	32	13		32	
1919	13	9			
1920	4	3			
Second World War					
1937			9		13
1938	7			17	
1939	16	2		25	
1940	49	2	21	44	17
1941	55	12		56	25
1942	54	34	75	69	36
1943	57	44	76	76	47
1944	56	45	69		64
1945	47	38			
1946	19	10			
1947	11	5			
1948	8	5	18		
1949	8	6	17		
1950	8	5	16		
1951	10	11	17		
End of the Cold War					
1987	5	6			
1988	4	6			
1989	4	6			
1990	4	5			
1991	4	5			
1992	4	5			
1993	4	4			
1994	3	4			
1995	3	4			
1996	3	3			
1997	3	3			

Sources: Feinstein, Temin, and Toniolo (1994); US Department of State, www.state.gov/www/global/arms/bureau%5Fac/reports%5Fac.html.

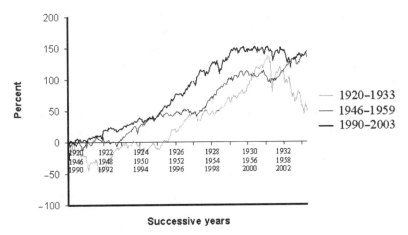

Figure 10.1 Dow-Jones Industrial Average returns, 1920:1946:1990 to 1933:1959:2003 alignment
Source: Dow-Jones Industrial Average (intraday data), http://www.globalfindata.com.

Our paper was written at the start of the 1990s, and it therefore contained a high ratio of speculation to data. This work comes a decade later, and I hope to redress this balance. I have surveyed half a dozen aspects of the economy to search for parallels and differences between the 1990s on the one hand and the 1920s and 1950s on the other. The dimensions are: the stock market and its interpretations, international capital flows, the distribution of income, international trade, and exchange rate policies.

10.2 Comparisons

An obvious parallel between the decades is shown in figure 10.1. I show there the progress of the Dow-Jones Industrial Average over the three decades. The most obvious point is that the rises were all but indistinguishable in these three postwar decades. There have been many reasons given for the stock market to rise that way, and I will discuss a few of them, but surely one good reason is the end of a major war. This kind of climactic event is liable to give rise to many years of euphoria, and it seems to have done so in each of these decades.

The euphoria of the 1920s is well known for the irony of history. President Calvin Coolidge bid adieu to Congress at the end of 1928 with the statement that "[t]he requirements of existence have passed beyond the standard of necessity into the region of luxury" (Coolidge, 1928). Thomas Lamont, Secretary of the Treasury under President Herbert Hoover, agreed in September 1929: "Not only has there been, since 1921, an unusually prolonged period substantially free from so-called crises . . . [T]his result must be attributed to greater foresight on the part of business men producing and selling commodities as well as on the part of buyers of goods" (Angly, 1931). And, of course, Irving Fisher agreed, saying in October 1929: "Stock prices have reached what looks like a permanently high plateau. I do not feel there will soon, if ever, be a fifty or sixty point break below present levels" (Angly, 1931).

The postwar prosperity after the Second World War is remembered with more fondness. The end of both the Great Depression and the war seemed to provide for a new beginning. Dean Acheson, Secretary of State throughout the 1940s, entitled his memoirs *Present at the Creation* (Acheson, 1969). President Harry Truman, in his first postwar public statement in Germany, said, "If we can put this tremendous machine of ours, which has made victory possible, to work for peace, we can look forward to the greatest age in the history of mankind" (McCullough, 1992, p. 429). I do not regard these statements as hyperbole, or the rise in stock prices shown in figure 10.1 as a boom, because prosperity and rapid economic growth continued well after the first postwar decade.

The spread of roads, suburbs, and hospitals changed the landscape of the United States. The demographic reaction from the depression and war gave rise to the baby boom that now haunts our budget projections for Medicare and Social Security. New international organizations and new exchange rate regimes provided hope for economic and political security. These hopes were modified by the Korean War, but not dashed as the United States and Europe continued to expand economically. Even postwar Germany recovered quickly from a temporary currency problem (Temin, 1995).

The 1990s also opened with a ringing announcement of the opportunity before us. The end of the Cold War may not have had the emotional appeal of the "War to end all wars," but it did echo the sense of a new dawn. As in 1919 and 1945, the political map was redrawn. Leaders of old countries needed to formulate policies to deal with new and newly constituted countries. President George H. W. Bush began his State of the Union Speech in January 1991 by noting that "[t]he end of the cold war has been a victory for all humanity." He closed the speech by speaking of a "new world order" (Bush, 1991a). He extended these themes in another speech to Congress on 6 March 1991: "Twice before in this century, an entire world was convulsed by war. Twice this century, out of the horrors of war hope emerged for enduring peace. Twice before, those hopes proved to be a distant dream, beyond the grasp of man. [. . .] Now, we can see a new world coming into view. A world in which there is the very real prospect of a new world order" (Bush, 1991b).

Accompanying the new world order, the apparently inexorable rise of the stock market was heralded in the United States as the sign of a "new economy." The symbol of the new economy was IT or ICT. The growth of the internet and of computer ownership went hand in hand, giving rise to new ways of doing business and improving the operations of older practices (Lamoreaux, Raff, and Temin, 2003). In the language of economics, this became a "general-purpose technology," transforming a wide range of economic activities (Helpman, 1998). In the language of the street, it became simply "technology," as in the description of the late stages of the stock market rise as a "technology bubble."

Alan Greenspan stated the optimism of the decade well (2000):

When historians look back at the latter half of the 1990s a decade or two hence, I suspect that they will conclude we are now living through a pivotal period in American economic history. New technologies that evolved from the cumulative innovations of the past half-century have now begun to bring about dramatic changes in the way goods and services are produced and in the way they are distributed to final users. Those innovations, exemplified most recently by the multiplying uses of the Internet, have brought on a flood of startup firms, many of which claim to offer the chance to revolutionize and dominate large shares of the nation's production and distribution system.

The new economy of the 1990s has echoes of the new economy of the previous postwar decades. The boom of the 1920s was labeled as the coming of a new economy by its participants. As in the 1990s, the defining innovation was a means of communication: the radio. More importantly for growth in the economy was the spread of electric motors. Electricity, of course, had been discovered long before the 1920s, but its effect on the economy took several decades. Paul David (1991) has argued that this delay was to be expected. If an electric motor simply replaced a steam engine, there would be only a small effect on productivity. If, however, a factory was reorganized to take advantage of separate motors at each machine, replacing a central steam engine, then more gains were to be expected. But this reorganization could not take place as soon as electricity became available. There was an inevitable delay while people absorbed the implications of the innovation and then reorganized activities accordingly.

The decade following the Second World War may be thought of as one of adapting to the automobile. This is a consumer good rather than a producer good, but it transformed a system nonetheless. The analogue of new factory layout was the federal highway system, constructed after the war ended. It gave rise to new suburban locations, symbolized for ever as Levittown. And it gave rise, in an exuberant response to the release from wartime shortages, to the great gas-guzzling, finned cars of the 1950s (Offer, 1998).

It is possible that the boom of the 1990s was due to similar causes. Personal computers became available in the 1970s, and there was much talk of the "paperless office." But the spread of computers was slow. More importantly, business practice was not altered in response to the initial availability of distributed computing power. Only after people began to understand what computers can and cannot do did they reorganize their business activities. The boom of the 1990s may have been the result.

The timing, I suggest, was also related to war. In the First World War, and the sharp recession that followed, industrial construction was reduced. The adoption of new plans incorporating electric motors therefore was not smooth. The interaction with war meant that the new factories adapted to electricity were opened in something of a rush in the 1920s. In the Second World War automobile production halted, as the manufacturing sector was directed towards wartime production. Only after the war did the automobile achieve its widespread influence on the economy, leading to highways, suburbs, and related construction. Something similar may have happened with computers. Progress was slow as long as the attention of computer scientists and related professions was directed towards the Cold War, and peacetime uses of computers were slighted. With the end of the Cold War the internet and other advances could burst into full flower.

I have continued the lines in figure 10.1 beyond the end of the decade, to suggest that the period of euphoria and rising expectations has not typically lasted more than a decade. In all three cases the advances of the postwar decade were checked at the decade's end. In the continuing prosperity of the 1960s, the pause in the growth of the stock market was barely noticed. In the depression of the 1930s, the fall in the stock market was not only noticed, but accused of causing the depression. In our time, the stock pause has not gone on long enough to tell us where it is going, although most people now are optimistic. They appear to be getting more optimistic as the stock market climbs out of its low point, but there is no sense that the heady days of the 1990s will return any time soon.

Joseph Stiglitz is an exception to this resumed optimism, characterizing the decade of the 1990s as a replay of the excesses of the 1920s and anticipating the worst now. He argues that finance has become the new center of attention in the economy and that the bubble in the stock market was both cause and effect of changes in the economy as a whole. The link between General Motors and the economy that was proclaimed in the aftermath of the Second World War has now been replaced by the link between Goldman Sachs and the economy. Stiglitz decries this view, along with many specific policies, and argues that it gave rise to a boom and bust at the end of the Cold War (Stiglitz, 2003, pp. 275–6).

A second parallel with the end of the First World War is in the extent of capital flows among rich countries. A lot has been written about the decline and rise of globalization in the early twentieth century (Obstfeld and Taylor, 2003; Temin, 1999). But there were extensive capital flows in the 1920s, in the aftermath of the First World War. The magnitude of these postwar flows is shown in table 10.2, where I have shown the international capital flows between the largest lenders

Table 10.2 *Capital flows of the largest lenders and borrowers, 1924–1930*

	$ millions	
Country	Credits	Debits
United States	5250	
United Kingdom	1300	
France	1340	
Germany		4190
Australia		1310
Argentina		770
Austria		860
Italy		710
Total	9060	9060

Source: Feinstein and Watson (1995, tables 3.3 and 3.4).

and borrowers of the 1920s. The countries shown in table 10.2 accounted for over 85 percent of the total estimated world capital flows.

The biggest lender was the United States, and the largest borrower was Weimar Germany. Given the magnitudes, it is clear that most of these capital flows consisted of lending by the United States to Germany. "[F]or a while it seemed that there was no limit to the appetite of American issuing houses and their investors for German bonds, regardless of the purposes for which the loans were raised, or for the interest to be earned from placing money on short-term deposit with German banks" (Feinstein and Watson, 1995, 115). This flow gave rise to an imbalance in the international payments system that could not be sustained. Ritschl (2003) argues that the Germans knew this rate of international borrowing could not be sustained, that they borrowed in full knowledge that they would not pay back the loans.

In the 1990s the United States was the great borrower, not the great lender. Some relevant data appear in table 10.3. The similarity with the 1920s is that there were large capital flows to a leading industrial economy that was going on a spending spree and absorbing savings from outside its borders. The difference, of course, is that the large borrower is different. The United States appears to be absorbing savings from around the world, although chiefly from Japan. This international imbalance cannot continue for ever; it is like the imbalance of the 1920s. The question that then arises is whether the United States, like Ritschl's Germany, may be borrowing in bad faith.

In any case, large capital movements to rich countries create an imbalance that has to be corrected. Will this be done now by a soft or hard landing? We

Table 10.3 *Capital flows of the largest lenders and borrowers, 1990–1999*

| | $ billions | |
Country	Credits	Debits
Japan	994	
China	232	
Switzerland	193	
France	143	
Singapore	107	
Italy	76	
United States		1169
United Kingdom		180
Australia		153
Germany		125
Total	1745	1627

Source: IMF, 2004. Flows calculated as the balance on goods, services, income, and transfers.

have examples of both types. The parallel with postwar decades suggests that the Great Depression, the "mother of hard landings," is the only way to resolve such an imbalance. But the experience of the United States in the 1980s, after the Reagan spending spree, indicates that soft landings are perfectly feasible. The flexibility of the world economic system now as opposed to the tight control of the gold standard – the prevalence of floating exchange rates as opposed to that of fixed rates in the 1920s – gives us hope that a soft landing is likely. This does not mean that there will be no cost, only that the reallocation of resources can be effected without dealing also with the collapse of the economy as a whole.

The third parallel is in the distribution of income in the world's largest economy. The data are striking. The highly unequal incomes of the 1920s were followed by a great compression during the tumultuous years that followed. And incomes have been approaching 1920s levels of inequality again today. I compare the distribution in the United States for the 1920s, 1950s, and 1990s in the first column of table 10.4. I have selected only one index among many for simplicity and comparability; the picture is the same no matter how you slice the data, and, of course, the sources give far more detail.

The richest 1 percent of the American population earned about 20 percent of the total in the 1920s, but only about 10 percent in the 1950s. This share has risen to about 15 percent in the 1990s, with a rising trend. For comparison,

Table 10.4 *Percentage income shares of the top 1 percent of the population*

Year	United States	United Kingdom	France	Netherlands
1918		19.24		
1919		19.59		
1920	14.46		17.95	20.59
1921	15.47		17.32	18.29
1922	16.29		17.87	16.84
1923	14.99		18.91	16.48
1924	16.32		17.96	17.36
1925	17.60		18.16	17.78
1926	18.01		17.82	18.00
1927	18.68		17.45	18.37
1928	19.60		17.27	18.63
1929	18.42		16.15	18.09
1950	11.36		8.98	12.05
1951	10.52	10.89	9.00	
1952	9.76	10.20	9.16	12.43
1953	9.08	9.72	9.00	11.79
1954	9.39	9.67	9.14	11.65
1955	9.18	9.30	9.33	11.21
1956	9.09	8.75	9.37	
1957	8.98	8.70	9.37	10.54
1958	8.83	8.76	9.01	11.48
1959	8.75	8.60	9.46	10.59
1990	12.98	9.80	8.23	5.48
1991	12.17	10.32	7.97	5.48
1992	13.48	9.86	7.75	5.43
1993	12.82	10.36	7.65	5.20
1994	12.85	10.60	7.71	5.29
1995	13.33	10.77	7.70	2.34
1996	13.85	11.88	7.57	5.36
1997	14.32	12.06	7.76	5.43
1998	14.58	12.54	7.76	5.27
1999		12.99		5.36

Sources: Atkinson (2002); Atkinson and Salverda (2003); Piketty (2001); Piketty and Saez (2003).

the richest decile of the American population earned 40 to 45 percent of total income in the 1920s. In the 1950s this number was about 32 percent, and in the 1990s it was again about 40 percent (Piketty and Saez, 2003). Clearly, the size of the income share of the richest groups has varied widely, and much of the change can be explained by trends that reach over a longer period of time.

US income inequality began shrinking in the 1930s and reached its nadir about 1968. It has been increasing more or less since then. The long-run increase in income inequality is explained by changes in the labor market and in household composition. There has been a shift in employment opportunities away from the manufacturing sector, which earlier provided high-wage opportunities for unskilled labor, to the service sector. This development has been driven by technological progress and by globalization, including both the immigration of low-skilled labor and the outsourcing of some jobs. The demand for high-skilled workers has risen, and a gap between those with higher and lower education has emerged. Other factors contributing to this gap are a decline in the proportion of workers belonging to unions, a decline in the real value of the minimum wage, the increasing use of temporary workers, and an increasing need for computer skills. Economists tend to see biased technical change at the bottom of this process, while more popular observers see globalization (Collins, 1998).

Another big factor is changes in living arrangements. Divorces, separations, births out of wedlock, and the increasing age at first marriage have all led to a shift away from married-couple households towards single-parent and non-family households, which typically have lower incomes. Also, the increasing tendency for men with higher earnings to marry women with higher earnings has contributed to widening the gap between high-income and low-income households (Weinberg, 1996).

A comparison with other OECD countries must, however, weaken some of the above explanations, because they should apply to all these countries (Gottschalk, 1997). Since 1970 the growth in inequality in the United States has been considerably greater than in all other OECD countries except for the United Kingdom. This difference is suggested in the other columns of table 10.4, which show income distributions for the United Kingdom, the Netherlands, and France. The decline in the income share of the top 1 percent between the 1920s and the 1950s is clear in all three countries. The subsequent rise appears in the UK data, but not in the Dutch or French data. In fact, the share of the top 1 percent in Dutch income continued to decline after the 1950s.

There is no simple explanation for these national differences, but it may help to recall that these were all postwar decades. It was common after the First World War for European governments to renegotiate their social contract. In consideration of the efforts extended by working men, they were given a greater voice in governance, which probably had some impact on the distribution of income (Eichengreen and Temin, 2000). The Great War was less of a strain for the United States, and there was no comparable renegotiation there. Similar revisions were undertaken after the Second World War, perhaps with less political struggle (Eichengreen, 1996). And almost no revisions appear to have taken place in the 1990s; in fact, there seems to have been a reversion to the pattern of the 1920s in the United States and Britain. Perhaps a Cold War does not have the effects on the social compact that a fighting one does; there is no analogue of the mass participation of ordinary working people.

Returning to similarities between the 1920s and the 1990s, and looking at the growth of the US top income share instead of at its relative size, we see that there is increasing inequality in both periods. There could be similar forces driving these trends, since we don't know if inequality in the 1990s was increasing for the same reasons as in the 1970s or 1980s, and the 1920s were not part of a longer period with rising inequality, so they stand out compared to other periods. Robert Keller (1973) has argued that the 1920s stood out from all other decades in the twentieth century (before the 1990s) because capital's share of income increased. This was due to growth in a few capital-intensive industries that made an impact on income distribution. The trend today owes something to technology and something to tax policies. There is no increasing trend in the 1920s or 1990s in the French and Dutch data. There is an increasing trend in the 1990s in the United Kingdom.

Continuing in this list of similarities with earlier postwar decades, I look at international trade in agriculture. As noted in our earlier paper, the world market for agricultural goods was disrupted by war and characterized by oversupply in the 1920s. This led to economic distress among agricultural exporters and protection among importers. A similar development took place in the 1990s. The end of the Cold War, coupled with great technological progress in agriculture, resulted in an increased supply of basic grains and fibers. In a free world market, trade would have increased and prices fallen.

This, of course, is not the history of the last decade. The OECD countries have protected their native agriculture at great cost, and not allowed consumers to enjoy the fruits of international specialization in this part of the economy. The vehicles for this protection were the programs of agricultural support built up in the aftermath of the Second World War. The United States expanded its agricultural supports that had been initiated in the depression and fallen into disuse in the prosperity of the war. The European countries constructed their Common Agricultural Policy (CAP), which has been used to protect their farmers. The contrast between the UK response to increases in world agricultural supplies in the late nineteenth century and in the late twentieth century is quite remarkable. The cost of this agricultural protection has grown to be vast.

Total costs of agricultural supports for a few countries are shown in table 10.5. In recent years the United States has spent just under $100 billion a year support-ing its agriculture, while the European Union has spent over $100 billion each year for the same purpose. These supports do not go equally to each farmer, but it gives an idea of their outsize magnitude by calculating the average subsidy per farmer in the United States and European Union. The agricultural labor

Table 10.5 *Agricultural supports by the United States and European Union*

	2001 $ billions	
Year	United States	European Union
1990	71.4	132.8
1991	75.6	153.6
1992	80.9	147.2
1993	86.0	128.3
1994	80.6	128.7
1995	70.5	145.9
1996	77.2	140.2
1997	76.3	127.2
1998	91.3	132.7
1999	99.5	128.9
2000	92.8	100.0

Source: OECD, total support estimate by country, available at www.oecd.org/dataoecd/2/18/4420681.xls.

force in the United States is about 3.2 million, making the average subsidy for everyone working on American farms close to $30,000. This is an amazingly large distortion in the US economy, and a massive distortion to world agricultural markets as well. The agricultural labor force in the old European Union (omitting recent additions in Eastern Europe) is 8 million, making the average subsidy only $12,500. This is a smaller distortion for each farmer, but of course there are many more of them. One observer has called these supports the "great trade robbery" (Sharma, 2003).

Some of the costs to less developed countries were revealed in the recent collapse of the WTO talks in Cancun. The issue on which the talks faltered was trade in cotton fibers. This largely tropical crop is not grown at all in Europe, although it is grown extensively in the southern and western United States. The Europeans saw it as the camel's nose entering into the CAP tent and opposed the reduction of support programs vigorously. The United States had the luxury of standing on the sidelines while looking out for its own farmers. The result was that the march towards free international trade that has been progressing since the Second World War has screeched to a halt.

The misallocation of resources may be even larger than is shown by market activity. The high level of agricultural support in the United States promotes agriculture, which uses water. The result has been a rapid depletion of the Ogallala aquifer that underlies the Great Plains. If we considered the true social cost of producing cotton in the American West, we should tax it instead of subsidizing it. It is hard to know how to value this cost and set a tax level, for two reasons. First, the water problem is a non-market cost; we need to discover a way to value it. Many Cassandras predict an agricultural collapse, while other economists recall earlier Cassandras and dismiss these predictions of doom. Second, agriculture is depleting water supplies and underground aquifers all over the world. It is hard to know how much the geographic misallocation of agriculture due to subsidies in advanced countries affects the world's water supplies (Easterlin, 1996, chap. 11; Glennon, 2002; Brown, 2003).

Is the distortion of agricultural markets a problem? Charles Kindleberger has argued in his classic history of the Great Depression that the collapse of agricultural cartels in the late 1920s was an important cause of the economic collapse. They were part of the general deflation that heralded the fall in aggregate demand. There is a problem with this argument, for agricultural prices are only one component of the general price level. A fall in agricultural prices, therefore, is a decline in a relative price, not the aggregate price level. How could a change in relative prices have a macroeconomic effect? Kindleberger asserts that agricultural exporters, typically poor countries, were constrained by their loss of farm income to reduce their expenditures. Agricultural importers, typically industrial countries, should have expanded by the increase in their real incomes, but they did not. Why not? Kindleberger appeals first to money illusion and then to the delay with which consumers would realize that their incomes had risen and adjust their spending – a delay that might be very long indeed if tariffs or quotas were imposed to cushion the effect of low prices on domestic farmers (Kindleberger, 1986, p. 91). We might add tight monetary policies to this list. A more recent paper places the fall in agricultural prices as the primary cause of the Great Depression, albeit indirectly through a fog of econometric exercises (Madsden, 2001).

There does not appear to be the same risk at the end of the 1990s as there was at the end of the 1920s, for the simple reason that private cartels have been replaced by government ones. The subtext of the Cancun conference was that the OECD governments were not about to relinquish their agricultural supports, no matter how distortionary they are or how much harm they do to the rest of the world. Domestic politics, strongly affected by the allocation of representatives during a former era when agriculture was important, trumps all. The importance of agricultural trade for this chapter is revealed in how little interest there is in reforming a bad economic policy.

On the other hand, the depletion of the water supplies and other resources may be a problem. There is no parallel with other postwar decades because the world economy has been growing steadily, if a bit unevenly, over time. We were consuming less than the capacity of global biosphere in earlier postwar decades, but we reached its limit in the 1980s. During the decade of the 1990s the world consumed above the capacity of the global biosphere – that is, it consumed the inherited capital of the planet. The pumping of irreplaceable aquifers is only the most easily understood example of this consumption of capital. A collection of scientists estimated that consumption had risen to 120 percent of the global biosphere's capacity by 1999. Their conclusion was summarized in a graph that shows an irregularly rising line labeled "Number of Earths Used by Humanity" set against a horizontal line at 1.00 labeled "Number of Earths Available." The first line crosses the second around 1980 and remained above it in the 1990s (Wackernagel et al., 2002). Unlike the problems of agricultural trade, the problems of agricultural production are risky and worrisome. They might even appear in retrospect as the most serious problems of the 1990s.

Exchange rate chaos was characteristic of the early 1920s. There were floating exchange rates left over from the war, and most European countries found it hard to return to fixed rates. This was due only partly to the conviction of the gold standard that fixed rates had to be unaltered from before the war. France, which disregarded this convention, took until 1926 to stabilize its currency. There were, of course, periods of hyperinflation during this period, and contemporary economists blamed floating exchange rates for these excesses. Planners aimed to avoid this kind of chaos after the Second World War, and the Bretton Woods system offered stable exchange rates without writing them in stone. When even that amount of flexibility did not appear to be enough to avoid problems in the postwar reconstruction, the Europeans were allowed to form the European Payments Union, which promoted trade among its members while limiting payments to the United States. The result was to create a floating shadow price of dollars in Europe, considerably above the official exchange rate. This was known at the time as the "dollar shortage."

The European Union spent the 1990s trying to recreate something very much like the European Payments Union. There are fixed exchange rates within Europe – that is, within the eurozone, which includes much of Continental Europe. But the exchange rate with the United States is not fixed. There is no official price of dollars and therefore no explicit dollar shortage. Instead, the price of dollars is allowed to float, and any "dollar shortage" in the 1990s was simply a rise in the value of the dollar. The eurozone has created problems reminiscent of the 1920s within Europe, but kept the flexibility vis-à-vis the United States of the 1950s.

10.3 Conclusions

I have shown that the 1990s have lived up to their advance billing as a postwar decade. They have exhibited some of the same kinds of excesses and some of the same kinds of disequilibria. Postwar exuberance showed most clearly in the US stock market; disequilibrium shows most clearly in the sustained capital flows between industrialized countries. The question, of course, is how long these trends of the 1990s can endure.

Stein's Law (from Herbert Stein, chairman of Nixon's Council of Economic Advisors) was designed for such a problem; it states: "Things that can't go on for ever, don't." This "law" appears designed for the current trend in the international location of savings and spending – and possibly for the total volume of consumption as well. If we assume that a correction will have to take place, then we come to the critical question. Will it be a hard landing, like the Great Depression? Or will it be a soft landing, like the conversion of the dollar surplus into the dollar glut?

I cannot claim to know the future. We can hope that the flexible dollar will allow the United States to have a soft landing, as it did in the 1980s, when it had the same kind of deficits in the federal budget and the balance of payments. The value of the dollar will continue to fall. Those Americans who like to purchase imported cars or travel abroad will notice the change in price, but there will be no threat of financial meltdown or international crisis. As in the 1980s, however, the soft landing may be dependent on a change in US policy that signals a reversal of the disequilibrium trend. There is no way to predict how soon such a change might begin. The longer it waits, the greater the chance of a hard landing – that is, a financial crisis that will make the needed readjustments more difficult and painful.

Note

I am grateful for the research assistance of Hai Nhu Nguyen, Hans Holter, and Alexei Zykov, under the Massachusetts Institute of Technology's Undergraduate Research Opportunities Program.

11 What is happening to the welfare state?

Peter H. Lindert

11.1 Introduction

It has been a quarter-century since the election of Margaret Thatcher ushered in an era of conservative assault on big government and the welfare state. This quarter-century has seen a wave of enthusiasm for cutting taxes and transfers, privatizing state industry, and trimming union power. It has produced at least fifteen English-language books with "crisis of the welfare state" or "welfare state in crisis" or "waning of the welfare state" in their titles. The Anglo-American press has repeatedly written off the welfare state as an obsolescing failure.

Hence the title of this chapter. Did the 1990s, and the start of this century, reveal that the welfare state is in retreat? How is it coping with the inexorable rise in the elderly share of every nation's population? The tentative findings are these.

(1) The welfare state is not an endangered species among the industrialized OECD countries. While its growth clearly slackened after 1980, social transfers continue to take a slowly rising share of GDP. Ireland and the Netherlands are the main exceptions that have cut social transfers as a share of GDP.

(2) We can use experience from the 1980s and 1990s to judge how population aging and the pension crisis will affect government budgets in this century. The countries with the very oldest populations have already begun to cut the relative generosity of their transfers to the elderly *per elderly person*. They did not, however, cut the average shares of public pensions or other transfers in GDP. Using behavioral regression patterns to project the same behavior up to the point where each country has 20 percent of its population over sixty-five, and noting current retirement policies, suggests how OECD countries will respond to the rise of the elderly population.

(3) There are a few welfare states in the Second and Third Worlds, and more of them will probably emerge as their populations age and prosper. Some, but not all, of the transition countries in central and Eastern Europe have high elderly shares in their total population, and are clinging to historically

generous pensions. Latin American and Middle Eastern countries are also making higher social transfers than the OECD countries offered at similar stages of development.

(4) Some developing countries, however, have regressive tax-transfer systems subsidizing public elites. These may (hopefully) erode as more egalitarian pensions and transfers rise.

The boundaries of this chapter are set by my definitions of "social transfers" and the "welfare state." Social transfers consist of these kinds of tax-based government spending:

– basic assistance to poor families, alias "poor relief" (before 1930), "family assistance," "welfare" (in the United States), or "supplemental income";
– unemployment compensation, alias "the dole";
– public pensions, excluding those for government and military employees;[1]
– public health expenditures; and
– housing subsidies.[2]

Such tax-based transfers tend to redistribute income somewhat progressively. Their progressivity is not uniform or easily measured, however. I define a welfare state as a country resembling those European countries that the media often call welfare states. These countries devote 20 percent of GDP or more to social transfers, and that 20 percent threshold defines a welfare state for present purposes. The welfare state does not include any other government interventions, such as government regulation or ownership of industry, worker protection laws, wage and price controls, or import barriers.

11.2 Who has retreated and reformed in the OECD core since the 1980s?

To judge whether the welfare state is an endangered species, we can begin with a straightforward survival analysis, of the type pioneered by George Stigler in the field of industrial organization. In our complicated world the sustainability of a type of firm, or institution, or policy often depends on more influences than a model can summarize and measure. Distrustful of our ability to judge economies of scale from production functions and other model-dependent constructs, Stigler proposed a straightforward Darwinian test: what sizes of firms tended to survive, and what sizes tended to disappear? While many economists might discount such a test as "merely descriptive," it is a useful starting point.[3] How well have different sizes of welfare states survived? Did social transfers tend to retreat as shares of GDP, or in their generosity to targeted recipients? Did they retreat especially rapidly in the top-spending countries, suggesting that large welfare states are proving unsustainable?

The OECD experience since 1980 is surveyed in table 11.1, where Panel (A) maps the changes between 1980 and 1998 (the latest OECD estimates), and Panel (B) maps those between 1988 and 1998, two years that were both in the

Table 11.1 *How social transfers have changed in the OECD since the 1980s*

(A) Twenty-one OECD countries, 1980–1998

	Changes in percentage shares of GDP					Changes in percentage support ratios	
	All social transfers	Public health	Unemployment compensation	Welfare	Public pensions and disability	For the elderly	For the unemployed
Average change	3.8	0.3	0.5	0.8	2.2	7.3	0.1
Change in standard deviation	−0.6	−0.7	−0.2	0.2	0.7	1.1	1.9
How many countries showed a decline?	2	6	6	4	4	6	11
Which countries?	Ireland −1.8	Sweden −4.0	Denmark −1.5	Netherlands −0.7	Netherlands −2.2	Netherlands −21.5	Netherlands −31.5
	Denmark −0.1	Ireland −3.9	United Kingdom −0.7	Austria −0.7	Ireland −1.4	New Zealand −8.9	United Kingdom −17.2
		Netherlands −2.0		United Kingdom −0.3	New Zealand −0.6	Ireland −7.4	New Zealand −8.0
		Denmark −2.0		United States −0.2	United States −0.1	Australia −4.5	Austria −6.6
		Italy −3.0				United States −4.2	Canada −6.1
		Austria −0.0				France −3.5	Belgium −4.9
							United States −4.4
							Japan −3.8
							Germany −3.4
							Australia −1.4
							Ireland −0.2

Table 11.1 (cont.)

(B) Twenty-one OECD countries, 1988–1998

	Changes in percentage shares of GDP					Changes in percentage support ratios	
	All social transfers	Public health	Unemployment compensation	Welfare	Public pensions and disability	For the elderly	For the unemployed
Average change	1.9	0.2	0.0	0.4	1.4	3.9	-0.3
Change in standard deviation	-0.4	-0.4	-0.2	0.1	0.7	1.7	1.8
How many countries showed a decline?	3	7	11	9	3	4	14
Which countries?	Ireland -4.8 Netherlands -3.2 Sweden -1.2	Sweden -3.9 Ireland -1.5 Denmark -1.2 Netherlands -1.2 Finland -0.8 Italy -0.5	Ireland -1.3 Spain -0.7 Denmark -0.6 Canada -0.6 United Kingdom -0.5 Belgium -0.4	Sweden -0.8 Austria -0.4 United Kingdom -0.3 Ireland -0.3 Netherlands -0.2 Belgium -0.1	Ireland -1.8 Netherlands -1.7 New Zealand -0.6	Netherlands -15.1 Ireland -10.4 New Zealand -6.9 United States -0.6	Netherlands -20.5 New Zealand -11.5 United Kingdom -9.6 Canada -8.9 Austria -7.5 Belgium -4.0

Table 11.1 (cont.)

Belgium −0.1	France −0.3	Greece −0.1	Germany −3.1
	Italy −0.2	Japan −0.0	Australia −2.8
	United States −0.2	New Zealand −0.0	Japan −2.7
	Netherlands −0.1		
	Norway −0.1		Ireland −1.9
			Sweden −1.9
			Spain −1.2
			United States −1.1
			Norway −0.4

NB: The twenty-one OECD countries covered here are Australia, Austria, Belgium, Canada, Denmark, Finland, France, Germany, Greece, Ireland, Italy, Japan, the Netherlands, New Zealand, Norway, Portugal, Spain, Sweden, Switzerland, the United Kingdom, and the United States. Support ratio for the elderly = (benefits/person over 65) / (GDP/person over 16). Support ratio for the unemployed = Allard's "net reservation wage," which she calculates as (replacement rate as a share of average wage)×(coverage rate)×(take-up rate)×(duration of benefits up to one year, as a fraction of a year). "−0.0" = a tiny decline, closer to zero than −0.05.

Sources: www.sourceoecd.oecd.org, downloaded November 2003, and OECD (1998); Age distributions – United Nations (2001) and US Department of Commerce (various dates); support ratio for the unemployed – Allard (2003).

middle of business cycle upswings.[4] The top row in each panel gives the main survival result, confirming the Stiglerian survival of large social transfers. On the average, the twenty-one core OECD countries slightly *raised* their share of social transfers in GDP, both during the Thatcher–Reagan 1980s and during the 1990s. Total social transfers rose by the equivalent of 3.8 percent of GDP for the whole 1980–1998 era, and 1.9 percent after 1988. Pensions and disability payments accounted for over half the overall increase, though all programs rose as a share of GDP in either period. Across all countries, even the support ratios of pensions per old person and unemployment compensation per unemployed person failed to decline significantly on the average, as shown in the last two columns.

Was there convergence or divergence in different countries' commitments to social transfers? The standard deviations in the second row of each panel paint a mixed picture. Expenditure shares for public health and unemployment compensation converged slightly, while those for welfare and pensions diverged. Overall, total social transfers converged slightly, suggesting that countries tended to trade off health and unemployment expenditures against welfare and pensions.

Despite the slight overall rise of social transfers as a share of GDP, there were some exceptions worth noting. Among countries, the two leading "reformers" were Ireland from about 1983 on, and the Netherlands from 1993 on. Among kinds of social transfers, which got cut most? Unemployment compensation stagnated, both as a share of GDP and as a support ratio, comparing benefits per unemployed person to the average wage rate. The average stagnation, however, hides an important divergence in national experiences. As shown in the last column of table 11.1, about half the countries cut the generosity of unemployment compensation, led by the Netherlands, the United Kingdom, New Zealand, and Austria. Many of these countries tightened up the eligibility rules for compensation, as one would expect in an era adopting free-market reforms. How do we reconcile the cuts in relative support for the unemployed in about a dozen countries with the lack of any overall drop in the share of unemployment compensation in GDP? Part of the reconciliation is that the countries cutting the support ratio for the unemployed had rising unemployment on the average, so that the support could stay about the same as an average share of either labor earnings or GDP. The rest of the reconciliation lies in the fact that a nearly equal number of countries – especially Greece, Italy, and Portugal – raised the generosity of their support for the average unemployed person.[5] Welfare spending was not severely cut, in general.

The most important changes, both recent and future, are those in public pensions. As the media constantly remind us, something has to give when a pay-as-you-go (PAYGO) pension system combines with an ever-aging population.

Faced with population aging, or with any other budgetary strain, a country has these four budgetary choices:

(1) raise tax rates on current workers' earnings and property;

(2) cut non-pension transfers per young person;

(3) cut pension benefits per pensioner of a given age; or

(4) raise the official ages at which benefits are granted.

All four options are being hotly debated in every industrialized country.[6]

The movements of the 1980s and 1990s already reveal how aging democracies are likely to dole out the medicine of pension reform. The industrialized countries have not returned to a fully funded or a private pension system, with the partial exception of the United Kingdom under Margaret Thatcher.[7] The main reason seems to be that switching back to these relatively sound systems would impose a double burden on the transitional generation that has to pay for the retirements of both a previous generation and itself. In addition, private pension systems are themselves showing a lot of strain in the face of population aging and volatile asset markets.

Stuck with PAYGO, the OECD democracies have shown some tendencies in the 1980s and 1990s that are likely to continue. Table 11.2 illustrates these tendencies, which are borne out by multivariate analysis. Most countries have not cut the share of GDP spent in taxes on social transfers, nor have they cut social transfers to the young. The share of GDP going to the elderly in the form of pensions and medical aid has also been stable on the average.

In a few countries in the 1980s and 1990s the elderly experienced cuts in the support ratio *per elderly person*, as shown in the next to last column of table 11.1 and in the four panels of figure 11.1's portrait of some countries' pension support ratios. The three countries that have cut the relative generosity of support for the elderly are those featured in panel (A), namely the Netherlands, New Zealand, and Ireland. The Netherlands in the 1990s slashed its average support for the elderly, as evident in the next to last column. The share of pension payments in GDP hardly fell at all, however, because of the rise in the share of the population over sixty-five. The magnitude of the cuts would be hidden if one looked only at the literature on pension reforms as such, since support for the over-65 elderly was not cut. Rather, the country retreated from its excessive disability payments and other subsidies to early retirement. Back in 1990 less than 40 percent of men in the fifty-five to sixty-four age bracket worked. Over 33 percent were on disability pay, and the remaining 27 percent were collecting other payments, especially the special early retirement (*Vervroegde Uittreding*, or VUT) payments. Sharp reforms of this system in the mid-1990s explain the decline in the support ratio for the elderly, since disability payments were counted as support for the elderly in table 11.1. New Zealand achieved a significant but gentler pension reform by raising the normal retirement age to sixty-five between 1989 and 2001, and by indexing benefits to prices rather

Table 11.2 Old-age tensions in OECD countries: projecting pension support and social transfers to 2020, using the aging effect alone

	Share of total population that is older than 65			Predicted changes from 1990 to 2020 due to the rise in the share of the elderly (over-65s) in total population			
	1990	Projected to the year	Projected share	In public pensions, percentage of GDP	In (pensions/elderly), percentage of (GDP/capita)	In total social transfers, percentage of GDP	In non-pension transfers, percentage of GDP
(A) Shorter-range projections for OECD countries surpassing 20 percent elderly before 2020							
Italy	14.5	2005	19.2	−0.3	−28.4	0.4	0.7
Japan	12.0	2005	18.6	1.2	−24.4	0.7	−0.5
Greece	13.7	2010	19.4	−0.1	−32.0	0.5	0.6
Finland	13.4	2015	19.0	0.3	−27.9	0.5	0.2
France	14.0	2015	18.9	0.1	−26.1	0.4	0.3
Spain	13.4	2015	19.0	0.3	−27.9	0.5	0.2
Sweden	17.8	2015	20.0	−1.4	−22.8	0.0	1.4
Switzerland	14.3	2015	18.7	0.1	−23.6	0.4	0.3

Table 11.2 (cont.)

	Share of total population that is older than 65			Predicted changes from 1990 to 2020 due to the rise in the share of the elderly (over-65s) in total population			
	1990	Projected to the year	Projected share	In public pensions, percentage of GDP	In (pensions/ elderly), percentage of (GDP/capita)	In total social transfers, percentage of GDP	In non-pension transfers, percentage of GDP
(B) OECD countries still just nearing the 20 percent elderly share by 2020							
Australia	11.2	2020	15.9	1.8	−6.4	0.6	−1.2
Austria	15.0	2020	18.7	−0.1	−22.0	0.3	0.5
Belgium	15.1	2020	20.0	−1.2	−36.7	0.3	1.5
Canada	11.2	2020	18.1	1.7	−19.8	0.8	−0.9
Denmark	15.6	2020	19.0	−0.5	−23.1	0.2	0.7
Germany	15.0	2020	20.0	−1.2	−36.9	0.3	1.5
Ireland	11.4	2020	15.9	1.8	−6.4	0.6	−1.2
Netherlands	12.8	2020	20.1	−0.4	−41.5	0.6	0.9
New Zealand	11.1	2020	18.2	1.7	−20.6	0.8	−0.9
Norway	16.3	2020	18.2	−0.2	−12.5	0.1	0.4
Portugal	13.6	2020	19.0	0.2	−27.7	0.5	0.3
United Kingdom	15.7	2020	19.1	−0.6	−23.8	0.2	0.8
United States	12.4	2020	16.3	1.4	−8.2	0.5	−0.9

NB: The age effects on pensions/GDP, the pension support ratio, and total social transfers are based on cubic functions of the elderly share. Twenty-one-country OECD regressions for 1978–1995 (without full fixed effects) have been used from Lindert (2004, appendix E).

Source: Percentages of persons over sixty-five – United Nations (1998).

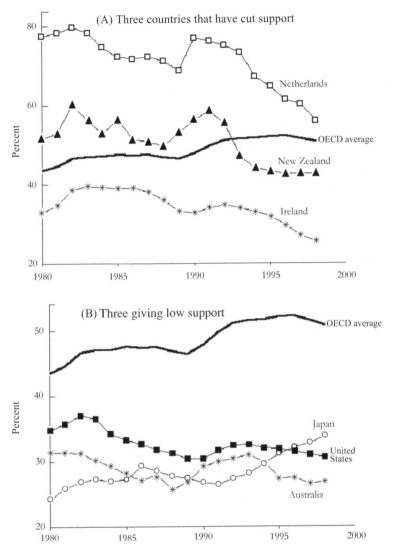

Figure 11.1 Support ratios for the elderly in selected countries since 1980
NB: Support ratio for the elderly = (benefits/person over 65)/(GDP/person over 16).
Source = same as for table 11.1.

than to wages after 1993 (Kremers, 2002, pp. 308–9). Ireland achieved its reduction in the pension support ratio in similarly gentle fashion, by leaving pensions indexed to the cost of living instead of to the soaring wage rates of that country's boom in the 1990s.

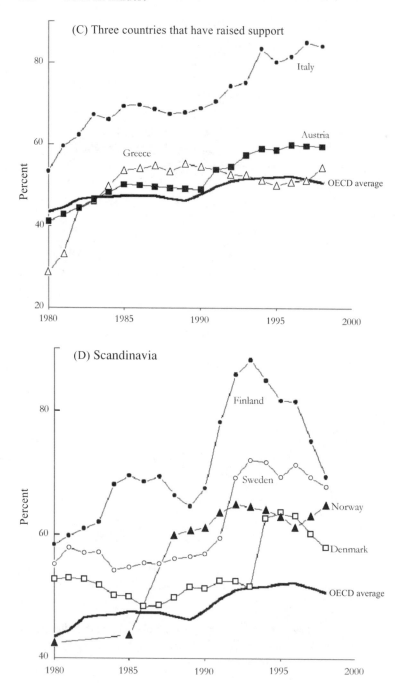

Figure 11.1 *(cont.)*

The pension support levels of other countries differed in both level and trend. Five countries have kept their level of old-age support below the OECD average. In addition to Australia, Japan, and the United States, all pictured in panel (B) of figure 11.1, Canada and Portugal have also kept their spending down since 1980 and earlier. By contrast, at least three countries – Austria, Greece, and Italy – have been scaling up their benefits for the elderly more rapidly than the average OECD country. The Scandinavian countries and Finland have maintained high levels of support.

The most frequent cutback in the 1980s and 1990s was in the generosity of benefits to the unemployed, as shown in the last column of each panel in table 11.1. The Netherlands led in such cuts, largely by trimming the use of disability claims and early retirement packages for persons still officially listed as being in the labor force. Other large cuts in the unemployment support ratio were imposed by the Thatcher government in the United Kingdom and by the government of New Zealand.

While the exceptional cases of transfer-cutting reforms make important topics in their own right, the main conclusion is clear enough. Since 1980 social transfers have not declined as a share of GDP. The welfare states have not yet flunked Stigler's (or Darwin's) survival test, either among all twenty-one countries or among the group of initially high spenders.

11.3 Extrapolating budget pressures into the twenty-first century

The welfare states that have survived the 1980s and 1990s might still suffer budget cuts, however, as the population aging continues. In an older world, something has to give in the PAYGO pension systems that now dominate. Whose budget crises will be the worst? Will the high-spending welfare states fare worse than others? We can indeed identify which countries are most in trouble, given their rates of aging and their current policies. Three main sources of budgetary trouble for social transfer programs, or for anything else in the government budget, are:
(1) population aging, in a world of initially generous transfers to the elderly;
(2) a history of early-retirement subsidies, which will be unsustainable as the population ages; and
(3) any general source of bigger government budget deficits, such as war or massive tax cuts.
Looking at these three sources allows us to name those OECD countries that are under the most pressure in the years ahead.

The pitfalls of forecasting are less treacherous when we are forecasting on the basis of movements in the age distribution. These movements can be projected further ahead than military, political, and economic movements. Let us consider which countries are aging most rapidly, what aging meant for public budgets in

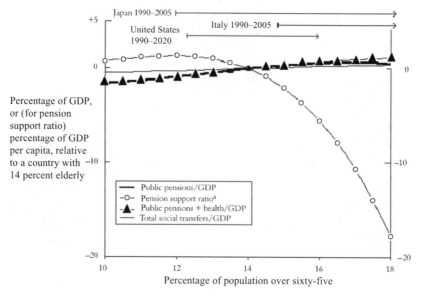

Figure 11.2 How population aging affected pensions and other social transfers in the OECD, 1978–1995

a: Pension support ratio = (public pensions/elderly)/(GDP per capita).

the pre-1998 political experience, and what budget pressure this combination implies, before turning to the extra problems posed by early-retirement subsidies and by soaring overall budget deficits.[8]

Some nations are aging more quickly each year than others. In the 1980s the oldest countries tended to be Scandinavian. Over the first quarter of the twenty-first century it will be a race between Italy and Japan. Italy will win by mid-century, and be saddled with the oldest population in the OECD, according to the UN's projections. Yet the aging trend is common to all OECD countries, not just to these leaders.

What the aging implies for budgets cannot be determined mechanically by applying the current pension rates to a rising elderly share, as many authors of scare stories have done.[9] Rather, the budgetary effect depends on how the political system reacts to the budgetary stress of population aging. Here our best guide is pre-1998 experience, when the Scandinavian governments had already confronted a large elderly population share, while Japan, North America, and other countries still had young populations.

Statistically controlling for other determinants of social budgets in 1978–1995 yields the predicted pattern of age effects shown in figure 11.2.[10] Let us follow the curves to the right of the point where the elderly (over-65) share of the population was only 10 percent. The three curves projecting transfers as shares of GDP are all steady or slightly rising. Public pensions do not seem to be "over the hill" as a tax burden measured as a share of GDP. They are, however, "over the hill" in terms of pension support per elderly person. Figure 11.2 suggests, when other things have been held equal, that the elderly will see fruits of their gray power erode in per person terms as their population share rises towards 18 percent.

What the pre-1998 patterns imply for individual countries early in this century is suggested by table 11.2, which pushes the age effects beyond the sample limit of 18 percent over sixty-five to conjecture about a world in which 20 percent have passed that sixty-fifth birthday. Country by country, the age trends yield specific numbers shaped by the curves of figure 11.2. Again, the aging effect taken alone implies that none of these twenty-one countries will cut the share of GDP it spends on transfers. Taxpayers will apparently get no relief, and non-pension transfers will not be cut. Rather, the burden in most countries is likely to fall on pensions per elderly person.[11] Australia, Ireland, the United States, and Norway will have the lightest burdens, because they are relatively young and still not aging rapidly, thanks in part to immigration.

Among the countries that are aging quickly, fewer need to see a crisis looming than the set of countries with minus signs for the pension support ratio in table 11.2. The reason is that some of them have already been doing their homework by taking the logical approach to longer life expectancy. The logical approach, for public pensions as well as for private pensions, is to extend the retirement age. An increasingly healthy and productive senior population can stay at work longer. Two countries that have faced this issue already are not welfare states: Japan and the United States tend to keep their workers employed to more advanced ages than most OECD countries. The other leading countries with wisely extended work ages, however, are the welfare states of Scandinavia, particularly Norway and Sweden. As best we can project, population aging looks less ominous in these cases.

Countries where the political balance has yielded to pressures to buy out seniors by subsidizing early retirement have asked for additional budgetary trouble. Starting in the 1960s several European countries invited their workers in the fifty to sixty-four age range, and especially those over sixty, to retire early. The implicit tax on staying at work peaked at the start of the 1990s. The incentives to quit work varied. Most European countries formalized an early retirement age, the fifty-fifth birthday for Italians and the sixtieth for others. Belgium and France gave the fifty-five to sixty-four age group extra unemployment and lay-off benefits. The Germans before 1982, the Italians before 1984, and the Dutch before 1995 offered especially generous disability benefits, making it easy for workers to claim that they had a job-related disability.

Table 11.3 *Heading the wrong way: employment rates since 1980, for men of ages fifty-five to sixty-four*

Country	Percentage of men aged 55–64 who were employed in			Net change, 1980–1999
	1980	1990	1999	
France	65.3	43.1	38.9	−26.4
Spain	71.6	57.3	52.7	−18.9
Italy (ages 50–64)	72.1	63.7	54.6	−17.6
Canada	73.3	59.0	55.9	−17.4
Germany	64.0	56.6	48.0	−16.0
Netherlands	61.0	44.2	46.0[e]	−15.0
Greece	69.6[a]	58.8	55.4[e]	−14.2
Finland	55.1	46.5	41.1	−14.0
Belgium	47.7[a]	34.3	35.1	−12.5
Ireland	72.1[b]	59.5	61.6	−10.5
Sweden	77.4	74.3	67.0	−10.4
Portugal	74.2	66.3	64.5	−9.8
Australia	66.3	59.0	57.7	−8.6
Norway	79.5	70.6	73.5	−6.0
Denmark	63.4[a]	65.7	60.1	−3.3
United Kingdom	62.6[c]	62.4	59.4	−3.1
Japan	82.2	80.5	79.5	−2.7
United States	67.0	63.9	65.1	−1.9
New Zealand	n.a.	78.9	78.6	n.a.
Switzerland	n.a.	85.2[d]	78.9	n.a.

[a] 1983.
[b] 1981.
[c] 1984.
[d] 1991.
[e] 1998.
Source: OECD (2000, part 3).

Such golden handshakes are a main reason why men have been retiring earlier and earlier. Table 11.3 shows this trend for twenty countries. In 1980, when the data series begin, Belgium and Finland stood out as countries where men retired earlier. Between 1980 and 1999 men in the fifty-five to sixty-four age group cut back on work in all countries. French men were world leaders in quitting work earlier than their predecessors had done back in 1980, catching up with Belgium in the level of early retirement. Men in Spain, Italy, Canada, Germany, and the Netherlands also cut back heavily on work, though the Netherlands has since reversed this trend. This shift away from older men's work, which was only partly offset by the rise in older women's work, further strained budgets in these countries.

So far, the combination of aging trends and early retirements suggests that Italy may be the country in which the pension system is in the most trouble, followed by France and Belgium. The Italians seem to have realized as much in the 1990s. For Italy, public pension coverage for private employees had won great victories back in the late 1960s. It was around 1969, in response to the financial distress of postwar funded schemes, that the government gave cost of living protection to all pensions, tied pensions to employees' high final salaries, and set up the means-tested *pensione sociale* as a safety net for all the elderly (Brugiavini, 1999). At that time, Italy's age distribution was not unusual among the more developed countries. By the early 1990s even politicians recognized the implications of Italy's having one of the world's lowest birth rates, excellent life expectancy, and not much immigration. Small reforms designed to improve the social security budget were passed in 1992 and 1995. Yet these limited reductions take effect only in this century, and the basic mathematics of Italian pensions remains problematic. Beyond Italy, the group of countries with the greatest danger might be Austria, Belgium, Finland, France, Germany, Greece, the Netherlands, and Spain.[12]

The budget pressures that can crush social programs need not relate to aging or to retirement policy alone, however. They can come from any source. In a PAYGO world, whatever raises the overall government deficit and national debt relative to annual GDP can force a country either to raise taxes or to cut back on any kind of spending, including pensions and other social transfers. Even if pensions are ostensibly protected in a special ring-fenced fund, a desperate government can always breach the ring-fence. The country subject to the most pressure from its overall budget deficit is Japan, where the deficit has been equivalent to about 8 percent of GDP. The United States has suddenly vaulted into second place in the deficit/GDP ranks since 2002, thanks to President Bush's mixture of spending hikes and tax cuts.

Combining all the leading sources of budgetary pressure suggests that the countries where social transfers will be under the most strain in the early twenty-first century will be Japan and Italy – Japan because of rapid aging plus the 8 percent budget deficit, and Italy because of rapid aging plus the folly of early-retirement subsidies. The budget pressures do not correlate with having a welfare state.

A broader point about the nature of budgetary pressures needs emphasis here. The countries may adjust, and apparently have adjusted, in ways that have a zero cost in terms of GDP even if the adjustment imposes a heavy burden on a particular group. This lesson emerges from twentieth-century experience. The net GDP cost of major changes in pensions or other social transfers looks like zero. Whatever happens to pension policy appears to involve offsetting gains and burdens that net out to zero. There is indeed a pensions "crisis," in the sense that some major changes will take from one generation and give to another. Yet these intergenerational effects net out to a virtually zero cost in terms of GDP (Lindert, 2004, chaps. 10 and 18, and appendix E).

11.4 What should we expect in the transition economies?

The transition countries of Eastern Europe and Central Asia face a social policy crisis more severe than the pensions crisis in the OECD. Three historical pressures are pushing the transition countries to cut their social transfers, including their pensions. First, in the 1990s they were emerging from a communist legacy demanding high levels of social spending. Second, their populations were almost as old as those of the average OECD country. Having a large share of elderly people, just like having a communist legacy, tilts a country's policies towards supplying more safety nets at government expense. Third, these countries became even poorer in the disruption of the early 1990s.

It would not have been surprising to see all of them slash their social budgets and fall back to the historical path followed by OECD countries of similar income levels and elderly shares, such as Greece. Yet nothing was simple in Eastern Europe and Central Asia in the 1990s, and a counter-pressure made some of them *raise* the shares of GDP spent on the elderly and the poor. The new post-communist governments desperately needed political support, or at least acquiescence, from the general public. Since the elderly tend to be politically vocal, their demands for safety nets were not so easily suppressed. What emerged was a variety of social policy responses in different countries.

The best starting point for surveying the turbulence in social policy in the 1990s is the Soviet prototype as it had evolved by the 1980s. Soviet social policy famously provided comprehensive social programs, with greater spending of resources on child care, schooling, public health, public housing, and pensions than one would have predicted of a non-socialist country with the same income level and age distribution. In addition, jobs were so secure and so unproductive that many received what might be called unemployment compensation on the job, as in the familiar Soviet expression "they pretend to pay us, and we pretend to work."

Pension spending may have crept slowly upwards as a share of GDP in the Soviet bloc in the 1960s, around the time that it was also rising in the OECD countries. In the Soviet Union, collective farmers were belatedly added to the national pension scheme in 1961. With the retirement age set as low as fifty-five for women and sixty for men, the number of recipients of old-age support and privileges greatly exceeded the over-65 population. In the 1970s and 1980s budgetary pressures started to thin out the support per elderly person, even though pension spending remained a high share of national product (McAuley, 1979, pp. 260–301; Conner, 1997; Kramer, 1997). With similar pension developments throughout the bloc, by the late 1980s cash pensions amounted to the equivalent of about 6 to 9 percent of GDP in all republics, except in the young populations of Romania and Muslim Central Asia (Subbarao et al., 1997, p. 40). In addition, the elderly were given housing and other aid in kind.

The collapse of the Soviet Union and the communist regimes of Eastern and Central Europe in 1989–1991 caused political turmoil and an economic slump. The new regimes reacted differently on the social transfer front. Some cut back, as one might expect in hard times and in the collapse of the whole system of taxation. So it was for pension spending in Belarus, Estonia, Kazakhstan, Moldova, and Ukraine, and for non-pension cash transfers in Bulgaria, the Czech Republic, Romania, and – again – Estonia and Ukraine. Yet other countries moved in the opposite direction between the late 1980s and 1993/94, raising social entitlements to unprecedented levels even as their economies slumped. Poland and Hungary stood out, raising the shares of GDP spent on both pensions and other cash transfers. Pensions also jumped as a share of GDP in Bulgaria, Romania, Slovenia, and Uzbekistan, and non-pension transfers rose in Russia. Such upward ratcheting of transfer shares was probably the result of the initial slump in GDP, a need to buy support for new regimes, and the continued rapid aging of the population. The peculiarity of the situations in the transition countries is underlined by comparing their shares of transfers in GDP since the late 1980s with both a global view for 1990 and the longer sweep of history. Figures 11.3 and 11.4 set the larger regional differences into perspective. Each figure helps us focus on some national and regional oddities by projecting social transfers against either the old-age share or GDP per capita.

The transition economies of Eastern Europe and the former Soviet Union retain a stronger commitment to social transfers than other parts of the world, for any given age distribution and level of income. The same peculiarity emerges in most cases – whether one looks at pensions or at the total transfers shown here, whether one projects them against age shares or against GDP per capita, and whether one compares the transition economies to the long flow of OECD history or to Third World countries around the year 1990. To illustrate, let us turn first to figure 11.3, comparing total transfers as a share of GDP with what one might expect given the elderly share of the total population. In the lower right, we see the flow of OECD history from 1880 through 1995, for the generous pensions of welfare state Sweden and for the lower-spending United States and Japan. Most countries of the former Soviet bloc clearly devote a greater share of GDP to public pensions than Sweden, or the United States, or Japan, or other OECD countries ever did at comparable incomes or age distributions. Their commitment to public transfers also exceeds that of East Asian countries (the triangles) or other developing countries (the crosses). What is most peculiar is

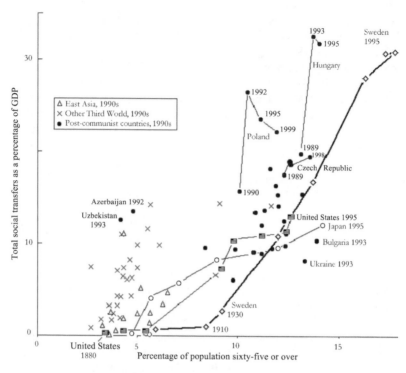

Figure 11.3 Age and total social transfers around the world in the 1990s, versus historical paths 1880–1995

the differential departure from the late 1980s norm of spending 6 to 9 percent on public pensions. Most of the transition economies (the dark dots) kept their shares from rising, as mentioned. Yet the public pension shares in Hungary and Poland had jumped by 1993 to levels that rivaled the pension commitments of Western Europe's welfare states. Public pensions were also strikingly high in Azerbaijan and Uzbekistan in the depths of the slump. Similar contrasts between these countries and others stand out in figure 11.4.

Are these high commitments sustainable? The peak commitments of the early 1990s were partly an artificial by-product of the deep slump in GDP per capita. The same stickiness that kept countries from slashing benefits as rapidly as GDP fell should also keep them from raising benefits as rapidly as GDP recovers. So the support should drop as a share of GDP. The pension support ratio should fall even more rapidly, as the population continues to age. In fact, that tendency to retreat towards world standards of support was already in motion in Poland and Hungary by the turn of the century.[13] To judge from skimpy data, it seems

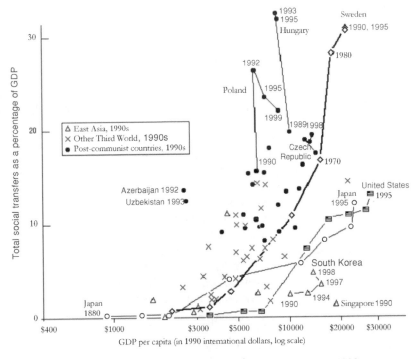

Figure 11.4 Income and total social transfers around the world in the 1990s, versus historical paths 1880–1995

likely that the retreat towards the Swedish historical curve will continue in these countries.

11.5 What should we expect in the developing countries?

Today's developing countries typically spend more on social transfers, including pensions, than was spent in the earlier history of the advanced OECD countries at similar levels of purchasing power and at similar shares of elderly in the population. So say either the positions of the dots and lines in figures 11.3 and 11.4 or the underlying numbers (Lindert, 2004, appendix F). To illustrate, let us compare Sweden in 1930, just before the Social Democrats first came to power, with some developing countries around 1990. Back in 1930 Sweden spent only 2.6 percent of GDP on social transfers, at a time when it had a relatively aging population (2 percent were over the age of sixty-five). Compared to the Sweden of 1930, the following developing countries were poorer and had younger populations around 1990, yet paid a *greater* share of GDP in taxes for social transfers than Sweden's earlier 2.6 percent: Costa Rica (10.9 percent), Panama (9.8 percent), Tunisia (7.0 percent), Sri Lanka (5.3 percent), Egypt (4.4 percent), and Bolivia (3.3 percent, by the central government only). The same was true for some other developing countries as well.

Within the Third World, two large regions seem to spend more than two others. Latin American and the Middle East generally spend more on the elderly, the disabled, the unemployed, and the poor than either Africa or South and East Asia. The lower social spending of Africa and the Indian subcontinent can be explained in large part by differences in income levels and age distribution. Yet one particular contrast stands out even after we have controlled for income and age. East Asia – that is, Asia east of India and Bangladesh – taxes and spends less than Latin America or the Middle East, the two regions that dominate the set of developing country dots (crosses) in figures 11.3 and 11.4. The contrast is blurred in the age perspective of figure 11.3, since the East Asian countries tend to have young populations. Yet in the income perspective of the other two figures, the contrast comes back to us: why should East Asia, which is more prosperous, pay a lower average tax rate for social transfers?

Many observers of the regional differences have imagined a contrast between a tougher and more virtuous East Asia and a more welfare-dependent Euro-American community. Is there a separate anti-welfare East Asian culture? How old is it? Will it last?

The imagined separate Asian culture was trumpeted in the literature on Japan as "number one," which was peaking in popularity just before Japan's asset markets crashed so resoundingly between 1989 and 1991, leading to Japan's "lost decade" of stagnation and policy stalemate in the 1990s. In the 1970s and 1980s many Japanese and foreigners thought that Japan had achieved the world's number one welfare state without government, by having families take care of themselves out of savings and mutual aid. The premise of high private savings is correct, of course, though Japan's data have never revealed any peculiar mutual aid or co-residence between the generations since the Second World War. Returning to figures 11.3 and 11.4, we see that Japan's historical time path of pensions and other social transfers was indeed near the bottom of the range of OECD paths, well below that followed by Sweden. Yet it was not far below that of the low-spending United States and Switzerland, complicating the task of distilling a historical lesson about Asian culture.

Louder and more sustained than the drumbeat on behalf of Japanese values has been the emphasis on anti-welfare Confucian values in the predominantly Chinese countries. In these countries twentieth-century leaders often preached the Confucian traditional emphasis on the family as the main source of support in times of need. That was even true of the government of Mao Zedong, at most times, despite the obvious tension between elevating the family and elevating the state and the wisdom of its leader. Similarly, in Singapore, former President

Lee Kuan Yew and the ruling People's Action Party (PAP) seldom pass up the opportunity to reassert the superiority of his "Asian values" over the Western disease of "welfarism." His successor, President Ong Teng Cheong, repeated the PAP sermon thus when opening Singapore's Parliament in 1994 (as cited in Tremewan, 1998, p. 78):

Developed countries in Europe, Australia, New Zealand, and Canada once proudly called themselves welfare states. Now they have to revamp their welfare systems in order to remedy the disastrous side effects of state welfare: weakened family bonds, diminished incentives to work, and impoverishment of the country's finances . . . Their problems confirm that we have chosen the right path.

To chart the social program trajectories of Third World countries requires a statistical look at their recent history. We need data from countries that have followed consistent definitions for several years. For most developing countries the international agencies supply insufficient data, both because they report social transfers only for one or two benchmark years and because those few data are not sufficiently explained in the publications of the ILO or the IMF. In regressions not presented here I have assembled relatively reliable data for twenty-one developing countries in the years 1975, 1980, 1985, 1990, and 1995.[14] To allow for possible simultaneous feedbacks between GDP per capita and the social transfer behavior, I used a two-stage simultaneous equation generalized least squares (GLS) framework. As it happens, the feedbacks proved negligible in this case: GDP per capita did not greatly affect the social transfer shares, and social transfers had no effects on the level or growth of GDP per capita. Social transfer shares were strongly raised by population aging, and strongly reduced by ethnic fractionalization. Democracy made no clear difference in this sample. These results are broadly consistent with past studies, though the jury is still out on the effects of democracy and autocracy.[15]

The effects of population aging among Third World countries have been very different from those revealed by the recent history of the OECD countries. This younger population side of the hill contrasts with the ageing OECD side shown back in figure 11.2. Among developing countries, where the over-65 population share never exceeded 12.3 percent, a more elderly population strongly raises both pension and non-pension transfers as a share of GDP. Among the youngest populations, up to an elderly share of about 10 percent, aging even slightly raises the support ratio *per elderly person*, perhaps as a reflection of the early stirrings of gray power. The strong positive effect of aging on social transfers suggests that we can once again forecast transfer trends up to the year 2020, this time for younger Third World countries. To interpret the predicted trends, however, we should first note how countries' starting points differed back in, say, 1990.

In fact, there is a significant difference between regions in their 1990 behavior towards social transfers, even when other variables are held equal. South and

East Asia do indeed spend significantly less on all kinds of social transfers than Latin America.[16] Does that mean that Asia has a separate anti-transfer culture, as Singaporean officials insist? Or is it Latin America (and perhaps the Middle East) that has the truly separate culture, in this case a positive political tendency towards social transfers? Let us recast this question into the forecasting question that motivates it: as both Asia and Latin America age, would we expect Asia to spend less than the welfare states had spent earlier, or would we expect them to spend just as much while Latin America spends more?

Some courageous guesses are offered in table 11.4, on the basis of different countries' starting points in 1990, their aging trends, and the non-linear age effects fitted to the whole sample of twenty-one countries for five benchmark years. The guesses, or projections, for each country extend out to one of two horizons. If the country reaches the year 2020 with fewer elderly than 12.3 percent of the total population, then table 11.4 reports its predicted behavior in 2020, based solely on its 1990 behavior plus an estimated age effect. The 12.3 percent share is used because this is the maximum elderly population share observed in the 1975–1995 sample. If the population over sixty-five reaches the 12.3 percent limit before 2020 then the forecast refers to that earlier year with 12.3 percent of the population over age sixty-five. This choice is designed to avoid going beyond the observed sample of historical experiences. Such earlier aging was observed in the cases of Uruguay, Israel, Singapore, Taiwan, and South Korea (which is outside the sample, but appears in table 11.4 anyway). For the other countries the projections run to 2020.

The estimated age effects for developing countries imply that any aging country will experience rising shares of pensions and other social transfers, with little change in the pension support ratio. Pensioners will not fall behind, say the predictions, while their greater numbers will extract rising shares of GDP from taxpayers (or from non-social government spending). The projections imply that the downward pressure on pension support that we witnessed in the OECD pattern will not have visited the developing countries by 2020.

Will any of these developing countries have become a "near-welfare state" by 2020, spending (say) 15 percent of GDP or more on social transfers? Combining countries' starting points with their rates of aging yields the forecasts in the last column of table 11.4. By 2020 there should be half a dozen welfare states, or near-welfare states, in this group. The clearest cases are two countries that had already crossed the 15 percent threshold in the early 1990s: Israel and Uruguay. What table 11.4 adds in these two cases is the interpretation that their welfare state status has been, and will be, reinforced by population aging. Chile will also have become a near-welfare state by 2020. A caveat about the forecast for Chile is that the high level of government pensions may reflect conditions not usually

Table 11.4 *Developing countries: projecting pension support and total social transfers to 2020 or the sample's age boundary, using the aging effect alone*

	Share of population over 65		Predicted changes from 1990 to 2020, or to the sample-maximum 12.3% elderly share, due only to the rise in the share of the elderly (over-65s) in total population			Implied ratios in 2020, or at the sample-maximum 12.3% share, which equal actual 1990 levels plus the changes predicted by age effects		
	1990	Projected to 2020	In public pensions, percentage of GDP	In (pensions/ elderly), percentage of (GDP/capita)	In total social transfers, percentage of GDP	In public pensions, percentage of GDP	In (pensions/ elderly), percentage of (GDP/capita)	In total social transfers, percentage of GDP
Argentina	8.9	11.5	3.6	-0.2	5.4	6.7	34.9	9.3
Bolivia	3.6	5.4	1.8	0.7	1.8	3.0	34.6	4.1
Brazil	4.3	8.7	1.7	0.5	3.3	6.2	105.3	8.7
Colombia	4.2	8.0	1.6	0.6	2.7	2.3	17.5	4.4
Chile	6.1	11.0	3.2	-0.2	6.1	11.2	131.1	17.9
China	5.6	10.8	3.0	-0.1	5.9	n.a	n.a	n.a
Ecuador	4.1	7.3	1.6	0.6	2.3	3.3	42.3	4.6
El Salvador	12.0	6.4	-5.6	0.2	-9.2	-5.2	10.9	-8.1
Guatemala	3.2	4.5	1.8	0.7	1.7	2.2	11.3	2.9
India	4.3	7.2	1.3	0.5	2.0	1.6	6.1	2.3
Indonesia	3.9	7.0	1.8	0.7	2.4	1.9	3.6	2.5
Israel	9.1	13.4	5.8	-0.1	8.1	12.8	76.3	23.5

Table 11.4 (*cont.*)

	Share of population over 65		Predicted changes from 1990 to 2020, or to the sample-maximum 12.3% elderly share, due only to the rise in the share of the elderly (over-65s) in total population			Implied ratios in 2020, or at the sample-maximum 12.3% share, which equal actual 1990 levels plus the changes predicted by age effects		
	1990	Projected to 2020	In public pensions, percentage of GDP	In (pensions/elderly), percentage of (GDP/capita)	In total social transfers, percentage of GDP	In public pensions, percentage of GDP	In (pensions/elderly), percentage of (GDP/capita)	In total social transfers, percentage of GDP
Malaysia	3.7	7.0	2.1	0.8	2.6	4.7	73.5	5.4
Mexico	4.0	7.9	1.8	0.6	2.9	2.6	19.9	6.1
Panama	5.0	9.0	1.3	0.2	3.0	6.8	111.6	12.8
Philippines	3.3	6.0	2.5	1.0	2.6	3.2	21.3	3.5
Singapore	5.6	15.6	6.8	−0.1	10.8	9.4	45.8	13.4
South Korea	5.0	13.5	7.2	0.1	11.3	7.3	3.6	13.7
Thailand	4.3	10.0	2.7	0.4	5.2	2.7	0.4	5.2
Taiwan	6.2	>12.3	6.6	−0.2	10.4	6.6	28.3	14.8
Turkey	4.3	8.5	1.6	0.5	3.1	5.0	78.2	9.5
Uruguay	11.6	12.8	2.1	0.0	2.6	11.3	80.4	13.9
Venezuela	3.6	7.7	2.3	0.9	3.3	2.8	14.2	4.7

NB: For the five countries passing the sample-maximum elderly population share of 12.3 percent before 2020, the years in which they passed or probably will pass that level are: Uruguay, 1995; Israel, 2018; Singapore, 2013; Taiwan, *circa* 2010 (a guess); and South Korea, 2017. The age effects on pensions/GDP, the pension support ratio, and total social transfers are based on cubic functions of the elderly share. The twenty-one countries in that sample are those listed above, excluding China and South Korea.

Source: Percentages of persons over sixty-five – United Nations (2001).

associated with the egalitarian welfare state. As of 1990 President Pinochet had bought out a whole cohort of pensioners with generous state support in order to placate opposition to the eventual shift from PAYGO to funded and privatized pensions.

In East Asia, there should be at least three new near-welfare states by 2020, say the forecasts. These are Taiwan, South Korea, and even Singapore itself. All three countries will have neared, but not yet surpassed, the 15 percent mark when their elderly shares reached the sample-maximum 12.3 percent. Taken at face value, the regression estimates and the forecasts deliver two conclusions about the distinctive anti-welfare culture of East Asia. On the one hand, yes, East Asia looked like a distinctively low spender in the 1975–1995 experience, even after controlling for other factors; either that, or Latin America looked like a distinctively high spender. On the other hand, the strong age effect should propel Singapore, Taiwan, and South Korea towards welfare state status by 2020, even before they become as elderly or as rich as today's European welfare states. Whatever might be distinctively anti-transfer about their culture may well be outweighed by the pro-transfer era in which we live – an era in which governments tax and transfer more than did Japan, the United States, and even Sweden before the Second World War. While these forecasts are as shaky as the average forecast, their implication seems plausible.

11.6 A different kind of transfer problem in developing countries

Today's developing countries have had some severe social transfer crises, but not for the same reasons as the leading OECD countries. Most social budget troubles in the Third World come from political sources like those that have put so much pressure on the budgets of formerly communist countries. Most crises have been by-products of the general breakdown of government budgets, though some have been exacerbated by special inequities in pension finance. That is, instead of the usual causation running from population aging to pension crisis and general budget crisis, as in the leading countries, pension crises in the Third World come as much from the larger political and budget breakdowns as they do from population aging.

The initial motivation for Third World public pensions, and unemployment compensation, also differs from earlier European history, even before any crisis has built up. The driving force is less often egalitarian help to the poor and more often schemes to transfer income from the general taxpayers to the well-connected elite, especially in Latin America. In Brazil, for example, the pension privileges for legislators, civil servants, and military daughters had become ruinously generous by the mid-1990s. A congressman or a career civil servant could retire in his late thirties, with a lifelong pension not far below his earlier rate of pay. In fact, he could even get a new job and still keep receiving the full pension for the rest of his life. Subsequent governments have trimmed this leaky pension program, but it is still generous, and low-income taxpayers have to pay a large part of the bill. Thus, the immediate pension task of populist President Lula is not to launch a bold increase in pension transfers but to cut back on the existing pension transfers, which redistribute income from the general population to the public sector elite.

We are beginning to understand that the elitist nature of many Third World transfer systems is a global phenomenon. One tell-tale sign of elitism in "public" pensions is that they do not cover agricultural laborers or casual workers. Many are specific to government officials and the relatively well-off industrial and commercial sectors.[17] The generosity of pensions for the elite is one reason why Third World "public" pensions seem to claim such a high share of GDP even under non-democratic governments.[18]

Such public sector pensions take their hits in general budget crises, long before the population has aged much. The crises are usually due to the general overspending and under-taxing of Third World governments, and the pensions are cut as part of the usual medicine, regardless of whether it is administered by the IMF.

11.7 Conclusions: global convergence and divergence in social transfers

In 2020, which countries will still be spending a smaller share of national product on social transfers than they do today, and which countries will be spending a greater share? A safe initial prediction is that, by 2020, most countries cutting the share of GDP spent on social transfers and public education will be troubled countries. The way to keep social spending from rising over the first half of the twenty-first century would be to have no growth in average real income, no gain in life expectancy, and no shift towards democracy.

The most likely candidates for this dubious "slim budget" distinction would be countries that fall apart, such as Somalia or Sierra Leone. Indeed, most of sub-Sahara Africa, afflicted with rising AIDS mortality and extractive dictatorships, is the region where social transfers will remain meager. In social transfers, as in other respects, the main global divergence may be the widening gap between an expanding world and a stagnant Africa.

By contrast, there is likely to be convergence in the shares spent on social transfers and public education in the rest of the world. The twentieth century saw a convergence of income growth and in life expectancy. The income convergence took the form of having successive waves of newly industrializing countries reform their economic institutions and catch up with the leading countries. At first the fast-growing catchers-up were European countries and Japan, followed later by the East Asian Tigers, and a few Latin American success cases. Population aging should also promote convergence in such shares outside Africa.

As a corollary, there is no sign of a global "race to the bottom," either in the 1980s or since 1990. That is, nothing even faintly suggests that countries are scrambling to reduce the tax rates implied by their social budgets, to compete for mobile factors of production. Nations have not been recoiling from the cost of the tax-and-transfer package, either since 1990 or earlier.

Notes

1. It is desirable to exclude contributory pensions – that is, the amounts paid by oneself or one's employer. They are not a controversial redistribution of resources but, rather, just part of one's employment contract. It is not easy, however, to remove all employer and employee contributions from the expenditure data. As a smaller step toward isolating non-contributory payments, I have tried to exclude government employee, and military, pensions from the measures used here.
2. The underlying data sets do not permit us to add "tax expenditures" (tax reductions) to the social transfers.
3. See Stigler (1958). For a critique and updated application of the Stigler survivor analysis, see Giordano (2003).
4. The OECD, the ILO, the IMF, and the US Social Security Administration have all had difficulty developing social transfer data that are comparable across countries and over time. For the twenty-one core OECD countries, I have preferred a spliced series based on these penultimate OECD set of estimates. In what follows the estimates from the OECD's (1999) CD-Rom are preferred for these core twenty-one countries through 1995, and the latest OECD estimates are spliced onto this base for years from 1995 on. I did not prefer the latest OECD estimates for the whole 1980–1998 time-span. The latest set of estimates contains a major change of series for all countries at 1990, and peculiar behavior in its Swiss and UK series. The ILO estimates on *The Cost of Social Security* (various issues) seem even shakier and are not available annually. The IMF figures contained in its publication *Government Finance Statistics* are highly aggregated and under-explained.
5. On the changes in eligibility for benefits, see Grubb (2000). For an in-depth discussion of all dimensions of change in unemployment policy, see Allard (2003).
6. In the United States context, such discussions rightly include Medicare along with pensions, since this country faces an even worse crisis in health care than in pensions. Nonetheless, in order to focus on common international patterns, this chapter sets the health care crisis to one side. As table 11.1 shows, a grand average of OECD countries reveals less strain on health care expenditures than on pensions.
7. On the recent history of British pension policy, see Blundell and Johnson (1999), Disney and Johnson (2001, chap. 9), and Blake (2002).
8. For the fuller view, see Gruber and Wise (1999) and Lindert (2004, chap. 8).
9. For an American scare story based on mechanical projections, see Kotlikoff and Burns (2004). Their huge $44 trillion shortfall in Social Security and Medicare comes mainly on the Medicare side, and mainly in the second half of the

twenty-first century. Yet, on the Social Security front, some modest adjustments in the retirement age should suffice to restore balance.

10. The twenty-one countries used in the 1978–1995 sample period are those listed in table 11.1. The panel estimation used three-year averages for 1978–1980, 1981–1983, . . . , 1993–1995. For a fuller view of the determinants of postwar social budgets, see Lindert (2004, chaps. 7, 8, and 16, and appendix E).

11. The double-digit percentage drops in the support ratio for the average pensioner may look implausibly large. Bear in mind, though, that they merely match the large percentage rises in the population share of the elderly.

12. So says a combination of the OECD employment ratios for 1998/9 in table 11.3 and the studies by Blöndal and Scarpetta (1999) and Gruber and Wise (1999).

13. The fallback in Poland's social transfer shares is evident in figures 11.3 and 11.4. For Hungary it is evident in separately available figures for public pensions as a share of GDP. See Rocha and Vittas (2002). All the pressures that seem likely for Hungary and Poland have already been manifest for East Germany. The government of reunified Germany has paid a high social budget price, and reunification will continue to heighten both the budgetary pressure for cuts and the political resistance to them.

14. The twenty-one "developing countries" are Argentina, Bolivia, Brazil, Colombia, Chile, Ecuador, El Salvador, Guatemala, Mexico, Panama, Uruguay, Venezuela, India, Indonesia, Israel, Malaysia, Philippines, Singapore, Thailand, Taiwan, and Turkey.

15. See Alesina, Baqir, and Easterly (1999), Alesina, DiTella, and MacCulloch (2001), Alesina et al. (2002), Mulligan, Gil, and Sala-i-Martin (2002), and Lindert (2004, chaps. 7, 16, and 17, and appendices D and E). One reason why democracy might still have a positive effect on social transfers is that the Third World samples giving the null result (like the current sample) lack data for distinguishing the share of the population that has political voice. The available democracy indices, such as Polity, miss this dimension, which proved so important in the past history of the OECD countries.

16. For expositional convenience, this paragraph welcomes Turkey as a new member of Latin America. Israel was given its own separate dummy variable, and can be set aside here.

17. On Brazil's runaway public sector pensions, see Fritsch (1999), Paes de Barros, and Foguel (2000), DeFerranti et al. (2004, chap. 9), Medici (2004), and World Bank (2004). On the restrictive coverage of public pensions around the globe, see Sala-i-Martin (1996, pp. 281–6).

18. Mulligan, Gil, and Sala-i-Martin (2002). The elitist bias may also explain how the pension support ratios for Brazil, Chile, and Panama are projected to exceed 100 percent by 2020. They were already nearly that high in 1990, because they were pensions for people with salaries well above the national average.

12   The American economic policy environment of the 1990s: origins, consequences, and legacies

Michael A. Bernstein

One phrase perhaps best summarizes the origins, consequences, and legacies of the economic policy environment of the 1990s: tax cuts. The passion for tax cuts as a kind of "Holy Grail" of a "new classical" economics was so intense that even the major political parties, towards the end of Ronald Reagan's second presidential term, could find little about which to disagree on that score. All that was left was political pandering to targeted constituencies. For the Republicans, that meant emphasizing the usefulness of tax reduction for upper-income groups and the broadening of the argument to include proposals for reductions in the prevailing levy on capital gains; for the Democrats, the riposte was to focus on what was beguilingly labeled "middle-class tax relief." Both parties flirted with radical suggestions to eliminate the entire structure of income taxation itself – usually toying with half-baked ideas concerning the implementation of a single- (or "flat-") rate income tax or a national sales (or "value added") tax. With genuine justification, an observer new to the scene might have concluded, during the 1988 presidential campaign especially, that John Maynard Keynes (not to mention his like-minded colleagues and students) had never published a word.[1]

Like most nostrums, tax reduction created more problems than it solved. Federal spending, whether engrossed by military initiatives such as those undertaken during the Reagan presidency, or propelled by transfer payment programs long on the books, rose in both absolute terms and on a per capita basis throughout the 1980s and early 1990s. A rising national debt seemed only to make more obvious the failures (and the failings) of supply-side economics and its attendant pieties. It was hardly surprising, therefore, that conservatives increasingly focused their attention on disbursements themselves. Within this context arose a great offensive against economic statecraft, the continuation of an attack originally launched by the Reagan tax cuts – the proposal for a balanced budget amendment to the United States constitution.[2]

A hardy perennial in the garden of conservative economic ideas, the balanced budget amendment became decidedly fashionable in 1985, when the National

Governors Association passed a resolution favoring its adoption. Ever since it has been the catalyst for a great deal of campaign posing and a consistent addition to the list of bills pending before each Congress. While it has consistently failed in passage, it remains a talisman of the Right, appropriately so given the fact that it would, by statute, eliminate the essential instrument of Keynesian fiscal policy from use by the Treasury, a kind of final nail in the Keynesian coffin. No wonder, then, that it has been and remains an object of great admiration among conservatives, equally loathsome to liberals. Far more striking than the obvious reactions it has provoked across the political spectrum, such as the debate around the tax cut strategies of the 1980s and 1990s, have been the muddled claims proffered in its defense – arguments that have made and that continue to make a mockery of the ideal of professionalized economic expertise in service to the state.[3]

For fairly obvious political reasons, critics of Keynesian-style spending techniques focused their attacks on absolute levels of indebtedness. Large numbers, especially those rendered in red, were impressive instruments of persuasion in the dismantling of the mixed economy. Yet, as any banker would know, let alone economic specialists, debt burden could only be meaningfully evaluated with reference to the ultimate ability to pay. In this context, the national debt, representing a claim on the wealth and income streams of future generations, necessarily had to be measured with reference to gross domestic product itself. As a share of annual income, debt reveals its true lading. By this measure, American public finance, while obviously deranged in the wake of the Vietnam era, had since the early 1980s shown tangible improvement – not surprisingly, because the ratio of annual deficits to GDP had steadily fallen from a high of 6.3 percent in 1983 to 1.4 percent in 1996. Looking at the debt as a whole, in 1995 the national shortfall stood at $3.6 trillion, just over 50 percent of a $7 trillion GDP. This compared quite favorably with a debt/GDP ratio of over 100 percent at the end of the Second World War – interestingly enough, the beginning of a period of growth and expansion in the national economy that was historically unprecedented. In this context, the central target variable would link any rate of growth in the level of debt to the rate of growth of the macroeconomy – a notion altogether obscured in the public debates surrounding a balanced budget amendment.

The sheer obtuseness of the public discussions concerning government finance in the late 1980s and early 1990s prompted a fair number of professional economists to act. In January 1997 the late James Tobin (then emeritus at Yale University and a Nobel Laureate) led an effort to petition Congress on the matter. Calling the proposed balanced budget amendment "unsound and unnecessary," the document was ultimately signed by some 1200 colleagues (eleven of them Nobel Memorial Prize winners). At the end of that month it was presented on Capitol Hill. Above and beyond the misunderstandings the petition sought to expose, it also expressed the conviction that "[t]he Constitution is not the place to put specific economic policy." Reaction to this professional foray into the realm of public debate was inconsequential. The signatories of the "Economists' Statement Opposing the Balanced Budget Amendment" found themselves prophets with neither honor nor influence.

Yet the debate over the national debt held within it an important if fairly unwelcome lesson for social scientists who coveted a place in public affairs. Instruments of economic policy, most especially those having to do with government finance, were – clearly – first and foremost political creations. No public outcry, for example, shook Washington in the fall of 1945, when the financial obligations incurred in the wake of four years of international conflict assumed dimensions that, in the short run, altogether dwarfed the productive capacity of the nation's markets. A remarkable degree of political solidarity concerning war aims had prevented it. Similarly, throughout the 1980s and 1990s it was politics rather than economics that not only framed policy outcomes but, more to the point, set the terms of public debate. If economists found themselves demoralized and confused by the indifference that met their arguments and prognostications, they might have been forgiven their lament. Theirs was a discipline, the product of a century of intellectual and social evolution, that fostered in its practitioners the notion that they could decisively separate ideology from analysis. It was, as a result, in matters of national policy made virtually superfluous.

In point of fact, the transformation of the nation's political landscape in the wake of the Vietnam era had subverted the very foundations of the liberalism that had made sense out of the "new economics." An emphasis on the political–economic issues that had framed the high tide of activist government since the New Deal had provided a community of professionals with both the means and the ends to deploy their expertise. As soon as social issues concerning opportunity and equality occupied center stage, most vividly in the formulation of a "war on poverty," American liberalism ran headlong into the abiding national puzzle of race and ethnicity. A backlash was the inevitable result – one that shifted a dynamic emphasis on productivity and plenty during the 1950s and 1960s into a static refrain concerning the costs and benefits, the winners and losers in market outcomes, during the 1980s and 1990s. So dependent had the promise of liberalism been upon sustained growth as a vehicle of redistributive betterment and justice that the first signs of macroeconomic instability robbed it of its voice and its authority. Indeed, by the last years of the century, the New Deal order was dead, and with it the hopes and achievements of the new economics.[4]

Perhaps it was predictable, given the rightward turn of American politics in the late twentieth century, that professional economics would itself regress and retrench. A kind of naivety coupled with an unbridled enthusiasm had propelled the discipline's leading lights to make claims on its behalf it could not redeem. Once events, and the ideological shifts they provoked, overtook the statecraft that economists had so painstakingly fashioned, their flanks were wholly exposed to an unrelenting and unparalleled assault. Reversion to classical principles, a rejection of heterodox notions, an insistence on a professional deportment unable and unwilling to join with the ideological issues in dispute, and a contentment with a return to scholarly detachment were understandable if pathetically timid reactions.[5]

It has long been a conviction of those who study the history of the sciences that moribund intellectual traditions may be overcome only by the effective articulation of alternatives. For modern American economics the possibilities for such a restructuring were by the late 1990s, precisely because of the effectiveness of the professionalizing processes that had obtained since the turn of the century, few and far between. A select few at leading colleges and universities continued to wield enormous influence over the distribution of research grants, their own ranks replenished from a hiring process disproportionately focused on the graduates of a small number of highly regarded training programs, including their own. Any examination of publication practices in the field would serve to demonstrate as well that the dissemination of research results remained powerfully concentrated in the hands of an elite few. It is a striking yet hardly surprising finding that, at the height of the economic instability occasioned by the Vietnam War, the OPEC oil price shocks, and the downward trends in productivity enhancement experienced throughout the 1970s, alumni of only seven graduate programs in the discipline authored well over half the scholarly articles published in the nation's three leading economics journals. Such disciplinary inbreeding was hardly conducive to the elaboration of alternative paradigms.[6]

If, by the 1990s, economics was a social scientific discipline in fast retreat from a public role it had sought for decades, it was clearly not the case that the influence of all its practitioners was on the wane. Supply-side theorists, in ways far out of proportion with their achievements, continued to enjoy a prominence and an authority in economic debate that was virtually hegemonic. Anti-Keynesian rhetoric became ever more fashionable; calls for parsimony in governmental expenditure policy, often phrased in ways approximating a morality play, went virtually unchallenged. No better signal of the sea change that had taken place could be found than the news, broadcast in the fall of 1997, that a young Harvard University economics professor, N. Gregory Mankiw, would receive a $1.25 million advance from a major textbook publisher to produce a new volume in which Keynes's name barely appeared once. As advance copies of the text made their way into the hands of reviewers, even *Business Week* magazine could express alarm at the widening popularity of what it derisively called "feel-good economics."[7]

There was, of course, a genuine logic to the whole process. Linked with the marvelously abstract claims of rational expectations theory, supply-side economics had succeeded in making a compelling case for the ineffectiveness of national policies that sought to intervene in the nation's markets. Indeed, the argument had been taken a step further by claiming that, even if the government sought to manipulate economic outcomes, it would succeed only in generating perverse results: stimulatory spending would ultimately reduce consumption, steps to increase employment would actually generate more idleness, aggregate policies to enhance technological change and productivity would in the end reduce the total supply of goods and services. Thus situated within the analytical domain of supply-side theory, economic statecraft was stymied. Why do anything when activism brought no appreciable benefits? A new laissez-faire doctrine found the largest possible audience, and the hope for a reorientation of economic analysis that would have made sense of the disturbing events of the 1970s and 1980s, while remaining true to a commitment that had characterized the profession since the 1930s, went unrequited.[8]

Over three decades ago the eminent historian William Appleman Williams, reflecting upon the entire span of the nation's past, noted that policy appeals based on the principle of laissez-faire were, more often than not, actually premised on a slightly different conviction – that of "laissez-nous-faire." Arguments militating in favor of reduced government involvement in economic life usually reduced themselves to strategies, on the part of particular elites, to secure opportunities with which to exercise greater control over resources, the workforce, and households. Williams's thesis had particular relevance with respect to the transformations in economic thinking that prevailed in the United States by the 1990s. As the Keynesian consensus of the postwar era dissolved, and as it was replaced by an increasingly detached social theory that actively condemned governmental activism in the market place, the economics profession became less and less an engaged social scientific community in the public service and more and more a mouthpiece for a particular, interest-based agenda. No longer ministers to statist power, many economists reinvented themselves as privy councilors to private wealth.[9]

Since the economic turmoil of the early 1970s indicting government for the nation's material woes had become an ever more expansive enterprise. Dismantling the Keynesian apparatus of the federal government had been only part of this project. Eager to ferret out any plausible cause of inefficiency and inflated costs in the national economy, analysts, political leaders, policy advocates, and pundits became increasingly preoccupied with the perceived burdens of governmental regulation in the market place. Deconstructing a variety of federal statutes and agencies, along the lines specified by an offensive against such statist intervention in economic affairs, became a significant parallel strategy in the eradication of Keynesian practice. Proponents of what was dubbed "privatization" argued that such reforms in the ways government did business would lead to greater efficiency in the allocation of scarce resources. By leaving decisions to businesspeople and other expertly trained individuals in the private sector, it was claimed, an appropriate system of incentives and capabilities would yield a more optimal distribution of services and a more inspired utilization of scarce public monies.[10]

Deregulation had a bipartisan gestation, its birth facilitated by the anti-taxation attitudes fostered during the economic uncertainties of the 1970s. It was Jimmy Carter's presidential administration, building upon some initial and tentative steps taken by Gerald Ford's White House, that launched the first systematic efforts to reassess and ultimately eliminate to whatever extent possible federal oversight in the finance, telecommunications, and transportation sectors. The initial forays were predominantly focused in the aviation industry, culminating in the closure of the Civil Aeronautics Administration when Congress passed the 1978 Airline Deregulation Act. Hard on the heels of that landmark legislative decision came the 1982 settlement between the Antitrust Division of the Department of Justice and AT&T, an agreement that began the systematic deregulation of the nation's telecommunications infrastructure. Shortly thereafter the Reagan administration began reconfiguring the government's role in the nation's banking industry – an effort that had profound consequences in the savings and loan sector for years to come. By the time George H. W. Bush took office the momentum of the deregulatory process had grown very large indeed. Declaring a moratorium on all new federal regulations early in 1992, the President also asked his deputy, Vice-President Dan Quayle, to chair a new Council on Competitiveness as an informal "super-arbiter" of national regulatory issues.[11]

While the Quayle Council lasted only a year, liquidated in its infancy by Democrat Bill Clinton in one of his first acts as President, the political movement of which it stood as a striking exemplar continued. So irresistible was the appeal of deregulation rhetoric that policy initiatives were proposed and often enacted without due consideration of either their justification or their consequences. Increasingly, mainstream American economists made themselves part of this process – often eager to formulate techniques for its implementation, rarely willing to confront many baseless assertions deployed on its behalf. Nowhere was this strange reality made more manifest than in the transformation of the regulatory environment within which the nation's banking industry did its work.

Beginning with the Ford and Carter presidencies, operational rules for banks, brokerage houses, and savings and loan institutions were relaxed. Among brokerages, deregulation resulted in a proliferation of discount offices that allowed investors to avoid the expenses and commissions associated with more traditional houses. Among banks, the elimination of many restrictions on the geographic range of their operations stimulated competitive entry throughout many states – although by the early 1990s a reconcentration of assets through bank mergers began in earnest. In the savings and loan industry, however, deregulation contributed to a crisis of mammoth proportions.[12]

It was in the period before deregulation, when rising interest rates and the proliferation of money market investment funds made it increasingly difficult for savings banks to offer depositors competitive rates of return, that the savings and loan catastrophe had its roots. As the rates paid on such alternative investments as money market funds dramatically increased (in no small measure pushed upwards by the process of inflation that began in 1973), "Regulation Q," a federal rule limiting the maximum rate of interest that could be paid on savings and other demand deposits, made it virtually impossible for savings and loan institutions (S&Ls) to attract funds. Ironically, interest rate regulation had begun in 1933 when the Federal Reserve System implemented the first version of Regulation Q. The goal had been precisely to prevent the competitive shopping around for interest returns and to encourage depositors to place their funds in institutions selected on the basis of reputations for solvency and safety.

Banking industry lobbyists, not surprisingly, wished to eliminate Regulation Q. In 1980 the Carter administration, ostensibly seeking to aid a troubled industry, eased interest rate restrictions by means of the Depository Institutions Deregulation and Monetary Control Act (known, by insiders, as the "Diddymac"). The new law abolished geographic restrictions on the investment activities of S&Ls, thereby bringing a national market within the purview of individual institutions that had operated locally for decades. It also provided for deposit insurance of up to $100,000 for every savings account in the system – tendered by the Federal Savings and Loan Insurance Corporation (FSLIC), a derivative of the Federal Deposit Insurance Corporation (FDIC). S&Ls were no longer tied to deposits generated in their immediate communities but, rather, could attract deposits from far away by offering through brokers the high rates of interest made possible by deregulation itself.

Geographic deregulation created a national market in unregulated savings deposits, as, for the first time, S&Ls were allowed to offer account and credit privileges and other banking services nationwide. FSLIC guarantees simultaneously created a false sense of security within the S&L industry itself. The thrifts responded by investing in speculative commercial ventures in the hopes of shoring up their profitability – profitability that had been compromised for over a decade by Regulation Q. Thrifts' net income, as a share of their total assets, had averaged only 0.5 percent throughout the late 1970s; it fell to 0.1 percent by 1980 and turned negative in 1981 and 1982. Home mortgage business, the mainstay of the industry since the Great Depression, dropped off. Indeed, it became increasingly (and uncharacteristically) common for the S&Ls to provide full financing for a broad spectrum of investments with little or no down payment.[13]

A further difficulty emerged in this reformed environment. Thrifts found that the interest they earned on traditional mortgages provided insufficient funds to pay the higher interest rates they were now allowed to offer on an array of financial instruments. Some institutions thus began to use up their own liquid reserves to make good the difference. In 1982 fifty thrifts nationwide failed – a rate unprecedented since the Second World War. Congress, reflecting bipartisan concern for the S&L sector, responded with another revision of law. The Garn–St Germain Bill, signed into law by President Ronald Reagan in 1982, having gone "through Congress like a dose of salts, with virtually no hearings in either Senate or House Banking Committees," further loosened the restrictions on the kinds of investments S&Ls could make. The Federal Home Loan Bank Board, later reconstituted as the Office of Thrift Supervision, also participated in this strategy by reducing, virtually to zero, the minimum amount of capital that a bank was required to have on hand to underwrite particular investments.[14]

In the savings and loan industry, the deregulation of the 1970s and 1980s generated hasty, at times foolish, and even corrupt decision-making. Operating in unrestricted and almost unknown territory, S&Ls became involved in questionable investment schemes, many of them unsecured, some very risky. Moreover, in the late 1980s, as the real estate market softened (especially in the South and the Southwest due to troubles in the oil, mining, and aviation industries), thrifts found even their traditional avenues of investment painfully encumbered. Thus began a series of savings and loan failures that had no equal since the 1930s. Unable to make good their obligations to depositors, S&Ls exhausted their deposit insurance and approached Congress for relief. The full dimensions of the "bailout" ultimately necessary to restore the industry to firm footing were nothing short of mind-boggling.[15]

Deregulation, at least in the financial sector, thus failed its proponents. Undertaken at the behest of an energetic and vocal academic and political constituency, it created vast costs in addition to its purported benefits. Regulatory reform, in this sense, responded far less to the lobbying of public interest groups than to the efforts of cadres of new entrepreneurs (such as Carl Icahn in aviation, and Charles Keating and Michael Milken in finance) to gain access to particular markets and to enjoy and exploit new levels of statist influence and visibility. There were no mass demonstrations on Pennsylvania Avenue, Northwest, to deregulate major sectors of American industry. In the hands of a smaller cadre, deregulation became an essential part of the doctrine of laissez-nous-faire.

The savings and loan debacle did nothing to stem the ardor of public officials for continued deregulation of the banking industry as a whole. By the spring of 1997 Clinton administration specialists had prepared legislative proposals to allow insurance companies, banks, and securities firms to do business in one another's markets. A practice long banned by the 1933 Glass–Steagall Act, which had been fashioned in response to the reckless management of investment funds that had helped make the crash of 1929 a catastrophe, the intermingling of banking and other financial operations had remained under close federal scrutiny for decades.

It was, to be sure, not simply the financial sector in which the consequences of deregulation expressed themselves in such negative ways – nor where the vast majority of the economics profession continued to stand mute, except in those contexts in which it could facilitate the deregulatory process itself. In the airline industry, where deregulation advocates had long pointed to apparent successes in the expansion of service and the lowering of fares, such that an ever-growing proportion of the nation's population used air transport year after year, elimination of the Civil Aeronautics Administration generated a less than impressive record of economic accomplishment. From the early 1980s until 1988 the number of independent airline companies fell by more than half; the number of independent regional airlines declined from 250 to 170. In the same time period over 300 small towns lost commercial aviation service altogether. As major companies, in the deregulated environment, created "hub" facilities, price competition in those particular markets virtually disappeared. Concerns about hard-pressed companies skirting safety regulations, manipulating labor practices, and delaying maintenance schedules proliferated nationwide. By the late 1990s the industry had reconcentrated itself in the wake of significant mergers. Complaints about price-fixing thus escalated. While many transportation economists had been quick to applaud the implementation of airline deregulation, virtually none of them spoke up about the problems that emerged in the newly configured industry.[16]

Interestingly enough, the impacts of deregulation in the transportation sector were not all negative. Many airline companies, at least in the early years of the new policy regime, sustained 25 percent reductions in their operating costs; consequently, average fares fell by almost a third. In trucking, costs were reduced by a very impressive 75 percent. Rate reductions were not as large but were nonetheless significant. Finally, in railroads, both rates and cost structures fell by a half; service improved as well, with 20 percent reductions in transit times overall (Kahn, 1990; Winston, 1993; Shepherd, 2001). In most cases, however, all these improvements in the transportation sector's performance proved to be temporary.

Telecommunications afforded a particularly large and complex territory for deregulatory initiatives, especially given the dissemination of new technologies (ranging from the personal computer to remote cellular phones, to digital television, to the internet) throughout the business world and a large proportion of the nation's households. By ending the AT&T monopoly of the nation's telephone and telegraph market, the 1982 consent decree clearly led to a rapid drop in long-distance toll rates. Much like the immediate impact of airline deregulation, the divestiture led to a marked increase in the nation's use of long-distance telephony. At the same time, and again ignored by economists who had mobilized in favor of the break-up of AT&T, the cross-subsidization of local phone costs by long-distance revenues, long claimed by AT&T itself, was lost. Local phone services became increasingly expensive; by the late 1990s the costs of installing household phones had run sufficiently high as to cause consternation on the part of advocates of lower-income groups. Payphone access was similarly restricted, through both higher costs per call and a reduction in the number of phones available for public use. For the first time, fees were imposed for using directory assistance. Many consumer groups were left wondering if the nation's households were left better off or not. No such self-interrogation appears to have occurred in the economics community.[17]

Deregulation of the telecommunications sector also brought a massive restructuring of the firms within it.[18] The liberalization of ownership laws, which had for decades sought to mitigate the potential for oligopolistic control, was the proximate cause. New auction rules, implemented by the Federal Communication Commission (FCC) to allocate spectrums for wireless technologies, among other innovations, furthered the easing of governmental oversight of the industry as a whole. Allegations of bid rigging emerged almost as soon as the FCC arbitrage began. The economic expertise that had fostered the creation of these new auction procedures was absent from the efforts to police its equitable enforcement. Meanwhile, the many smaller companies spawned by the AT&T antitrust decision began, by the late 1990s, a merger initiative to reclaim both market share and its attendant control. The difference, this time, was that the federal regulatory apparatus to oversee such newly constituted large industry actors was gone.[19]

Any misgivings that some may have had about the trend and impact of national economic policy in the early 1990s were only faintly heard. By mid-decade a dramatic boom began in US stock and allied financial markets, which continued, in almost uninterrupted fashion, until the terrorist attacks of September 2001. The presumption that the run-up would last for ever infected the sensibilities of Americans drawn from all walks of life. In 1995 alone more than $100 billion was invested in the stock market – and investment in speculative capital simply increased from there. Many working people placed their entire retirement nest eggs into 401(k) plans and Investment Retirement Accounts. "Daytrading," a highly volatile enterprise in which literally millions could be lost in seconds, became a fad. With the proliferation of virtual, electronic market places, many individuals tried their hands at such gambling – while often lacking the time, training, and financial security to underwrite their excessive risk-taking. Meanwhile, electronic commerce took off, with spectacular run-ups in the stock values of firms that existed solely "online," most of which had never executed a genuine transaction nor met a formal delivery date for their output. By the early months of 2001 the Dow-Jones Industrial Average had broken 10,000 – a previously unimagined plateau.

Economic booms never last for ever, and that which had defined the US economy's prospects from the 1990s to the turn of the twenty-first century was no different. By the early summer months of 2001 warning signs marred virtually every market horizon. Energy prices accelerated upwards; stock market values softened, as profit-seekers cashed in on the high values generated in the boom; manufacturing output slowed; and lay-offs began to rise. Then, with the 11 September attacks in New York City, western Pennsylvania, and Washington, DC, the upper turning point was clearly reached.

In the midst of the economic slide after 9–11 it became increasingly obvious that the national economy, working in a dramatically unregulated and "tax-revenue-poor" environment in which the federal government's capacity for countercyclical management had been decisively curtailed, had become really quite frail. Strikingly enough, the very timidity of the fiscal spending proposals brought before Congress to deal with the downturn gave ample testimony to that fact. Even the most aggressive pump-priming bills, debated on Capitol Hill, embraced spending targets that approximated a mere 1 to 2 percent of gross domestic product. The fragile nature of the nation's infrastructure, in the face of the terrorist attacks, was also demonstrated by the inability of the Federal Aviation Administration to make rapid adjustments to the disarray occasioned in airline operations by the attacks themselves, and this fragility was further portrayed by the chaotic response of an enervated public health apparatus in the face of a series of horrifying, yet unexplained contaminations of the national postal system by letters laced with anthrax.

As if the recession after 9–11 and related economic dislocations were not enough, by early 2002 yet another dramatic incident further evidenced the frailty of the national market place in the wake of deregulation and the application of supply-side economics. Enron Corporation, one of the largest firms in the country, with major interests in energy trading and distribution networks, filed for bankruptcy early in January. As liquidation proceedings documented, it rapidly became clear that the company had run up its stock values through a wide array of manipulations, falsified accounting records, and outright deceit. The accounting giant, Arthur Anderson Company, became implicated in the debacle when it was revealed that its auditors not only participated in the subterfuge but also began the systematic shredding of documents when it became clear that the end was near.

The dismantling of Keynesian-style fiscal management (the policy hallmark of the Cold War era) and the deregulation of the nation's market places, which began during the high tide of the Reagan presidency, had an enduring impact on the ability of the government both to maintain cyclical stability in the face of economic shocks and to sustain regulatory vigilance and control of financial and other related practices. As a consequence, especially after the 11 September attacks, the federal government found itself incapable of taking matters decisively in hand.

Making war against Iraq, strangely enough, simply had the effect of interfering further with Washington's ability to manage the nation's economic affairs. The conservative constituency brought to power in the closely contested (and deeply controversial) 2000 presidential election had insisted on pursuing a conservative agenda in domestic affairs that conflicted decisively with the fiscal realities of unilateral ambitions abroad. Throughout most of the Cold War era, successive presidential administrations (drawn from both major political parties) had yoked high levels of public spending for military and diplomatic initiatives overseas with measured countercyclical policies directed towards balanced and fair economic growth at home. Yet the very "victory" in the Cold War with the Soviet Union severed this link between an active role in the world and socio-economic progress at home. While the aggressive foreign policy ambitions remained, the progressive domestic agenda did not.

In many respects, the collapse of the Cold War coalition that brought conservatives determined to confront Soviet influence in the wider world together with liberals focused on social needs at home was the direct result of the "success" of the Cold War itself. Liberals themselves, ironically enough, contributed to this remarkable script of political economic deconstruction. Eager to criticize the errors of American foreign policy in the wake of the debacle of the Vietnam War, the Left nonetheless neglected to explore, in a thorough and rigorous fashion, the close economic and political connections between military-industrial spending, the anti-communist containment strategy, and social welfare initiatives that had defined the "New Deal order" since the end of the Second World War. As a result, the primary mechanisms of fiscal and monetary control that had fostered the progressive social agendas of the Cold War era were ripe pickings for a conservative insurgency determined to destroy the vestiges of the New Deal while remaining committed to the anti-communist containment goals of the past.

Of course, after the collapse of the Soviet Union and the devolution of its satellite states, the global containment strategies of the United States were no longer focused on the activities of a crippled and bankrupt Red Army and Navy. Indeed, "containment" in the 1990s and in the early twenty-first century was all about the pursuit of pro-capitalist policies throughout the world. Whether anti-Soviet containment had been an aggressive or a defensive foreign policy posture in the era after the Second World War has long been a subject of debate among historians and political scientists; subsequently, by contrast, "containment" of the world's regions on behalf of capitalist American interests was the core foreign policy stance fashioned by the US government.

To be sure, following the end of major military operations in Iraq in 2003 there have emerged some rather crude examples of the ways in which a new conservative coalition seeks to tie foreign policy to domestic concerns. The award of reconstruction contracts to individual corporations, most of which had as their primary retainers major leaders in the American government (most notably and notoriously Vice-President Dick Cheney), gave concrete testimony to the derangement of the Cold War era consensus regarding public spending strategies and anti-communist containment. Over $0.5 billion alone engrossed the Bechtel Corporation as it executed a contract to rebuild Iraqi infrastructure for which it never had to bid; similarly, Vice-President Cheney's former employer, the Halliburton Corporation, earned as much as $7 billion to restore Iraqi oil fields to full production. These singular examples of political–economic corruption stood in sharp contrast to Cold War projects such as the Marshall Plan, which had sought to benefit an entire national economy in the project of postwar reconstruction in Western Europe.

Needless to say, the postwar reconstruction of Iraq took place on a world stage markedly different from that of 1948. Over a half-century ago the US economy stood alone, among the major industrialized nations, as the source of manufacturing output and skilled labor. By the end of the 1990s, by comparison, US policy was no longer oriented towards containing (a non-existent) communist influence but, rather, towards limiting the influence of foreign capital in its competition with American wealth in world markets. When, in May 2003, WorldCom Corporation, one of the disgraced entities in the accounting scandals that had plagued the American economy since 2000, won a contract to build Iraq's first cellphone network, the effort was born as much of a determination to bring the money for the project home to a US firm as it was to exclude prime foreign competitors from reaping any benefits at all. Part of the legislation passed in Congress to frame the disbursement of public monies for postwar reconstruction in Iraq tried to require that any new telecommunications networks utilize technological standards developed by American, rather than European, firms.

A profound disjunction between US foreign policy and the domestic management of economic needs placed the Bush administration in the grips of a profound dilemma. While it pursued its foreign strategies, tied as they were to exceedingly conservative fiscal and monetary policies at home, the US government struggled to articulate a coherent economic agenda. Unemployment persisted in certain troubled sectors, capital markets were roiled by scandals and mismanagement, and the international value of the dollar weakened steadily as global financial markets become increasingly concerned about insipid economic performance and unstable credit markets in the country as a whole. Where earlier Cold War presidential administrations had consistently found ways to stimulate economic growth and employment at home while containing Soviet and Chinese influence overseas, the federal government sought to reconcile its divergent and contradictory policy impulses. Born of decades of tax cutting and deregulation, that impasse is properly understood as the most significant legacy of the economic policy environment of the 1990s and even earlier decades.

Notes

For comments on a previous draft of this chapter, I am very grateful to Thomas M. Geraghty, Paul Rhode, Gianni Toniolo, and the participants at the conference on "Understanding the 1990s: the economy in long-run perspective," held at the Terry Sanford Institute for Public Policy of Duke University, Durham, NC, 26–7 March 2004.

1. George H. W. Bush's travails as the nation's forty-first President provided a unique example of the "new classical economic chickens" coming home to roost. Within the first year of his term it became obvious that federal tax cuts had so unbalanced the federal ledger that the nation's capital markets were at risk given the enormous amounts of borrowing undertaken by the Treasury. Forced ultimately to ask for a tax increase, the President found himself hounded by the right wing of his own party as the 1992 campaign approached. Most analysts believe these intra-party struggles played a significant part in weakening Bush's bid for re-election. Bill Clinton's subsequent triumph, as the first Democrat to reach the White House in twelve years, was a striking representation – in the political realm – of the inherent contradictions to be found in a national fiscal policy recast by "Reaganism." See, in this regard, Passell (1990). No less an authority than Richard Darman, director of the Office of Management and Budget under President Bush, ultimately claimed that the combination of Reagan tax cuts and increased military spending constituted the largest and most undisciplined addition to federal debt in the nation's history (Darman, 1996).

2. In his memoir, *Who's in Control?*, Richard Darman argues that the massive rise in the national debt during the 1980s was far more the result of increased military spending than it was due to the cost of social spending (especially anti-poverty) programs. It is well worth noting that, at the same time, a rhetorical sleight of hand took place so subtle as to provoke little if any comment. Increasingly, politicians, economists, and voters alike spoke of what were once called "transfer payments" (such as Medicare, Medicaid, Aid to Families with Dependent Children, Food Stamps, and Social Security) as "entitlements." The former label, of course, was freighted with operational and technical meaning drawn from the national income accounts themselves. By contrast, the latter evoked notions of engrossment at public expense by those possibly unworthy. Just as one could be "entitled" to something, one could just as arguably be "unentitled." Thus, it became easier to speak of program elimination, zero-base budgeting, means-testing, and an array of efforts at fiscal contraction literally unthinkable a decade or more earlier. In such simple yet profound changes in word choice, conservatives found yet another weapon in their determination to disestablish the mixed economy of the postwar era. See Davies (1996).

3. In its most typical renditions, the proposed amendment would mandate a three-fifths majority in the Congress to pass any exceptions to a balanced budget in any given

year – a legislative threshold that would effectively cripple any efforts towards deficit spending save for those in times of war. At the 1985 National Governors Association convention, it was Arkansas's Bill Clinton who stood as one of the most resolute Democratic supporters of the amendment proposal. His position changed quickly upon his election as President.

4. A particularly compelling discussion of the century's progress of American liberalism, framed more with reference to intellectual rather than political economic contexts, is Gerstle (1994). See also Brinkley (1995) and Fraser and Gerstle (1989).

5. See Taylor (1995), as well as Alston, Kearl, and Vaughan (1992). American Economic Association president Gerard Debreu offered interesting speculations about the tendencies of modern economists to indulge an introverted formalism in his presidential address in 1991 (Debreu, 1991).

6. The authorship "shares" reported in a 1983 study for the period 1973–1978 were, respectively, 54 percent in the *American Economic Review*, 58 percent in the *Journal of Political Economy*, and 74 percent in the *Quarterly Journal of Economics* (Canterbery and Burkhardt, 1983). On the articulation of alternative scientific "paradigms," the classic reference is Kuhn (1970). A decade ago Hyman Minsky once argued that the scholarly debates among Keynesians and monetarists during the 1970s were really nothing of the sort. Given that "the competing camps used the same economic theory," the substance of their dispute was minor and the potential outcomes of its resolution hardly innovative (Minsky, 1986). Independent of the formulation of opinion within the economics profession, there is the broader issue of how public attitudes on economic matters were and are framed. The entire question of the role of the "financial press" and of non-profit organizations in both setting the terms of public debate on policy issues and influencing public understanding of them is a significant matter for further historical inquiry. In this regard, see, for example, Parsons (1990) and Stefancic and Delgado (1996). See also Parry (1996). Above and beyond the power of policy pundits and the media, there is also the puzzle of how individuals gain access to the necessary information and skills to formulate appropriate and sophisticated positions on economic questions – an issue made all the more complex by the fact that such questions often require quantitative skills sorely lacking in large proportions of the electorate. See Bernstein (1990).

7. See Coy (1997). Mankiw's text, *Principles of Economics*, was issued by Harcourt, Brace.

8. Gardiner Means, early in 1975, had put it well to his friend and colleague Richard Goodwin (a professor at the University of Cambridge then visiting at Harvard). "Traditional theory cannot explain what is happening," he wrote, "and therefore cannot supply the prescription for dealing with it. What is needed is reorientation of thinking as drastic as the shift from Ptolemaic to Copernican[.]" Given his own scholarly record and public policy career, Means clearly did not have supply-side theory in mind when he wrote these words. Indeed, he closed his letter to Goodwin by reflecting that "for more than 40 years, [he] has been trying to play the part of an economic Copernicus." See Means to Goodwin (1975).

9. It is interesting to consider that, at the very time that such changes in the outlook of the profession took place, opportunities for the employment of economists in

the private sector increased dramatically. No doubt a parallel development, in this regard, was the transition in the aspirations of new generations of students, who sought out careers in the corporate world rather than, as their predecessors had done a few decades before, positions in the government service. Equally intriguing is the fact that the anti-statism of this new cadre of young economists had close formal (if not substantive) similarities with that of an earlier generation who had, as a "new Left," excoriated government professionals as servants of a malicious power elite. On the notion of "laissez-nous-faire," see Williams (1961).

10. A particularly vivid, if strident, representation of these arguments is Lee (1996). An historical perspective on American attitudes regarding regulation is provided by Peritz (1996). The strange ironies inherent in privatization strategies were revealed on a local level late in 1996 in San Diego, California. In the wake of the public ratification of Proposition 218, a ballot measure requiring local governments to seek voter approval for all tax and fee increases, both Standard and Poor's and Moody's downgraded San Diego's credit ratings. As a result, the costs of bond financing for the city rose. An effort allegedly undertaken to reduce the tax burdens of the city's residents thus generated an outcome that will, over time, increase them. See LaVelle (1996).

11. See, for example, Risen and Jehl (1992); Chen (1992); and Risen (1993). Thomas Petzinger, Jr., provides a thorough survey of the impacts of deregulation in the American aviation industry (Petzinger, 1996).

12. Much of this argument, and that which follows, is derived from Bernstein (1994).

13. Data on thrifts' income were generated by the Federal Home Loan Bank Board and the Office of Thrift Supervision. See White (1991).

14. The words are those of Martin Mayer, in Mayer (1990).

15. The "bailout" was undertaken by a newly created agency, the Resolution Trust Corporation (RTC). Whether some of the legislative machinations around the operations of the RTC involved criminal conduct, as suggested in a flurry of investigative activity concerning the "Keating Five" (Senators Alan Cranston of California, Dennis DeConcini of Arizona, John Glenn of Ohio, John McCain of Arizona, and Donald Riegle of Michigan), who, some alleged, supported bailout efforts in exchange for campaign contributions and other emoluments, was never thoroughly investigated. Similarly unresolved allegations were made concerning the activities of Member of Congress Fernand St Germain (Democrat, Rhode Island), who had personally led the move to raise insurance deposit thresholds. Critics suggested that St Germain orchestrated lavish dinners and receptions (often peopled with hired escorts) at which S&L lobbyists could mingle with congressional representatives. See, for example, Adams (1991), and, more recently, Calavita, Pontell, and Tillman (1997). Ironically enough, Reagan administration efforts to reduce federal payrolls also seriously weakened the number of personnel available at the Treasury and the Federal Reserve Board to provide oversight and enforcement of federal regulations regarding banking practice. This cost-cutting strategy thus further contributed to the crisis in the S&L industry.

16. By 1996 the nation's airways were dominated by three major carriers: American, Delta, and United. This was hardly the scenario envisioned (nor extolled) by the

proponents of deregulation two decades earlier. In the struggle for business, many aviation companies developed "frequent flyer" programs in the 1980s – systems designed to tie customers to particular airlines through a schedule of ticket rebates that were as confusing and anti-competitive in their use as they were frequently revised and manipulated when the number of potential claimants was large. On these matters, see Peltz (1996, 1997).

17. See, for example, Moffat (1992); Shiver (1996b, 1997b, 1997c); and Brooks (1997).

18. Indeed, beginning in the mid-1980s a new merger wave took place in major sectors of American industry. These consolidations represented some of the most significant and telling outcomes of "deregulation." Gulf Oil completed a $13.4 billion alliance with Standard Oil of California in 1984; Kraft merged with Philip Morris in 1988 in a deal similarly valued; RJR Nabisco bought Kohlberg Kravis Roberts in a $25 billion negotiation in 1989; and Warner Communications absorbed Time, Inc. for $14.11 billion two years later. In 1996 there was a virtual "merger fever," which witnessed the consummation of six major takeovers: Bell Atlantic Corporation appropriated Nynex Corporation for $22.7 billion; Disney Company, Capital Cities/ABC for $19 billion; SBC Communications, the Pacific Telesis Group for $16.7 billion; WorldCom, MFS Communications for $14.4 billion; Wells Fargo, the First Interstate Bancorp for $14.2 billion; and Boeing, McDonnell Douglas for $13.3 billion. Here, too, Reagan-era "downsizing" of federal agencies appeared to have played an important part – most significantly with respect to the enfeebled Antitrust Division of the United States Department of Justice.

19. See, for example, *Los Angeles Times* (1996a); Shiver (1996a); *Los Angeles Times* (November 1996); Los Angeles Times (March 1997); Los Angeles Times (1996b); Shiver (1997c, 1997d); and Kaplan and Mulligan (1997). On Veterans Day 1997 MCI Communications and WorldCom announced their agreement to merge; the $37 billion deal constituted the largest corporate consolidation in the nation's history; see Shiver (1997f). The 1996 Telecommunications Act also raised a variety of concerns linked to freedom of access and freedom of speech on the internet, along with frustrations that the reconcentration of ownership in telecommunications would continue unabated; see Shiver (1997a), and McChesney (1997). By the end of October 1997 the Federal Communications Commission had completed the auction of 525 wireless licenses, with bids totaling $13.07 billion. Needless to say, rhetorical justification for auction processes such as this one emphasized the revenue enhancement they could also generate to help balance the federal budget; see *Los Angeles Times* (1997c). Paul Milgrom was one of the leading economists who designed the auction processes used by the FCC; see Milgrom (1996). William Vickrey of Columbia University received the 1996 Nobel Memorial Prize in Economic Science, in part, for work he had done on auction theory.

References

Abramovitz, Moses. 1956. Resource and output trends in the United States since 1870. *American Economic Review* 46, 5–23.

1986. Catching up, forging ahead, and falling behind. *Journal of Economic History* 36, 385–406.

1993. The search for the sources of growth: areas of ignorance, old and new. *Journal of Economic History* 53 (2), 217–43.

Abramovitz, Moses, and Paul A. David. 1973. Reinterpreting American economic growth: parables and realities. *American Economic Review* 63, 428–39.

2000. American macroeconomic growth in the era of knowledge-based progress. In Stanley L. Engerman and Robert E. Gallman (eds.). *The Cambridge Economic History of the United States*, Vol. III. Cambridge: Cambridge University Press, 1–92.

Acemoglu, Daron. 1998. Why do new technologies complement skills? Directed technical change and wage inequality. *Quarterly Journal of Economics* 113, 1055–89.

2002. Technical change, inequality and the labor market. *Journal of Economic Literature* 40, 7–72.

Acemoglu, Daron, and Simon Johnson. 2003. *Unbundling Institutions*. Working Paper no. 9934, National Bureau of Economic Research, Cambridge, MA.

Acheson, Dean. 1969. *Present at the Creation: My Years in the State Department*. New York: Norton.

Adams, Donald. 1970. Some evidence on English and American wage rates, 1790–1860. *Journal of Economic History* 30, 499–520.

Adams, James Ring. 1991. *The Big Fix – Inside the S&L Scandal: How an Unholy Alliance of Politics and Money Destroyed America's Banking System*. New York: Wiley.

Aghion, Philippe, Mathias Dewatripont, and Patrick Rey, 1997. Corporate governance, competition policy and industrial policy. *European Economic Review* 41, 797–805.

Ahmad, Nadim, François Lequiller, Pascal Marianna, Dirk Pilat, Paul Schreyer and Anita Wolf. 2003. *Comparing Labor Productivity Growth in the OECD Area. The Role of Measurement*. Statistics Working Paper no. 2003/5 Organisation for Economic Co-operation and Development, Paris.

Aiginger, Karl. 2004. *Copying the US or Developing a New European Model.* Paper prepared for the Spring Seminar of the UN Economic Commission for Europe, United Nations, Geneva.

Aitken, Brian, and Ann E. Harrison. 1999. Do domestic firms benefit from foreign direct investment? Evidence from Venezuela. *American Economic Review* 89, 605–18.

Alesina, Alberto, Reza Baqir, and William Easterly. 1999. Public goods and ethnic divisions. *Quarterly Journal of Economics* 114, 1243–84.

Alesina, Alberto, Arnaud Devleeschauwer, William Easterly, Sergio Kurlat, and Romain Wacziarg. 2002. *Fractionalization.* Working Paper no. 9411, National Bureau of Economic Research, Cambridge, MA.

Alesina, Alberto, Rafael DiTella, and Robert MacCulloch. 2001. Inequality and happiness: are Europeans and Americans different? *Brookings Papers in Economic Activity* 2, 187–277.

Allard, Gayle. 2003. *Jobs and Labor Market Institutions in the OECD.* Doctoral dissertation, University of California, Davis.

Alston, Richard M., J. R. Kearl, and Michael B. Vaughan. 1992. Is there a consensus among economists in the 1990s? *American Economic Review* 82, 203–20.

Amsden, Alice H. 1989. *Asia's Next Giant: South Korea and Late Industrialization.* New York: Oxford University Press.

Angly, Edward. 1931. *Oh Yeah?* New York: Viking Press.

Atack, Jeremy, Fred Bateman, and Robert A. Margo. 2004. Skill intensity and rising wage dispersion in nineteenth-century American manufacturing. *Journal of Economic History* 64, 172–92.

Atkinson, Anthony B. 2002. *Top Incomes in the United Kingdom over the Twentieth Century.* Discussion Papers in Economic and Social History no. 43, University of Oxford.

Atkinson, Anthony B., and Wiemer Salverda. 2003. *Top Incomes in the Netherlands and the United Kingdom over the Twentieth Century.* Working Paper no. 14, Amsterdam Institute for Advanced Labour Studies.

Autor, David. 2004. Labor market intermediation: what it is, why it is growing, and where it is going. *NBER Reporter* (September), 7–10.

Baily, Martin N. 2003. Comments and discussion [on paper by Robert J. Gordon]. *Brookings Papers on Economic Activity* 2, 280–7.

Bairoch, P. 1982. International industrialization levels from 1750 to 1980. *Journal of European Economic History* 11, 269–331.

Balke, Nathan S., and Robert J. Gordon. 1986. Appendix B: Historical data. In Robert J. Gordon (ed.). *The American Business Cycle: Continuity and Change.* Chicago: University of Chicago Press for the National Bureau of Economic Research, 781–850.

Barro, Robert J., and Xavier Sala-i-Martin. 1995. *Economic Growth.* New York: McGraw-Hill.

Basu, Susanto, and John Fernald. 1995. Are apparent productive spillovers a figment of specification error? *Journal of Monetary Economics* 36, 165–88.

Basu, Susanto, John Fernald, Nicholas Oulton, and Sylaja Srinivasan. 2003. The case of the missing productivity growth, or, does Information Technology explain why productivity accelerated in the United States but not the United Kingdom? In *NBER Macroeconomics Annual 2003*, 9–63.

Baumol, W. J. 1967. Macroeconomics of unbalanced growth: the anatomy of urban crisis. *American Economic Review* 57, 415–26.

Bayoumi, Tamim, and Markus Haacker 2002. *It's Not What You Make, It's How You Use IT: Measuring the Welfare Benefits of the IT Revolution Across Countries*. Working Paper no. 02/117, International Monetary Fund, Washington, DC.

Bayoumi, Tamim, Douglas Laxton, and Paolo Pesenti. 2004. *Benefits and Spillovers of Greater Competition in Europe: A Macroeconomic Assessment*. Working Paper no. 10416, National Bureau of Economic Research, Cambridge, MA.

Becker, Gary S., Tomas J. Philipson, and Rodrigo R. Soares. 2003. *The Quantity and Quality of Life and the Evolution of World Inequality*. Working Paper no. 9765, National Bureau of Economic Research, Cambridge, MA.

Bell, Linda A., and Richard B. Freeman. 2001. The incentive for working hard: explaining hours worked differences in the U.S. and Germany. *Labour Economics* 8, 181–202.

Bernanke, Ben S., and Mark Gertler. 2000. *Monetary Policy and Asset Price Volatility*. Working Paper no. 7559, National Bureau of Economic Research, Cambridge, MA.

2001. Should central banks respond to movements in asset prices? *American Economic Review* 91, 253–7.

Bernanke, Ben S. and Frederic Mishkin. 1997. Inflation targeting: a new framework for monetary policy. *Journal of Economic Perspectives* 11, 97–116.

Berndt, Ernst R., Ellen R. Dulberger, and Neal J. Rappaport. 2000. *Price and Quality of Desktop and Mobile Personal Computers: A Quarter Century of History*. Working paper, Alfred P. Sloan School of Management, Massachusetts Institute of Technology, Cambridge, MA.

Bernstein, Michael. 1990. Numerable knowledge and its discontents. *Reviews in American History* 18, 151–64.

1994. The contemporary American banking crisis in historical perspective. *Journal of American History* 80, 1382–96.

Berry, Thomas Senior. 1988. *Production and Population Since 1789: Revised GNP Series in Constant Dollars*. Bostwick Paper no. 6. Richmond, VA: Bostwick Press.

Bertolini, Leonardo, and Allan Drazen. 1997. Capital account liberalization as a signal. *American Economic Review* 87, 138–54.

BIS. 1998. *Central Bank Survey of Foreign Exchange and Derivatives Market Activity*. Basel: Bank for International Settlements.

Blake, David. 2002. The United Kingdom: examining the switch from low public pensions to high-cost private pensions. In Martin Feldstein and Horst Siebert (eds.). *Social Security Pension Reform in Europe*. Chicago: University of Chicago Press, 317–48.

Blanchard, Olivier. 1993. Movements in the equity premium. *Brookings Papers on Economic Activity* 2, 75–138.

2004. The economic future of Europe. *Journal of Economic Perspectives* 18, 3–26.

Blanchard, Olivier, and Francesco Giavazzi. 2003. Macroeconomic effects of regulation and deregulation in goods and labor markets. *Quarterly Journal of Economics* 118, 879–909.

Blanchard, Olivier, and Mark W. Watson. 1982. Bubbles, rational expectations and financial markets. In Paul Wachtel (ed.). *Crises in the Economic and Financial Structure*. Lexington, MA: DC. Heath and Company, 295–315.

Blau, Francine D., and Lawrence M. Kahn. 2002. *At Home and Abroad: U.S. Labor-Market Performance in International Perspective*. New York: Russell Sage Foundation.

Bleaney, Michael, and Akira Nishiyama. 2002. Explaining growth: a contest between models. *Journal of Economic Growth* 7, 43–56.

Blinder, Alan. 2002. Comments on U.S. monetary policy during the 1990s. In Jeffrey A. Frankel and Peter R. Orszag (eds.). *American Economic Policy in the 1990s*. Cambridge, MA: MIT Press, 44–51.

Blöndäl, Sveinbjörn, and Stefano Scarpetta. 1997. Early retirement in OECD countries: the role of social security systems. In *OECD Economic Studies* no. 29. Paris: Organisation for Economic Co-operation and Development, 1–27

Blume, Marshall, and Irwin Friend. 1978. *The Changing Role of the Individual Investor*. New York: Wiley.

Blundell, Richard, and Paul Johnson. 1999. Social security and retirement in the United Kingdom. In Jonathan Gruber and David Wise (eds.). *Social Security Programs and Retirement around the World*. Chicago: University of Chicago Press for the National Bureau of Economic Research, 403–36.

Boltho, Andrea. 2003. What's wrong with Europe? *New Left Review* 22, 5–26.

Boltho, Andrea, and Gianni Toniolo. 1999. The assessment: the twentieth century – achievements, failures, lessons. *Oxford Review of Economic Policy* 15, 1–17.

Bordo, Michael, and Olivier Jeanne. 2002. *Boom-Busts in Asset Prices, Economic Instability, and Monetary Policy*. Working Paper no. 8966, National Bureau of Economic Research, Cambridge, MA.

Bordo, Michael, Barry Eichengreen, and Douglas Irwin. 1999. Is globalization today really different than globalization a hundred years ago? In *Brookings Trade Policy Forum 1999*, 1–72.

Bordo, Michael, Barry Eichengreen, Daniela Klingebiel, and Soledad Maria Martinez Peria. 2001. Is the crisis problem growing more severe? *Economic Policy* 32, 51–82.

Bosworth, Barry P., and Susan M. Collins. 2003. The empirics of growth: an update. *Brookings Papers on Economic Activity* 2, 113–206.

Boskin, Michael J., Ellen R. Dulberger, Robert J. Gordon, Zvi Griliches, and Dale Jorgenson. 1996. *Final Report of the Advisory Commission to Study the Consumer Price Index*, S. Prt. 104–72. Washington, DC: US Government Printing Office.

Bourguignon, François, and Christian Morrisson. 2002. Inequality among world citizens: 1820–1992. *American Economic Review* 92, 727–44.

Brady, Dorothy S. 1966. Price deflators for final product estimates. In Dorothy S. Brady (ed.). *Output, Employment, and Productivity in the United States After 1800*. New York: Columbia University Press, 91–116.

Brauer, Jurgen, and John T. Marlin. 1992. Converting resources from military to non-military uses. *Journal of Economic Perspectives* 6, 145–64.

Brenner, Robert. 2002. *The Boom and the Bubble*. Verso Press.

2003. Towards the precipice. *London Review of Books* 25 (6 February), 3.

Bresnahan, Timothy F., and Manuel Trajtenberg. 1995. General purpose technologies: engines of growth? *Journal of Econometrics* 65, 83–108.

Brinkley, Alan. 1995. *The End of Reform: New Deal Liberalism in Recession and War*. New York: Knopf.

Broadberry, Stephen N., and Douglas A. Irwin. 2004. *Labor Productivity in the United States and the United Kingdom During the Nineteenth Century*. Working Paper no. 10364, National Bureau of Economic Research, Cambridge, MA.

Brooks, Nancy. 1997. Pac Bell hikes coin-call rate. *Los Angeles Times*. 18 October, D1, D3.

Brown, Lester R. 2003. *Plan B: Rescuing a Planet under Stress and a Civilization in Trouble*. New York: Norton.

Brugiavini, Agar. 1999. Social security and retirement in Italy. In Jonathan Gruber and David Wise (eds.). *Social Security Programs and Retirement around the World*. Chicago: University of Chicago Press for the National Bureau of Economic Research: 181–238.

Brynjolfsson, Erik, and Lorin M. Hitt. 2000. Beyond computation: Information Technology, organizational transformation and business performance. *Journal of Economic Perspectives* 14, 23–48.

Burnside, Craig, and David Dollar. 2000. Aid, policies, and growth. *American Economic Review* 90, 847–68.

Bush, George H. W. 1991a. *Address before a Joint Session of the Congress on the State of the Union*. 29 January. Available at www.presidency.ucsb.edu/site/docs/doc_sou.php?admin=41&doc=3.

1991b. *Address Before a Joint Session of the Congress on the Cessation of the Persian Gulf Conflict*. 6 March. Available at www.presidency.ucsb.edu/site/docs/pppus.php?admin=041&year=1991&id=030600.

Cairncross, Frances. 2001. *The Death of Distance*. Boston: Harvard Business School Press.

Calavita, Kitty, Henry N. Pontell, and Robert H. Tillman. 1997. *Big Money Crime: Fraud and Politics in the Savings and Loan Crisis*. Berkeley: University of California Press.

Campbell, John Y. 1999. Comment. In Ben S. Bernanke and Julio S. Rotemberg (eds.). *NBER Macroeconomics Annual*. Cambridge, MA: MIT Press, 253–62.

Campbell, John Y., and John H. Cochrane. 1999. By force of habit: a consumption-based explanation of aggregate stock market behavior. *Journal of Political Economy* 107, 205–51.

Campbell, John Y., and Robert J. Shiller. 1988. Stock prices, earnings, and expected dividends. *Journal of Finance* 43, 661–76.

Campbell, John Y., and Tuomo Vuolteenaho. 2004. *Inflation Illusion and Stock Prices*. Working Paper no. 10263, National Bureau of Economic Research, Cambridge, MA.

Canterbery, Ray, and Robert Burkhardt. 1983. What do we mean by asking if economics is a science? In Alfred Eichner (ed.). *Why Economics Is Not Yet a Science*. Armonk, NY: M. E. Sharpe, 15–40.

Card, David, and John E. DiNardo. 2002. Skill-biased technological change and rising wage inequality: some problems and puzzles. *Journal of Labor Economics* 20, 733–83.

Cecchetti, Stephen. 2003. *What the FOMC Says and Does When the Stock Market Booms*. Mimeo, Brandeis University, Waltham, MA.

Cecchetti, Stephen, Hans Genberg, John Lipsky, and Shushil Wadhwani. 2000. *Asset Prices and Central Bank Policy*. Geneva Report on the World Economy 2, Centre for Economic Policy Research, London.

Center for Research on Securities Prices. 2002. *CRSP Database*. Center for Research on Securities Prices, University of Chicago.

Chandler, Alfred D. 1977. *The Visible Hand: The Managerial Revolution in American Business*. Cambridge, MA: Belknap Press.

Chen, Edwin. 1992. White House pushes deregulation. *Los Angeles Times*. 31 January, D4.

Chen, Shaohua, and Martin Ravallion. 2004. *How Have the World's Poorest Fared since the Early 1980s?* Policy Research Working Paper no. WPS3341 World Bank, Washington, DC.

Chiswick, Barry, and Timothy Hatton. 2003. International migration and the integration of labor markets. In Michael Bordo, Alan Taylor and Jeffrey Williamson (eds.). *Globalization in Historical Perspective*. Chicago: University of Chicago Press, 65–120.

Christofides, Charis, Christian Mulder, and Andrew Tiffin. 2003. *The Link between Adherence to International Standards of Good Practice, Foreign Exchange Spreads and Ratings*. Working Paper no. 03/74, International Monetary Fund, Washington, DC.

Clarke, Stephen V. O. 1967. *Central Bank Cooperation, 1924–1931*. New York: Federal Reserve Bank.

Cochrane, John H. 1991. Volatility tests and efficient markets: a review essay. *Journal of Monetary Economics* 27, 463–85.

Collins, Susan M. (ed.). 1998. *Imports, Exports, and the American Worker*. Washington, DC: Brookings Institute.

Cohen, Jessica, William Dickens, and Adam Posen. 2001. Have the new human resource management practices lowered the sustainable unemployment rate? In Alan B. Krueger and Robert M. Solow (eds.). *The Roaring Nineties*. New York: Russell Sage Foundation, 219–59.

Conner, Walter D. 1997. Social policy under Communism. In Ethan B. Kapstein and Michael Mandelbaum (eds.). 1997. *Sustaining the Transition: The Social Safety Net in Postcommunist Europe*. New York: Council on Foreign Relations: 10–45.

Coolidge, Calvin. 1928. *Sixth Annual Message Written to Congress*. 4 December. Available at www.polsci.ucsb.edu/projects/presproject/idgrant/sou_pages/coolidge6su.html.

Cortada, James W. 2004. *The Digital Hand: How Computers Changed the Work of American Manufacturing, Transportation, and Retail Industries*. New York: Oxford University Press.

Coy, Peter. 1997. Let's not take feel-good economics too far. *Business Week*. 20 October.

Crafts, Nicholas. 1999. Implications of financial crisis for East Asian trend growth. *Oxford Review of Economic Policy* 15, 110–31.

2002. The Human Development Index, 1870–1999: some revised estimates. *European Review of Economic History* 6, 395–405.

2003. *Quantifying the Contribution of Technological Change to Economic Growth in Different Eras: a Review of the Evidence*. Working Paper in Economic History no. 79/03, London School of Economics.

Crafts, Nicholas, and Markus Haacker. 2003. *Welfare Implications of HIV/AIDS*. Working Paper no. 03/118, International Monetary Fund, Washington, DC.

Crafts, Nicholas, and Kai Kaiser. 2004. Long term growth prospects in transition economies: a reappraisal. *Structural Change and Economic Dynamics* 15, 101–18.

Darby, Michael R. 1984. The U.S. productivity slowdown: a case of statistical myopia. *American Economic Review* 74, 301–22.

Darman, Richard. 1996. *Who's in Control? Polar Politics and the Sensible Center*. New York: Simon and Schuster.

David, Paul A. 1975. *Technical Choice, Innovation, and Economic Growth*. Cambridge: Cambridge University Press.

1977. Invention and accumulation in America's economic growth: a nineteenth-century parable. In *International Organization, National Policies, and Economic Development*, supplement to *Journal of Monetary Economies* 6, 179–228.

1990. The dynamo and the computer: an historical perspective on the modern productivity paradox. *American Economic Review* 80, 355–61.

1991. Computer and dynamo: the modern productivity paradox in a not-too-distant mirror. In *Technology and Productivity: The Challenge for Economic Policy*. Paris: Organisation for Economic Co-operation and Development, 315–48.

2004. *The Tale of Two Traverses: Innovation and Accumulation in the First Two Centuries of U.S. Economic Growth*. Gallman lecture, presented at conference on "Understanding the 1990s: the economy in long-run perspective," Duke University, Durham, NC, 26–7 March.

David, Paul A., and Gavin Wright. 2003. General purpose technologies and surges in productivity: historical reflections on the future of the ICT revolution. In Paul A. David and Mark Thomas (eds.). *The Economic Future in Historical Perspective*. Oxford: Oxford University Press, 135–66.

Davies, Gareth. 1996. *From Opportunity to Entitlement: The Transformation and Decline of Great Society Liberalism*. Lawrence: University Press of Kansas.

De Long, J. Bradford, Andrei Shleifer, Lawrence H. Summers, and Robert J. Waldmann. 1990. Noise trader risk in financial markets. *Journal of Political Economy* 98, 703–38.

De Serres, Alain 2003. *Structural Policies and Growth: A Non-Technical Overview*. Working Paper no. 355, Economics Department, Organisation for Economic Co-operation and Development, Paris.

Debreu, Gerard. 1991. The mathematization of economic theory. *American Economic Review* 81, 1–7.

DeFerranti, David, Guillermo E. Perry, Francisco H. G. Ferreira, and Michael Walton. 2004. *Inequality in Latin America: Breaking With History?* Washington, DC: World Bank.

De Long, J. Bradford. 2003. India since independence: an analytical growth narrative. In Dani Rodrik (ed.). *In Search of Prosperity: Analytical Narratives on Economic Growth*. Princeton, NJ: Princeton University Press, 184–204.

DeLong, J. Bradford, and Barry Eichengreen. 2002. Between meltdown and moral hazard: the international monetary and financial policies of the Clinton administration. In Jeffrey A. Frankel and Peter R. Orszag (eds.). *American Economic Policy in the 1990s*. Cambridge, MA: MIT Press, 191–254.

Denison, Edward F. 1962. *The Sources of Economic Growth in the United States and the Alternatives before Us*. New York: Committee for Economic Development.

Devine, Warren D., Jr. 1983. From shafts to wires: historical perspectives on electrification. *Journal of Economic History* 43, 347–72.

Dice, Charles Amos. 1929. *New Levels in the Stock Market*. New York: McGraw-Hill.

DiNardo, John E., Nicole M. Fortin, and Thomas Lemieux. 1996. Labor market institutions and the distribution of wages, 1973–1992: a semiparametric approach. *Econometrica* 64, 1001–44.

Disney, Richard, and Paul Johnson (eds.). 2001. *Pension Systems and Retirement Incomes across OECD Countries*. Cheltenham: Edward Elgar.

Dollar, David, and Aart Kraay. 2004. Trade, growth and poverty. *Economic Journal* 114, F22–F49.

Donaldson, R. Glen, and Mark Kamstra. 1996. A new dividend forecasting procedure that rejects bubbles in asset prices: the case of 1929's stock crash. *Review of Financial Studies* 9, 333–83.

Douglas, Paul H. 1930. *Real Wages in the United States, 1890–1926*. Chicago: University of Chicago Press.

Douglas, Paul H. and Florence T. Jennison. 1930. *The Movement of Money and Real Earnings in the United States, 1926–1928*. Chicago: University of Chicago Press.

DuBoff, Richard B. 1964. *Electric Power in American Manufacturing, 1889–1958*. Ph.D. Dissertation, University of Pennsylvania, PA.

Dun and Bradstreet, Inc. 2002. *D&B Million Dollar Directory*. Bethlehem, PA: Dun and Bradstreet, Inc.

Dunning, John. 1983. Changes in the level and structure of international production: the last one hundred years. In Mark Casson (ed.). *The Growth of International Business*. London: Allen and Unwin, 84–139.

Easterlin, Richard. 1996. *Growth Triumphant*. Ann Arbor: University of Michigan.

Easterly, Williamson, Ross Levine and David Roodman. 2003. *New Data, New Doubts: A Comment on Burnside and Dollar's "Aid, Policies and Growth" (2000)*. Working Paper no. 9846, National Bureau of Economic Research, Cambridge, MA.

Edelstein, Michael. 1990. What price Cold War? Military spending and private investment in the US, 1946–1979. *Cambridge Journal of Economics* 14, 421–37.

Edison, Hali J., Michael Klein, W. Luca Ricci, and Torsten Sloek. 2002. *Capital Account Liberalization and Economic Performance: Survey and Synthesis*. Working Paper no. 9100, National Bureau of Economic Research, Cambridge, MA.

Eichengreen, Barry. 1992a. *Golden Fetters: The Gold Standard and the Great Depression, 1919–1939*. New York and Oxford: Oxford University Press.

1992b. The origins and nature of the Great Slump revisited. *Economic History Review* 45, 213–39.

1996. Institutions and economic growth in Europe after World War II. In Nicholas Crafts and Gianni Toniolo (eds.). *Economic Growth in Europe since 1945*. Cambridge: Cambridge University Press, 38–72.

2000. U.S. foreign financial relations in the twentieth century. In Stanley L. Engerman and Robert E. Gallman (eds.). *The Cambridge Economic History of the United States*, Vol. III. Cambridge: Cambridge University Press, 463–504.

Eichengreen, Barry, and David Leblang. 2002. *Capital Account Liberalization and Growth: Was Mr Mahathir Right?* Working Paper no. 9427, National Bureau of Economic Research, Cambridge, MA.

Eichengreen, Barry, and Kris Mitchener. 2003. *The Great Depression as a Credit Boom Gone Wrong*. Working Paper no. 137, Bank for International Settlements, Basel.

Eichengreen, Barry, and Alan Taylor. 2003. *The Monetary Consequences of a Free Trade Area of the Americas*. Working Paper no. 9666, National Bureau of Economic Research, Cambridge, MA.

Eichengreen, Barry, and Peter Temin. 2000. The gold standard and the Great Depression. *Contemporary European History* 9, 183–207.

Fairris, David. 1997. *Shopfloor Matters*. London: Routledge

Fama, Eugene F., and Kenneth R. French. 1988. Dividend yields and expected stock returns. *Journal of Financial Economics* 22, 3–25.

Federal Reserve Bank of St Louis. 2002. *FRED Database*. Federal Reserve Bank of St Louis, MO.

Feinstein, Charles H., Gianni Toniolo, and Peter Temin. 1994. Three shocks, two recoveries: historical parallels for the end of the Cold War. *Rivista di Storia Economica* 11, 297–316.

Feinstein, Charles H., and Katherine Watson. 1995. Private international capital flows in Europe in the inter-war period. In Charles H. Feinstein (ed.). *Banking, Currency, and Finance in Europe Between the Wars*. Oxford: Oxford University Press, 94–130.

Feldstein, Martin, and Charles Horioka. 1980. Domestic savings and international capital flows. *Economic Journal* 90, 314–29.

Field, Alexander J. 1987. Modern business enterprise as a capital saving innovation. *Journal of Economic History* 47, 473–85.

1992. The magnetic telegraph, price and quantity data, and the new management of capital. *Journal of Economic History* 52, 401–13.

1996. The relative productivity of American distribution, 1869–1992. *Research in Economic History* 16, 1–37.

2003. The most technologically progressive decade of the century. *American Economic Review* 93, 1399–1413.

2004. *The Origins of US Multifactor Productivity Growth in the Golden Age.* Working paper, Leavey School of Business, Santa Clara University, CA.

2005. *The Impact of World War II on US Productivity Growth.* Paper presented at the Centre for Economic Policy Research/Centre de Recerea en Economia International workshop on "War and the macroeconomy," Universitat Pompeu Fabra, Barcelona, 29–30 June.

2006a. Technical change and US economic growth during the interwar period. *Journal of Economic History*, 66.

2006b. The equipment hypothesis and US economic growth. *Explorations in Economic History*, 44.

Fischer, Stanley, Ratna Sahay, and Carlos A. Vegh. 1998. *From Transition to Market: Evidence and Growth Prospects.* Working Paper no. 98/52, International Monetary Fund, Washington, DC.

Fisher, Irving. 1930. *The Stock Market Crash – And After.* New York: Macmillan.

Fisher, Lawrence. 1966. Some new stock market indexes. *Journal of Business* 39 (1, part 2 supplement), 191–225.

Fishlow, Albert. 1965. *American Railroads and the Transformation of the Antebellum Economy.* Cambridge, MA: Harvard University Press.

Flavin, Marjorie A. 1983. Excess volatility in the financial markets: a reassessment of the empirical evidence. *Journal of Political Economy* 91, 929–89.

Flood, Robert P., and Robert J. Hodrick. 1990. On testing for speculative bubbles. *Journal of Economic Perspectives* 4, 85–101.

Fogel, Robert. 1964. *Railroads and American Economic Growth: Essays in Econometric History.* Baltimore: Johns Hopkins University Press.

Foss, Murray F. 1981. Long-run changes in the workweek of fixed capital. *American Economic Review* 71, 58–61.

1985. Changing utilization of fixed capital: an element in long-term growth. *Monthly Labor Review*, 108(5), 3–8.

Foster, Lucia, John Haltiwanger, and C. J. Krizan. 2002. *The Link between Aggregate and Micro Productivity Growth: Evidence from Retail Trade.* Working Paper no. 9120, National Bureau of Economic Research, Cambridge, MA.

Frankel, Jeffrey, and Andrew Rose. 1996. Currency crashes in emerging markets: empirical indicators. *Journal of International Economics* 41, 351–66.

Fraser, Steven, and Gary Gerstle (eds.). 1989. *The Rise and Fall of the New Deal Order: 1930–1980.* Princeton, NJ: Princeton University Press.

Friedman, Milton, and Anna J. Schwartz. 1963. *A Monetary History of the United States, 1867–1960.* Princeton, NJ: Princeton University Press for the National Bureau of Economic Research.

Fritsch, Peter. 1999. Golden years: in Brazil, retirement has become a benefit nearly all can enjoy. *Wall Street Journal.* 9 September, 1.

Fukuyama, Francis. 1992. *The End of History and the Last Man.* New York: Free Press.

Gali, Jordi, and Roberto Perotti. 2002. Fiscal policy and monetary integration in Europe. *Economic Policy* 17, 533–72.

Gallup, John L., Jeffrey D. Sachs, and Andrew D. Mellinger. 1999. Geography and economic development. *International Regional Science Review* 22, 179–232.

Gao, Bai. 2001. *Japan's Economic Dilemma: The Institutional Origins of Prosperity and Stagnation*. Cambridge: Cambridge University Press.

Gates, Bill. 1999. *Business @ the Speed of Thought*. New York: Warner Books.

Gelos, Gaston, and Shang-Jin Wei. 2002. *Transparency and International Investor Behavior*. Working Paper no. 02/174, International Monetary Fund, Washington, DC.

Gerstle, Gary. 1994. The protean character of American liberalism. *American Historical Review* 99, 1043–73.

Giordano, James. 2003. Using the survivor technique to estimate returns to scale and optimum firm size. *Topics in Economic Analysis & Policy* 3(1), 23 (available at www.bepress.com).

Glassman, James, and Kevin Hassett. 1999. *The Dow 36,000: The New Strategy for Profiting from the Coming Rise in the Stock Market*. New York: Times Business.

Glennerster, Rachel, and Yongseok Shin. 2003. *Is Transparency Good for You, and Can the IMF Help?* Working Paper no. 03/132, International Monetary Fund, Washington, DC.

Glennon, Robert. 2002. *Water Follies: Groundwater Pumping and the Fate of America's Fresh Waters*. Washington, DC: Island Press.

Golden, Lonnie. 1996. The expansion of temporary help employment in the U.S., 1982–1992. *Applied Economics* 28, 1127–41.

Goldin, Claudia. 1998. America's graduation from high school: the evolution and spread of secondary schooling in the twentieth century. *Journal of Economic History* 58, 347–74.

2001. The human-capital century and American leadership: virtues of the past. *Journal of Economic History* 61, 263–92.

Goldin, Claudia, and Lawrence Katz. 1998. The origins of technology-skill complementarity. *Quarterly Journal of Economics* 113, 693–732.

Goldin, Claudia, and Robert A. Margo. 1992. The great compression: the wage structure in the United States at mid-century. *Quarterly Journal of Economics* 107, 1–34.

Goldin, Claudia, and Kenneth Sokoloff. 1982. Women, children and industrialization in the early republic. *Journal of Economic History* 42, 741–774.

Gordon, Robert Aaron. 1951. Cyclical experience in the interwar period: The investment boom of the "Twenties." In *Conference on Business Cycles*. New York: National Bureau of Economic Research 163–214.

1961. *Business Fluctuations*, 2nd edn. New York: Harper and Brothers.

1974. *Economic Instability and Growth: The American Record*. New York: Harper and Row.

Gordon, Robert. J. 1969. $45 billion of U.S. private investment has been mislaid. *American Economic Review* 59, 221–38.

1982. Why stopping inflation may be costly: evidence from fourteen historical episodes. In Robert E. Hall (ed.). *Inflation: Causes and Effects*. Chicago: University of Chicago Press, 11–40.

1990. *The Measurement of Durable Goods Prices*. Chicago: University of Chicago Press.

1997. The time-varying NAIRU and its implications for economic policy. *Journal of Economic Perspectives* 11, 11–32.

1998. Foundations of the Goldilocks economy: supply shocks and the time-varying NAIRU. *Brookings Papers on Economic Activity* 2, 297–333.

1999. U.S. economic growth since 1870: one big wave? *American Economic Review* 89, 123–8.

2000a. Interpreting the "one big wave" in US long-term productivity growth. In Bart van Ark, Simon Kuipers, and Gerard Kuiper (eds.). *Productivity, Technology, and Economic Growth*. Boston: Kluwer, 19–65.

2000b. Does the new economy measure up to the great inventions of the past? *Journal of Economic Perspective* 14, 49–74.

2002. Comments. *Brooking Papers on Economic Activity* 2, 245–60.

2003a. Exploding productivity growth: context, causes, and implications. *Brookings Papers on Economic Activity* 2, 207–96.

2003b. *Macroeconomics*, 9th edn. Boston: Addison-Wesley.

2003c. *Five Puzzles in the Behavior of Productivity Investment, and Innovation*. Unpublished Papers.

2004a. *Two Centuries of Economic Growth: Europe Chasing the American Frontier*. Discussion Paper no. 4415, Centre for Economic Policy Research, London.

2004b. *Why Was Europe Left at the Station when America's Productivity Locomotive Departed?* Discussion Paper no. 4416, Centre for Economic Policy Research, London.

Gordon, Robert J., and John M. Veitch. 1986. Fixed investment in the American business cycle, 1919–83. In Robert J. Gordon (ed.). *The American Business Cycle: Continuity and Change*. Chicago: University of Chicago Press for the National Bureau of Economic Research, 267–357.

Gordon, Robert J., and James Wilcox. 1981. Monetarist interpretations of the great depression: evaluation and critique. In Karl Brunner (ed.). *The Great Depression Revisited*. Boston: Martinus Nijhoff, 49–107.

Gottschalk, Peter. 1997. Inequality, income growth, and mobility: The basic facts. *Journal of Economic Perspectives* 11, 21–44.

Greenspan, Alan. 2000. *Technology Innovation and its Economic Impact*. 7 April. Available at www.federalreserve.gov/boarddocs/speeches/2000/20000407.htm.

Griliches, Zvi, and Ernst R. Berndt. 1993. Price indexes for microcomputers: an exploratory study. In M. F. Foss, M. E. Manser and A. H. Young (eds.). *Price Measurements and Their Uses*. NBER Studies in Income and Wealth 5. Chicago: University of Chicago Press, 63–93.

Groningen Growth and Development Centre. 2005. *Total Economy Database*. Available at www.ggdc.net/deseries/totecon.shtml.

Grubb, David. 2000. Eligibility criteria for unemployment benefits. In *OECD Economic Studies* no. 31. Paris: Organisation for Economic Co-operation and Development, 147–81.

Gruber, Jonathan, and David Wise (eds.). 1999. *Social Security Programs and Retirement around the World*. Chicago: University of Chicago Press for the National Bureau of Economic Research.

Gust, Christopher, and Jaime Marquez. 2002. *International Comparisons of Productivity Growth: the Role of Information Technology and Regulatory Practices*.

International Finance Discussion Paper no. 727, Board of Governors of the Federal Reserve System, Washington, DC.

Habakkuk, H. J. 1962. *American and British Technology in the Nineteenth Century.* Cambridge: Cambridge University Press.

Hall, Robert E., and Charles I. Jones, 1999. Why do some countries produce so much more output per worker than others? *Quarterly Journal of Economics* 114, 83–116.

Hausmann, Ricardo, and Eduardo Fernandez-Arias. 2000. *Foreign Direct Investment: Good Cholesterol?* Unpublished manuscript, Research Department, Inter-American Development Bank, Washington, DC.

Hayashi, Fumio, and Edward Prescott. 2002. The 1990s in Japan: a lost decade. *Review of Economic Dynamics* 5, 206–35.

Heaton, John, and Deborah Lucas. 1999. Stock prices and fundamentals. In Ben S. Bernanke and Julio S. Rotemberg (eds.). *NBER Macroeconomics Annual.* Cambridge, MA: MIT Press, 213–242.

Helpman, Elhanan (ed.). 1998. *General Purpose Technologies and Economic Growth.* Cambridge, MA: MIT Press.

Helpman, Elhanan, and Manuel Trajtenberg. 1998. A time to sow and a time to reap: growth based on general-purpose technologies. In Elhanan Helpman (ed.). *General-purpose Technologies and Economic Growth.* Cambridge, MA: MIT Press, 55–83.

Hickman, Bert G. 1974. What became of the building cycle? In Paul A. David and Melvin Reder (eds.). *Nations and Households in Economic Growth: Essays in Honor of Moses Abramovitz.* New York: Academic Press, 291–314.

Hicks, John R. 1950. *A Contribution to the Theory of the Trade Cycle.* Oxford: Clarendon Press.

Homer, Sidney, and Richard Sylla. 1991. *A History of Interest Rates*, 3rd edn. New Brunswick, NJ: Rutgers University Press.

Hobsbawm, Eric J. 1994. *Age of Extremes: The Short Twentieth Century 1914–1991.* London: Pantheon Books.

Hopenhayn, Hugo A. 1992. Entry, exit, and firm dynamics in long run equilibrium. *Econometrica* 60, 1127–50.

ILO. Various issues. *The Cost of Social Security.* Geneva: International Labour Organization.

   2003. *Key Indicators of the Labour Market*, 3rd edn. Geneva: International Labour Organization.

IMF. 1997. *World Economic Outlook. Globalization: Opportunities and Challenges.* Washington, DC: International Monetary Fund.

   Various issues. *World Economic Outlook.* Washington, DC: International Monetary Fund.

   2004. *International Financial Statistics.* Washington, DC: International Monetary Fund (available at http://libraries. mit.edu/get/ifs).

Investment Company Institute. 2003. *Mutual Fund Fact Book,* 43rd edn. Investment Company Institute, Washington, DC.

Jacoby, Sanford M. 1983. Industrial labor mobility in historical perspective. *Industrial Relations* 22, 215–28.

1985. *Employing Bureaucracy: Managers, Unions, and the Transformation of Work in American Industry, 1900–1945.* New York: Columbia University Press.

James, John A., and Jonathan S. Skinner. 1985. The resolution of the labor-scarcity paradox. *Journal of Economic History* 45, 513–40.

Jerome, Harry. 1930. *Mechanization in Industry.* New York: National Bureau of Economic Research.

Johnson, Haynes. 2001. *The Best of Times: America in the Clinton Years.* New York: Harcourt.

Jones, Charles I. 1995. Time series tests of endogenous growth models. *Quarterly Journal of Economics* 110, 495–525.

Jorgenson, Dale, and Kevin Stiroh. 1999. Information Technology and growth. *American Economic Review* 89, 109–15.

2000. Raising the speed limit: U.S. economic growth in the information age. *Brookings Papers on Economic Activity* 31 (1), 125–211.

Jorgenson, Dale, Mun Ho, and Kevin Stiroh. 2003. *Lessons from the US Growth Resurgence.* Paper prepared for the First International Conference on the Economic and Social Implications of Information Technology, US Department of Commerce, Washington, DC, 27–28 January.

Jovanovic, Boyan, and Peter L. Rousseau. 2001a. *Vintage Organization Capital.* Working Paper no. 8166, National Bureau of Economic Research, Cambridge, MA.

2001b. Why wait? A century of life before IPO. *American Economic Review* 91, 336–41.

2002a. Moore's law and learning-by-doing. *Review of Economic Dynamics* 4, 346–75.

2002b. Stock markets in the new economy. In Chong-En Bai and Chi-Wa Yuen (eds.). *Technology and the New Economy.* Cambridge, MA: MIT Press, 9–48.

Kahn, Alfred. 1990. Deregulation: looking backward and looking forward. *Yale Journal of Regulation* 7, 325–54.

Kaplan, Karen, and Thomas S. Mulligan. 1997. Telephone giants AT&T, SBC discuss $50-billion merger. *Los Angeles Times.* 28 May, A1, A18.

Katz, Lawrence F., and David H. Autor. 1999. Changes in the wage structure and earnings inequality. In Orley Asherfelter and David Card (eds.). *Handbook of Labor Economics* Vol. IIIA. Amsterdam: Elsevier, 1463–555.

Katz, Lawrence F., and Alan B. Krueger. 1999. The high-pressure US labor markets of the 1990s. *Brookings Papers on Economic Activity* 1, 1–87.

Kaufmann, Daniel., Aart Kraay, and Massimo Mastruzzi. 2003. *Governance Matters III: Governance Indicators for 1996–2002.* Policy Research Working Paper no. 3815, World Bank, Washington, DC.

Keegan, John. 1989. *World War II.* London: Hutchinson.

Keller, Robert. 1973. Factor income distribution in the United States during the 1920s: a reexamination of fact and theory. *Journal of Economic History* 33, 252–73.

Kelley, Etna M. 1954. *The Business Founding Date Directory.* Scarsdale, NY: Morgan and Morgan.

Kendrick, John. 1961. *Productivity Trends in the United States.* Princeton, NJ: Princeton University Press.

Keynes, John Maynard. 1936. *The General Theory of Employment, Interest and Money*. London: Macmillan.

Kindleberger, Charles P. 1986. *The World in Depression*, rev. edn. Berkeley: University of California Press.

Kleidon, Allan W. 1986. Variance bounds tests and stock price valuation models. *Journal of Political Economy* 94, 953–1001.

Kleinknecht, Alfred. 1987. *Innovation Patterns in Crisis and Prosperity: Schumpeter's Long Cycle Reconsidered*. New York: St. Martin's Press.

Klenow, Peter, and Andres Rodriquez-Clare. 1997. Economic growth: a review essay. *Journal of Monetary Economics* 40, 597–617.

Kneller, Richard, Michael Bleaney, and Norman Gemmell. 1999. Fiscal policy and growth: evidence from OECD countries. *Journal of Public Economic* 74, 171–90.

Kortum, Samuel, and Josh Lerner. 1998. Stronger protection or technological revolution: what is behind the recent surge in patenting? *Carnegie-Rochester Conference Series on Public Policy* 48, 247–304.

Kotlikoff, Laurence J., and Scott Burns. 2004. *The Coming Generational Storm*. Cambridge, MA: MIT Press.

Kramer, Mark. 1997. Social protection policies and safety nets in East–Central Europe: dilemmas of the postcommunist transformation. In Ethan B. Kapstein and Michael Mandelbaum (eds.). *Sustaining the Transition: The Social Safety Net in Postcommunist Europe*. New York: Council on Foreign Relations, 46–123.

Kremers, Jeroen J. M. 2002. Pension reform: issues in the Netherlands. In Martin Feldstein and Horst Siebert (eds.). *Social Security Pension Reform in Europe*. Chicago: University of Chicago Press, 291–316.

Krugman, Paul. 1994. Competitiveness: a dangerous obsession. *Foreign Affairs* 73, 28–44.

Krusell, Per, Lee E. Ohanian, José-Victor Rios-Rull, and Giovanni L. Violante. 2000. Capital–skill complementarity and inequality: a macroeconomic analysis. *Econometrica* 68, 1029–53.

Kugler, Maurice. 2000. *The Diffusion of Externalities from Foreign Direct Investment: Theory ahead of Evidence*. Working paper, University of Southampton.

Kuhn, Thomas. 1970. *The Structure of Scientific Revolutions*. Chicago: University of Chicago Press.

Kuznets, Simon S. 1961a. *Capital in the American Economy: Its Formation and Financing*. Princeton, NJ: Princeton University Press.

1961b. *Annual Estimates, 1869–1955*. Manuscript. Johns Hopkins University, Baltimore, MD.

1966. *Modern Economic Growth: Rate, Structure, and Spread*. New Haven, CT: Yale University Press.

Lamont, Owen. 1998. Earnings and expected returns. *Journal of Finance* 53, 563–87.

Lamoreaux, Naomi, Daniel M. G. Raff, and Peter Temin. 2003. Beyond markets and hierarchies: toward a new synthesis of American business history. *American Historical Review* 108, 404–33.

LaVelle, Philip. 1996. City suffers costly slash in credit ratings. *San Diego Union Tribune.* 6 December, A1, A27.

Leamer, Edward, and Michael Storper. 2001. *The Economic Geography of the Internet Age.* Working Paper no. 8450, National Bureau of Economic Research, Cambridge, MA.

Lebergott, Stanley. 1964. *Manpower in Economic Growth: The United States Record since 1800.* New York: McGraw-Hill.

Lee, David S. 1999. Wage inequality in the United States during the 1980s: rising dispersion or falling minimum wage? *Quarterly Journal of Economics* 114, 977–1023.

Lee, Susan. 1996. *Hands Off: Why the Government is a Menace to Economic Health.* New York: Simon and Schuster.

Lindert, Peter H. 2004. *Growing Public: Social Spending and Economic Growth since the Eighteenth Century* (two volumes). Cambridge: Cambridge University Press.

Lipsey, R. G., C. Bekar, and K. Carlaw. 1998. What requires explanation? In E. Helpman (ed.). *General Purpose Technologies and Economic Growth.* Cambridge, MA: MIT Press, 15–54.

Lopez-Cordova, Ernesto, and Mauricio Mesquita Moreira. 2003. *Regional Integration and Productivity: The Experiences of Brazil and Mexico.* Discussion Paper no. 14, Inter-American Development Bank, Washington, DC.

Los Angeles Times. 1996a. Court blocks rule on local phone rivalry. 16 October, D1, D6.

1996b. FCC may loosen ownership rules. 8 November, D4.

1997a. FCC to auction wireless licenses. 12 March, D3.

1997b. Merger of Baby Bells clears hurdle. 25 April, D10.

1997c. Also, . . . 29 October, D3.

Lucas, Robert E. 1990. Why doesn't capital flow from rich to poor countries? *American Economic Review, Papers and Proceedings* 80, 92–6.

2000. Some macroeconomics for the 21st century. *Journal of Economic Perspectives* 14, 159–78.

Lucking-Reiley, David and Daniel F. Spulber. 2001. Business to business electronic commerce. *Journal of Economic Perspectives* 14, 3–22.

Maddison, Angus. 1996. Macroeconomic accounts for European countries. In Bart van Ark and Nicholas Crafts (eds.). *Quantitative Aspects of Postwar European Economic Growth.* Cambridge: Cambridge University Press, 27–83.

2001. *The World Economy: A Millennial Perspective.* Paris: Organisation for Economic Co-operation and Development.

2003. *The World Economy: Historical Statistics.* Paris: Organisation for Economic Co-operation and Development.

Madsden, Jakob B. 2001. Agricultural crises and the international transmission of the Great Depression. *Journal of Economic History* 61, 327–65.

Mankiw, N. Gregory. 2002. U.S. monetary policy during the 1990s. In Jeffrey A. Frankel and Peter R. Orszag (eds.). *American Economic Policy in the 1990s.* Cambridge, MA: MIT Press, 19–43.

Margo, Robert A. 1991. The microeconomics of Depression unemployment. *Journal of Economic History* 51, 331–41.

Mathieson, Clive. 2002a. Telecoms waste $500bn on fibre cables. *TimesOnline* 13 February. Available at www.timesonline.co.uk/article/0,,5-206870,00.html.

2002b. Investment in fibre cable fails to light up the world. *TimesOnline* 13 February. Available at www.timesonline.co.uk/article/0,,630-206695,00.html.

Mayer, Martin. 1990. *The Greatest-Ever Bank Robbery: The Collapse of the Savings and Loan Industry*. New York: Collier.

McAuley, Alastair. 1979. *Economic Welfare in the Soviet Union: Poverty, Living Standards, and Inequality*. Madison: University of Wisconsin Press.

McChesney, Robert. 1997. Digital highway robbery. *The Nation*. 21 April, 22–24.

McCullough, David G. 1992. *Truman*. New York: Simon and Schuster.

McKinsey Global Institute. 2001. *US Productivity Growth 1995–2000: Understanding the Contribution of Information Technology Relative to other Factors*. McKinsey Global Institute, San Francisco. Available at www.mckinsey.com.

2003. *Offshoring: Is It a Win-Win Game?* McKinsey Global Institute, San Francisco.

Means, Gardiner, to Richard Goodwin. 1975. *Papers of Gardiner Means*. Franklin D. Roosevelt Library: Hyde Park, New York. Box 68, 18 January, Folder: Correspondence – G.

Medici, André. 2004. *The Political Economics of Reform in Brazil's Civil Servant Pension Scheme*. Technical Report on Pensions no. 002, Inter-American Development Bank, Washington, DC.

Mehra, Rajnish, and Edward C. Prescott. 1985. The equity premium: a puzzle. *Journal of Monetary Economics* 15, 145–61.

Meltzer, Allan H. 2003. *A History of the Federal Reserve*, Vol. I. Chicago: University of Chicago Press.

Mensch, Gerhard. 1979. *Stalemate in Technology: Innovations Overcome the Depression*. Cambridge, MA: Ballinger.

Midelfart-Knarvik, Karen H., Henry G. Overman, Stephen J. Redding, and Anthony J. Venables. 2000. *The Location of European Industry*. Economic Paper no. 142, European Union Commission, Brussels.

Milgrom, Paul. 1996. *Auction Theory for Privatization*. Cambridge: Cambridge University Press.

Minsky, Hyman P. 1986. *Stabilizing an Unstable Economy*. New Haven, CT: Yale University Press.

Mishkin, Frederic S., and Eugene N. White. 2003. U.S. stock market crashes and their aftermath: implications for monetary policy. In William C. Hunter, George G. Kaufman, and Michael Pomerleano (eds.). *Asset Price Bubbles: The Implications for Monetary, Regulatory, and International Policies*. Cambridge, MA: MIT Press, 53–79.

Moffab, Susan. 1992. Right call? 10 years later, AT&T split favors business. *Los Angeles Times*. 7 January, D1, D7.

Moore, Gordon E. (1965). Cramming more components onto integrated circuits. *Electronics* 38 (19 April).

Moser, Petra, and Tom Nicholas. 2004. Was electricity a general–purpose technology? Evidence from historical patent citations. *American Economic Review* 94, 388–94.

Mowery, David C. 1981. *The Emergence and Growth of Industrial Research in American Manufacturing, 1899–1946*. Ph.D. dissertation, Stanford University, CA.

Mowery, David, and Nathan Rosenberg. 1998. *Paths of Innovation: Technological Change in 20th-Century America*. Cambridge: Cambridge University Press.

2000. Twentieth-century technological change. In Stanley Engerman and Robert Gallman (eds.). *The Cambridge Economic History of the United States*, Vol. III. Cambridge: Cambridge University Press, 803–926.

Mulligan, Casey, Ricard Gil, and Xavier Sala-i-Martin. 2002. *Social Security and Democracy*. Working Paper no. 8958, National Bureau of Economic Research, Cambridge, MA.

Nelson, Richard, and Gavin Wright. 1992. The rise and fall of American technological leadership: the postwar era in historical perspective. *Journal of Economic Literature* 30, 1931–64.

Neumayer, Eric. 2003. Beyond income: convergence in living standards, big time. *Structural Change and Economic Dynamics* 14, 275–396.

Nickell, Stephen. 2003. *A Picture of European Unemployment: Success and Failure*. Discussion Paper no. 577. Centre for Economic Performance, London School of Economics.

Nicoletti, Giuseppe, and Stefano Scarpetta. 2003. Regulation, productivity, and growth: OECD evidence. *Economic Policy* 36, 9–72.

Nicoletti, Giuseppe, Andrea Bassanini, Ekkehard Ernst, Sébastien Jean, Paulo Santiago, and Paul Swaim. 2001. *Product and Labour Market Interactions in OECD Countries*. Working Paper no. 312, Economics Department, Organisation for Economic Co-operation and Development, Paris.

Nordhaus, William D. 1997a. Traditional productivity estimates are asleep at the (technological) switch. *Economic Journal* 107, 1548–59.

1997b. Do real output and real wage measures capture reality? The history of lighting suggests not. In Timothy Bresnahan and Robert Gordon (eds.). *The Economics of New Goods*. Chicago: University of Chicago Press, 29–70.

2000. New directions in national economic accounting. *American Economic Review, Papers and Proceedings* 90, 259–63.

2002. Productivity growth and the New Economy. *Brookings Papers on Economic Activity* 2, 211–44.

North, Douglass C. 1990. *Institutions, Institutional Change and Economic Performance*. Cambridge: Cambridge University Press.

O'Brien, Anthony Patrick. 1989. A behavioral explanation for nominal wage rigidity during the Great Depression. *Quarterly Journal of Economics* 104, 719–35.

Obstfeld, Maurice, and Alan M. Taylor. 2003. Globalization and capital markets. In Michael D. Bordo, Alan M. Taylor, and Jeffrey G. Williamson (eds.). *Globalization in Historical Perspective*. Chicago: University of Chicago Press, 138–45.

2004. *Global Capital Markets: Integration, Crisis and Growth*. Cambridge: Cambridge University Press.

OECD. 1981. *Long-Term Trends in Tax Revenues of OECD Member Countries.* Paris: Organisation for Economic Co-operation and Development.

1998. *Social Expenditure Database 1980–1995.* CD-Rom. Paris: Organisation for Economic Co-operation and Development.

1999. *Social Expenditure Database, 1980–1996.* CD-Rom, Paris: Organisation for Economic Co-operation and Development.

2000. *Labour Force Statistics 1979–1999.* Paris: Organisation for Economic Co-operation and Development.

2001. *Knowledge, Work Organization and Economic Growth.* Paris: Organisation for Economic Co-operation and Development.

2002. *Revenue Statistics 1965–2001.* Paris: Organisation for Economic Co-operation and Development.

2003a. *The Sources of Economic Growth.* Paris: Organisation for Economic Co-operation and Development.

2003b. *Economic Outlook.* Paris: Organisation for Economic Co-operation and Development.

2003c. *Employment Outlook.* Paris: Organisation for Economic Co-operation and Development.

Offer, Avner. 1998. The American automobile frenzy of the 1950s. In K. Bruland and P. K. O'Brien (eds.). *From Family Firms to Corporate Capitalism: Essays in Business and Industrial History in Honour of Peter Mathias.* Oxford: Oxford University Press, 315–53.

Oliner, Stephen D., and Daniel E. Sichel. 2000. The resurgence of growth in the late 1990s: is Information Technology the story? *Journal of Economic Perspectives* 14, 3–22.

2002. Information technology and productivity: where are we now and where are we going? *Economic Review, Federal Reserve Bank of Atlanta* (3rd quarter), 15–44.

Olmstead, Alan L., and Paul W. Rhode. 2000. The transformation of Northern agriculture, 1910–1990. In Stanley L. Engerman and Robert E. Gallman (eds.). *The Cambridge Economic History of the United States*, Vol. III. Cambridge: Cambridge University Press, 693–742.

2002. The Red Queen and the Hard Reds: productivity growth in American wheat, 1800–1940. *Journal of Economic History* 62, 929–66.

O'Mahoney, Mary. 2002. *Productivity in the EU, 1979–1999.* London: HM Treasury.

O'Mahoney, Mary, and Bart Van Ark (eds.). 2003. *EU Productivity and Competitiveness: An Industry Perspective – Can Europe Resume the Catching-up Process?* Luxembourg City: European Commission, Directorate-General for Enterprise.

O'Rourke, Kevin H., and Jeffrey G. Williamson. 1999. *Globalization and History: The Evolution of a Nineteenth-Century Atlantic Economy.* Cambridge, MA: MIT Press.

Osterman, Paul. 1980. *Getting Started: The Youth Labor Market.* Cambridge, MA: MIT Press.

Owen, Laura. 1995. Worker turnover in the 1920s: what the labor-supply arguments don't tell us. *Journal of Economic History* 55, 822–41.

Paes de Barros, Ricardo, and Miguel Nathan Foguel. 2000. Focalização dos Gastos Públicos Sociais e Erradicação da Probreza. In Ricardo Henriques (ed.). *Desigualdade e Pobreza no Brasil*. Rio de Janeiro: IPEA, 719–39.

Panagariya, Arvind. 2004. *India in the 1980s and 1990s: A Triumph of Reforms*. Working Paper no. 04/43, International Monetary Fund, Washington, DC.

Parente, Stephen L., and Edward C. Prescott. 2000. *Barriers to Riches*. Cambridge, MA: MIT Press.

Parry, Robert. 1996. Who buys the right? *The Nation*. 18 November, 5–6.

Parsons, Wayne. 1990. *The Power of the Financial Press: Journalism and Economic Opinion in Britain and America*. New Brunswick, NJ: Rutgers University Press.

Passell, Peter. 1990. The tax-rise issue: Bush rationale vs. economists. *New York Times*, 10 May.

Patterson, Robert T. 1965. *The Great Boom and Panic, 1921–1929*. Chicago: Henry Regnery Company.

Peltz, James F. 1996. Airline mergers '90s-style might stand a better chance this time. *Los Angeles Times*. 5 December, D1, D9.

   1997. Justice Dept. reviews claims of airlines' price squeeze. *Los Angeles Times*, 12 February, D1, D3.

Peritz, Rudolph. 1996. *Competition Policy in America, 1888–1992: History, Rhetoric, Law*. New York: Oxford University Press.

Petzinger, Jr., Thomas. 1996. *Hard Landing: The Epic Contest for Power and Profits That Plunged the Airlines Into Chaos*. New York: Times Business.

Piketty, Thomas. 2001. *Income Inequality in France, 1901–1998*. Discussion Paper no. 2876, Centre for Economic Policy Research, London.

Piketty, Thomas, and Emmanuel Saez. 2003. Income inequality in the United States, 1913–1998. *Quarterly Journal of Economics* 118, 1–39.

Plotnick, Robert D., Eugene Smolensky, Eirik Evenhouse, and Siobhan Reilly. 2000. The twentieth-century record of poverty and inequality in the United States. In Stanley L. Engerman and Robert E. Gallman (eds.). *The Cambridge Economic History of the United States*, Vol. III. Cambridge: Cambridge University Press, 249–99.

Prescott, Edward C. 2004. *Why do Americans Work so much more than Europeans?* Working Paper no. 10316, National Bureau of Economic Research, Cambridge, MA.

Pritchett, L. 1997. Divergence big time. *Journal of Economic Perspectives* 11 (3), 3–17.

Rangazas, Peter. 2002. The quantity and quality of schooling and US labor productivity growth, 1970–2000. *Review of Economic Dynamics* 5, 932–64.

Redding, Stephen J., and Anthony J. Venables. 2002. *Explaining Cross-Country Export Performance: International Linkages and Economic Geography*. Discussion Paper no. 549, Centre for Economic Performance, London School of Economics.

   2004. Economic geography and international inequality. *Journal of International Economics* 62, 53–82.

Rees, Albert. 1960. *New Measures of Wage-Earner Compensation in Manufacturing, 1914–1957*. Occasional Paper no. 75, National Bureau of Economic Research, Cambridge, MA.

Risen, James. 1993. Clinton kills controversial Quayle panel. *Los Angeles Times*. 23 January, A14.

Risen, James, and Douglas Jehl. 1992. Bush to call for freeze on new regulations. *Los Angeles Times*. 21 January, A1, A14.

Ritschl, Albrecht. 2003. "Dancing on a volcano": the economic recovery and collapse of Weimar Germany. In Theo Balderson (ed.). *The World Economy and National Economies in the Interwar Slump*. Basingstoke: Palgrave Macmillan, 105–42.

Rocha, Roberto, and Dimitri Viltas. 2002. The Hungarian pension reform: a preliminary assessment. In Martin Feldstein and Horst Siebart (eds.). *Social Security Pension Reform in Europe*. Chicago: University of Chicago Press, 365–400.

Rodrik, Dani. 1997. *Has Globalization Gone Too Far?* Washington, DC: Institute for International Economics.

Rodrik, Dani, and Arvind Subramanian. 2003. *From "Hindu Growth" to Productivity Surge: The Mystery of the Indian Growth Transition*. Mimeo, John F. Kennedy School of Growth, Harvard University, Cambridge, MA.

Romer, Christina. 1990. The Great Crash and the onset of the Great Depression. *Quarterly Journal of Economics* 105, 597–624.

Romer, Paul M. 1987. Crazy explanations for the productivity slowdown. In *NBER Macroeconomics Annual 1987*. Cambridge, MA: MIT Press, 163–202.

Rostow, W. W. 1960. *The Stages of Economic Growth: A NonCommunist Manifesto*. Cambridge: Cambridge University Press.

Sachs, Jeffrey, and Andrew Warner. 1995. *Economic Convergence and Economic Policies*. Working Paper no. 5039, National Bureau of Economic Research, Cambridge, MA.

Sala-i-Martin, Xavier. 1996. A positive theory of social security. *Journal of Economic Growth* 1, 277–304.

2002. *The World Distribution of Income (Estimated from Individual Country Distributions)*. Working Paper no. 8933, National Bureau of Economic Research, Cambridge, MA.

Samuelson, Paul A. 1939. Interactions between the multiplier analysis and the principle of acceleration. *Review of Economics and Statistics* 21, 75–8.

Sapir, André, Philippe Aghion, Giuseppe Bertola, Martin Hellwig, Jean Pisani-Ferry, Dariusz Rosati, José Vinals, and Helen Wallace. 2003. *An Agenda for a Growing Europe: Making the EU Economic System Deliver*. Brussels: European Commission.

Sato, Kazuo. 2002. From fast to last: the Japanese economy in the 1990s. *Journal of Asian Economics* 13 (March–April), 213–35.

Saxonhouse, Gary R. and Robert M. Stern. 2003. The bubble and the lost decade. *World Economy* 26 (March), 267–81.

Schmookler, Jacob. 1966. *Invention and Economic Growth*. Cambridge, MA: Harvard University Press.

Schumpeter, Joseph A. 1939. *Business Cycles*. New York: McGraw-Hill.

Segal, Lewis M., and Daniel G. Sullivan. 1997. The growth of temporary services work. *Journal of Economic Perspectives* 11, 117–36.

Sharma, Devinder. 2003. *WTO and Agriculture: the Great Trade Robbery*. Paper presented at debate on international politics: Agricultural Stumbling Block for the WTO? Legislative Assembly, Berlin, 2 September (available at www.mindfully.org/WTO/2003/Trade-Robbery-WTO-Sharma2sep03.htm).

Sharpe, Andrew, and Leila Gharani. 2000. The productivity renaissance in the US service sector. *International Productivity Monitor* 1, 6–8.

Shepherd, William. 2001. Airlines. In Walter Adams and James Brock (eds.). *The Structure of American Industry*. Boston: Prentice Hall, 199–223.

Shiller, Robert J. 1981. Do stock prices move too much to be justified by subsequent changes in dividends? *American Economic Growth* 71 (2), 421–35.

1991. *Market Volatility*. Cambridge, MA: MIT Press.

2000. *Irrational Exuberance*. Princeton, NJ: Princeton University Press.

Shever, Jr., Jube. 1996a. Justice Dept. approves merger of PacTel, SBC Communications. *Los Angeles Times*. 6 November, D1, D9.

1996b. New rules will let pay phone rates climb. *Los Angeles Times*. 9 November, A1, A19.

1997a. Was telecommunications reform just another act? *Los Angeles Times*. 3 February, D1, D6.

1997b. Deregulation of phones stirs hornet's nest. *Los Angeles Times*. 28 April, D1, D4.

1997c. US probes alleged fixing of bids for FCC licenses. *Los Angeles Times*. 1 May, D1, D5.

1997d. AT&T rate cut clears way for FCC reforms. *Los Angeles Times*. 5 May, D1, D2.

1997e. New federal rules expected to result in pay phone hikes. *Los Angeles Times*. 7 October, D1, D22.

1997f. MCI, WorldCom agree to record $37-billion merger. *Los Angeles Times*. 11 November, A1, A15.

Simon, Curtis J. 2001. The supply price of labor during the Great Depression. *Journal of Economic History* 61, 877–903.

Sinn, Stefan. 1992. Saving–investment correlations and capital mobility: on the evidence from annual data. *Economic Journal* 102, 1171–83.

Sirkin, Gerald. 1975. The stock market of 1929 revisited: a note. *Business History Review* 49, 223–31.

Solow, Robert M. 1957. Technical change and the aggregate production function. *Review of Economics and Statistics* 39, 312–20.

1987. We'd better watch out. *New York Times Book Review* (12 July), 36.

Staiger, Douglas, James H. Stock, and Mark W. Watson. 1997. The NAIRU, unemployment, and monetary policy. *Journal of Economic Perspectives* 11, 33–49.

Stefancic, Jean, and Richard Delgado. 1996. *No Mercy: How Conservative Think Tanks and Foundations Changed America's Social Agenda*. Philadelphia: Temple University Press.

Stigler, George J. 1958. The economies of scale. *Journal of Law and Economics* 1, 54–71.

Stiglitz, Joseph E. 2003. *The Roaring Nineties*. New York: Norton.

Stiroh, Kevin. 2001. Is IT driving the US productivity revival? *International Productivity Monitor* 2, 31–36.

Subbarao, K., Aniruddha Bonnerjee, Jeanine Braithwaite, Soniya Carvalho, Kene Eze-menari, Carol Graham, and Alan Thompson. 1997. *Safety Net Programs and Poverty Reduction: Lessons from Cross-Country Experience*. Washington, DC: World Bank.

Taylor, John B. 1995. Changes in American economic policy in the 1980s: watershed or pendulum swing? *Journal of Economic Literature* 33, 777–84.

Temin, Peter. 1976. *Did Monetary Forces Cause the Great Depression?* New York: Norton.

    1995. The "Koreaboom" in West Germany: fact or fiction? *Economic History Review* 48, 737–53.

    1999. Globalization. *Oxford Review of Economic Policy* 15, 76–89.

    2000. The Great Depression. In Stanley L. Engerman and Robert E. Gallman (eds.). *The Cambridge Economic History of the United States*, Vol. III. Cambridge: Cambridge University Press, 301–28.

    2002. The golden age of european growth reconsidered. *European Review of Economic History* 6, 3–22.

Tremewan, Christopher. 1998. Welfare and governance: public housing under Singapore's party-state. In Roger Goodman, Gordon White, and Huck-ju Kwon (eds.). 1998. *The East Asian Welfare Model: Welfare Orientalism and the State*. London: Routledge, 77–105.

Triplett, Jack E. and Barry P. Bosworth. 2003. Productivity measurement issues in services industries: "Baumol's Disease" has been cured. *Federal Reserve Bank of New York Economic Policy Review* (September), 23–34.

UN 1965. *The Growth of World Industry, 1938–1961*. New York: United Nations.

    1998. *World Population Prospect: The 1996 Revision*. New York: United Nations, Population Division.

    2001. *World Population Prospects: The 2000 Revision*, Vol. I: *Comprehensive Tables*. New York: United Nations, Population Division.

UNCTAD. 1983. *Handbook of International Trade and Development Statistics*. New York: United Nations.

    2000. *World Investment Report*. New York: United Nations.

    2002. *Handbook of Statistics*. New York: United Nations.

    2003. *World Investment Report*. New York: United Nations.

UNDP. 2001. *Human Development Report*. New York: United Nations.

    2003. *Human Development Report*. New York: United Nations.

UNIDO. 2002. *International Yearbook of Industrial Statistics*. Vienna United Nations Industrial Development Organization.

US Bureau of the Census. 1975. *Historical Statistics of the United States, Colonial Times to 1970*. Washington, DC: Government Printing Office.

US Bureau of the Census. Various issues. *Current Population Survey*. Washington, DC: Government Printing Office.

US Bureau of Economic Analysis. 2002. *Survey of Current Business*. Washington, DC: Government Printing Office.

2004. *Gross Product Originating by Industry*. Available at www.bea.gov.

US Bureau of Labor Statistics. 2002. *Online Database*. Available at www.bls.gov/data.

2005. *Labor Force Statistics from the Current Population Survey*. Available at http://data.bls.gov/servlet/SurveyOutputServlet.

US Council of Economic Advisers. 1990. *Economic Report of the President*. Washington, DC: Government Printing Office (available at http://w3.access.gpo.gov/eop/).

1992. *Economic Report of the President*. Washington, DC: Government Printing Office (available at http://w3.access.gpo.gov/eop/).

2001. *Economic Report of the President*. Washington, DC: Government Printing Office (available at http://w3.access.gpo.gov/eop/).

2003. *Economic Report of the President*. Washington, DC: Government Printing Office (available at http://w3.access.gpo.gov/eop/).

2004. *Economic Report of the President*. Washington, DC: Government Printing Office (available at http://w3.access.gpo.gov/eop/).

US Department of Commerce. Various dates. *Statistical Abstract of the United States*. Washington, DC: Government Printing Office.

2001. *Statistical Abstract of the United States*. Washington, DC: Government Printing Office.

US Department of Education. 1993. *120 Years of Education: A Statistical Portrait*. Washington, DC: Government Printing Office.

Van Ark, Bart, Johanna Melka, Nanno Mulder, Marcel Timmer, and Gerard Ypma. 2003. *ICT Investments and Growth Accounts for the European Union*. Research Memorandum no. GD-56, Groningen Growth and Development Centre.

Venables, Anthony J. 1996. Equilibrium locations of vertically linked industries. *International Economic Review* 37, 341–59.

2001. Geography and international inequalities: the impact of new technologies. *Journal of Industry, Competition and Trade* 1, 135–60.

Visco, Ignazio 1994. *La crescita economica in Europa: ritardi e opportunità*. Mimeo, Bank of Italy, Rome.

Vissing-Jorgensen, Annette. 1999. Comment. In Ben S. Bernanke and Julio S. Rotemberg (eds.). *NBER Macroeconomics Annual*. Cambridge, MA: MIT Press, 242–53.

Wackernagel, Mathis, Niels B. Schulz, Diana Deumling, Alejandro Callejas Linares, Martin Jenkins, Valerie Kapos, Chad Monfreda, Jonathan Loh, Norman Myers, Richard Norgaard, and Jorgen Randers 2002. Tracking the ecological overshoot of the human economy. *Proceedings of the National Academy of Science* 99, 9266–71.

Wade, Robert. 1990. *Governing the Market*. Princeton, NJ: Princeton University Press.

Wall Street Journal. 2003. Behind surging productivity, the service sector delivers. 7 November.

Weinberg, Daniel H. 1996. A brief look at postwar U.S. income inequality. In *Current Population Reports*, 60–191 (available at www.census.gov/prod/1/pop/p60-191.pdf).

Weinstein, Michael. 1980. *Recovery and Redistribution under the NIRA.* Amsterdam: North-Holland.

West, Kenneth D. 1988. Dividend innovations and stock price volatility. *Econometrica* 56, 37–61.

White, Eugene N. 2000. Banking and finance in the twentieth century. In Stanley L. Engerman and Robert E. Gallman (eds.). *The Cambridge Economic History of the United States*, Vol. III. Cambridge: Cambridge University Press, 743–802.

White, Lawrence. 1991. *The S&L Debacle: Public Policy Lessons for Bank and Thrift Regulation.* New York: Oxford University Press.

Wigmore, Barrie A. 1985. *The Crash and Its Aftermath: A History of Securities Markets in the United States, 1929–1933.* Westport, CT: Greenwood Press.

Williams, John B. 1938. *The Theory of Investment Value.* Cambridge, MA: Harvard University Press.

Williams, William Appleman. 1961. *The Contours of American History.* Chicago: World Publishing.

Williamson, Jeffrey G. 1973. Late nineteenth-century American retardation: a neoclassical analysis. *Journal of Economic History* 33, 581–607.

Williamson, John, and Molly Mahar. 1998. *A Survey of Financial Liberalization.* Essay in International Finance no. 211, International Finance Section, Department of Economics, Princeton University, NJ.

Winston, Clifford. 1993. Economic deregulation: days of reckoning for microeconomists. *Journal of Economic Literature* 31, 1263–89.

Winters, L. Alan 2004. Trade liberalization and economic performance: an overview. *Economic Journal* 114, F4–F21.

World Bank. 1995. *World Development Report.* Washington, DC: World Bank.

  2001. *Global Economic Prospects and the Developing Countries.* Washington, DC: World Bank.

  2002. *Global Development Finance.* Washington, DC: World Bank.

  2004. *Brazil: Sustaining Equitable Income Security for Old Age.* Washington, DC: World Bank, Social Protection Unit.

World Bank. Annually. *World Development Report.*

Wright, Gavin. 1999. Can a nation learn? American technology as a network phenomenon. In Naomi Lamoreaux, Daniel M. G. Raff, and Peter Temin (eds.). *Learning By Doing in Markets, Firms, and Countries.* Chicago: University of Chicago Press, 295–326.

WTO. 2001. *International Trade Statistics.* Geneva: World Trade Organization.

Yang, Shinkyu, and Erik Brynjolfsson. 2001. *Intangible Assets and Growth Accounting: Evidence from Computer Investments.* Working paper, Massachusetts Institute of Technology, Cambridge, MA.

Yates, P. L. 1959. *Forty Years of Foreign Trade.* London: Allen and Unwin.

Young, A. 2003. Gold into base metals: productivity growth in the people's republic of China during the reform period. *Journal of Political Economy* 111, 1220–61.

Zlotnik, Hania. 1998. International migration, 1965–96: an overview. *Population and Development Review* 24, 429–68.

Author index

Subject index